Sovereignty, Civic Participation, and Constitutional Law

This book brings recent insights about sovereignty and citizen participation in the Belgian Constitution to scholars in the fields of law, philosophy, history, and politics.

Throughout the Western world, there are increasing calls for greater citizen participation. Referendums, citizen councils, and other forms of direct democracy are considered necessary antidotes to a growing hostility towards traditional party politics. This book focuses on the Belgian debate, where the introduction of participatory politics has stalled because of an ambiguity in the Constitution. Scholars and judges generally claim that the Belgian Constitution gives ultimate power to the nation, which can only speak through representation in parliament. In light of this, direct democracy would be an unconstitutional power grab by the current generation of citizens. This book critically investigates this received interpretation of the Constitution and, by reaching back to the debates among Belgium's 1831 founding fathers, concludes that it is untenable. The spirit, if not the text, of the Belgian Constitution allows for more popular participation than present-day jurisprudence admits.

This book is the first to make recent debates in this field accessible to international scholars. It provides a rare source of information on Belgium's 1831 Constitution, which was in its time seen as modern constitutionalism's greatest triumph and which became a model for countless other constitutions. Yet the questions it asks reverberate far beyond Belgium. Combining new insights from law, philosophy, history, and politics, this book is a showcase for continental constitutional theory. It will be a valuable resource for academics and researchers in constitutional law, political and legal philosophy, and legal history.

Brecht Deseure is a post-doctoral researcher at King's College London, UK.

Raf Geenens is an associate professor of ethics and legal philosophy at KU Leuven's Institute of Philosophy.

Stefan Sottiaux is a professor of constitutional law and human rights at KU Leuven's Faculty of Law.

Routledge Research in Constitutional Law

This series features thought-provoking and original scholarship on constitutional law and theory. Books explore key topics, themes and questions in the field with a particular emphasis on comparative studies. Where relevant, titles will engage with political and social theory, philosophy and history in order to offer a rounded analysis of constitutions and constitutional law. Series Editor: David Marrani.

Available titles in this series include:

Constitution-making and Human Rights in the Sudans
Edited by Lutz Oette and Mohamed Abdelsalam Babiker

Constitutional Law, Religion and Equal Liberty
The Impact of Desecularization
Azin Tadjdini

Kant, Global Politics and Cosmopolitan Law
The World Republic as a Regulative Idea of Reason
Claudio Corradetti

Diversity of Law in the United Arab Emirates
Privacy, Security and the Legal System
Kristin Kamøy

Sovereignty, Civic Participation, and Constitutional Law
The People versus the Nation in Belgium
Edited by Brecht Deseure, Raf Geenens, and Stefan Sottiaux

For more information about this series, please visit:
www.routledge.com/Routledge-Research-in-Constitutional-Law/book-series/CONSTLAW

Sovereignty, Civic Participation, and Constitutional Law

The People versus the Nation in Belgium

Edited by
Brecht Deseure,
Raf Geenens,
and Stefan Sottiaux

Routledge
Taylor & Francis Group
LONDON AND NEW YORK

First published 2021
by Routledge
2 Park Square, Milton Park, Abingdon, Oxon OX14 4RN

and by Routledge
605 Third Avenue, New York, NY 10158

Routledge is an imprint of the Taylor & Francis Group, an informa business

British Library Cataloguing-in-Publication Data
A catalogue record for this book is available from the British Library

Library of Congress Cataloging-in-Publication Data
Names: Deseure, Brecht, 1985- editor. | Geenens, Raf, 1979- editor. | Sottiaux, Stefan, 1976- editor.
Title: Sovereignty, civic participation, and constitutional law: the people versus the nation in Belgium/edited by Brecht Deseure, Raf Geenens and Stefan Sottiaux.
Description: Milton Park, Abingdon, Oxon; New York, NY: Routledge, 2021. | Series: Routledge research in constitutional law | Includes bibliographical references and index.
Identifiers: LCCN 2020046394 (print) | LCCN 2020046395 (ebook) | ISBN 9780367483593 (hardback) | ISBN 9781003039525 (ebook)
Subjects: LCSH: Constitutional history–Belgium. | Constituent power–Belgium. | Constitutional law–Belgium. | Political participation–Belgium. | Representative government and representation–Belgium. | Sovereignty.
Classification: LCC KJK2504 .S68 2021 (print) | LCC KJK2504 (ebook) | DDC 342.493–dc23
LC record available at https://lccn.loc.gov/2020046394
LC ebook record available at https://lccn.loc.gov/2020046395

ISBN: 978-0-367-48359-3 (hbk)
ISBN: 978-0-367-71228-0 (pbk)
ISBN: 978-1-003-03952-5 (ebk)

Typeset in Galliard
by Deanta Global Publishing Services, Chennai, India

Contents

Acknowledgements

This book is the outcome of a four-year research project (2015–2019) at the faculties of philosophy and law of KU Leuven (Belgium). This project was directed by Raf Geenens (Institute of Philosophy) and co-directed by Stefan Sottiaux (Faculty of Law), but involved a much larger team, composed of historian Brecht Deseure as a post-doctoral fellow and five very talented PhD students in philosophy and law: Olga Bashkina, Bas Leijssenaar, Christophe Maes, Nora Timmermans, and Ronald Van Crombrugge. We happily take this opportunity to thank all team members for a most pleasant collaboration. We thank Brecht in particular for his help in editing this volume. Apart from our research team, we would like to thank the many conversation partners we had in this project. Throughout these four years, our thinking has been substantially enriched by the input of numerous guests and visitors, and by those who have been so kind to act as hosts or jury members for our PhD students. It is impossible to list everyone, but special thanks are due to Andrew Arato, Anat Ascher, Marnix Beyen, Jan Clement, Bram Delbecke, Annelien De Dijn, Henk de Smaele, John Dryzek, Jason Frank, Arthur Ghins, Stefaan Marteel, Markus Prutsch, John Parkinson, Helena Rosenblatt, Nenad Stojanović, Johan Tollebeek, Steven Van Hecke, Miguel Vatter, Neil Walker, and Els Witte. In preparing this edited volume, we have been lucky to count on the invaluable assistance of Pierpaolo Betti (who helped with endnotes, bibliographies, and many other important details) and Allegra Reinalda (who corrected and improved our English wherever necessary). We would also like to thank our funders: FWO (Research Foundation Flanders) and KU Leuven's Research Fund. Without their generous financial support, this research project would have been impossible. Finally, it should be mentioned that this is the second volume that comes out of this project. The first book, *Sovereignty in Action*, contains more philosophical research on the notion of sovereignty and was published in 2019. (RG and SS)

Contributors

Olga Bashkina is a doctoral researcher at KU Leuven's Institute of Philosophy. She specialises in the history of political ideas and in constitutional theory and maintains a vivid interest in critical theory and contemporary political theory. Olga holds degrees in philosophy and political science from KU Leuven, the European University at St Petersburg, and St Petersburg State University.

Brecht Deseure obtained his PhD in history from the University of Antwerp in 2011 with a dissertation on the politics of history pursued by the French republican and Napoleonic governments. His research interests include political culture, history and memory, constitutional history, historical theory, and political philosophy. During several years, he has done post-doctoral research on the 1831 Belgian Constitution at the universities of Passau and Leuven. He now works as a researcher at King's College London, where he investigates the transnational dynamics of radical translation in the revolutionary era.

Raf Geenens is associate professor of ethics and legal philosophy at KU Leuven's Institute of Philosophy. He has held visiting positions at Columbia University, École des Hautes Études en Sciences Sociales, and Queen Mary University. Raf is currently the principal investigator of a research project on constitutions and collective identity and he is in the process of completing a monograph on Claude Lefort. He previously edited, together with Helena Rosenblatt, *French Liberalism. From Montesquieu to the Present Day* (Cambridge University Press, 2012).

Bas Leijssenaar is a PhD researcher (funded by FWO, Research Foundation Flanders) at KU Leuven's Institute of Philosophy. His research concerns sovereignty, constituent power, American pragmatism, and philosophical reflections on the Anthropocene. He recently edited, with Neil Walker, a volume titled *Sovereignty in Action* (Cambridge University Press, 2019).

Christophe Maes holds master's degrees in law (2007) and history (2010), both from KU Leuven. He obtained his PhD in law in 2020 from KU Leuven with a dissertation on the notion of sovereignty in the Belgian Constitution of 1831 and in Belgian legal scholarship (1831–1960s). His research interests include constitutional thought, democratic theory, and intellectual history, with a specific focus on sovereignty, political representation and the separation of state powers. Christophe's current research concerns the role of constitutional identity in Belgium.

Stefaan Marteel obtained his PhD from the European University Institute in Florence with a dissertation which was recently published as *The Intellectual Origins of the Belgian Revolution. Political Thought and Disunity in the Kingdom of the Netherlands* (Palgrave, 2020). Stefaan taught political history at the Radboud University Nijmegen from 2011 to 2015 and is currently an unaffiliated historian. He is preparing a book on the contemporary relevance of republican political thought (to be published with Garant in 2021).

Markus J. Prutsch is a senior investigator and administrator at the European Parliament, and an associate professor of modern and contemporary history at Heidelberg University. A historian and political scientist, Markus holds a PhD from the European University Institute in Florence, and has directed several international research projects. His work has been awarded at various occasions, and he is a fellow of the Heidelberg Academy of Sciences and Humanities and a member of the Global Young Academy.

Stefan Sottiaux is a professor of constitutional law and human rights law at KU Leuven. He obtained a Magister Juris from Oxford (2000) and a PhD from Antwerp (2006). His research interests include federalism, comparative human rights law, discrimination law, and methods of judicial decision-making. He is a member of the Antwerp Bar and has experience in defending clients before the European Court of Human Rights, the European Court of Justice, and the Belgian Constitutional Court.

Nenad Stojanović is a Swiss National Science Foundation (SNSF) professor of political science at the University of Geneva. He is currently working on an SNSF project titled 'A non-populist theory of direct democracy' and conducts field experiments combining sortition, deliberative mini-publics, and direct democracy (www.demoscan.ch). His past projects include a study of electoral discrimination and a doctoral thesis on the concept of quota (*Dialogue sur les quotas*, Presses de Sciences Po, 2013).

Nora Timmermans has studied law and philosophy at KU Leuven. She is a PhD fellow at KU Leuven's Institute of Philosophy since 2015. Her doctoral research on collective subjectivity and popular power in French political liberalism is funded by FWO, Research Foundation Flanders. Nora has held visiting scholarships at the City University of New York and Tilburg University. Her research expertise includes constitutional theory, the history of democratic thought, and contemporary democratic theory.

Ronald Van Crombrugge graduated as a master in law from KU Leuven in 2015. He is now enrolled as a doctoral student at KU Leuven's Centre for Public Law, where he specialises in political theory and the law of politics. In recent years, he has been a visiting research fellow at the Australian National University and the Max Planck Institute for Comparative Public Law and International Law.

1 A simple sentence

Towards a new interpretation of sovereignty in the Belgian Constitution

Raf Geenens, Brecht Deseure, and Stefan Sottiaux

Writing an entire book about a single sentence might sound like the kind of pedantic exercise that only career academics can get excited about. However, the purpose of this book is to show that one short sentence can make a world of difference. This book's central object is a seven-word statement in Belgium's Constitution. Translated from Dutch, French, or German (Belgium's official languages) into English, its length goes down to just six words and it reads as follows: "All powers emanate from the Nation". The original formulation, written in French in the fall of 1830, goes like this: "*Tous les pouvoirs émanent de la Nation*".[1] This sentence is part of article 25 (now article 33)[2] of Belgium's written Constitution, a Constitution that has the merit of remaining in force, with many of its essentials untouched, for almost 200 years now. It was officially proclaimed on 7 February 1831, and, perceived by contemporaries as unusually liberal, it became a model for countless other constitutions in the course of the nineteenth century. The historian Horst Dippel notes that the Belgian Constitution was, in its time, seen as modern constitutionalism's "greatest triumph" (Dippel, 2005, p. 165).

Not much is left of this reputation today. Hardly any international constitutional theorist is knowledgeable about Belgium's Constitution and in studies of the period the Belgian Constitution is sometimes simply left out. One purpose of this book is certainly to rekindle interest in Belgium's Constitution and to make available recent insights and developments (which are often only published in Dutch or French) to international audiences. Yet, we will do so by focusing on this one short sentence about the source of all powers. There are good reasons for this narrow focus. This sentence is, in a way, the cornerstone of the Belgian Constitution because it points out the purported origin of all the

1 In Dutch, the sentence reads, "*Alle machten gaan uit van de Natie*". In German, it reads as follows: "*Alle Gewalten gehen von der Nation aus*". The Constitution was translated into Dutch by the provisional government immediately after its promulgation, but the Dutch version only received the force of law in 1967. Until that year, only the French version was officially recognised. The official German version dates from 1991.

2 In full, article 25 reads as follows: "All powers emanate from the Nation. They are to be exercised as prescribed by the Constitution". This article has stood unchanged in Belgium's Constitution since 1831.

constitutional powers and institutions. As such, this statement is indicative of the way Belgium's founding fathers thought about the legitimacy of their exercise and about the legitimacy of the state they were establishing. This is important, as the Belgian Constitution was written at a time when European countries were going through a complex and often painful transition from monarchical to parliamentary governments. In the reports of the constituent assembly (the 'National Congress'), where Belgium's founding fathers were drafting and discussing the new Constitution between November 1830 and February 1831, one can witness their intellectual struggle as they sought to create a monarchy in which the monarch would not be sovereign.[3] This puzzle of constitutional engineering was not easy to solve, but they did eventually solve it in an elegant manner. A crucial element in their solution was article 25: "All powers emanate from the Nation".

This sentence is all the more important because of its role in recent debates about citizen participation. In Belgium, as elsewhere, there are increasing calls for greater citizen involvement in politics. Referendums, citizen councils, and other forms of participation are considered necessary antidotes to traditional representative institutions, which are said to be going through a crisis of legitimacy.[4] In Belgium, blame is typically placed on political parties, whose power is seen as excessive and in need of being checked (cf. Dewachter, 2001; 2014). But it is not obvious where such checks can come from. As all political institutions are populated by professional politicians, they always tend to come under party control.[5] This is what makes citizen participation so attractive in Belgium: it promises to be a counterweight against the dominance of parties and professional politicians. However, all attempts to introduce forms of direct democracy, especially referendums, have been blocked by the Council of State and the Constitutional Court, precisely through reference to article 25 of the Constitution. It sounds, of course, paradoxical that the very article that was meant to sanction the authority of the Belgian people is now used to block the participation of citizens in government. The main reason for this volte-face is the gradual emergence, from the late 1800s onwards, of a peculiar interpretation of article 25. The statement that "All powers emanate from the Nation" came to be construed as an expression of the principle of 'national sovereignty', a principle that purportedly excludes all forms of citizen participation. This idiosyncratic understanding of sovereignty

3 The National Congress was Belgium's 200-strong, provisional legislative assembly, elected in November 1830 and dissolved in July 1831. Its central task was to write and ratify a constitution for the new state. A smaller commission prepared a first, rough draft (see Van den Steene, 1963) but the general assembly also took its task to heart. Reliable and relatively complete transcripts of the meetings of the constituent assembly were published in five volumes by Emile Huyttens in 1844.

4 Although, as political scientists note, it is not always easy to distinguish myth from reality in this purported 'legitimacy crisis'. See Van Ham et al. (2017).

5 Even in Belgium's Constitutional Court, supposedly an external check on the political system, party power looms large. The seats are attributed to the parties in accordance with the election results. See *Parl. St. Senaat* 2007–2008, 9 October 2007, 18.

continues to dominate legal and political thinking in Belgium, leaving little room for democratic innovation.

The core purpose of this book is to put into question this dominant understanding of article 25. Several chapters in the book will demonstrate that the 'national sovereignty' interpretation of article 25 is flatly anachronistic, as the very idea of 'national sovereignty' played no role whatsoever in the thinking of the Belgian drafters in 1830–1831. Consequently, we will seek to construct a more appropriate interpretation of the statement that "All powers emanate from the Nation" and we will explore to what extent this corrected understanding of article 25 can open the door to greater citizen involvement in Belgian politics.

It should be noted that this book is the outcome of an interdisciplinary research project that was conducted at KU Leuven from 2015 to 2019. The goal of this project was precisely to investigate the historical meaning of article 25 and to plot the practical consequences of a corrected interpretation of the constitutional text. Most chapters in this book are written by philosophers, lawyers, and historians at KU Leuven who were involved in this research project; just three chapters were solicited from outside authors. Although the chapters are drawn from a relatively small pool, it does not follow that all authors share the same position. There have been various conflicts of interpretation throughout our research project, and in this book we have not tried to gloss them over. Nor is this book meant to be the final word on the topic of sovereignty in the Belgian Constitution. In our research, we have been humbled by the number of sources, earlier interpretations, and cross-linkages with similar debates in other countries. While remaining open to the possibility that other, more refined interpretations of article 25 will appear in the future, we are nevertheless convinced that this book presents the most accurate and complete analysis of the Belgian concept of sovereignty to date. As the different chapters in this book show, the topic of sovereignty opens onto many other discussions, for instance, about representation, constitutional change, and national identity. It is therefore our keenest hope that this book will encourage further and more extensive research, not just on sovereignty, but on the rich heritage of Belgium's Constitution in its entirety.

In this first chapter, we will limit ourselves to the following. In the next section, we provide a brief overview of the dominant interpretation of article 25. In the subsequent section, we outline the case against this classic interpretation, and we introduce the working hypothesis that has guided our attempt to construct a more plausible interpretation. In the chapter's concluding section, we will say something more about the structure of the book and present the different chapters.

The national sovereignty myth

There seems to have been little controversy about article 25 among the drafters in 1830–1831. But this article did soon become an object of disagreement. In the decades after 1831, the sentence stating that "All powers emanate from the Nation" was sometimes understood in a Rousseauist vein, sometimes in light of the ideas of Benjamin Constant. Some understood it as an expression of Doctrinaire liberalism, while still others held that the statement was vacuous because the drafters lacked a genuine understanding of sovereignty. As Chapter 11 will demonstrate, these and other interpretations vied in public law manuals without a clear victor in sight until, from the 1950s on, opinions coalesced around one specific interpretation. Starting with the first edition of André Mast's influential public law textbook, published in the summer of 1950 (Mast, 1950, pp. 66–68),[6] ever more authors came to agree as to what the drafters of the Belgian Constitution genuinely intended when writing that all powers emanate from the nation. This consensus can be summarised as follows. The drafters wanted to break with theological or absolutist justifications of sovereignty, which they saw as potential threats to liberty. Yet, they did not grant sovereignty to the 'people', understood as the set (or a subset) of all currently living citizens. Instead, they granted sovereignty to the 'nation', an abstract, transhistorical entity that encompasses not only currently living citizens but also earlier and future generations of citizens. The former option would be 'popular sovereignty' (typically associated with Rousseau), whereas the latter option is 'national sovereignty' (purportedly originating with Sieyès). Both types of sovereignty were supposedly propagated by the French Revolution, but the Belgian founders – just like the French drafters of 1791 – consciously picked national sovereignty.

This choice for the nation as the subject of sovereignty has a number of 'elitist' implications. (i) Given that the nation does not materially exist, it can only express itself by means of representative institutions. Thus, direct democratic procedures are excluded, as only careful deliberation by representatives can reveal the will of the nation. (ii) National sovereignty provides a potential argument against universal suffrage, since voting is not a fundamental 'right' of the citizens but only a means (or a 'function') to appoint the most competent representatives of the nation. iii) In the exercise of their mandate, representatives are not bound to the opinions or interests of their voters, since they are representing the nation rather than the actual electorate.

Today, most public law textbooks insist that the Belgian drafters made a conscious choice for national sovereignty, possibly with these three 'elitist' implications clearly in mind (see e.g. Alen and Muylle, 2011, pp. 120–130; Gilissen, 1958, pp. 11–12; Mast, 1981, pp. 27–30; Rimanque, 2005, pp. 100–101; Senelle, 1974, pp. 66–68; Tilleman and Alen, 1992, p. 11; Uyttendaele, 2001, pp. 25–31; Vande Lanotte and Goedertier, 2013, pp. 203–218; Velaers, 1999, pp. 228–233; Wigny, 1952, pp. 224–225). In contrast to this general consensus,

6 André Mast was a professor of public law at Ghent University and is probably the most influential Dutch-language interpreter of the Constitution in post-war Belgium. It is noteworthy that his (hand-typed) textbook was first published months after Belgium's first and only statewide referendum (12 March 1950). This non-binding referendum concerned the return of the exiled King Leopold III and brought the country to the brink of dissolution. In the francophone literature, the 'national sovereignty' interpretation can first be found in Wigny (1952, pp. 224–225).

a small number of contemporary scholars maintain that the Constitution sanctions the principle of popular sovereignty, in line with the 'Rousseauist' tradition (De Meyer, 1985, p. 134; De Witte, 2003, p. 353),[7] or that the Belgian drafters simply had no theoretically coherent view on sovereignty (Delpérée, 1987, p. 301; Velu, 1986, p. 78).[8] Yet, the overwhelming consensus reads that the drafters opted for 'national sovereignty'.

The consensual emphasis on 'national sovereignty' has important practical effects. Most significantly, it provides a key argument against the constitutionality of direct citizen participation, in particular of referendums. Since 1985, the Belgian Council of State has consistently declared legislative proposals to introduce binding and non-binding referendums at the federal, regional, and community levels unconstitutional, as a violation of the principle of national sovereignty enshrined in article 25 (Opinion of 15 May 1985, *Parl. St. Kamer* 1983–1984, no. 783/2, 8).[9] This reading of article 25 has often been confirmed, with respect to both ordinary legislative referendums and 'constitutional' referendums (e.g. referendums concerning the transfer of sovereign powers to supranational bodies). Thus, in its opinion on a proposed referendum concerning a constitution for Europe, the Council recalled that the Belgian Constitution "is grounded not in a system of popular sovereignty but in a system of national sovereignty, in which the Nation is represented by the established powers". In consequence, "methods of direct democracy on the federal, the regional and the community levels" are not allowed (Opinion of 29 November 2004, *Parl. St. Kamer* 2003–2004, no. 0281/004, 4–5). In a similar vein, most scholars opposing the use of referendums refer to the concept of sovereignty in article 25 as an important argument against referendums (see e.g. Alen and Muylle, 2011, pp. 121–126; Rimanque, 2005, p. 101; Velaers, 1999, pp. 149–166). It should be added that 'national sovereignty' is not the only legal line of reasoning against the introduction of direct democracy. The second major argument introduced by the Council of State, and supported by legal doctrine, is based on the second sentence of article 25, which states that the powers emanating from the nation shall be exercised in accordance with the procedures laid down in the Constitution. As the constitutional text states that legislative power is exercised by the king, the Chamber of Representatives, and the Senate, but does not mention direct citizen participation, there seems to be no room for referendums (see Opinion of 15 May 1985,

7 The claim that the Belgian drafters sought to express a republican or Rousseauist conception of sovereignty not only is made by contemporary scholars but can also be found in Pirenne's seminal history of Belgium, and some older public law textbooks seem to read the Constitution in a similar tone. See e.g. Pirenne (1926); Giron (1884); Errera (1909).

8 Although Tilleman and Alen (1992) put forward the 'national sovereignty' interpretation, Alen also writes that, all in all, the Belgian drafters were not really occupied with the abstract juridical or philosophical aspects of sovereignty (see Alen, 1984, p. 207).

9 The Council of State confirmed this view in its subsequent opinions. See e.g. Opinion of 30 October 2002, *Parl. St. Vl. Parl.* 2002–2003, no. 1176/2, 7; Opinion of 29 November 2004, *Parl. St. Kamer* 2003–2004, no. 0281/004, 4.

Parl. St. Kamer 1983–1984, no. 783/2, 5–8; Opinion of 30 October 2002, *Parl. St. Vl. Parl.* 2002–2003, no. 1176/2, 8; Opinion of 29 November 2004, *Parl. St. Kamer* 2003–2004, no. 0281/004, 5).

There is broad consensus among Belgian constitutional scholars that, for these two reasons, binding referendums are unconstitutional.[10] The fact that the current constitutional framework does not allow for referendums evidently does not preclude a constitutional amendment. Actually, in an attempt to overcome the constitutional hurdles against citizen participation, the Constitution was already amended twice. Today, it provides for non-binding referendums at the local level (since 1999) and the regional level (since 2013). At the national level, however, referendums remain impossible. Note that the assumption of 'national sovereignty' in principle also excludes other forms of non-representative democracy, such as citizen participation in the legislative process through deliberative councils. National sovereignty implies that the representatives united in parliament are the exclusive channel for the expression of the national will. Given this view, it is only logical not to discriminate between different forms of non-representative decision-making and thus to also exclude as unconstitutional any transfer of legislative tasks to participatory bodies.[11]

In addition to the legal considerations, there is, of course, a range of philosophical, political, and empirical arguments for and against the use of referendums and/or forms of participatory democracy.[12] Let us just mention one non-legal argument that is of special relevance in the Belgian context. As the Council of State observed in an *obiter dictum* in its 1985 Opinion, the use of referendums at the federal level might jeopardise the "harmonious coexistence" of the French and the Flemish Communities, the two largest linguistic Communities in multilingual Belgium, as it would bring the differing political preferences of these Communities to the fore (Opinion of 15 May 1985, *Parl. St. Kamer* 1983–1984, no. 783/2, 18). This consideration – even when not always explicitly mentioned – has certainly played an important role in keeping the door closed to more direct forms of democracy in Belgium, as it is usually assumed that elite compromises offer the best prospects for stability in this divided country.

Towards a different interpretation

The consensual understanding of sovereignty in the Belgian Constitution has many advocates, yet the working hypothesis of this book reads that it amounts

10 With respect to non-binding referendums, some dissenting voices argue that these would not violate the Constitution, see Popelier (2001, pp. 265–269) or Vande Lanotte and Goedertier (2013, pp. 207–208).

11 For further discussion of participation in the Belgian legal context, see Lancksweerdt (2009) and Schram (2012).

12 For an overview of the debate in Belgium, see Van Damme et al. (2012).

to little more than a myth that needs to be dismantled.[13] What are the arguments that are typically put forward in favour of the 'national sovereignty' interpretation? An important, if not the principal, argument is the supposed parallel between the 1831 Belgian understanding of sovereignty on the one hand, and the notion of sovereignty that is enshrined in the revolutionary French Constitution of 1791 on the other. Defenders of the consensual understanding point out that the phrasing of article 25 ("All powers emanate from the Nation") was inspired by article 2 of the third section of the French Constitution of 1791, which contains similar wording ("The Nation, from which all powers emanate"). This might be true (cf. Van den Steene, 1963; Gilissen, 1968). Unfortunately, many authors conclude from this that both constitutions must share the same conception of sovereignty, namely 'national sovereignty' as described above. There are various reasons to reject this conclusion.

On a textual level, it can be mentioned that in the 1791 Constitution, article 2 is preceded by article 1, which deals explicitly with sovereignty. In this article, sovereignty is defined (as "indivisible", "inalienable", and "imprescriptible") and it is stated that "sovereignty belongs to the nation" and can never be exercised by "a section of the people" or "an individual". In the Belgian Constitution, one does not find a single trace of this article on sovereignty. This strongly suggests that the Belgian drafters were not particularly interested in importing the 1791 understanding of sovereignty into the Belgian Constitution. More generally, it is doubtful that the Belgian drafters would have stuck to sovereignty as it was understood in the early years of the French Revolution. Ideas on sovereignty and constitutional government had evolved considerably in these four decades. Discussions during the French Revolution involved heavy, 'Rousseauist' questions such as how to discover the general will and how to represent sovereignty given that it should not be divided or alienated. These questions dovetailed with the general concern of setting up a strong central authority that would empower the people as the new subject of sovereignty. In 1831, the debate had moved on decidedly, among other reasons because of the experiences of the Revolution and the first Empire.

Furthermore, when the National Congress discussed the issue of sovereignty (which happened only rarely), there was no mention of the idea of 'national sovereignty', nor was there a trace of opposition between defenders of 'national sovereignty' and defenders of 'popular sovereignty' (Huyttens, 1844a, pp. 215–216, 1844b, p. 15). To the contrary, debaters in the National Congress stated that a representative, constitutional monarchy was always based on the "sovereignty of the people", or even that *all* modern societies were based on the "sovereignty of the people", without meeting any resistance or correction (Huyttens, 1844a, pp. 216, 603). This strongly indicates that no one in the National Congress was aware of a possible conceptual distinction between national sovereignty and

13 For previous criticisms of the myth, see De Smaele (2000), Geenens and Sottiaux (2015), and Deseure (2016).

popular sovereignty. This is also confirmed by the fact that the congressmen consistently used 'people' and 'nation' interchangeably. If the choice for the term 'nation' was as momentous as later interpreters claim, it is doubtful that the two terms would not have been carefully differentiated from one another (Huyttens, 1844a, pp. 188, 208–209, 228, 443, 1844b, p. 28).[14] Although our book shows that semantic evidence should be treated carefully, the fact remains that the constituent debates contain no trace of the underlying differentiation between the concrete people and the abstract nation implied by the national sovereignty thesis.

Although these considerations need to be further developed (as they will be in the remainder of this book), they already suggest that the national sovereignty myth is, historically speaking, questionable and that a sounder interpretation of sovereignty in the Belgian Constitution is needed. This requires re-embedding the Constitution in the political-philosophical debates of its day and investigating the intellectual sources of the Belgian founding fathers. These sources are almost invariably French liberal philosophers, whose ideas were eagerly absorbed in Belgium during the years of opposition against King William I.[15] The guiding hypothesis throughout this book reads that the conception of sovereignty that the drafters wrote into the Belgian Constitution can best be understood in light of the paradigm of French political liberalism as it developed in the aftermath of the French Revolution[16] and, more specifically, in light of the work of Benjamin Constant. With regard to other aspects of the Belgian constitutional edifice, such as ministerial responsibility and freedom of the press, it has by now been established that they are intellectually very much indebted to Constant.[17] We hypothesise that, with regard to the key notion of sovereignty, the Belgian Constitution is similarly – if not more strongly – rooted in French restoration liberalism, in particular in the ideas of Constant.

Structure of the book

This book consists of 15 chapters, divided into three parts. Part I lays the conceptual groundwork by investigating the intellectual context of post-revolutionary

14 In the same vein, it can be noted that the 1831 Dutch translation of the Constitution translated 'nation' by 'people' in this article and that the term 'National Congress' (in French: '*Congrès national*') was formally rendered in Dutch, in 1831, as '*Volksraad*' ('Council of the People').

15 In 1815, William Fredrick, Prince of Orange-Nassau, became king of the newly united Kingdom of the Netherlands (including the contemporary Netherlands, Belgium, and Luxembourg). His autocratic style of rule, combined with a perceived preference for the North and with religious differences, led to fierce resistance in the southern territories (the former Austrian Netherlands and the Prince-Bishopric of Liège), where the mood was dominated by the Catholic church on the one hand and by a liberal-minded, mostly francophone bourgeoisie on the other. An unexpected rapprochement between Catholics and liberals enabled the 1830 Revolution and the proclamation of an independent Belgian state.

16 Cf. Geenens and Rosenblatt (2012).

17 Van Velzen (2005) and Delbecke (2012).

constitutionalism, with a special focus on the notion of sovereignty. Nineteenth-century liberal theorists were confronted with the particular challenge of integrating sovereignty into their systems. The concept was tainted by unwelcome notions of omnipotence, the risks of which had been illustrated by old regime monarchical absolutism on the one hand and by the popular despotism of the French Revolution on the other. While the legacy of Rousseau and Sieyès continued to loom large, Restoration liberals such as Constant and Guizot came up with new approaches to the origin and distribution of power within society. On the Catholic side, the liberal-minded priest Lamennais and the reactionary nobleman Maistre formulated diametrically opposed answers to the challenges offered by the concept of sovereignty in post-revolutionary society.

Markus Prutsch's chapter provides an overview of constitutional ideas and practices in the Restoration period. Even though the collapse of the Napoleonic order in 1814 symbolised a victory over the Revolution and its principles, it proved impossible to negate the revolutionary legacy. A key challenge was to reconcile monarchical claims to sovereignty with modern, post-revolutionary political principles. This dilemma gave rise to a specific form of constitutional monarchy, for which the *Charte constitutionnelle* of the restored Bourbon monarchy in France provided the example: the *Charte* established a representative constitutional system while retaining many of the monarch's traditional prerogatives. Yet, constitutional monarchism proved a fragile compromise, with a dualism between Crown and parliament – and thus a latent systemic conflict. This chapter outlines the genesis and characteristic features of post-Napoleonic 'constitutional monarchism' and examines its role for nineteenth-century constitutionalism. Moreover, it makes clear how constitutional monarchism was put under pressure by various evolutions, such as the growing importance of the press, the weakening of traditions, and the growing desire of citizens to be involved in politics, which ultimately made this model untenable. In a way, this is the evolution that occurred in the Southern Netherlands at an accelerated pace from 1815 to 1830. After their subjection to the autocratic tendencies of William I, intellectuals and journalists in the Southern Netherlands rapidly matured into constitutional theorists who, pulling the broader public along, devised their own brand of parliamentary-constitutional monarchy.

Alongside Montesquieu, whose influence on the Belgian founding fathers has already been ascertained (De Dijn, 2012), Benjamin Constant (1767–1830) was the author most cited in the constituent debates. In her chapter, Nora Timmermans investigates Constant's understanding of sovereignty. She finds that Constant's political theory is nowadays read and understood in light of the common liberal-democratic view that governmental authority should be popularly grounded yet limited by fundamental norms. As a result, the focus is mostly on Constant's claim that popular sovereignty has a limited rather than an absolute extension, and that certain fundamental rights are, by definition, outside its scope. The positive flipside of that conception, i.e., what Constant took popular sovereignty to mean within those limits, is underdeveloped. On the basis of Constant's 1815 *Principles of Politics*, this chapter reconstructs and reflects upon

Constant's conception of popular sovereignty. The main claim is that Constant distinguishes between 'governmental power' and 'sovereign power'. This latter concept refers to the specific power to establish or withdraw the legitimacy of government through assent. This is not a collective power: it is exercised by the individual and consists of critical judgment.

Next to Constant, the abbé Sieyès (1748–1836) was a key influence on all nineteenth-century debates about sovereignty. In her chapter, Olga Bashkina looks at Sieyès' work to investigate the origins of the national sovereignty doctrine. Even though Raymond Carré de Malberg cites him as the original theorist of national sovereignty, Bashkina notes that Sieyès himself was critical of the concept of 'sovereignty'. Nevertheless, Sieyès' work can shed new light on the opposition between popular and national sovereignty. The chapter suggests that his thinking can be divided into two paradigms: an immanent and a transcendent one. While Sieyès' thought shifted from an immanent to a transcendent understanding of the nation, ideas from both paradigms influenced theories of sovereignty in the nineteenth and twentieth centuries. By reading Sieyès in light of the relation between the immanent and the transcendent paradigm, this chapter questions the alleged incompatibility of popular and national sovereignty.

Against the general background sketched in the book's first section, Part II focuses on the Belgian Revolution and the drafting of the Belgian Constitution. Belgium's founding fathers were profoundly influenced by French liberal thinkers such as Montesquieu and Benjamin Constant. This fact is widely recognised, but very little research deals with its theoretical and conceptual implications. Belgium does not possess a genuine tradition of constitutional theory and history, resulting in a fragmentary and limited knowledge of the intellectual and theoretical background of the constitution's 133 articles. This section of the book goes some way towards remedying this. It starts with an overview of the intellectual context before 1830. Subsequent chapters investigate the key notions underlying the 1830–1831 constitutional construction, such as nation, people, liberty, sovereignty, constituent power, participation, and representation.

The intellectual context of the 1815–1830 period, which culminated in the break-up of the Restoration state of the 'united' Kingdom of the Netherlands, is provided by Stefaan Marteel. In his chapter, he reconsiders the debates of 1830–1831 in light of the development of liberal and Catholic strands of thinking from 1815 to 1830. He argues that two factors in particular were decisive in the emergence of a specific liberal-constitutional culture in the southern part of the Netherlands (especially in comparison with the North): the reaction of Belgian political thinkers to the 'imposed' nature of the union with the North (and its constitutional foundation) on the one hand, and the particularly strong influence of Benjamin Constant on the other. After considering the way in which pre-revolutionary ideas were expressed in the Belgian Constitution of 1831, Marteel charts the evolution of the different political strands that emerged in the wake of the constituent moment. In doing so, the chapter throws new light on the ideological rapprochement between liberals and Catholics, which fundamentally determined the founding fathers' choices in 1830–1831.

In his chapter, Christophe Maes investigates liberal political thought before and during the Belgian Revolution, with a specific focus on the notion of liberty. Although the Belgian Constitution was drafted by a minority of liberals and a majority of Catholics, its theoretical groundwork is most strongly indebted to liberal thought. In many constitutional choices, priority was given to liberty: the members of the 1830–1831 constituent assembly aimed to form a stable political system that would ensure the people's freedom and happiness through the limitation of political authority and the protection of individual rights. How this goal was to be achieved, however, remained a major object of discussion within the assembly, as there existed divergent views on the notion of liberty. This chapter looks into the relation between the drafters' understanding of liberty and their advocacy for specific institutions and shows that the influence of Germaine de Staël and Benjamin Constant was crucial in this regard.

A second important concept is 'constituent power'. In their chapter, Bas Leijssenaar and Christophe Maes combine a politico-theoretical and a legal-historical approach to analyse how the Belgian constituent assembly understood its own 'constituting' role. The first section of their chapter analyses the different ways in which constituent power can be interpreted and practiced. The second part applies these distinctions to the 1830–1831 debates and investigates the implicit and explicit conceptions of constituent power with which the congressmen operated. The chapter shows that strong ideological disagreement existed on the constituent role of the people, especially between the republican minority on the one hand and the liberal and Catholic majority on the other. According to the majority view, constituent power was to be institutionally and constitutionally domesticated. Although the congressmen were committed to the people's deep-seated right of resistance against oppressive rule, this did not imply a right for the people to assume a constituent role at any given moment. The Belgian Constitution was not based on the active consent of the people but merely 'emanated' from the people's passive consent.

In the next chapter, Brecht Deseure and Christophe Maes return to the 1830–1831 debates – both the public debate in the press and the formal debate in the national constituent assembly – in order to elucidate a number of key terms: sovereignty, people, and nation. Based on a systematic and in-depth reading of the original sources, they argue that the conceptual distinction between people and nation, which is crucial for the national sovereignty doctrine, was not present in 1830–1831. The term 'sovereignty' was rarely explicitly discussed by the congressmen, but the evidence shows that they regarded the people as the only source of sovereignty. The real fault line was not between national and popular sovereignty, but between divisible and indivisible sovereignty. The dominant opinion adhered to the former option, resulting in a liberal conception of state power.

Finally, the relation between sovereignty and representation is discussed. Christophe Maes and Brecht Deseure argue that the congressmen attributed a position of legislative primacy to the two chambers of parliament because these concentrated, in their midst, all the individual wills of the people and could therefore express the wish of the nation. Yet, parliament was not the only representative of the national wish, nor was it considered completely self-contained. Parliament's expression of the national wish was subject to constant evaluation by public opinion. When the assembly failed to respond to popular grievances, other representatives were qualified to address the issue. The king could disband the Chamber or pronounce his veto when the national interest required it. The jury, assessing press crimes and political crimes, could correct oppressive governmental action. And if all of this failed, the nation could resist and directly take matters into its own hands. This confirms the popular character of sovereignty in the Belgian constitutional system.

Part III of the book connects the philosophical and historical findings of the preceding chapters to contemporary debates on citizen participation, democratic renewal, and constitutional change. If one replaces the national sovereignty interpretation of the Belgian Constitution with a 'Constantian' reading, which emphasises the republican and participatory elements, there might be room for introducing forms of direct democracy. Although this was evidently not the option pursued by the founding fathers, we argue that it might nevertheless dovetail with the spirit of the Constitution. In contemporary Belgian politics, where party headquarters have become the most important centres of power, participatory or deliberative democratic procedures may constitute a valuable and even vital reinforcement of the power of citizens and of public opinion.

Several scholars have already criticised the distinction between national and popular sovereignty. Olga Bashkina's chapter on Raymond Carré de Malberg substantiates this critique and applies it to the Belgian case. She situates Carré de Malberg's theory in its historical context and explains the key concepts that structure his thinking. Moreover, she shows not only how his early formulation of national sovereignty allowed him to make a strong case against direct citizen participation but also how, later, he drastically shifted his position and even endorsed referendums. Returning to the Belgian Constitution, Bashkina asks whether Carré de Malberg's conception of sovereignty remains useful for the Belgian context.

In the next chapter, Christophe Maes, Brecht Deseure, and Ronald Van Crombrugge demonstrate that there is not one well-defined, sovereignty interpretation which undergirds Belgian constitutional thinking. Instead, sovereignty has been interpreted and redefined under the influence of new societal circumstances and at the service of changing political goals. This chapter traces the variety of sovereignty interpretations in Belgian textbooks and jurisprudence from 1831 to the present. It shows the broad variation along different theoretical and ideological lines that existed up until the consolidation of the national sovereignty doctrine around the middle of the twentieth century.

With the national sovereignty myth dispelled, a positive approach to citizen participation in Belgium becomes possible. Ronald Van Crombrugge explores how Belgian democracy can give a more prominent place to citizen participation. To this end, the chapter draws inspiration from recent initiatives at the sub-state level in Belgium to reinvigorate democracy. It discusses several examples of democratic innovation happening in Flanders, Wallonia, Brussels, and Ostbelgien, while also paying attention to the additional hurdles citizen participation is likely to face at the federal level, given Belgium's deeply divided nature.

Nenad Stojanović's chapter is written from the perspective of political science. Stojanović investigates the possibility of referendums in a linguistically divided society. Can other multilingual countries provide inspiration for the Belgian case? Stojanović gives a positive answer to this question. One of the reasons for the success of the Swiss multilingual polity is the routine use of direct democracy. Frequent referendums work as a unifying factor: everyone participates, and at each referendum new cleavages and coalitions arise, creating cross-cutting forms of conflict and loyalty. At the same, the divisions that appear in referendums dispel the populist illusion of a unitary 'popular will'. Moreover, participation in referendums can become a reason for national pride and a component of national identity. The comparative perspective developed in this chapter is relevant not only for Belgium but also for other countries that are culturally or linguistically divided.

Using a similar, comparative approach, Ronald Van Crombrugge explores the possibilities for democratic constitutional change in Belgium. One of the defining characteristics of modern constitution-making is the involvement of citizens in the drafting and ratification of a new or amended constitution. In Belgium, however, constitutional change has remained off-limits for citizens and is primarily the business of political party leaders and technocrats. This chapter argues against the elite-led nature of constitutional change in Belgium and refutes the dominant arguments in the constitutional doctrine which posit that the existing amendment procedure does not allow for citizen participation. Instead, it claims that an approach to citizen participation grounded in a communicative understanding of political representation is compatible with the existing constitutional structure. The chapter then looks at two recent examples of democratic constitution-making – Iceland and Ireland – for concrete inspiration and concludes by asking how these lessons could be practically applied in Belgium.

Raf Geenens sums up the major findings of the book in the concluding chapter. The chapter starts by providing a comprehensive interpretation of article 25 in light of the intellectual and political circumstances of 1830–1831. This interpretation is further substantiated by looking again at the debates in contemporary newspapers and by situating it in the drafters' broader constitutional project. In the second half of this chapter, the traditional doctrine of national sovereignty is extensively examined and the complete case against this doctrine is laid out. Finally, the chapter returns to the question of referendums, which has become the litmus test for interpretations of article 25. In line with the arguments developed in the previous chapters, it is concluded that referendums, although certainly not favoured by Belgium's founding fathers, could nevertheless be part of a coherent continuation of their project in contemporary circumstances.

Bibliography

Alen, A. (1984) *Rechter en bestuur in het Belgische publiekrecht: de grondslagen van de rechterlijke wettigheidskontrole* (Vol. I). Deventer and Boston: Kluwer.

Alen, A. and Muylle, K. (2011) *Handboek van het Belgisch staatsrecht*. Deventer and Boston: Kluwer.

De Dijn, A. (2012) 'A Pragmatic Conservatism. Montesquieu and the Framing of the Belgian Constitution (1830–1831)', *History of European Ideas*, 28(4), pp. 227–245. DOI: 10.1016/s0191-6599(02)00045-1.

De Meyer, J. (1985) *Staatsrecht*. Leuven: KU Leuven.

De Prins, D. (2011) *Handboek politieke partijen*. Bruges: Die Keure.

De Smaele, H. (2000) *'Omdat we uwe vrienden zijn': religie en partij-identificatie, 1884–1914*. Faculty of Arts, Unpublished PhD thesis. Leuven: KU Leuven.

De Witte, B. (2003) 'Do Not Mention the Word: Sovereignty in Two Europhile Countries, Belgium and the Netherlands', in Walker, N. (ed.) *Sovereignty in Transition*. Oxford: Hart Publishing, pp. 351–366. DOI: 10.5040/9781472562883.ch-015.

Delbecke, B. (2012) *De lange schaduw van de grondwetgever. Perswetgeving en persmisdrijven in België (1831–1914)*. Ghent: Academia Press.

Delpérée, F. (1987) *Droit constitutionnel. Tome I. Les données constitutionnelles*. Brussels: Larcier.

Dewachter, W. (2001) *De mythe van de parlementaire democratie. Een Belgische analyse*. Leuven: Acco.

Dewachter, W. (2014) *De trukendoos van de Belgische particratie*. Kalmthout: Pelckmans.

Dippel, H. (2005) 'Modern Constitutionalism, an Introduction to a History in Need of Writing', *Legal History Review*, 73(1–2), pp. 153–170. DOI: 10.1163/1571819054088670.

Errera, P. (1909) *Traité de droit public belge*. Paris: Giard et Brière.

Geenens, R. and Rosenblatt, H. (eds.) (2012) *French Liberalism. From Montesquieu to the Present Day*. Cambridge: Cambridge University Press. DOI: 10.1017/cbo9781139084178.

Gilissen, J. (1958) *Le régime représentatif en Belgique depuis 1790*. Brussels: La Renaissance du livre.

Gilissen, J. (1968) 'La Constitution belge de 1831: ses sources, son influence', *Res Publica*, 10, pp. 107–141.

Giron, A. (1884) *Le droit public de la Belgique*. Brussels: Manceaux.

Huyttens, E. (1844a) *Discussions du Congrès National de Belgique 1830–1831. Tome premier*. Brussels: Société Typographique Belge.

Huyttens, E. (1844b) *Discussions du Congrès National de Belgique 1830–1831. Tome deuxième*. Brussels: Société Typographique Belge.

Lancksweerdt, E. (2009) *Handboek burgerparticipatie*. Bruges: Die Keure.

Mast, A. (1950) *Overzicht van het grondwettelijk recht. Deel I*. Antwerp: Standaard Boekhandel.

Mast, A. (1981) *Overzicht van het Belgisch grondwettelijk recht*. Ghent: Story-Scientia.

Pirenne, H. (1926) *Histoire de la Belgique. Tome VI. La conquête française, le consulat et l'Empire, le Royaume des Pays-Bas, la Révolution belge*. Brussels: Lamertin.

Popelier, P. (2001) *Democratisch regelgeven*. Antwerp: Intersentia.

Rimanque, K. (2005) *De grondwet toegelicht, gewikt en gewogen*. Antwerp: Intersentia.

S.A. (n.d.a) *Parlementaire Stukken Kamer van Volksvertegenwoordigers* (Parliamentary documents of the Chamber of Representatives) [*Parl. St. Kamer*].

S.A. (n.d.b) *Parlementaire Stukken Senaat* (Parliamentary documents of the Senate) [*Parl. St. Senaat*].

S.A. (n.d.c) *Parlementaire Stukken Vlaams Parlement* (Parliamentary documents of the Flemish Parliament) [*Parl. St. Vl. Parl.*].

Schram, F. (2012) 'Juridische benadering van participatie' in Van Damme, J. et al. (eds.) *Participatie: What's in a Name? Een multidisciplinaire kijk op maatschappelijke participatie*. Bruges: Vanden Broele.

Senelle, R. (1974) *Commentaar op de Belgische grondwet*. Brussels: Ministerie van Buitenlandse Zaken.

Tilleman, B. and Alen, A (1992) 'General Introduction', in Alen, A. (ed.) *Treatise on Belgian Constitutional Law*. Deventer and Boston: Kluwer, pp. 1–25.

Uyttendaele, M. (2001) *Précis de droit constitutionnel belge. Regards sur un système institutionnel paradoxa*. Brussels: Bruylant.

Van Damme, J. et al. (eds.) (2012) *Participatie: What's in a Name? Een multidisciplinaire kijk op maatschappelijke participatie*. Bruges: Vanden Broele.

Van den Steene, W. (1963) *De Belgische Grondwetscommissie (oktober-november 1830): tekst van haar notulen en ontstaan van de Belgische grondwet*. Brussels: KVAB.

Van Ham, C., Thomassen, J., Aarts, K., and Andeweg, R. (eds.) (2017) *Myth and Reality of the Legitimacy Crisis: Explaining Trends and Cross-National Differences in Established Democracies*. Oxford: Oxford University Press. DOI: 10.1093/oso/9780198793717.001.0001.

Van Velzen, P. (2005) *De ongekende ministeriële verantwoordelijkheid. Theorie en praktijk 1813–1840*. Nijmegen: Wolf Legal Publishers.

Vande Lanotte, J. and Goedertier, G. (2013) *Handboek Belgisch publiekrecht*. Bruges: Die Keure.

Velaers, J. (1999) *De grondwet en de Raad van State, Afdeling Wetgeving*. Antwerp: Maklu.

Velu, J. (1986) *Droit public. Tome premier: le statut des gouvernants*. Brussels: Bruylant.

Wigny, P. (1952) *Droit constitutionnel*. Brussels: Bruylant.

Publications without a specific, personal author (such as newspapers and official documents) are listed under S.A.

Part I

Intellectual context

2 Constitutionalism in Restoration Europe

Markus J. Prutsch

Introduction

The period after 1814 can legitimately claim to have been "the age of constitutions" (Rotteck, 1830, p. 172), with a wide range of hopes and expectations being projected onto constitutional law, and constitutional questions gaining a historically unprecedented prominence throughout Europe – notwithstanding, or rather because of, the fall of the Napoleonic Empire.

Napoleon Bonaparte's (1769–1821) extensive Europe-wide reform and constitutionalisation agenda, symbolised by the creation of constitutional model states such as the Kingdom of Westphalia, was clearly recognised as being a power-political tool for making French hegemonic policies legitimate. Consequently, 'Napoleonic constitutionalism', including the release of written constitutions in the French sphere of influence, was not necessarily perceived as progress, but rather as an instrument of foreign domination: an assessment confirmed by the fact that none of the constitutions created under French influence developed into a functioning political system. Yet, while a sobering experience in many respects, 'Napoleonic constitutionalism' still cultivated the desire to set up constitutions. Demands for constitutionalisation gained additional momentum through the fact that the Napoleonic modernisation agenda gave rise to obvious improvements in the fields of administration and law, which might be given a conclusive form by being encased in a constitutional mould. Especially the introduction of the *Code Napoléon* signalised that the codification of the public realm was an irreversible process, and the fact that Napoleon's reform policies were imitated even in those parts of Europe that were not under direct French influence, such as Prussia,[1] demonstrated growing awareness that merely maintaining pre-revolutionary conditions was neither desirable nor likely to be possible.

The fall of the French Empire in spring 1814 made the question of how to deal with the revolutionary and Napoleonic legacy a most pressing one; in particular, it raised the question of how the issue of 'sovereignty' should be tackled, that is, how regimes could be legitimised and put on a solid basis. Perhaps the

1 For French influences on these reform projects in Germany, see Fehrenbach (1981).

main challenge in this regard was how to reconcile European princes' claim to preserve their monarchical sovereignty with post-revolutionary societies' expectations, especially their hopes for a constitutional state guaranteeing civil liberties and allowing for political participation. At the Congress of Vienna – in contrast to the widespread perception of the age after 1814 as having been merely 'reactionary', characterised by the attempt to go back to pre-1789 political and social conditions – it was generally felt that rigid neo-absolutism denied the *zeitgeist* and was therefore not a long-term solution.[2] In comparison, providing a 'constitutional answer' of some sort appeared as a more appropriate and less risky solution since it offered a potential bridge between the diverging aspirations of rulers and ruled. Yet, *what* concrete 'constitutional answer' to provide, and which constitutional model to follow, was obviously a delicate question.

With this in mind, the chapter seeks to answer the following questions:

1. What were the constitutional alternatives available in post-1814 Europe?
2. How far can the concept of 'constitutional monarchism' be claimed to have been a genuine political innovation and the dominant constitutional model of the Restoration period?
3. What were the prospects of institutionalising 'constitutional monarchism' in the longer term, and how can its status be assessed within the context of European constitutional developments, especially vis-à-vis the alternative of a parliamentary monarchy?[3]

Constitutional models in post-Napoleonic Europe

In the wake of the American and especially the French Revolution, an increasing number of constitutions saw the light of day. Within the range of constitutions that had been tested by 1814, two 'models' are particularly noteworthy: on the one hand, the large group of 'revolutionary constitutions', characterised by their emphasis on the principle of popular sovereignty and comprising not only the constitutional texts of the American (the constitutions of the American states since 1776 and the Federal Constitution of 1787) and French revolutions (the constitutions of 1791, 1793, 1795, and the Consular Constitution of 1799, as well as – though with certain qualifications – the Imperial Constitution of 1804), but also the Spanish Constitution of 1812 and the Norwegian Constitution of 1814; on the other hand, the somewhat specific model of the (unwritten) 'English Constitution'.

2 In his final report on the Congress of Vienna, Talleyrand described the unanimous disappointment felt by the European powers at the neo-absolutist way in which Ferdinand VII had returned to the Spanish throne in 1814: 'Rapport fait au Roi pendant son voyage de Gand à Paris' (June 1815). In Pallain (1881, p. 474).

3 This text is inspired by and largely based on the findings of my monograph on constitutional monarchism in post-Napoleonic Europe (Prutsch, 2013).

Revolutionary constitutions embodied the spirit of the revolutionary age in its essence: that power ultimately resides with the sovereign nation and that monarchs are accordingly a *pouvoir constitué* rather than a *pouvoir constituant* (if not to be replaced altogether by elected temporary officeholders such as a president). While revolutionary constitutions were not without any advocates in post-Napoleonic Europe, they were clearly struggling with widespread reservations and often open hostility not only among the political class, but also among large parts of the population that were still heavily under the impression of the preceding decades of war and unrest. Memories of the excesses of the French Revolution gave rise to the idea that constitutional systems based on revolutionary principles were arbitrary, unsteady, and hence inappropriate. It is thus not surprising that French constitutional models in particular had a bad reputation, since in their case scepticism towards the impetus of revolutionary constitutionalism as such converged with a distinct Francophobe mood after the Napoleonic Wars. However, non-French revolutionary constitutions were unable to gain much public support either. The main obstacle to an unbiased perception of these was the 'popular principle' on which they were based; this principle was manifest either in a radical republican form, as in the case of the American Constitution of 1787, or in a form that considerably limited monarchical power, as in the Cádiz Constitution of 1812 and the Eidsvoll Constitution of 1814. In addition, available information about practically all these constitutions was vague, insufficient, or highly biased, thus fundamentally standing in the way of an informed debate.

In contrast, knowledge about the 'English Constitution' was considerably better, despite the fact that this knowledge was based on the specific assessments of only a few authors, mainly Montesquieu (1689–1755), William Blackstone (1723–1780), and Jean Louis Delolme (1740–1806). Overall, the British constitutional system enjoyed a good reputation throughout Europe and was seen as a symbol of stability and political ethos. Notwithstanding the positive connotation of the English Constitution among both liberals and conservatives, their views diverged when it came to the question of whether this model should actually be imported as the legal basis for the constitutionalisation of other nations. While many liberals in Europe tended to answer this question in the affirmative, most conservatives referred to its unique 'home-grown' character and hence the non-transferability of the British constitutional system. At the root of conservative scepticism was the conviction that the English Constitution might be a splendid act of political reasoning for the British Isles, but was far too 'progressive' for other contexts – especially as far as the strong role of parliament vis-à-vis that of the monarch was concerned.

Anxiety about the suitability of foreign models for domestic constitutionalisation processes more generally was ingrained in a third – heterogeneous – group of constitutions that had emerged by (or were about to emerge soon after) 1814, featuring specific national variants of constitutional government that often harked back to a traditional corporatist understanding of society and political decision-making. Examples of such constitutions include not only the parliamentary-corporatist Swedish Constitution of 1809, but also many of the later *landständische* constitutions in the German Confederation.[4] By their very nature, these constitutions were difficult to implement in other settings.

In 1814, with no existing constitution both sufficiently universal *and* acceptable to the ruling classes, prospects of a real trans-European constitutional model were bleak. In the midst of this situation, a major constitutional innovation took place that had the potential to turn into such a model – tellingly in France. It was there, in the motherland of European revolutionary constitutionalism, that in spring 1814 Louis XVIII (1755–1824) managed to reinstate the Bourbon dynasty by means of what might best be characterised as 'constitutional monarchism'.[5] Wise enough to realise that "the restoration of the ancient line can mean any thing [*sic*!] else but the restoration of the ancient constitution of the monarchy" (*State and Prospects of Europe*, 1814c, p. 14 f.), he withstood the temptation to restore the monarchy with all its previous powers. Instead, the Bourbon Restoration largely rested on a constitutional tightrope act embodied by the *Charte constitutionnelle* ('Constitutional Charter').

Set up under Louis' personal direction as the new constitution of the country and formally proclaimed on 6 May 1814 (*Charte constitutionnelle*, 1814a), the *Charte* incorporated the legal achievements of the previous decades and established a modern representative system that involved the French nation in the political process. In this respect, the *Charte* included many of the liberal aspirations laid down in a constitutional draft prepared by the French Senate in the wake of Napoleon's deposition, which had been intended as the legal grounds for the restoration of the Bourbons (*Constitution française*, 1814b). At the same time, however, the *Charte* was based on a completely different ideology than the so-called 'Senatorial Constitution', namely on the doctrine that the *pouvoir constituant* and all state authority resided in the person of the king, thus, at least theoretically, rejecting a separation of powers. The most obvious expression of 'monarchical sovereignty' was the way the *Charte* was enacted, namely by royal *octroi*, rather than being voted upon by a parliament or confirmed by a popular plebiscite. The affirmation of what Friedrich Julius Stahl later termed the 'monarchical principle'[6] was the demarcation by which the new constitution was clearly distinguishable not only from its revolutionary predecessors but also

4 The German noun *Landstände* – and the adjective derived from it, *landständisch* – traditionally signifies the assembly of representatives of the estates of the realm, called together for purposes of passing legislation or deliberation. They are also known by the name *Landtag*. In post-Napoleonic Germany, however, the usage of the term *landständisch* was anything but consistent: while there was almost an omnipresent reference to *landständische Verfassung*, there was neither much agreement as to what this actually meant (and which features characterised such a constitution), nor even a clear understanding of the distinction between 'representative' and *landständische* constitutions.

5 See, e.g., Anderson (1967, p. 39 f. and 78 f.). On 'constitutional monarchism' – which might also justifiably be termed 'monarchical constitutionalism' – in post-Napoleonic Europe, see Prutsch (2013). See also Prutsch (2014; 2018; 2019).

6 For the first comprehensive theory of the 'monarchical principle' see Stahl (1845).

from the English constitutional system.[7] Rather, the *Charte* was in the spirit of Samuel von Pufendorf's (1632–1694) panegyric for a *monarchia limitata*, which he had sharply differentiated from *res publica mixta* in *De jure naturae et gentium* (1672)[8] by resorting to Hugo Grotius' (1583–1645) concept of 'limited monarchy'.[9] For Pufendorf, the *res publica mixta* and the division of sovereign power – in his eyes a "typical *faux pas* of Political Aristotelians" (Bödeker, 2002, p. 235) – exemplified the *res publica irregularis*. The only 'regular' polity was the *monarchia limitata*, in which the monarch was bound to certain laws and the consent of the nobles and the representatives of the nation, but continued to embody undivided sovereignty. This was of central importance for Pufendorf, who vehemently denounced the idea that supreme sovereignty must be crippled in a limited monarchy, even if the limits on the monarch were validated by a constitutional contract.[10]

The obvious contradiction between constitutional government and the undivided monarchical authority manifest in the *Charte* can be overcome by the distinction of *ius* and *exercitium*, that is, by the idea that political power is monopolised by the Crown, but its execution in part left to other subordinate constitutional institutions. While the provisions of the new constitution were nothing short of a full concession to the existing political and legal realities, at least in argumentative terms, the monarch was able to keep up appearances of constitutionalism as an act of voluntary grace and merely a variation of monarchical rule. In line with this logic, it was natural that the constitution's founding fathers avoided using the term *constitution*, charged as it was with revolutionary connotations. Instead, they sought an alternative and finally agreed upon *Charte*.[11] Rooted in the language of the Old Regime, the term stressed both awareness of tradition and the fact that the new order was not a mere continuation of existing constitutional documents, but was in fact a phenomenon *sui generis*.

While, at first glance, the term 'constitutional monarchism' seems to squeeze two seemingly contradictory concepts together, a closer examination reveals that it is exactly this apparent contradiction that represents the soul of the constitutional system established by the *Charte constitutionelle*. It was created out of a necessary compromise between 'old' and 'new' France, and for that reason it ultimately served as a potential means to overcome the political fragmentation

7 The 'monarchical principle' found its clearest expression in the preamble of the Constitutional Charter. See *Charte constitutionnelle* (1814). A detailed analysis can be found in Sellin (2008).

8 See Pufendorf (1692, Book 7, Ch. 5, Para. 13 and Book 7, Ch. 6, Para. 6–12). On concepts of *monarchia limitata* from Grotius to Pufendorf, see Dreitzel (1991, vol. 1, pp. 94–99).

9 See Grotius (1625), especially Book 1 Ch. 3. The term *monarchia limitata*, however, is not yet explicitly used by Grotius.

10 See Pufendorf (1692, Book 7 Ch. 6. Para. 10).

11 See Rémond (1965, p. 268 f.). See also Gangl (1966, p. 273 f.). Jacques-Claude Comte de Beugnot (1761–1835), a leading figure in the royal commission entrusted with drafting the actual text of the new constitution, took the credit for having urged for the term *Charte*. See Beugnot (1866, vol. 2, p. 218 f.).

of post-Napoleonic France. It is true that the *Charte* was less 'democratic' (especially regarding the actual number of those being granted franchise) than the constitutions drawn up during the Revolution or the senatorial draft. But taken as a whole and given the contemporary political challenges, the *Charte* was in some respects more 'balanced' and 'viable' than its predecessors.

Not only was the Crown the sole holder of executive power, but it also had a dominant position in the legislative process, disposing of a set of constitutional tools to exert influence on the composition and activity of the parliament as well as the judiciary. Nevertheless, monarchical power was far from unrestricted, and despite the king's leading role, he could no longer rule devoid of parliament without violating the provisions of the constitution. Many of the royal prerogatives such as the right of initiative in the legislation and the right to dissolve the second chamber were certainly powerful, but they could not obscure the fact that every bill and every budget proposal required the approval of both chambers. Moreover, the catalogue of fundamental rights set down in the *Charte* codified a legal space which could not, at least in theory, be violated by the executive power. Critics might still object that the new constitutional system was unable to entirely satisfy any particular political group in France, but this undecidedness could also be considered its very advantage.

In summary, it can be argued that constitutional monarchism as put into practice by the French *Charte* was a genuine innovation, representing a fragile but appropriate response to the demands of the post-Napoleonic age. However, this is with the important proviso that 'innovation' should not and must not be seen as an 'unprecedented novelty', but as a sagacious reshuffling of existing doctrines and institutions: natural and positive law, 'revolutionary' and 'classical' constitutionalism, liberalism and conservatism, parliamentarism and monarchism, representative government and monarchical sovereignty, civil rights and royal prerogatives. With the proclamation of the *Charte constitutionnelle*, an archetypal constitutional model undoubtedly saw the light of day. But which role would *Charte*-constitutionalism, shaped by and developed under its own unique 'French' conditions, play beyond the borders of France?

'Constitutional monarchism' as *the* post-1814 model? The case of Germany

The potential appeal of constitutional monarchism was the way in which it provided a viable alternative to revolutionary constitutionalism, offering a somewhat fragile but functional compromise capable of mastering the pressing political challenges of the post-Napoleonic age. In particular, the Crown – while defending claims to be the sovereign and institutional power hub – could position itself in a tradition of 'royal adaptability' and 'modernity', thus making 'Restoration' a dynamic adjustment concept rather than a synonym for outward repudiation of the revolutionary and Napoleonic legacy.[12] And indeed, a large number of

12 For such an interpretation of Restoration, see, e.g., Sellin (2001; 2017).

European nineteenth- and early twentieth-century constitutions can be classified as following the model of 'constitutional monarchism' as represented by the French *Charte*. Among them are those of the United Kingdom of the Netherlands (1815), the Kingdom of Poland ('Congress Poland'; 1815), the Southern German states of Bavaria, Baden, and Württemberg (1818 and 1819, respectively), Spain (1834), Greece (1844), Denmark (1849), Austria (1861/1867), the German Empire (1871) and Russia (1906), to name but a few.

Yet, it would be misleading to infer that there was an immediate and linear 'transfer' of the French *Charte* to those countries eventually opting for a monarchical-constitutional legal framework. In fact, attitudes towards any constitutional model were nuanced, as were motivations for constitutional takeovers. All in all, the perception and transfer of constitutional ideas and texts was an intricate process, and often much less 'informed' than one might expect. Germany, a keen implementer of constitutional monarchism and one of its most consistent defenders until the First World War, is a case in point and, at the same time, characteristic of the often diverging dynamics of public discourse and governmental politics.

When considering constitutional discourse in Germany around 1814, one can observe that among the middle class(es), interest in constitutional matters had been growing gradually since the second half of the eighteenth century. The *Befreiungskriege* had served as a catalyst, and after the victory over Napoleon, *Verfassung* was on everyone's lips. Conflict over 'constitution' and 'non-constitution' became *the* distinguishing hallmark of *Vormärz* Germany. Most contemporaries were aware that constitutionalism was not an issue specific to Germany. Instead, across Europe the *zeitgeist* of the period begged for 'harmony' between monarchical power and the widespread desire for freedom and liberty:

> Since [...] the social order in all realms and states of Western Europe is, with minor variations, basically the same, they are all facing the same task. One might certainly argue as to the nature of this task; but what always really matters is to harmonize princely power and liberty in such a way that they are no longer in conflict.
>
> (*Ueber den historischen Standpunkt bei dem Verfassungs-Werke*, 1817, p. 252)

However, one would be wrong to presume that awareness of the 'international' nature of the constitutional question resulted in some kind of 'pan-European' discourse, or an unbiased approach to foreign constitutional alternatives. Despite the intensity of intellectual debate in Germany, the perception of foreign political and constitutional 'models' was characterised by a lack of information, selectivity, and widespread scepticism, as was characteristic for the rest of Europe, too. Many non-German constitutional documents available at the time were largely disregarded in public debate. This holds true not only for the constitutions of the Nordic countries (the Swedish Constitution of 1809, the Norwegian Constitution of 1814), the United Kingdom of the Netherlands (1814) and

Congress Poland (1815), but also, with certain reservation, for the Spanish Cádiz Constitution of 1812 and the United States Constitution of 1787. Rather, the German *Bürgertum*'s interest in foreign constitutional systems was predominantly focused on two countries: France and Great Britain.

Still, knowledge of these two countries could not by any means be regarded as comprehensive,[13] and the way their political systems were perceived was anything but unanimously positive. French revolutionary constitutionalism based on popular sovereignty met with open hostility and was regarded as the opposite of a 'balanced' constitution. As a matter of fact, the Constitution of 1791 and even more so the constitutional documents of 1793 and 1795 as well as the Napoleonic Constitutions of 1799, 1802, and 1804 could be taken as classic examples of 'negative reception'. Antipathy against the Revolution could be conveniently combined with general anti-French resentments nurtured by the experience of the Napoleonic Wars: "If one asks [...] what general opinion agrees upon unconditionally and unanimously: it is hate and contempt of France" (Görres, 1854–1874, vol. 2, p. 13). This rejection was common among both conservatives and liberals. Many of the latter certainly accepted the fundamental principles of the (French) Revolution, such as a written constitution, the abolition of feudal privileges, and guarantees of civil rights. However, more often than not, liberals disclaimed any association whatsoever with the Revolution, and rarely would they come out wholly in favour of revolutionary constitutionalism. In contrast, the English Constitution enjoyed a good reputation across political camps in Germany. Nevertheless, while some liberals deemed Britain's constitutional system a worthy model for the constitutionalisation of Germany, most contemporaries argued that its 'home-grown' nature made it non-transferable. Above all, the British parliamentary system was considered incompatible with German historical traditions, particularly strong executive power.

Against this background, the *Charte* seemed to present a more favourable model, since it incorporated many worthwhile elements of the English Constitution, for example bicameralism, yet preserved monarchical sovereignty. However, enthusiasm for the French Charter among the German intelligentsia remained subdued. There were favourable comments on the constitutional text and recognition that the *Charte* was a useful means for pacifying the country under the restored Bourbon monarchy as well as that it was probably the best constitution France had manufactured so far. But any unreserved acknowledgement of the Charter as a model for Germany was foredoomed to failure on account of widespread Francophobia.

Biased reception and fragmentary knowledge of foreign constitutions and political systems – characterised moreover by frequent confusion of constitutional ideal and existing practice – made foreign constitutions at best a stockroom of

13 In 1818, for example, the Bavarian writer and jurist Johann Christoph von Aretin (1773–1824) felt obliged to encourage his fellow countrymen to intensify their study of French and English constitutional law. See Aretin (1818, vol. 1, p. 54).

arguments for political debate, not legal models for lasting institutional solutions. At the same time, the language of *landständische Verfassung*, which swamped the press around 1814/1815, embodied the emerging trend of self-referential political discourse and growing demands for 'national constitutions':

> The actual wording of a constitution and legislation may be the same in different nations; but they never produce the same results, which are more the outcome of the spirit and character of the people. Words can be transferred but not the spirit, which only develops and evolves in and through life.
>
> (*Allgemeine politische Annalen*, 1821–1824, vol. 10, p. 71, F. Murhard)

The idea that a constitution was the product of specific national conditions was to remain a – if not *the* – most crucial element in public constitutional discourse over the next few decades, both in Germany and beyond.

Public constitutional discourse, however, was just one side of the coin, practical politics the other. Even though most German intellectuals were themselves closely involved in state administration or worked for politicians, the ideas and objectives of intellectuals and state authorities were by no means the same. The former tended towards the legalisation of state power and the extension of political rights. The latter, however, wanted the consolidation of rule, which had to be accomplished with a minimum of political concessions. For the ruling class, the need to transform politics and polity had become clear during the Napoleonic age, resulting in a range of reform processes throughout Europe, including Germany. Demands for reform, however, had not been fully met, and at the end of the Napoleonic era, German rulers could no longer turn a blind eye to the 'constitutional problem'. During the Congress of Vienna, the promise to set up constitutions in all German states was finally put down in writing in the German Federal Act. But this promise was so vaguely expressed – "All Confederal states will be given a *landständische* constitution" (article 13) – that it was neither clear nor certain when, how, or if it would be fulfilled at all.[14] Nonetheless, prospects for constitutionalisation were better than ever before, especially in those German states confronted with burning domestic and foreign policy challenges like the Southern German *Mittelstaaten* ("medium-sized states") of Bavaria, Baden, and Württemberg. The question which remained was what these new constitutions should look like. While it was certain that 'revolutionary constitutionalism' would attract the ruling classes even less than the intelligentsia, monarchs were presumably more open to foreign models in general and French-style constitutional monarchism in particular; for them, the constitutional question was above all a pragmatic one and '(monarchical) class consciousness' still more relevant than 'national consciousness'. With pragmatic considerations of securing and

14 *Deutsche Bundesakte vom 8. Juni 1815.* Printed in Huber (1978, pp. 84–90). Art. 13: "In allen Bundesstaaten wird eine Landständische Verfassung statt finden".

stabilising political power prevailing, the appeal of the *Charte* is not particularly surprising. Considering that the English Constitution could be regarded as being either too 'home-grown' or handing over too much competence to parliament, and *landständische Verfassung* more of a slogan than a feasible model, constitutional monarchism as exemplified by the *Charte* was simply 'constitutional common sense' – and hence the only real alternative if a formal written constitution *and* the continued political preponderance of the Crown were the ultimate goals.

Prospects of constitutional monarchism and its role for European constitutionalism

This observation leads us to the question concerning the long-term 'potential' of constitutional monarchism and its role within the context of European constitutional history, especially in relation to the alternative of a parliamentary monarchy.

Constitutional monarchism can be argued to have been the most universal constitutional model after 1814. It found implementation in many different national contexts throughout Europe, representing a broad range of social, political, and cultural traditions. At the same time, not only were the motives for setting up monarchical-constitutional systems most diverse – securing the restoration of the monarchy (France 1814), consolidating rule in newly formed states and demonstrating foreign-political sovereignty (Southern Germany in 1818/1819), or making concessions to revolutionary movements (Prussia 1848 or Russia 1906) – but also the various monarchical-constitutional systems kept their distinctive features. They thus differed not only regarding the setup of the political institutions, civic rights granted, and franchise, but even regarding the definition and interpretation of the monarchical principle itself: the very nucleus of constitutional monarchism, which could be formulated more or less rigidly. In terms of performance, constitutional monarchism has encountered criticism both from contemporaries and in later scholarly research. Nevertheless, the legislative output of constitutional monarchism was not necessarily bad, and in many cases constitutional practice proved that such systems were able to tackle political, social, and economic reforms effectively. It is true, however, that the model of constitutional monarchism was particularly affected by the ongoing radical shifts in the way political power was legitimised and exercised.

Since the late seventeenth century, the general trend had been towards democratising, legalising, functionalising, and mediatising political rule, processes which intensified and accelerated during the nineteenth century. The democratic principle gained importance, which was manifest in growing demands for political participation, for civil rights, and for the introduction or extension of the franchise. It became progressively more difficult to argue for and justify the unrestricted political powers of the princes, whose role gradually changed from 'ruler' into responsible 'regent'.[15] This was all the more so since the political field was increasingly subjected to laws and left fewer and fewer legal 'black holes'. Accordingly,

15 On legitimisation – and indeed survival – strategies of European monarchies in the nineteenth century, see Sellin (2018).

it became more problematic, particularly for monarchs, to solve constitutional conflicts[16] without recourse to juridical arguments. During the revolutionary age, political confrontation had become radicalised in style and approach, and several constitutional conflicts were solved by open coups (France, Italy, the Netherlands, Switzerland). But after 1814, even in monarchical-constitutional systems, any assaults on existing constitutional regimes had to be supported by legal arguments. This was demonstrated by the attempts of King Charles X in France to justify the July Ordinances of 1830 and hence the *de facto* repeal of crucial constitutional provisions by referring to article 14 of the *Charte*.[17] In the second half of the century, constitutional conflicts were rarely solved by unilateral action on the part of the monarch. Long, drawn-out political and juridical struggles between monarch and parliament, as in Prussia (1862–1866) and Denmark (1884–1894), became the rule.

Parallel to the process of 'juridification' of the political realm was a drastic downgrading of established concepts of legitimacy. 'Tradition', the idea of an 'authority of the past', had been characteristic of the pre-modern age and served as a regulator for political life. In the modern age, however, the category of tradition was to be replaced by functionality[18] and originality, thus fundamentally changing the nature of politics. It was no longer possible to base political rule exclusively upon conviction about what had previously existed. Political institutions were forced to reassert their legitimacy through continuous activity and innovation. The concept of the 'divine right of kings' was no longer a solid basis for monarchical legitimacy. Monarchs – no matter how powerful they might be – were increasingly seen and judged rationally, and the awe which the officeholder had formerly commanded was now replaced by respect, which first had to be earned:

> No one any longer believes in the divine origin of the regent, no one any longer fears his physical power – thus there remains only the regard for him, the belief in the excellence of his intentions and the allegiance to institutions whose guardian he is and of which he is a part.
>
> (Andrian-Werburg, 1843, p. 178)

But the more rational the understanding of political institutions was, the clearer it became that monarchs were replaceable, especially if they did not live up to public

16 On the interplay of 'constitution' and 'conflict' in a long-term European perspective, see Müßig (2006).

17 Article 14 specified that "Le Roi est le chef suprême de l'Etat, il commande les forces de terre et de mer, déclare la guerre, fait les traités de paix, d'alliance et de commerce, nomme à tous les emplois d'administration publique, et fait les règlements et ordonnances nécessaires pour l'exécution des lois et la sûreté de l'Etat".

18 On the 'functional' character of the modern monarchy, particularly in the nineteenth century, see e.g. Böckenförde (1981, p. 159 f.); Dollinger (1985, p. 331 f.); Kirsch (1999, p. 389 f.; 2007).

expectations. In former times, monarchs might talk about freedom or constitutional government and yet continue to govern like despots. But in the nineteenth century, "the royal amateurs would now be taken at their word, and their pleasant speculations turned into anxious realities" (*Political State of Prussia*, 1846, p. 229). In fact, Louis XVIII's Restoration project was essentially based on the promise that the Bourbon monarchy was a better guarantee for the future development of the country than any other political alternative, which was, perhaps, the most central foundation stone on which Louis could confidently base his rule. All the more disastrous then, if this promise was not kept.

A no less demanding challenge for monarchical rule was the budding 'mediatisation' of Western society. The increasing importance of the press as a (mass) medium from the eighteenth century onwards ran parallel with the politicisation process among broader parts of the population and helped turn politics into an accessible 'mass market'. Political rule became more public – though not automatically more transparent – than ever before, and increasingly dependent on popular opinion created under the influence and within the framework set down by the press. Its capacity to set the 'political agenda' was clearly demonstrated during the French Restoration, when the press became one of the central players on the political stage. In such an environment, it became more important for political actors to win over the press or suppress it, to consider the impact their political decisions would have on the media, and to develop strategies on how to 'sell' and 'market' themselves and their political programmes. In this respect, the legitimacy of monarchical rule underwent crucial changes as well. Whether they liked it or not, the princes were now forced to live up to the expectations of the public. They were controlled rather than independent in their decisions and actions, and by the end of the nineteenth century, the ideal of an autonomous monarch had lost most of the foundations it may have once had.

Faced with such obstacles, the long-term prospects of constitutional monarchism were limited, even if the monarchical power maintained the ability and will to reform. It is certainly true that the monarchical-constitutional systems established in France, Germany, and other parts of Europe were not doomed to failure *a priori*, but had some potential for development. Despite this, however, the adaptability and reformability of these systems had clear limits. The more politics developed into a mass phenomenon and the more omnipresent the public desire and need to be actively involved in the political process was, the more anachronistic the concept of unrestricted monarchical sovereignty and authority became. As tradition lost its role as a cohesive element of monarchical rule, the more unstable the legitimacy of that rule became and the more exposed the monarch was to public discontent and criticism.

The dilemma was, basically, that in order to equip monarchical-constitutional systems to stand up to and surmount the challenges of the time through reform and evolution, the only reasonable way to go about it was to allow uncompromising democratisation and parliamentarisation, and to withdraw the monarch from the political frontline. Indeed, the need for such parliamentarisation and depoliticisation was recognised in contemporary political thought by writers such as Benjamin Constant (1767–1830), François-René de Chateaubriand (1768–1848), and Robert von Mohl (1799–1875).[19] If consistently applied, however, this meant that monarchs had to forgo their dominant political position, the typical feature of constitutional monarchism. Or, to put it another way: the only way to reform constitutional monarchism in the long term was by means of a change of regime, which would inevitably deprive the system of its very soul.

In this respect, constitutional monarchism – while giving the notion and practice of monarchy new vigour and perspective after 1814 – was forced to be a transitional phenomenon, representing neither a 'zero hour' nor 'the end' of European constitutionalism. In many cases, monarchical-constitutional systems paved the way for parliamentary forms of government. In these systems, there might still be a place for princes, but this would be predominantly as a head of state with a representative function, as a symbol of national unity, as a moral instance, or as an anchor of stability. They were, in any case, less and less an 'efficient part' of the constitution.[20] Parliamentary monarchies were more attuned to the 'rational principle' increasingly gaining ground in the nineteenth century, the progressing functionalisation of monarchy, and in particular the growing political aspirations of the middle classes. At the same time, for most contemporaries, parliamentary monarchy represented a potentially more appealing and stable alternative to republicanism, which continued to be negatively connoted throughout most of the century.

The revision of the French *Charte constitutionnelle* during the July Revolution of 1830 is a paragon for the structural shortcomings of constitutional monarchism and the transition from monarchical to parliamentary-monarchical constitutionalism.[21] The revolutionary crisis of 1830 culminated in the toppling of King Charles X (1757–1836) and a regime change, albeit one characterised not by a revolutionary transformation of the political system, but merely by a fundamental redesign of the monarchy, which was preserved as such. The revised *Charte* of 1830 reversed the power relation between the Crown and parliament, with the new King Louis-Philippe (1773–1850) becoming a *pouvoir constitué* with clearly limited prerogatives. The renunciation of the principle of monarchical sovereignty became manifest not only in Louis-Philippe's taking the oath to the new constitution at the Chamber of Deputies as a prerequisite for his ascending to the throne, but also in his being termed *Roi des Français* rather than the traditional *Roi de France*. Notwithstanding the redefinition of the monarchy, the defensive character of the regime change was beyond question. The dynastic rupture was

19 See, e.g., Constant (1814), Constant (1815), Chateaubriand (1814; 1816), and Mohl (1845; 1852).

20 See also Walter Bagehot's, in parts cynical, judgment of the British monarch's limited political role in the second half of the nineteenth century (Bagehot, 1867, pp. 57–117). For Bagehot, the monarch was only at the head of the "dignified part of the constitution", while the prime minister was at the head of its "efficient part" (ibid., p. 13).

21 On the revision of the *Charte constitutionnelle* in the crisis of 1830, which moved constitutional powers from the Crown to parliament, see Prutsch (2006).

kept to a minimum, with the Orléans branch succeeding the ruling Bourbon dynasty, and while the founders of the July Monarchy in 1830 were keen to limit royal power, they were anxious not to substitute the monarchical with the popular principle. Accordingly, the language of 'popular sovereignty' was consciously avoided, and a strict census suffrage was kept.

Shortly after the July Revolution, the transition towards parliamentary monarchy could also be witnessed north of the French border, namely in Belgium. Inasmuch as the French Revolution of 1830 inspired the uprising of the Southern Provinces of the United Kingdom of the Netherlands, there is an intrinsic link between the revised *Charte* of 1830 and the later Belgian Constitution of 1831 with regard to their formation and their content. Despite their respective specificities and the existing differences between them, both the *Charte* of 1830 and the Belgian Constitution of 1831 are exemplary for a burgeoning shift from monarchism to parliamentarism, with the Crown demoted to a mere 'constituted power' largely stripped of its pre-revolutionary legitimatory basis and prerogatives, and parliament increasingly turning into a constitutional centre of power. Yet, while the French July Monarchy collapsed in 1848, the Kingdom of Belgium – together with other cases – demonstrated the potential of parliamentary-constitutional monarchies to endure even in the long run, in some cases to the present day. This was possible because an evolutionary constitutional development towards increasing parliamentarisation and democratisation could be guaranteed, with the Crown withdrawing from day-to-day politics and contenting itself with the role of an 'authority in reserve'.

Conclusions

The period after the fall of Napoleon is often considered as animated by the attempt to revive the *Ancien Régime*, expressed by the term 'Restoration', which is meant to designate the anti-revolutionary period between 1814 and the later revolutions of 1830 and 1848, respectively. Yet, such an understanding of 'Restoration' is problematic, as Volker Sellin and other authors have demonstrated. On the one hand, it is doubtful whether 'Restoration' can be conceived as a uniform epoch of European history for the reason that the underlying conditions for various attempts at 'Restoration' varied considerably from country to country, as did their respective character and time frame. This is why 'Restoration' should be understood as a specific period within the history of monarchies rather than a clearly defined period of European history.[22] On the other hand, the time after 1814 has been demonstrated to have had considerable potential for innovation and was characterised by a distinctive revolutionary element itself – especially when it comes to constitutional matters.

22 See Sellin (2017, p. 122).

The model of constitutional monarchism exemplified by the French *Charte constitutionnelle* of 1814 can claim to have been a 'monarchical revolution': it was a device to renew and consolidate monarchical legitimacy by accepting central achievements of the Revolution, guaranteeing the rule of law, and granting subjects at least some effective political participation. This inherent ambivalence did not go unnoticed even among contemporaries, especially among those who had hoped for a complete shift away from the 'revolutionary spirit' after Napoleon's fall. One of them was Joseph de Maistre (1753–1821), who in a letter from St Petersburg dated 18 July 1814 clearly described the (French) Restoration as a continuation of the Revolution by other means:

> one would be entirely mistaken to think that Louis XVIII returned to the throne of his ancestors. He returned only to the throne of Bonaparte, which is already a great source of happiness for humanity, but we are far from repose. The revolution was initially democratic, then oligarchic, then tyrannical. Today it is royal, but it always follows its own path. The prince's art is to reign over the revolution and to softly suffocate it by embracing it. Directly contradicting the revolution or insulting it would be to risk reviving it and to lose oneself in the process.
>
> ('Saint-Pétersbourg, 6/18 juillet 1814'. In Blanc, 1860, vol. 1, p. 379)

This, too, underlines that the objectives of Restoration policies were essentially defensive in nature, aimed at the preservation of a monarchical form of government and especially what was later termed the 'monarchical principle'. Given that constitutions had been a central – if not *the* most fundamental – concern of both the American and French Revolution, it was simply consistent for Restoration policies to focus on constitutional issues as well. The central question was: how to react to the challenges of democracy without necessarily following the path of revolutionary constitutionalism? Constitutional monarchism, in its fusing of tradition and modernity and attempt to overcome the Revolution by a qualified 'internalisation' of some of its key legacies (thereby creating something qualitatively new), was a possible answer to that question in post-1814 Europe, and indeed the most successful of all: if there was anything like a trans-European constitutional model after 1814, it was that of constitutional monarchism.

Nevertheless, it was a model the concrete institutional expressions of which not only varied considerably from country to country, but also a model beset with a dangerous structural deficit, namely an immanent antagonism between the Crown and parliament resulting from the daring attempt to combine a modern representative constitution with a traditional monarchical concept of 'rule by one'. After all, constitutional monarchism represented the rearward battle of a traditional understanding of monarchical sovereignty and dynastic legitimacy in an age of democratic revolutions, with a clear trend for the 'democratic principle' gaining the upper hand in the long term. There was increasingly less appetite in nineteenth-century societies for monarchical omnipotence, especially if the perception was that monarchical prerogatives were abused to merely satisfy egotism and personal lust for power. Constitutional 'evolutions' were not impossible, but they did require the Crown to accept a progressing 'democratisation' of the monarchical system and thus its own political marginalisation. It was the lack of that preparedness on the part of the Crown that often paved the way for a revolutionary constitutional change – a change that did not necessarily imply the replacement of monarchy by alternative types of rule altogether, but could result in a forced transformation of monarchical government towards a parliamentary form as well.

Bibliography

Anderson, E.N. and Anderson, P.R. (1967) *Political Institutions and Social Change in Continental Europe in the Nineteenth Century*. Berkeley: University of California Press.

Andrian-Werburg, V.F. Freiherr von (1843) *Oesterreich und dessen Zukunft*. Hamburg: Hoffmann und Campe.

Aretin, J.C. Freiherr von [= Timonomus, B.] (1818) *Gespräche über die Verfassungs-Urkunde des Königreichs Baiern* (2 vols). München: K. Thienemann.

Bagehot, W. (1867) *The English Constitution*. London: Chapman and Hall.

Beugnot, A. (ed.) (1866) *Mémoires Du Comte Beugnot, Ancien Ministre (1783–1815)* (2 vols). Paris: Dentu.

Blanc, A. (ed.) (1860) *Correspondance diplomatique de Joseph de Maistre 1811–1817* (2 vols). Paris: Michel Lévy frères.

Böckenförde, E.-W. (1981) 'Der Verfassungstyp der deutschen konstitutionellen Monarchie im 19. Jahrhundert', in Böckenförde, E.-W. and Wahl, R. (eds.) *Moderne deutsche Verfassungsgeschichte (1815–1914)*. Königstein/Ts.: Athenäum, Hain, Scriptor, Hanstein, pp. 146–170.

Bödeker, H.E. (2002) 'Debating the "respublica mixta": German and Dutch political discourses around 1700', in van Gelderen, M. and Skinner, Q. (eds.) *Republicanism and Constitutionalism in Early Modern Europe*. Cambridge: Cambridge University Press, pp. 219–246. DOI: 10.1017/cbo9780511490750.012.

Chateaubriand, F.R.A. Vicomte de (1814) *Réflexions politiques sur quelques écrits du jour et sur les intérêts de tous les français*. Paris: Le Normant.

Chateaubriand, F.R.A. Vicomte de (1816) *De la monarchie selon la Charte*. Paris: Imprimerie des Amis du Roi.

Constant, B. (1814) *Réflexions sur les constitutions, la distribution des pouvoirs et les garanties, dans une monarchie constitutionnelle*. Paris: Nicolle, Gide.

Constant, B. (1815) *Principes de politique, applicables à tous les gouvernements représentatifs et particulièrement à la constitution actuelle de la France*. Paris: A. Eymery.

Dollinger, H. (1985) 'Das Leitbild des Bürgerkönigtums in der europäischen Monarchie des 19. Jahrhunderts', in Werner, K.F. (ed.) *Hof, Kultur und Politik im 19. Jahrhundert. Akten des 18. Deutsch-französischen Historikerkolloquiums Darmstadt vom 27.-30. September 1982*. Bonn: Röhrscheid, pp. 325–364.

Dreitzel, H. (1991) *Monarchiebegriffe in der Fürstengesellschaft. Semantik und Theorie der Einherrschaft in Deutschland von der Reformation bis zum Vormärz* (2 vols). Köln: Böhlau.

Fehrenbach, E. (1981) 'Verfassungs- und sozialpolitische Reformen und Reformprojekte in Deutschland unter dem Einfluss des napoleonischen Frankreich', in Berding, H. and Ullmann, H.-P. (eds.) *Deutschland zwischen Revolution und Restauration*. Königstein/Ts.: Düsseldorf: Athenäum; Droste, pp. 65–90.

Gangl, H. (1966) 'Die Verfassungsentwicklung in Frankreich 1814–1830', *Historische Zeitschrift*, 202(2), pp. 265–308. DOI: 10.1524/hzhz.1966.202.jg.265.

Görres, M. (ed.) (1854–1874) *Gesammelte Schriften* (9 vols). München: Literarisch-artistische Anstalt.

Grotius, H. (1625) *De jure belli ac pacis libri tres. In quibus jus naturae et gentium: item juris publici praecipua explicantur*. Paris: Buon.

Huber, E.R. (1978) *Dokumente zur deutschen Verfassungsgeschichte. 1. Deutsche Verfassungsdokumente 1803-1850*. Stuttgart: W. Kohlhammer.

Kirsch, M. (1999) *Monarch und Parlament im 19. Jahrhundert. Der monarchische Konstitutionalismus als europäischer Verfassungstyp – Frankreich im Vergleich*. Göttingen: Vandenhoeck & Ruprecht.

Kirsch, M. (2007) 'Die Funktionalisierung des Monarchen im 19. Jahrhundert im europäischen Vergleich', in Fisch, S., Gauzy, F. and Metzger, C. (eds.) *Machtstrukturen im Staat in Deutschland und Frankreich/Les structures de pouvoir dans l'État en France et en Allemagne*. Stuttgart: F. Steiner, pp. 81–97.

Mohl, R. von (1845) 'Constitutionelle Erfahrungen. Ein Beitrag zur Verfassungs-Politik', *Zeitschrift für die gesamte Staats-Wissenschaft*, 2(2), pp. 191–233.

Mohl, R. von (1852) 'Das Repräsentativsystem, seine Mängel und die Heilmittel. Politische Briefe', in Beyme, K. von (1966) (ed.) *Politische Schriften. Eine Auswahl*. Köln: Westdeutscher Verlag, pp. 118–224.

Müßig, U. (ed.) (2006) *Konstitutionalismus und Verfassungskonflikt: Symposion für Dieter Willoweit*. Tübingen: Mohr Siebeck.

Pallain, G. (ed.) (1881) *Correspondance inédite duPrince de Talleyrand et duRoi Louis XVIII pendant le Congrès de Vienne, publiée sur les manuscrits conservés au dépôt des Affaires étrangères avec préface éclaircissements et notes*. Paris: E. Plon.

Prutsch, M.J. (2006) *Die Charte constitutionnelle Ludwigs XVIII. in der Krise von 1830. Verfassungsentwicklung und Verfassungsrevision in Frankreich 1814 bis 1830*. Marburg: Tectum.

Prutsch, M.J. (2013) *Making Sense of Constitutional Monarchism in Post-Napoleonic France and Germany*. Basingstoke: Palgrave Macmillan. DOI: 10.1057/9781137291653.

Prutsch, M.J. (2014) '"Monarchical Constitutionalism" in Post-Napoleonic Europe', in Grotke, K.L. and Prutsch, M.J. (eds.) *Constitutionalism, Legitimacy, and Power: Nineteenth-Century Experiences*. Oxford: Oxford University Press, pp. 69–83. DOI: 10.1093/acprof:oso/9780198723059.003.0004.

Prutsch, M.J. (2018) 'Constitutionalism in Post-1814 Europe: Monarchy, Parliament and Sovereignty', *Giornale di Storia costituzionale/Journal of Constitutional History*, 35(1), pp. 33–47.

Prutsch, M.J. (2019) 'Constitutional Monarchism in Post-Napoleonic Europe', in Broers, M. and Caiani, A.A. (eds.) *A History of the European Restorations. Volume One: Government, States and Monarchy*. London: Bloomsbury, pp. 109–120. DOI: 10.5040/9781788318044.ch-008.

Pufendorf, S. Freiherr von. (1692) *Samuelis Pufendorfii de jure naturæ et gentium libri octo.* Lund [= Londini Scanorum]: Junghans.

Rémond, R. (1965) *La vie politique en France depuis 1789. Tome 1: 1789–1848.* Paris: A. Colin.

Rotteck, C. von. (1830) *Lehrbuch des Vernunftrechts und der Staatswissenschaften* (2 vols). Stuttgart: Franck; Hallberger.

S.A. (1814a) 'Charte constitutionnelle', *Bulletin des lois du Royaume de France*, 1(133), pp. 197–207.

S.A. (1814b) 'Constitution française', *Bulletin des lois du Royaume de France*, 1(13), pp. 14–18.

S.A. (1814c) 'State and Prospects of Europe', *Edinburgh Review*, 23(45), pp. 1–40.

S.A. (1817) 'Ueber den historischen Standpunkt bei dem Verfassungs-Werke', *Journal für Deutschland, historisch-politischen Inhalts*, 8, pp. 231–255.

S.A. (1821–1824) *Allgemeine politische Annalen.* Munich, Stuttgart, Tübingen.

S.A. (1846) 'Political state of Prussia', *Edinburgh Review*, 83(167), pp. 224–239.

Sellin, V. (2001) *Die geraubte Revolution. Der Sturz Napoleons und die Restauration in Europa.* Göttingen: Vandenhoeck & Ruprecht.

Sellin, V. (2008) 'Die Erfindung des monarchischen Prinzips. Jacques-Claude Beugnots Präambel zur Charte constitutionnelle', in Heinen, A. and Hüser, D. (eds.) *Tour de France. Eine historische Rundreise. Festschrift für Rainer Hudemann.* Stuttgart: F. Steiner, pp. 489–497.

Sellin, V. (2017) *European Monarchies from 1814 to 1906. A Century of Restorations.* Munich: De Gruyter Oldenbourg.

Sellin, V. (2018) *Violence and Legitimacy: European Monarchy in the Age of Revolutions.* Munich: De Gruyter Oldenbourg.

Stahl, F. J. (1845) *Das Monarchische Princip. Eine staatsrechtlich-politische Abhandlung.* Heidelberg: Mohr.

Publications without a specific, personal author (such as newspapers and official documents) are listed under S.A.

3 Benjamin Constant and the limits of popular sovereignty

Nora Timmermans

The first French theorist of liberal democracy

Over the past few decades, scholars of both political theory and intellectual history – and from both sides of the Atlantic – have managed to carve a position for Benjamin Constant (1767–1830) as a canonical political theorist, if not in his own right, at least as a crucial rung in the evolution of Western modern political thought. Helena Rosenblatt (2009) has shown that the ideas of Constant, who was active as a writer, philosopher, journalist, and politician, have been influential from the moment they were first formulated, albeit in different ways and directions. Yet, nowadays, it is especially Constant's keen eye for constitutional mechanics that is appreciated in the secondary scholarship. The scholarly interest in Constant's constitutional and political thought reflects the sense of crisis that has been haunting liberal democracy ever since the 1960s and that has taken different forms. Today, it is the worldwide success of populism and the growing number of authoritarian regimes that feed both the belief that liberal democracy is in urgent need of saving and the interest in Constant's political thought.

The first wave of Constant-interpretation was immersed within so-called 'Cold War liberalism'. Isaiah Berlin's 1958 essay 'Two Concepts of Liberty' (1969) is probably the most famous example of this approach. Keeping totalitarianism at bay was the central tenet of Western political thought after the Second World War, especially when the vivid memory of fascism was amplified by growing communist regimes in the East (Rosenblatt, 2009, pp. 369–373; Timmermans, 2019, pp. 184–188). In this context, interpreters tended to overemphasise Constant's distrust of politics, thereby reducing his political theory to a single argument for the primacy of 'negative liberty', i.e. of an area of individual existence where political interference is absent altogether (Berlin, 1969; Dodge, 1980).

Post-1968, the attention shifted towards the positive elements in Constant's political thought. Hofmann's publication of the manuscript *Les principes de politique applicable à tous les gouvernements* (1980) facilitated the shift by making one of Constant's most sophisticated political treatises, written between 1806 and 1810 but unpublished, for the first time widely accessible to scholars. The text develops much of the theoretical foundations that Constant draws on in his later works. The year 1980 also marked the start of the ambitious and ongoing project to publish Constant's *Oeuvres complètes*[1] and the publication of the influential interpretations of Constant's political theory by Stephen Holmes and Marcel Gauchet. Grange's publication of the *Fragments d'un ouvrage abandonné sur la possibilité d'une constitution républicaine dans un grand pays* (1991) added another fundamental, hitherto unpublished political treatise to the available body of Constant's work. The manuscript was written at about the same time as the 1806 *Principles* and elaborates for the first time – and in a republican framework – Constant's famous notion of '*le pouvoir neutre*' (Cf. Rolland, 2008).

The thus-expanded primary material was enthusiastically interpreted in the late 1990s and early 2000s. Biancamaria Fontana (1991), George Armstrong Kelly (1992), Lucien Jaume (1997), Tvzetan Todorov (1999), and Helena Rosenblatt (2008), among others, have made key contributions to the present understanding of Constant's political thought. Today, the contours of that understanding are well in place (e.g. Chopin, 2002, pp. 35–40; Delbouille, 2006, p. 260; Garsten, 2009, p. 92; Vincent, 2011, p. 110): Constant, together with his intellectual inspiration Germaine de Stael and the better known and widely read Alexis de Tocqueville, is considered to be at the origins of a French branch of political liberalism that brought about the first (French) theorists of 'liberal democracy' (cf. Geenens and Rosenblatt, 2012). The approach is eloquently summarised by Tzvetan Todorov:

> Constant invents neither the democratic (or republican) principle of the sovereignty of the people nor the liberal principle of the limitation of power. Nonetheless it is he who articulates them, who holds them up against the real-life experience of the Revolution, the Empire, and the Restoration, who thus gives flesh to abstractions. It is he who reveals their consequences and sometimes their dangers. Constant is one of the first, and one of the most brilliant, authors who chose, among all the options that arose at the time, the one that appears to us today to be obvious (even if we are far from fulfilling it in all its perfection) – Revolution without Terror, popular sovereignty with respect for personal freedoms. In this, he is the first French theorist of liberal democracy.
>
> (Todorov, 1999, p. 41)

Under the guise of divergent labels such as '*liberalisme du sujet*' (Jaume, 1997), 'political moderation' (Craiutu, 2012), or 'liberal republicanism' (Jainchill, 2008), contemporary interpreters tend to focus on Constant's conception of the *legitimacy* of political rule instead of on his supposed preference for the altogether absence of rule. Underlying this shift is the assumption that Constant "occupies an intriguing middle ground in comparison to other positions of his time" when

1 See Delbouille (2006, p. 260) and see Université de Lausanne's project webpage: https://www.unil.ch/ibc/fr/home/menuinst/publications/oeuvres-completes.html

it comes to "the tension between popular sovereignty and the restraints on sovereignty" (Geenens and Sottiaux, 2015, pp. 305–306). This "intriguing middle ground" is also the purported reason why Constant's political thought is not merely of historical interest but also of particular relevance for present-day political theory and practice (cf. Hofmann, 1980, p. 380; Holmes, 1980, p. 260; Todorov, 1999, p. 41). Constant represents the commonsensical position that governmental authority can and should be at once popularly grounded and limited by a more fundamental framework (be it normative, political, or constitutional).

This "intuitive" liberal democratic rendition is reflected in the abundant scholarly attention that has been given to Constant's conception of limited popular sovereignty, as a result of which the following passage has become the most quoted of Constant's entire oeuvre:

> There is, on the contrary, a part of human existence which by necessity remains individual and independent, and which is, by right, outside of any social competence. Sovereignty has only a limited and individual existence. At the point where independence and individual existence begin, the jurisdiction of sovereignty ends. If society oversteps this line, it is as guilty as the despot who has, as his only title, his exterminating sword.
>
> (Constant, 1815/1988, p. 177)

The passage itself is well known by now, but it raises two issues that are rarely addressed in the secondary literature. First, there is the issue that the boundaries of "social competence" need to be defined and justified. This distinct problem is not discussed here (I do not know of a comprehensive analysis of this issue, but Feldman [2008, pp. 682–689] offers some useful reflections). Secondly, Constant's statements regarding the limited character of sovereignty say very little about how sovereignty should be understood within those limits. This is the issue that this chapter seeks to address. Generally, it has been overlooked by the secondary literature. This negligence is to a certain extent excusable, given that, as we shall see, Constant himself only cursorily developed the positive side of the principle of popular sovereignty. But without a positive account of Constant's conception of popular sovereignty, the liberal democratic rendition of Constant's position will always remain something akin to an intuition rather than a full-fledged theorisation. This chapter favours the latter approach and aims to clear a path for it.

One positive reading promoted within the contemporary Constant literature is Bryan Garsten's analysis of Constant's theory of representative government (Garsten, 2009).[2] Garsten argues that Constant's theory aims to keep open and maximise the opportunities for the popular contestation of governmental representation. Constant's aim is contrasted with a more unilateral and superficial understanding of representative government, which would be "asking the government

2 Similar interpretations have been put forward by Gauchet (1995; 1997; 2005), Manent (1994), and Vincent (2011).

as a whole to represent the popular will as it can be found through any particular vote or poll" or "as it could be imagined to emerge from a process of deliberation or from an independent analysis of the public interest" (ibid., p. 91). Constant sought to "multiply and challenge governmental claims to represent the people" (ibid.) and did so for "fundamentally democratic reasons" (ibid., p. 92):

> In asking instead for a government to multiply and challenge representative claims, representative government aims (on this view) to provoke debate about precisely what the popular will is and thereby to prevent any one interpretation of the popular will from claiming final authority. It aims to foster and institutionalize popular impatience with our rulers, to both fuel and channel popular grievances against those in power.
>
> (Ibid., p. 91)

Constant's conception of representative government thus reflects "a fundamental and unchanging desire to find ways of institutionalizing resistance to centralizing and usurping authority" (ibid., p. 100). Although I fundamentally agree with Garsten's conclusions, which characterise Constant's position as 'liberal democratic' because it is pluralist and dynamic, I believe they are not sufficiently grounded in Constant's texts. My analysis serves both as a theoretical foundation and a critical examination of that liberal democratic assessment.

It starts with a reconstruction of Constant's understanding of the principle of popular sovereignty, starting from his 1815 *Principles of Politics.* Constant never used the term 'principle' light-heartedly and neither did he when discussing the principle of popular sovereignty. All of his theoretical endeavours are predicated on the assumption that there are principles to everything that exists. This is not to say that Constant has much patience for abstract theorising or metaphysics; the principles he has in mind are based on (his assessment of) political experience: they can be discovered, explained, and, most importantly, applied (Hofmann, 1980; Fontana, 1991, pp. 13–16). With the discovery of and adherence to principles, Constant seeks to ward off arbitrariness, i.e. "the absence of rules, limits, definitions, in one word, the absence of everything that is precise" (Constant, 1797/2003, p. 38). Arbitrariness, according to Constant, should be avoided at all costs, especially in politics. This is why he has always taken a special interest in debunking the falsities that his opponents have advertised under the guise of principles (cf. Constant, 1806/2003, p. 22). He does so by rigorously dissecting the terms and concepts they use. Even though I do not aim to disparage Constant's principle of popular sovereignty, I believe that bringing a similar conceptual rigour to bear on his own argumentation concerning this principle is the best way to reconstruct its meaning and its implications. This is what I do in the section 'Constant's Principle of Popular Sovereignty'. In the section 'Assent as Sovereign Power', I scrutinise two particular elements of the conception of popular sovereignty that results from my reconstruction in the first section: Constant's understanding of the collective subject of popular sovereignty and his arguments concerning the institutions needed for the exercise of popular sovereignty. As I argue in the concluding section, 'The

Political Implications of Popular Sovereignty', Constant avoids some of the problems usually associated with constitutionalism by limiting popular sovereignty to its critical dimension and detaching it from its constitutive dimension. But first, a few words about Constant's oeuvre are due.

Constancy in Constant's work?

As Biancamaria Fontana has accurately noted (Fontana, 1991, p. 11), one particular issue that every Constant scholar has to confront is the point of entry into his vast body of work. Constant wrote numerous political treatises (two of his more important ones even remained unpublished during his life) and published several pamphlets and many newspaper articles. He maintained an extensive correspondence with family, friends, and colleagues across Europe and his interventions in parliament are well documented.[3] In addition to the sheer size of his oeuvre, Constant enthusiastically copy-pasted within his own texts. It is therefore notoriously difficult to separate the wheat from the chaff in terms of the originality of his ideas.

Moreover, Constant has a reputation for being politically versatile. Active as a political actor from 1796 until 1830, his career spanned more than 30 years – the most turbulent ones of the post-revolutionary era. Other contemporary interpreters have done the work of analysing Constant's positions in light of their shifting political context. As I do not assess Constant's overall political evolution nor the theoretical consistency of his oeuvre as a whole here, it suffices to say that despite some discussion on when precisely Constant reached his mature theoretical position (for a short but useful overview, see Vincent, 2011, p. 18 and footnotes), most contemporary analyses argue for a certain degree of theoretical, if not political coherence in his work, thus rejecting the ad hominem criticism that Constant was an opportunistic turncoat (cf. Deguise, 1966, pp. 3–37; Deguise traces the formerly prevalent hyper-negative assessment of Constant's personality back to Saint-Beuve's detrimental portraits).

My reconstruction of Constant's conception of popular sovereignty starts from the first chapter of the 1815 *Principles of Politics (Principes de politique applicables à tous les gouvernements représentatifs et particulièrement à la constitution actuelle de la France)*, titled 'On the Sovereignty of the People'. This is the first published text where Constant posited his adherence to "the principle of the sovereignty of the people" in those precise terms. Unfortunately, Constant does not live up to his ambition of providing a "precise and exact definition" (Constant, 1815/1988, p. 175) of the principle of sovereignty. Its meaning needs to be reconstructed based on the subsequent argumentation in the first chapter. My objective is precisely to follow the internal logic of this particular text to reconstruct and interpret its argumentation. Pieced together, this argumentation turns out to be as simple as it is compelling, for it seems to adopt a logical more than a political rationale.

3 Constant was appointed as Tribune from 1799 until 1808 and elected as deputy from 1819 until 1822 and from 1824 until his death in 1830 (Wood, 1993, pp. ix–x).

That I follow the text's internal, conceptual logic also means that I intentionally refrain from the historical contextualisation of Constant's positions. The question of whether my reconstruction is representative of Constant's overall position nevertheless stands, especially since Constant seems to shift to a more conditional endorsement of popular sovereignty after 1815 (Constant, 1818/1872, p. 275). At the beginning of 1830, Constant even appears to have come to the unqualified rejection of popular sovereignty:

> Two systems have, throughout history, divided the world: the system of popular sovereignty that I deny and the system of divine right that I detest. [...] Let us ban the word sovereignty, properly speaking, from our vocabulary. There are, in society, needs to fulfil, faculties to exercise, liberties to guarantee. Unlimited sovereignty does not exist anywhere.
>
> (Harpaz, 1989, p. 176)

Kalyvas and Katznelson (1999) have argued that there was a fundamental evolution in Constant's views on political legitimacy, although they have identified a different tendency on the basis of different texts ("As Constant's thought matured, he moved from a primarily republican position, then to a purely liberal orientation, culminating in a more synthetic hybrid we call immanent liberalism, encompassing three apparently opposed principles of legitimacy: democratic, liberal, and traditional", Kalyvas and Katznelson, 1999, p. 514). According to their categorisation, the 1815 *Principles of Politics* that is my focal point is situated within the last stage of Constant's intellectual development. I, however, contend that there is more consistency in Constant's views on political legitimacy and that the later stage is fully compatible with the earlier ones (for this reason, I will occasionally draw on both earlier and later texts as well). Constant's understanding of sovereignty has always been at once popular and limited. Even in his very first pamphlets, published in 1796 and 1797 in support of the Directory, Constant argues against arbitrary power and in favour of constitutional limitations (e.g. Constant, 1796/2003). He thus consistently rejects a particular, unlimited understanding of popular sovereignty. Consequently, the shift indicated above exists only in the formulation of his position, not in its essence. As I show in this chapter, Constant endorses a similarly consistent positive conception of popular sovereignty, although it is a particular one.

Constant's principle of popular sovereignty

The opening paragraph of Constant's 1815 *Principles of Politics* reads as follows:

> Our present constitution formally recognizes the principle of the sovereignty of the people[4] that is the supremacy of the general will over any particular will.

4 Constant refers to the (in)famous *Acte additionnel aux Constitutions de l'Empire du 22 avril 1815*, also known as 'la Benjamine', written by Constant himself, at the request and under the supervision of Napoleon Bonaparte during the Hundred Days. In fact, the *Acte additionnel*

> Indeed this principle cannot be contested. In our days many have attempted to obscure it; the evils which were caused and the crimes which were committed on the pretext of enforcing the general will lend apparent strength to the reasonings of those who would like to assign a different source to the authority of governments. Nevertheless those reasonings cannot stand against the simple definition of the words they use. The law must be either the expression of the will of all, or that of the will of some.
>
> (Constant, 1815/1988, p. 175)

Constant identifies "the principle of the sovereignty of the people" with "the supremacy of the general will over any particular will". This identification needs to be understood in light of Constant's contention that "[t]here exist only two kinds of power in the world. The one, illegitimate, is force. The other, legitimate, is the general will" (ibid.). Constant argues that if power serves a particular will, it is always illegitimate because it must be based on force ["*la force*"] (ibid., note that Fontana's translation of both '*force*' and '*pouvoir*' into 'power' is imprecise at this point). If power serving a particular will would not be based on force, it would be "sanctioned by the assent of all" ['*l'assentissement de tous*'] (ibid.). In other words, it would no longer serve a particular will, but the general will. A particular will can thus only prevail on the basis of force. And because "force belongs to whoever takes it", it is senseless to call power that is based on force "legitimate" (ibid.).[5]

It follows that the principle of popular sovereignty or "the supremacy of the general will over any particular will" for Constant simply means that legitimate power should prevail over illegitimate power. And being "sanctioned by the assent of all" is a necessary condition for power to be legitimate. It is, of course, not a sufficient condition; in the 1815 *Principles of Politics* as well as in other texts, Constant stresses that the legitimacy of political power also depends on its limited extension (e.g. ibid., p. 177). Here, as I am only addressing the positive meaning of popular sovereignty, it is important to note that even if political power stays within its proper limits, it requires the sanction of the assent of all to be legitimate. Any kind of power that is not sanctioned by general assent simply amounts to force and is therefore illegitimate. Power sanctioned by the assent of all should prevail over power that is not sanctioned by the assent of all. Constant asserts that this basic provision holds true for every type of political system:[6]

makes no explicit mention of 'popular sovereignty', nor for that matter do the other constitutions of the Empire that the *Acte additionnel* is meant to supplement and modify. It merely states in the preamble: "In consequence, the following articles, forming an act supplementary to the constitutions of the Empire, shall be submitted for the free and solemn acceptance of all citizens throughout the whole extent of France" (https://www.napoleon-series.org/research/government/legislation/c_additional.html).

5 Here Constant's argument echoes Rousseau's analysis of 'The Right of the Strongest' in *The Social Contract* (Rousseau, 1762/2002, p. 158).

6 Constant does not make a distinction between assenting to the regime as a whole (the way it is organised) or its concrete policies. This has to do with the fact that, as I show, Constant's

> This principle applies to all institutions. Theocracy, royalty, aristocracy, whenever they rule men's minds, are simply the general will. When, on the other hand, they fail to rule them, they are nothing but force. In short there are only two sorts of power in the world: one, illegitimate, is force; the other, legitimate, is the general will. But while we recognize the rights of that will, that is, the sovereignty of the people, it is necessary, indeed imperative, to understand its exact nature and to determine its precise extent.
>
> (Ibid., p. 175)

The principle also works the other way around: in theory, given that it does not exceed its limits, every form of power that is properly sanctioned by the assent of all can be legitimate, regardless of how it is organised or exercised. Constant only excludes anarchy and despotism, which, according to him, cannot be the object of assent:

> This principle does not deny the legitimacy of any form of government. In some circumstances society may want a monarchy and in others a republic. So these two institutions may therefore be equally legitimate and natural. Those who declare one or the other illegitimate or against nature are either party mouthpieces and do not say what they think, or else they are ideological dupes and do not know what they are saying. There are only two forms of government, if we may even give them that title at all, which are essentially and eternally illegitimate, because no society could want them: anarchy and despotism.
>
> (Constant, 1806/2003, p. 7)

But what does it mean, for power to be sanctioned by the assent of all? In any case, it does not mean that power needs to be exercised through a particular form of government. Constant deems the principle of popular sovereignty to be a universal principle, valid for all governmental regimes. Constant's understanding of popular sovereignty hence does not require governmental power to be exercised by the people at large for it to be legitimate. Governmental power exercised by a small number of rulers (or a single one) can be equally legitimate if the requirements are met. In fact, although Constant spends the larger part of his political theory explaining how *governmental power* should be organised and exercised, this is of little relevance for his understanding of *popular sovereignty*.

I argue that a proper understanding of Constant's conception of popular sovereignty should be based on the implicit distinction that his framework makes between two kinds of political power, i.e. 'governmental power' and 'popular sovereignty'. I am aware that this distinction looks similar to Rousseau's well-known differentiation of 'sovereignty' and 'government' (cf. Tuck, 2016), or

conception of sovereign power does not have a constituent dimension. There is hence no other option than to express one's assent through the existing regime.

to the distinction between constituent power and constituted power that is at the centre of contemporary debates in constitutional and democratic theory (cf. Walker and Loughlin, 2008). But the resemblance is deceptive. It is true that Constant and Rousseau attribute an equally general application to the principle of popular sovereignty, deeming it to be at the basis of all legitimate political systems. But for Rousseau, the decisive feature of popular sovereignty is that the legislative power is exercised by the people as a collective body (Rousseau, 1762/2002, p. 179; Manin, 1997, pp. 74–75). The governmental form is determined by the body that exercises executive power. In a democracy, e.g., the whole or the majority of the people exercise both legislative and executive power and are thus both sovereign and government (Rousseau, 1762/2002, p. 199). Recently, it has been argued that Rousseau's definition of sovereignty thus identifies it with constituent power, i.e. with fundamental decisions about the organisation of society, whereas 'government' concerns everyday politics (Tuck, 2016; Colon-Rios, 2016).

Whether or not one accepts this 'constituent' reading of Rousseau, it does not overlap with the distinction that I identify in Constant's framework. For Constant, legislative power, even of the constituent kind, is situated in the sphere of 'governmental power' and can be exercised by a small minority. In other words, Constant's understanding of governmental power comprises both Rousseau's understanding of 'sovereignty' (legislative/constituent power) and Rousseau's understanding of 'government' (executive power/everyday politics). Constant's principle of popular sovereignty is thus not dependent on the manner of the exercise of executive power or legislative power. For Constant, popular sovereignty concerns a separate form of power that I call *sovereign power*. As I show in the remainder of the chapter, sovereign power is a proper though particular form of political power. Sovereign power means that the sanction of the assent of all establishes *the legitimacy of governmental power*. It does not have a constituent element. The implications of this understanding of popular sovereignty are discussed in the concluding section. First, the particular features of Constant's conception of sovereign power need to be examined.

Assent as sovereign power

The collective subject of sovereign power

The first feature that I examine is the collective, i.e. the popular element of Constant's understanding of sovereign power. Even though Constant's preoccupation with the individual and individual rights has often been emphasised in the secondary literature, except for the 'constructivist' rendition proposed by Garsten, his particular conception of the collective subject of popular sovereignty has not been given much attention. I argue that Constant theorises the subject of popular sovereignty as an aggregate of individuals, rather than as a 'body politic' (a political community in the sense of a single moral person with a separate, independent collective personhood and agency).[7]

Throughout his texts, Constant refers to the subject of popular sovereignty in rather vague and strongly varying terms: 'the association', 'society', 'the people', 'the nation', or even just 'all' ('*tous*'). When discussing popular sovereignty in the 1815 *Principles of Politics*, the most elaborate account Constant gives of its subject is, in fact, a negative one:

> In a society founded upon the sovereignty of the people, it is certain that no individual, no class, are entitled to subject the rest to their particular will. But it is not true that society as a whole has unlimited authority over its members. The universality of citizens is [the] sovereign in the sense that no individual, no faction, no partial association can arrogate sovereignty to itself, unless it has been delegated to it. But it does not follow from this that the universality of citizens, or those who are invested with the sovereignty by [it], can dispose sovereignly of the existence of individuals.
>
> (Constant, 1815/1988, pp. 176–177, modified translation)

It is clear by now that Constant focuses mostly on what sovereignty does not mean. And it certainly does not mean unlimited power. Constant rejects Rousseau's definition of the social contract as "the complete alienation of each individual with all his rights, without any reservations, to the community" precisely because it results in unlimited power (ibid., p. 177). Yet, Rousseau's definition of the social contract is closely intertwined with his conception of collective subjectivity and Constant's critique of the former cannot be understood apart from his critique of the latter. Rousseau's theory of popular sovereignty hinges on the fact that "the sovereign" constitutes a "body politic", a political community with a separate purpose, agency, and personhood; a collective entity that is not reducible to its individual members:

> Right away, in place of the particular individuality of each contracting party, this act of association produces a moral and collective body, composed of as many members as the assembly has voices, and which receives from this same act its unity, its common self (*moi*), its life, and its will. This public person, which is thus formed by the union of all the individual members, used to be called a *city*, and now is called *republic* or *body politic*.
>
> (Rousseau, 1762/2002, p. 164)

Such an understanding of collective subjectivity is crucial to Rousseau's goal

7 The distinction, with a long history in political thought, goes back to Roman private law, where a distinction existed between *universitas* (association) and *societas* (aggregate) as different types of collective entities (cf. Oakeshott, 1975).

> [t]o find a form of association that may defend and protect with the whole force of the community the person and property of every associate, and by means of which each, joining together with all, may nevertheless obey only himself, and remain as free as before.
>
> (Ibid., p. 163)

Some have taken Rousseau's conception of the body politic to favour a homogeneous, natural community (based on, e.g. ethnic ties) (e.g. Gauchet, 1997, pp. 51–64; Dunn, 2002, pp. 13–16). Yet, Rousseau explicitly confirms the constructed character of the body politic by arguing that the body politic comes about through the alienation of the aspiring members' individual sovereignty. Rousseau also repeatedly refers to "the sovereign" as a "moral" (Rousseau, 1762/2002, p. 164, 166) or "artificial" (ibid., p. 197) rather than a natural person. Neither does it follow from his definition of the body politic that Rousseau completely disregards the individual members and their rights: the power that the body politic has over its members may be absolute, but it cannot be arbitrary (ibid., p. 174). Rousseau's conception means first and foremost that "the sovereign" *qua* sovereign has a separate existence. The collective entity, although it is a moral person, is ontologically real.

Constant's understanding of collective subjectivity is very different from Rousseau's. To begin with, as we have seen in Constant's famous passage about limited sovereignty, the individual members do not transfer, let alone alienate, any of their rights to the collective entity. Individual rights should remain outside the scope of governmental power. As a consequence, they also remain outside the scope of sovereign power, which has the function of establishing the legitimacy of governmental power and is, in that sense, dependent upon the latter's extension. On this reading, it is thus, first and foremost, Constant's conception of governmental power that is limited, the limited conception of popular sovereignty is merely a consequence thereof.

Constant is not at all interested in the 'act' of aggregation itself. He takes society, i.e. the aggregate of individuals, as a given (Constant, 1821/2015, pp. 29–30). And the political organisation of that aggregate does not fundamentally change the position, the status, or the character of the individuals who are involved in it. Contrary to Rousseau, who considers the collective to be an artificial but real public person with concrete characteristics, Constant explicitly calls the sovereign "an abstract being":

> The repose and happiness of all is better guaranteed by the independence of each, in everything which is not harmful to others, than by any of the attempts, open or disguised, violent or equivocal, which are constantly repeated by authority and unfortunately blessed by some shortsighted philosophers, to endow society, that abstract and fictive being, at the expense of individuals, the sole real and sensible beings.
>
> (Ibid., p. 33)

For Constant, the collective does not have its own, separate reality. The collective subject of sovereign power is merely the sum of these individuals and not an independent collective person. In Constant's framework, the crucial step of Rousseau's social contract, i.e. the constitution of the body politic, is not taken. There is no constitution of a political community. As I argue in the concluding section, Constant's understanding of sovereign power does not have a constituent dimension.

The individual exercise of sovereign power

Popular sovereignty is thus attributed to an aggregated collectivity and it is exercised by the individual members. More precisely, they exercise it in their own name and on their own behalf rather than on behalf of the collective. Constant's sovereign power is the specific power of the *individual* to give their assent to governmental power. For Constant, sovereign power is thus a generalised form of individual assent rather than a collective power. This interpretation, although perhaps unconventional, is confirmed in one of Constant's earliest political texts. Because this particular text is not often discussed in the secondary literature, it is worth quoting the relevant passage at length:

> It is a universal principle, true in all times and circumstances, that no man can be bound except by the laws in which he has concurred. In a very restricted society, this principle can be applied in an immediate manner and does not need an intermediary principle to become a habitual practice. But in a different combination, in a very large society, we must add a new principle, a principle intermediary to that which we have just stated. This intermediary principle says that individuals can contribute to the formation of laws, either in person or by their representatives. Whoever wishes to apply the first principle to a large society without employing the intermediary, would inevitably upset it; but this upheaval, which would attest to the ignorance or ineptitude of the legislator, would prove nothing against the principle. The State would not be shaken because of the acknowledgment that each of its members must concur in the formation of laws, but because one was unaware that, in the surplus of a given number, the members must, in order to concur, be represented.
>
> (Constant, 1797/2003, p. 35, my translation)

The principle that "no man can be bound except by the laws in which he has concurred" refers to the principle of popular sovereignty. It restates the idea that only legitimate governmental power can create a legal obligation (whereas force or illegitimate power cannot). And governmental power can only be legitimate if it is sanctioned by the assent of all. The passage also emphasises the individual character of the *exercise* of that sovereign power: "this intermediary principle says that *individuals* can contribute to the formation of laws, either in person or by their representatives" [my emphasis].

Obviously, some form of institutional organisation is required to allow individuals to exercise sovereign power, i.e. express their assent.[8] As Constant stipulates, individual assent can be expressed either directly or through representation. Electing representatives amounts to the exercise of sovereign power: it is an expression of assent that establishes the legitimacy of their legislative (i.e. governmental) power. Contrary to what is usually assumed (e.g. on the basis of Constant's lecture on *The Liberty of the Ancients Compared with that of the Moderns*, 1988b), Constant does not argue that popular sovereignty necessarily requires representative government. Admittedly, given that France is a large society,[9] he does not spend much energy on the Rousseauian scheme wherein the individual members (permanently) participate in the legislative assembly in person. But he accepts it as a theoretically valid option. A different form of the direct expression of assent is included in the 1815 *Acte additionnel* that Constant drafted himself and to which he refers in the 1815 *Principles of Politics*: the *Acte* made it possible for the (enfranchised) population to directly ratify the constitution (cf. Laquièze, 2003).

Constant's representative system is a complex institutional arrangement with five *governmental* powers and refined checks and balances (Constant, 1815/1988, pp. 184–185). I focus exclusively on the elective segment of that arrangement as I am only interested in the exercise of *sovereign power*, i.e. the expression of assent. In the 1815 *Principles of Politics*, Constant advocates for the direct popular election of the second legislative chamber (ibid., pp. 201–213).[10] The question is who (or what) is represented by the elected representatives, given that the subject of sovereign power is not a body politic but an aggregate of individuals? When those individuals elect the representatives, they establish the legitimacy of their legislative power. As Constant stipulates, from that moment on, the power of the representatives becomes the general will (ibid., p. 175). The legislative power represents the general will, and the general will is represented by the legislative power. So, whereas the individual members cannot act on behalf of 'society' as a whole (they exercise sovereign power in their own name), the elected representatives can (they exercise governmental power in the name of the aggregate). Constant accepts this implication but in a qualified manner. The general will/interest needs to be understood as the aggregate of the individual wills (and only a limited part thereof), and it is thus composed of multiple concrete, separate interests:

8 My focus here is on the organisation/exercise of sovereign power and not on the organisation of governmental power. The latter is, for Constant, an issue that does not directly pertain to the principle of popular sovereignty.

9 The arguments that Constant provides in support of the representative system are mostly of a sociological nature (Constant, 1819/1988, pp. 314–315). Although they are very interesting in themselves, I leave them aside, as they do not touch upon the theoretical issues that I want to discuss in this text.

10 This chamber exercises "the representative power of public opinion" and shares the legislative power with the first, hereditary chamber.

> The general interest is nothing but the reunion, the conciliation of all the private interests that exist simultaneously. If the general interest was something else, it would a chimeric abstraction. [...] It is not necessary to claim so much contempt for private interests: these are the only real interests because society is nothing but the aggregation of the private individuals that are a member of it.
>
> (Constant, *Session des chambres de 1818 à 1819, Discussion sur le projet relatif aux pétitions.* Cited in Feldman [2008, p. 691, footnote 76])

With this view, Constant goes against the "very exaggerated idea of the general interest" (Constant, 1815/1988, p. 205) that prevailed in the post-revolutionary constitutional debates. As Lucien Jaume has argued (Jaume, 1998, pp. 161–166), the dominant position, defended by Sieyès and Cabanis among others, was that popular unity should be substantive and therefore handed down from above. This was the only way the unity of the general will could be achieved and guaranteed. The general will was not to be constructed by collecting and synthesising individual or sectional input; representatives were not to represent their electorate, they were chosen to determine 'the general will' on behalf of the nation as a whole. In other words, the dominant view corresponds to the understanding of the collective subject of popular sovereignty as a body politic. As a consequence, electoral colleges were generally preferred over the direct popular election of representatives. Constant's conception of sovereignty power, on the contrary, rejects the idea of a substantive popular unity whether it is presupposed bottom up or enforced top down.

The political implications of popular sovereignty

Based on this analysis of Constant's conception of popular sovereignty, I principally agree with Garsten's assessment of Constant's theoretical/political position as pluralist and dynamic, even though I think it is theoretically more precise to attribute these characteristics to Constant's conception of popular sovereignty instead of to his conception of representative government. Whereas Garsten claims that Constant theorises representative government as a correction to popular sovereignty (Garsten, 2009, p. 91), I have argued that Constant's representative system allows the individual members of the aggregation to express their assent, i.e. exercise their sovereign power. In my reading, popular sovereignty and representative government are thus not so much opposed but connected, although I believe that the connection, for Constant, is not a necessary one. Yet, overall, I agree with Garsten that Constant is not worried about the one-on-one transferral of popular will into governmental power but, on the contrary, heavily emphasised the possibility of contesting governmental power from below.

It is easy to see that Constant's conception of the aggregated subject of sovereign power endorses a significant degree of *pluralism*. Because he thinks of this subject (i.e. society) as the aggregate of its individual members, he can easily accept that society harbours multiple, different, and potentially conflicting interests. Constant does not believe that society is (or should be) characterised by unity or homogeneity: "variety is what constitutes an organisation, uniformity is mere mechanism. Variety is life, uniformity is death" (Constant, 1814/1988, p. 77). The fact that sovereign power is not exercised in the name of a collective in the sense of a body politic with its own purpose, agency, and personhood also helps to guarantee the possibility of *contesting* the legitimacy of governmental power. For Constant, submitting governmental power to the "assent of all", exercised by the individual members in their own name and on their own behalf, is a way to *prevent* particular groups from indefinitely usurping governmental power:

> The axiom of the people's sovereignty has been thought of as a principle of freedom. It is in fact a principle of constitutional guarantee. It aims to prevent any individual from seizing the authority which belongs only to the political society as a whole. It determines nothing, however, about the nature of this authority itself. It in no way adds to the sum of individual liberties, therefore, and if we do not turn to other principles for determining the extent of this sovereignty, freedom could be lost, despite the principle of the sovereignty of the people, or even because of it.
>
> (Constant, 1806/2003, p. 11)

It is precisely because the possibility of contestation needs to be guaranteed that Constant does *not* think of popular sovereignty as a principle of collective empowerment. It does not entail the constitution of a collective subject. The essence of sovereign power is individual judgment, rather than the formation and expression of collective will. Sovereign power does not concern the *constitution* of governmental power, but merely the possibility to approve or contest its legitimacy. In other words, it is crucial that 'governmental power' and 'sovereign power' are exercised by individuals in different capacities (the former in the name of society, the latter in their own name).

Paradoxically, this conception of sovereign power also introduces a bias in favour of the existing institutions. The fact that sovereign power is recast as the possibility of contestation has a conservative penchant, at least in Constant. It is hard to see how assent could be expressed or withdrawn except through the *existing* institutional framework. Although others like Rousseau and Sieyès have identified this as a fundamental problem for political theory (i.e. the infamous paradox of constituent power, cf. Walker and Loughlin, 2008), it is not an issue at all for Constant: sovereign power simply does not have a constituent dimension. The power to *constitute* governmental power is, according to Constant, not a part of popular sovereignty:

> There really is a prerogative – when we are speaking abstractly – that society does possess and does not delegate to the government, namely the right to change the organization of the government itself. To delegate this right

> would set up a vicious circle, since the government could use it to transform itself into a tyranny. But this very exception confirms the rule. If society does not delegate this prerogative, neither does it exercise it itself. Just as it would be absurd to delegate it, so it is impossible to exercise it and dangerous to proclaim it.
>
> (Constant, 1806/2003, p. 18)

In order to serve its purpose, i.e. "to prevent any one interpretation of the popular will from claiming final authority" (Garsten, 2009, p. 91), such a constitutive dimension is also unnecessary and could even be detrimental. As Constant writes, it could be used to transform the existent system into a tyranny with the risk of completely eliminating the power to contest the legitimacy of governmental power. The objective to keep the possibility for contestation open is realised at the cost of maintaining the institutional status quo. Constant's understanding of popular sovereignty thus entails genuine opportunities for contesting the legitimacy of governmental power while also working to keep the existing organisation of governmental power in place.

In conclusion, I want to emphasise that the way Constant understands popular sovereignty is a form of political power that is crucially important. Legitimacy requires that citizens can express or withdraw their assent to the regime and its concrete policies. Sovereign power, however, does not exhaust all the possible forms of political power. In fact, the crisis of democracy that keeps the interest in Constant's theory alive may require us to theorise (and practice) alternative forms of power that do have a constituent dimension and are less tied to the institutional status quo.

Bibliography

Berlin, I. (1969) 'Two Concepts of Liberty', in *Four Essays on Liberty*. Oxford: Oxford University Press, pp. 118–172.

Chopin, T. (2002) *Benjamin Constant. Le libéralisme inquiet*. Paris: Michalon.

Colon-Rios, J.I. (2016) 'Rousseau, Theorist of Constituent Power', *Oxford Journal of Legal Studies*, 34(4), pp. 885–908. DOI: 10.1093/ojls/gqw012.

Constant, B. (1796) *De la force du gouvernement actuel de la France et de la nécessité de s'y rallier*. Reprinted in: Tremblay, J.M. (ed.) (2003) *Québec: Les classiques des sciences sociales*. Available at: http://classiques.uqac.ca/classiques/constant_benjamin/des_reactions_politiques/des_reactions.html.

Constant, B. (1797) *Des réactions politiques*. Reprinted in: Tremblay, J.M. (ed.) (2003) *Québec: Les classiques des sciences sociales*. Available at: http://classiques.uqac.ca/classiques/constant_benjamin/des_reactions_politiques/des_reactions.html.

Constant, B. (1802) *Fragments d'un ouvrage abandonné sur la possibilité d'une constitution républicaine dans un grand pays*. Grange, H. (ed.) (1991). Paris: Aubier.

Constant, B. (1806) *Principles of Politics Applicable to all Governments*. O'Keeffe, D. (trans.) and Hoffman, E. (ed.) (2003). Indianapolis: Liberty Fund.

Constant, B. (1814) *The Spirit of Conquest and Usurpation and their Relation to European Civilization*. Translated in: Fontana, B. (ed.) (1988) *Political Writings*. Cambridge: Cambridge University Press.

Constant, B. (1815) *Principles of Politics Applicable to all Representative Governments.* Translated in: Fontana, B. (ed.) (1988) *Political Writings.* Cambridge: Cambridge University Press.

Constant, B. (1818) *Réflexions sur les constitutions et les garanties avec une esquisse de constition.* Reprinted in: Laboulaye, E. (ed.) (1872) *Cours de politique constitutionelle ou collection des ouvrages publiés sur le gouvernement répresentatif.* Paris: Librairie de Guillaumin et Cie.

Constant, B. (1819) *The Liberty of the Ancients Compared with that of the Moderns.* Translated in: Fontana, B. (ed.) (1988) *Political Writings.* Cambridge: Cambridge University Press.

Constant, B. (1821) *Commentary on Filangieri's Work.* Edited, translated, and introduced by Kahan, A.S. (2015). Indianapolis: Liberty Fund.

Craiutu, A. (2012) *A Virtue for Courageous Minds. Moderation in French Political Thought 1748–1830.* Princeton: Princeton University Press.

Deguise, P. (1966) *Benjamin Constant méconnu. Le livre 'De la religion'.* Genève: Droz.

Delbouille, P. (2006) 'Aux sources de la démocratie libérale: Benjamin Constant', *Revue d'Histoire Littéraire de la France*, 2(106), pp. 259-70.

Dodge, G. (1980) *Benjamin Constant's Philosophy of Liberalism. A Study in Politics and Religion.* Chapel Hill: University of North Carolina Press.

Dunn, S. (2002) 'Introduction. Rousseau's Political Triptych', in Dunn, S. (ed.) *The Social Contract and the First and Second Discourses.* New Haven: Yale University Press, pp. 1–35.

Feldman, J.P. (2008) 'Le constitutionnalisme selon Benjamin Constant', *Revue Française de Droit Constitutionnel*, 4(76), pp. 675–702. DOI: 10.3917/rfdc.076.0675.

Fontana, B. (1991) *Benjamin Constant and the Post-Revolutionary Mind.* New Haven: Yale University Press.

Garsten, B. (2009) 'Representative Government and Popular Sovereignty', in Shapiro, I., Stokes, S.C., Wood, E.J., and Kirshner, A.S. (eds.) *Political Representation.* New York: Cambridge University Press, pp. 90–110.

Gauchet, M. (1995) *La révolution des pouvoirs. La souveraineté, le peuple et la représentation: 1789–1799.* Paris: Gallimard.

Gauchet, M. (1997) 'Benjamin Constant. L'illusion lucide du libéralisme', in Gauchet, M. (ed.) *Ecrits Politiques.* Paris: Gallimard, pp. 12–110.

Gauchet, M. (2005) 'Constant: Le libéralisme entre le droit et l'histoire', in *La condition Politique.* Paris: Gallimard, pp. 277–304.

Geenens, R. and Rosenblatt, H. (eds.) (2012) *French Liberalism from Montesquieu to the Present Day.* New York: Cambridge University Press.

Geenens, R. and Sottiaux, S. (2015) 'Sovereignty and Direct Democracy: Lessons from Constant and the Belgian Constitution', *European Constitutional Law Review*, 11(2), pp. 293–320. DOI: 10.1017/S1574019615000188.

Harpaz, E. (1989) 'Un texte inconnu de Benjamin Constant. De la souveraineté', in Cockerham, H. and Ehrman, E. (eds.) *Ideology and Religion in French Literature. Essays in Honour of Brian Juden.* Camberley: Porphyrogenitus, pp. 173–179.

Hofmann, E. (1980) *Les 'Principes de politique' de Benjamin Constant. Tome I : La genèse d'une oeuvre et l'évolution de la pensée de leur auteur, 1789–1806. Tome II : Texte avec introduction et notes.* Genève: Droz.

Holmes, H. (1980) *Benjamin Constant and the Making of Modern Liberalism.* New Haven: Yale University Press.

Jainchill, A. (2008) *Reimagining Politics after the Terror. The Republican Origins of French Liberalism*. Ithaca: Cornell University Press.
Jaume, L. (1997) *L'individu effacé ou le paradoxe du libéralisme français*. Paris: Fayard.
Jaume, L. (1998) 'Le problème de l'intérêt général dans la pensée de Benjamin Constant', in Tilkin, F. (ed.) *Le Groupe de Coppet et le monde moderne. Conceptions–images–débats*. Liége: Presses universitaires de Liège, pp. 159–176.
Kalyvas, A. and Katznelson, I. (1999) '"We are Modern Men". Benjamin Constant and the Discovery of an Immanent Liberalism', *Constellations*, 6(4), pp. 513–539. DOI: 10.1111/1467-8675.00160.
Kelly, G.A. (1992) *The Humane Comedy. Constant, Tocqueville, and French Liberalism*. New York: Cambridge University Press.
Laquièze, A. (2003) 'Benjamin Constant et l'acte additionnell aux Constitutions de l'Empire du 22 avril 1815', *Historia Constitucional*, 4, pp. 197–234. http://hc.rediris.es/04/index.html.
Manent, P. (1994) *An Intellectual History of Liberalism*. Translated by Balinski, R. Princeton: Princeton University Press.
Manin, B. (1997) *The Principles of Representative Government*. New York: Cambridge University Press.
Oakeshott, M. (1975) *On Human Conduct*. Oxford: Oxford University Press.
Rolland, P. (2008) 'Comment préserver les institutions politiques? La théorie du pouvoir neutre chez B. Constant', *Revue Française d'Histoire des Idées Politiques*, 1(27), pp. 43–73. DOI: 10.3917/rfhip.027.0043.
Rosenblatt, H. (2008) *Liberal Values. Benjamin Constant and the Politics of Religion*. New York: Cambridge University Press.
Rosenblatt, H. (2009) 'Eclipses and Revivals: Constant's Reception in France and America, 1830–2007', in Rosenblatt, H. (ed.) *The Cambridge Companion to Constant*. Cambridge: Cambridge University Press, pp. 351–377.
Rousseau, J.J. (1762) *The Social Contract and the First and Second Discourses*. Edited, translated, and introduced by Dunn, S. (2002). New Haven: Yale University Press.
Timmermans, N. (2019) 'A Positive or Negative Conception of Sovereignty? Marcel Gauchet, Benjamin Constant and Liberal Democracy', in Leijssenaar, B. and Walker, N. (eds.) *Sovereignty in Action*. Cambridge: Cambridge University Press.
Todorov, T. (1999) *A Passion for Democracy: Benjamin Constant*. New York: Algora Publishing.
Tuck, R. (2016) *The Sleeping Sovereign. The Invention of Modern Democracy*. London: Cambridge University Press.
Vincent, S.K. (2011) *Benjamin Constant and the Birth of French Liberalism*. New York: Palgrave Macmillan.
Walker, N. and Loughlin, M. (eds.) (2008) *The Paradox of Constitutionalism. Constituent Power and Constitutional Form*. Oxford: Oxford University Press.
Wood, D. (1993) *Benjamin Constant. A Biography*. London: Routledge.

4 Abbé Sieyès

The immanent and transcendent nation

Olga Bashkina

Introduction

Formally ratified in February 1831, the Belgian Constitution established parliamentary monarchy with bicameral representation. The drafters of the Constitution sought to connect its legitimacy not to traditional or religious foundations but to society itself, which was expressed in the formulation of article 33 (originally article 25): "All powers emanate from the Nation. They are exercised in the manner established by the Constitution". The Constitution's until recently uncontested interpretation postulates that the meaning of sovereignty engrained in the Constitution by definition excludes all forms of direct democracy in favour of a representative government. This interpretation operates with a strict separation of the principles of direct democracy and representation that is expressed in two contrasting conceptions of sovereignty – popular and national sovereignty, respectively.

It seems that the predominantly accepted national sovereignty paradigm prevents democratic innovation and development in Belgium. It has been suggested that it is necessary to part with this dated conception of national sovereignty (Geenens and Sottiaux, 2015). One way to approach the issue of sovereignty in Belgium is to do it via conceptual analysis and the history of concepts. Which ideas influenced the meaning that is attributed to sovereignty in Belgium today? Several influences are usually named, but the two most common reference points for the origins of the national sovereignty paradigm are Abbé Sieyès, a political theorist from the time of the French Revolution, and French constitutional scholar Raymond Carré de Malberg.

Should the national sovereignty paradigm be abandoned in Belgium? To answer this question, I suggest looking at how one of the major influences of this conception – Abbé Sieyès – treated the issue of sovereignty. How did he understand the idea of national self-government through representation? Did he use the concept of sovereignty? Which conceptual problems did he encounter in theorising the idea of the free nation? Addressing these questions can shed new light on how to understand the idea of national sovereignty in Belgium. In what follows, I argue that Sieyès developed not one but *two theoretical paradigms* through which to understand the free nation.[1] Although he did not favour the concept of sovereignty as such, he developed influential insights that were later connected with the modern understanding of sovereignty. My interpretation suggests that Sieyès offered two major ideas that are both imprinted in the concept of sovereignty today. Yet, in the evolution of Sieyès' thought, these two ideas are conflicting and do not find a productive synthesis. Extrapolating the observations from the analysis of Sieyès' theory onto the Belgian context, at the end of this chapter, I conclude that in order to promote democratic development in Belgium, one does not need to reject the concept of national sovereignty. Instead, a more productive approach is the combination of popular and national sovereignty in one system.

Two conflicting paradigms

Perhaps the reference to Sieyès as the original theorist of national sovereignty is best traced to the work of the influential French constitutional scholar Raymond Carré de Malberg (1861–1935) (see Chapter 10). Carré de Malberg claimed that Sieyès "defined representative government, at the beginning of the new era of public law, with an accuracy and precision that has not been exceeded since then" (Carré de Malberg, 2003, II, p. 257). It is in Sieyès' ideas on national representation, which he opposed to direct democracy, that Carré de Malberg saw the origins of the national sovereignty paradigm. In contrast to Carré de Malberg's reading of Sieyès, today Sieyès is a prominent reference in radical democratic conceptions of popular sovereignty as constituent power (e.g. Kalyvas, 2005). According to this approach, Sieyès is part of a tradition of revolutionary democratic understanding of popular power coming from below. Which one is the real Sieyès then?

Historically, Sieyès' reception has been highly diverse. Sieyès significantly contributed to the continuous debate on new political forms during the revolutionary decade. Moreover, the author of the infamous pamphlet *Qu'est-ce que le tiers-état?* influenced subsequent thinking about democracy and democratic founding for two centuries onwards. His legacy carried over into classical nineteenth-century French liberalism, the constitutional controversies of the twentieth century, and twenty-first-century debates over democracy. Having lived till 1836, Sieyès was a direct witness to all major events of the revolutionary years in France: the Tennis Court Oath in 1789, the execution of the king in 1793, the establishment of the Directory in year III, and the coup of 18 Brumaire (see Laquièze, 2008). Forgotten during some periods, Sieyès' ideas have undergone several revivals, each of which has accentuated different aspects of his thought in light of the pressing debates of the time. In the nineteenth and twentieth centuries, debates that engaged with Sieyès included those over individual rights and the limitation of power (the Coppet Group: Madame de Staël and Benjamin

1 I am assuming conceptual interconnectedness between 'freedom' and 'sovereignty'.

Constant), national sovereignty (Adhémar Esmein, Léon Duguit, and Raymond Carré de Malberg), and constituent power (Carl Schmitt) (Laquièze, 2008). The scope of contemporary readings of Sieyès that are informed by the revived interest in democratic founding and constituent power is remarkable. From revolutionary thinker to theorist of constitutional limits, Sieyès exists in contemporary thinking in a variety of manifestations.

Not only is this diversity of interpretations indicative of the richness of Sieyès' thought, but it also gestures to a paradox at the heart of his theory of representation: While regarded as one of the first theorists of modern representation, some of his ideas appear to be anti-representational. Acclaiming the new revolutionary potential of the French nation, he says that "if a nation had to wait for a positive mode of being in order to become a nation, it would simply never have had an existence" (Sieyès, 2003, p. 136). Statements like this contribute to a line of thought that suggests that representation does not create the nation, which already exists, but only the national government. Yet, in other passages of *Qu'est-ce que le tiers-état?*, he asserts that the nation is "a body of associates living under a common law, represented by the same legislature" and that "a nation is made one by virtue of a common system of law and a common representation" (ibid., pp. 97–99). This would seem to suggest that he believes that the nation cannot speak other than through its representatives. These different inflections within his thinking have, in turn, found their home in different interpretations. On the one hand, because of Sieyès' extensive analysis of representation and the way in which he posits it at the centre of his politics, many assert that he follows the Hobbesian tradition in his argument about the nation (Forsyth, 1981; 1987; Hont, 1994). On the other hand, some fundamental claims made by Sieyès are ultimately anti-Hobbesian (Clavreul, 1982; Jaume, 1986; Laquièze, 2008). Consider, for example, the claim that "the nation exists prior to everything; it is the origin of everything. Its will is always legal. It is the law itself" or

> a nation is independent of all forms and, however it may will, it is enough for its will to be made known for all positive law to fall silent in its presence, because it is the source and supreme master of all positive law.
>
> (Sieyès, 2003, p. 138)

These claims, together with a powerful statement equating the Third Estate with the entire nation, cast Sieyès' theory of representation in a paradoxical light. They raise the question of whether Sieyès conceives of representation as the fundamental way of understanding political relations or whether the nation as a political agent can also be conceived and express itself in a pre-representational, direct way. The central problem is, in short, whether the nation is formed by the representative will from above or is expressing itself directly from below.

My interpretative approach departs from this more common debate on Sieyès' idea of representation. While, within this debate, the problem pertains to *how* the nation expresses itself (via representatives or directly), I am concerned with *what* is being expressed. While I too believe that the concept of representation is central for Sieyès, I choose to shift the focus of my enquiry away from the either/or of representation versus the direct will of the people and frame my interpretation in terms of immanence and transcendence. My reading in the present chapter offers a division of Sieyès' ideas into these two paradigms. Representation remains important for both paradigms since, for Sieyès, the idea of representation is fundamental. That is to say, what changes in his thought is not *how* he conceives the national will being expressed – either directly or by means of representation. Rather, what changes is *what* he thinks is being represented (and by whom) – immanent relations that already exist in a society or transcendent norms that should shape an ideal nation. In this chapter, I do not want to construct a system out of these paradigms. Rather, I want to think of them as two archetypes of thought that are both present in how we think about democracy today.

One final remark is due about the concept of sovereignty itself. I read Sieyès with regard to the tradition of national sovereignty that is central to the Belgian case analysed in this book. However, it is necessary to note that Sieyès himself was critical of the concept of sovereignty and almost never used it in his own work (see Rubinelli, 2016). He associated the term 'sovereignty' with the tradition of absolutist rule that he was trying to debunk with his work. In his mind, 'sovereignty' meant an absolute undivided highest power that was in conflict with the new liberal ideas of national representation that he proclaimed. Sieyès' conceptions of representation and constituent power were directed against the personal power of the monarch. For Sieyès, ascribing sovereignty to any group of people would mean advocating for a form of tyranny. Later in the nineteenth century, 'sovereignty' came to also mean an attribute of an abstract rather than a concrete agent – a nation rather than a monarch. This is not yet the case for Sieyès. Yet, even if he is critical of a particular meaning of the term 'sovereignty', Sieyès remains a recurring reference in discussions of sovereignty. Ideas that he framed in different concepts, e.g. constituent power, have enriched the meaning of various conceptions of sovereignty and continue to do so today.

Revolutionary immanence: Constituent power of the oppressed

Born in 1748, Abbé Sieyès pursued a religious career until 1788, when Louis XVI called for the convocation of the Estates-General in Paris. After publishing his renowned pamphlet *Qu'est-ce que le tiers-état?*, Sieyès was elected a representative of the Third Estate to the Estates-General, which was soon to become the National Constituent Assembly. Sieyès' pamphlet not only changed the course of debates at the time but also inspired the eventual revolutionary turn of events. Moreover, modern political categories continue to bear the mark of his innovative contribution (Guilhaumou, 2002). Yet, before developing his famous insights in *Qu'est-ce que le tiers-état?*, Sieyès had already experimented with big ideas in his pre-revolutionary studies in metaphysics and political economy. During his education at the Sorbonne, he was influenced by, among others, Gottfried Wilhelm Leibniz, Étienne Bonnot de Condillac, Adam Smith, and the school of the physiocrats. In my reading of Sieyès, I trace two lines of arguments from his pre-revolutionary writings – metaphysical (what Guilhaumou calls Sieyès' "*métaphysique du moi*" [Guilhaumou, 1999, pp. 513–535]) and economic – that influence Sieyès' thought in *Qu'est-ce que le tiers-état?*, especially the idea of constituent power. It is these ideas that I frame as the immanent paradigm.

Living force of society

Guilhaumou (1997) has pointed to the particular influence of Leibniz' monadology and his principle of individuation on Sieyès' *Le cahier métaphysique* (1773–1776). It is Leibniz's philosophy of physics and his conception of *vis via*, or living force, that appears in Sieyès' thought as *force vive*. Leibniz, in the famous controversy with Sir Isaac Newton, rejected Newton's first law of motion, according to which an object will obey the law of inertia, i.e. an object in motion stays in motion and an object at rest stays at rest unless it is acted upon by another force. In Newton's mechanistic system, the understanding of motion is predicated upon a causal understanding of movement, i.e. movement is conceived as only caused by another force.[2] In *Specimen Dynamicum*, Leibniz (1695/1989) develops a concept of *vis viva*, or living force, the earlier formulation of what we know now as the principle of the conservation of energy, according to which the energy of a system is not created or destroyed but is transformed within a system. Simply put, contrary to Newton, movement within a system does not presuppose an external cause; a system contains the constant principle of movement within itself. No outside transcendent source of motion and energy needs to be posited in order to account for the principle of movement of things – the cause of the movement is immanent in the moving thing.

In Sieyès' thought, this idea of living force reappears as *force vive* and is used in analysing the dynamics of a society. In *Letters to the Economists*, Sieyès writes that a society has an immanent force of its own:

> Society, independently of the power of nature which produces goods, must have a living force coproductive of wealth, and it is necessary that the elements of that force, united by society, produce more than they would if they remained isolated. The sum of the labors of all citizens forms the living force. If there is a citizen who refuses his portion of activity, he renounces his rights; no man may enjoy the labor of others without exchange. General labor is therefore the foundation of society, and the social order is nothing but the best possible order of labor.
>
> (Sieyès, 1985, p. 32)

Sieyès' theory of society rests on the analogy between a physical conception of living force and the economic theory of labour. Sieyès (2003, p. 95) argued

2 In *An Essay Concerning Human Understanding*, Locke articulated it as "bodies operate by impulse and nothing else" (*Essay*, II.viii.11).

extensively against the economic theory of the physiocrats who claimed that economic value is derived exclusively from agricultural labour. Instead, Sieyès considered that value derives from labour in general, which encompassed not only agricultural labour but also the labour of industrial and service workers as well as that labour used in social reproduction. This idea of general labour as a living force resembles Marx's later conception of living labour (*lebendige Arbeit*).[3] Similarly to Marx, living labour for Sieyès produces not only value but also social connections and sociability. In other words, this immanent force organises social relations before and prior to any external intervention.

This account of immanent social force can also be found in Sieyès' *Qu'est-ce que le tiers-état?*, where, in attempting to give a definition to the nation, he famously excludes the privileged classes from the definition of the nation for "a class like that is surely foreign to a nation because of its idleness" (ibid., p. 97). Sieyès' pamphlet is revolutionary because it exposes how there is a conflict between existing social relations and the political system of the *Ancien Régime.* This idea allowed Sieyès to formulate the revolutionary definition of the Third Estate as an entity that becomes a political subject because it performs "the activities that support society" (ibid., p. 95) but lacks political rights. For Sieyès, the Third Estate constitutes the living force of the social body because it performs the labour required for its subsistence, but the dominant system of social organisation does not recognise the Third Estate as equal and oppresses it. Sieyès argumentation in this pamphlet is operating within what I call the 'immanent paradigm' as it is built on highlighting the conflict between the existing immanent dynamic of relations in a society and a system of domination that ignores this built-in vitality.

Constituent power

Within this immanent paradigm, the emerging political subject can be conceived on the basis of existent social relations that are not reflected in the current political system. In the pamphlets of 1788 and 1789, the theme of the contradiction between social reality and political inequality is apparent. This is expressed in Sieyès' view that constituting a new people (*un peuple neuf*) requires first getting rid of all the privileges separating people. He explores this point in his piece *Essai sur les privilèges*, printed in 1788 and reprinted in 1789:

> It is the essence, the characteristic, of privilege to place the possessor of it beyond the boundaries of common right. [...] [People] seem ignorant that their property, thus increased, with all the additions which a new spirit of

3 "Labor not as an object, but as activity; not as itself value, but as the living source of value" (Marx, 1857/1993, p. 296); "Capital is dead labor, that, vampire-like, only lives by sucking living labor, and lives the more, the more labor it sucks. The time during which the laborer works, is the time during which the capitalist consumes the labor-power he has purchased of him" (Marx, 1867/1981, p. 342).

> industry has been able to accumulate in a social state, is in reality their own, and could never be considered as the gift of an extrinsic power. [...] The grant of any exclusive privilege to any person with respect to that which belongs to all would be to wrong the whole community for the sake of an individual; which is an idea at once the most unjust and the most absurd.
>
> (Ibid., pp. 70–71)

This point shows that privileges exist above the law (common or positive) because they operate as if no law can regulate them. While privileges can be instituted in the law itself, e.g. by legally establishing the division of society into social orders, privileges can also function tacitly as "the deplorable effect of long servitude on the human mind" (ibid., p. 70).

Having noted that the Third Estate constitutes the entire nation based on the living force of labour and that the unjust system of existing privileges oppresses the Third Estate, Sieyès can introduce his famous idea of *pouvoir constituant*:

> The nation exists prior to everything; it is the origin of everything. Its will is always legal. It is the law itself. [...] The first in order of precedence will be the constitutional laws. These laws are said to be fundamental, not in the sense that they can be independent of the national will, but because bodies that can exist and can act only by way of these laws cannot touch them. In each of its parts a constitution is not the work of a constituted power but a constituent power.
>
> (Ibid., p. 136)

Even though Sieyès does not spend much time defining the concept of constituent power, the concept has become influential in democratic and constitutional theory. While there is much debate around the meaning of the concept, 'constituent power' generally expresses the intuition that the people themselves should be the authors of the basic rules by which they are governed. Sieyès clearly makes this argument when he asserts that the unprivileged Third Estate can speak for the entire nation as the unjust laws imposed from above have been oppressing them for too long. In other words, in Sieyès' immanent paradigm, the exercise of constituent power by extraordinary representatives frames and expresses the grievances of an oppressed group and aims to change the dominant social and political order. Having made this argument for what I call revolutionary immanence, Sieyès confronts the question of how to combine in thought and in practice the assertion of the revolutionary potential of the people and the organisation of the new political system.

Antonio Negri, the well-known Marxist theorist of constituent power, acknowledges Sieyès for being the first to introduce labour as an exclusive theme in the discussion of constituent power (Negri, 2009, p. 212). For Negri, Sieyès' economic definition of society shapes the content of his other concepts, e.g. constituent power and representation. According to Negri, Sieyès represents society as "a laborious, unified and compact whole, standing on the social work organized by the bourgeoisie, and whose development is obstructed by the contradiction between labor and public functions, on the whole usurped by the aristocracy" (ibid.). Yet, Negri is critical of Sieyès for he believes that Sieyès' concept of labour and hence his conception of constituent power is inherently conservative. For Negri himself, constituent power is a concept that reflects class struggle and, thus, the transformation of social relations. For Sieyès, a new political order should conserve already existing labour relations rather than change them. Hence, Negri concludes, Sieyès' representative notion of constituent power prevents and suppresses actual revolutionary socio-economic change (ibid., p. 214).

Yet, Sieyès' immanent paradigm does justify revolutionary transformative action insofar as it allows for the transformation of the old oppressive system into a regime animated by a new conception of the people. The difference between Negri's and Sieyès' understandings of transformation lies in the fact that Sieyès does not advocate for direct action. Like Negri, Sieyès sees the foundation of transformative action as existing immanently in society; unlike Negri, he understands this action as representative in nature:

> Citizens who appoint representatives renounce and must renounce making laws themselves; they do not have a particular will to impose. If they dictated their wills, France would not be a representative state anymore, it would be a democratic state. The people, I repeat it, in a country that is not a democracy (and France cannot be a democracy), the people cannot speak, cannot act other than through their representatives.
>
> (*Archives parlementaires de 1787 à 1860*, pp. 594–595)

Nadia Urbinati has framed Sieyès as a theorist of the nation of electors; unlike Girondists such as Marquis de Condorcet, he did not conceive of elements necessary for a participatory democracy (Urbinati, 2006). It was Sieyès' anti-federalist position and praise of representation that made Carré de Malberg frame him as the first theorist of national sovereignty. While Sieyès does advocate for representation over direct action, his deeper concern is the exact nature of this representation: what should be represented and by whom? Once he uncovers the idea of the revolutionary principle immanent in society, he starts questioning who can embody and exercise this principle to transform society. It is in respect to this questioning that one can single out a transition period in Sieyès' thought in which he shifts from the immanent to the transcendent paradigm.

Transcendent nation: The project of a constitutional jury

Transition

The idea that Sieyès did not exclusively reject all forms of direct participation has been put forward by Olivier Beaud and Andrew Arato, who emphasise Sieyès' discussion of the preliminary constitution. Beaud posits that Sieyès' idea of constituent power is twofold: it consists of destructive (*déconstituant*) and constructive (*constituant*) moments (Beaud, 1994). The first moment consists of completely unbound negative will, while the second moment relies on democratically established procedures and rules. This distinction is important in order to see the connection between the allegedly radical and representative dimensions of Sieyès' constituent power. While radical constituent power pertains to negating privileges and oppressive relations, constructive constituent power establishes rules as to how to, among other things, change established rules democratically. Arato underlines how the originality of this idea lies in Sieyès emphasis on how democratic constituent power can be conceptualised between revolution and reform (Arato, 2017). In *Préliminaire de la Constitution françoise* (1789a), Sieyès talks about the process of drafting the first Constitution:

> The constitution which will be given to France, and which the necessity of circumstances must make provisionally obligatory for all, will be definitive, only after new deputies, regularly delegated to exercise solely constituent power, have it revised, reformed if necessary, and will have given it a national consent which the rigor of the principles demands.
>
> (Sieyès, 1789a, pp. 17–18)

Clearly, for Sieyès, a free people comes into being over time and through a process rather than in a single moment of original creation. He proposes several stages of constitution drafting and maintains that it is important to involve citizens in the process. Arato and Beaud, who identify the importance of this idea for Sieyès' thought, focus only on the drafting of the actual document of the constitution and the possibilities of increasing participation in it. Yet, this idea of constitution as a process has larger implications for Sieyès. In the foreword to the same publication, Sieyès inquires about what it means to give a constitution to a new people (*un peuple neuf*) (ibid., p. 16). For the principles proclaimed in the Declaration of Rights and in the Constitution to function, a society needs to be ready and aware of those principles. But those people whom these documents declare to possess civil and political rights have been subjected to "centuries of misfortune" (ibid.). That is why, Sieyès diagnoses, ideas like constituent power emanating from the nation, the abolition of privileges, equality, etc., first assert themselves as "transcendental metaphysics" (ibid., p. 6). When he states that society needs to mature in order to realise those ideas "not as a set of laws, but as a set of principles" (ibid., p. 3), Sieyès is implying that fundamental laws should not only be enforced upon the people but also be internalised and consciously accepted as their own laws.

In this regard, the idea of a preliminary constitution takes up a broader significance in Sieyès' thought. A constitution conceived in this way envisions the emergence of a free people over time, and it would rely on a system of representative institutions that serve a unifying and an enlightening function but do not replace the active citizenry. Sieyès adheres to the idea of progress as the approximation to the ideal of complete collective freedom. A new people comes about in the process of the gradual maturation of reason which is set off but not limited to the drafting of the constitutional document. In a different text from the same year (*Quelques idées de Constitution, applicables à la ville de Paris*), Sieyès advances that the category of active citizens, which he initially distinguished from passive citizens, will expand with time.[4] With the help of national education and the formation of new interests, people will be able to see past their individual concerns and acquire a shared concern for social issues (Sieyès, 1789b, p. 21). Thus, for Sieyès, constitutional principles should eventually become reflected in social reality. The idea of a preliminary constitution then speaks both to the possibility of redrafting the fundamental law of the community and to the eventual actualisation of the ideals of equality and liberty in practice. As to what such a constitution might look like – what combination of citizen participation and representative institutions it would involve – Sieyès does not give a clear answer. Nonetheless, he furnishes political theory with an original and lasting picture of constituent power that does not sever its representative and radical dimensions. For Sieyès, the changes propelled by the Revolution do not stop but evolve and influence society over time. This, in turn, means that institutions are not static but should be able to change as ideas do.

The project of a constitutional jury

The Sieyès of *Qu'est-ce que le tiers-état?*, a mouthpiece of the Revolution, theorised constituent power as the power of a nation to create for itself whatever laws it pleases. In the early years of debates around constitutional proposals, Sieyès developed the position that since the nation establishes its freedom over time, recurring constitutional amendments are required. Finally, after the end of the Reign of Terror, in the years of the Thermidorian Reaction (1794–1795), Sieyès was preoccupied with problems arising in a very different political context, and in his thought, the radical democratic potential of constituent power is replaced by the need to prevent the creativity of constituent power. In speeches made during these years, Sieyès explores how the stability of a constitutional order can be preserved. During Thermidor, Sieyès seeks to put an end to revolutionary experimentation and secure its results: equality, citizen rights, and liberties. If the Revolution itself cannot sustain what it has fought for, what can? Having proclaimed the equality and liberty of citizens, the Revolution resulted in the despotic reign of the few. With this in mind, Sieyès was preoccupied not with the task of democratic founding *qua* inventing new possibilities but with preserving what had already been established. For the purpose of demonstrating how a constitutional order can preserve citizen rights, Sieyès comes up with the project of a constitutional jury. This project is believed to be the first analogue of the contemporary constitutional court.

Seeking to protect the Constitution and secure its basic principles, Sieyès imagines a power that would exist above and be independent of the political process.

4 For more on the distinction between active and passive citizens, see Sewell (1994, ch. 5).

This neutral power would watch over the legislative process and, if necessary, regulate it to keep it aligned with the principles of citizen rights and equality. This project of a constitutional jury is connected with an earlier debate that Sieyès had with the drafters of the Constitution of 1791 (Jacques Guillaume Thouret and Antoine Barnave) over the question of the royal veto (Pasquino, 1998, pp. 11–13). Sieyès did not support the right of a monarch to veto laws drafted by the National Assembly, arguing that the king is not an elected representative of the nation and thus cannot intervene in the legislative process. In 1795, Sieyès theorises an alternative power to serve this neutral function. A constitutional jury, *un dépositaire conservateur de l'acte constitutionnel*, judges on the constitutionality of proposed laws and drafts *cahier de propositions* once every decade as a way of improving the Constitution (ibid., p. 195). He envisions three functions to be exercised by the jury:

> 1) that it faithfully watches over the safeguard of the constitutional 'deposit'; 2) that, sheltered from the pernicious passions, it takes into consideration all proposals that may serve to ameliorate the Constitution; 3) that, ultimately, it offers to civil liberties the possibility to appeal to natural equity on those serious occasions when the guardianship of the law will have forgotten its fair guarantees.
>
> (Goldoni, 2012, p. 6)

While I will not discuss all the organisational details and implications of such a constitutional jury, it is important to emphasise how this idea is aligned with Sieyès' conception of representation. As Marco Goldoni explains, the conception of representation that underlies Sieyès' idea of the jury is based on the idea of cooperation, rather than conflict. Sieyès thought of public powers as forming a unity of will and not a balance of powers representing different social interests. In this sense, the jury was to fulfil the function of an apolitical elite which guarantees that no political conflict gets in the way of national unity. A constitutional jury institutionalises democratic founding and "is presented as the building block of a system that keeps citizens' active participation to a vital minimum" (i.e. away from constitutional matters and only voting for ordinary representatives) (ibid., p. 22).

Moreover, this conception of the constitutional jury as taming social and political conflicts is paired with a conception of the nation that transcends the present generation and represents 'human nature'. Bronislaw Baczko has emphasised that Sieyès changes his take on the nation from 1789 to Year III from a concrete association of 25 million men to an abstract entity extending over successive generations (Baczko, 1988, pp. 98–125). In the speech where he presents his project of the constitutional jury, Sieyès discusses whether it is advisable to permit a constitutional reform. He defends the belief that amelioration instead of total renovation is best. It is at this point that he suggests that the idea of the nation expresses human nature rather than any particular temporal identity:

> Without wishing to dispute with future generations the right to do anything in this respect that suits them, it is permissible, and it is still a duty to remark that the true relations of a political constitution are with the nation that remains, rather than with such passing generation; with the needs of human nature, common to all rather than individual differences.
>
> (Bastid, 1939, p. 35)

What is this nation that remains? Marcel Gauchet theorises this as the two bodies of the people: the actual people and trans-temporal or constituent people (Gauchet, 1995, p. 42). The appearance of the transgenerational nation and the constitutional jury in the same text is not accidental. Sieyès here conceptualises positive achievements of the Revolution and speculates how the values of citizen rights and liberties can be practiced. Once identified, rights expressed in the Declaration of the Rights of Man and of the Citizen need to be safeguarded and perfected by the knowledge and experience of the centuries (*'les lumières et l'expérience des siècles'*). If these rights pertain to human nature itself, then their bearer can be conceived as an atemporal subject that transcends conflicts and differences.

Thus, over the course of the Revolution, Sieyès substantially changed his views on the principle that constitutes a free people. In the initial stages of the Revolution, characterised by the conflict between the immanent organisation of social relations and the *status quo* political system, he attributed revolutionary potential to the Third Estate. For it was the Third Estate that manifested itself as the critical subject in the act of the negation of the old social, political, and legal order. Thus, in Sieyès' earlier texts, a free people is constituted by the principle of radical conflict. In contrast, the conception of the nation that operates in Sieyès' later texts is predicated upon the assumed universality of human nature (as shared by the citizens of the nation-state and, most importantly, as interpreted by the jury). It posits that basic rights and liberties need to be protected from political conflict; the idea being that the people's freedom is ensured when constitutional change is restricted to a special constitutional organ.

This later position of Sieyès prefigures what today is framed as legal constitutionalism. According to legal constitutionalism, the proclamation and protection of individual rights and constitutional limits to power are definitive hallmarks of democracy. Constitutions are considered primarily to be legal documents that enshrine fundamental rights. The protection and interpretation of these fundamental rights are assigned to a counter-majoritarian institution, often a supreme or constitutional court (Bellamy, 2007). The argument for judicial review is usually motivated by counter-majoritarian reasons: majorities can pass oppressive legislation and turn into tyrannies. Additionally, there is an assumption that the law-making process needs to rely on the pre-established definition of rights to obtain guiding values. Rights themselves in this model are understood in a legal and not a political way and allow for little democratic contestation over their content and applicability. The role of interpreting the Constitution and the rights is assigned to judges who are thought of as standing above the political process. In this framework, constituent power is an elusive concept; it never fully emerges to challenge the constituted order and oftentimes "the question of constituent power simply does not arise" (Dyzenhaus, 2007, pp. 129–130). Pasquale Pasquino frames Sieyès' theory as the foundation of this framework. He praises Sieyès as the father of modern constitutionalism who explicated major concepts essential for modern democracies (Pasquino, 1998). Sieyès' influence is most noticeable, for Pasquino, in how his theory of the constitutional jury later became central for many constitutional regimes. Developed later in Sieyès' career, this theory frames the constitutional jury not only as the guarantor of the rights of human nature but also as the body that will defend them from the perils of politics (Pasquino, 2007).[5]

Conclusion

The shifts in Sieyès' thought are natural difficulties that arise when we theorise how democratic society and politics can exist. The two paradigms that I single out in Sieyès' thinking express equally important ideas for the democratic tradition. On the one hand, modern democracy, marked by the experience of the American and the French revolutions, contains elements critical towards the *status quo*. The interpretation of democracy that is attuned to this critical and oppositional dimension is, so to speak, an *immanent* one, that is, it understands

5 Following this reading, Pasquino insists that there is no other way to understand constituent power in Sieyès' work except as the power to authorise (so not the power to author the constitution). In this reading, the constituent power that is exercised by representatives does not presuppose that the people are actual authors of the constitution. The only way that constituent power can be understood in Sieyès' theory, Pasquino claims, is in the same way as the contemporary meaning of the constitution is, i.e. "a text establishing fundamental rights, their guarantee, and the basic rules for governing a given country" (Pasquino, 2016, p. 230). Authorisation can either mean electing a representative assembly (*ex ante*) or popular ratification (*ex post*). Sieyès did not theorise popular ratification, but authorisation in his theory should be understood as the election of extraordinary representatives. Pasquino uses Sieyès to justify the indispensable role of constitutional courts in contemporary democracies. He also combines it with the 'thin' conception of popular ratification (*ex ante*). In *The Sleeping Sovereign*, Tuck attempted to disassociate Sieyès with the paradigm of popular ratification. The point of Tuck's book is to demonstrate that there is an intellectual tradition of modern democracy that is based on the distinction of sovereignty and government. This tradition for Tuck runs as a motif through the works of Jean Bodin, Thomas Hobbes, Jean-Jacques Rousseau, and the thought of the American Revolution. It pertains to the plebiscitary model of popular sovereignty and should be considered, according to Tuck, the normative model for modern democracy. The distinction of sovereignty and government, expressed by Hobbes but fully developed by Rousseau, refers to the separation of the act of foundation and regular government. While government cannot but be representative, sovereignty manifested in the act of founding should always be direct. Tuck explains that direct democratic sovereignty does not author the constitution but authorises it. This means that the people in an ideal democracy, for Tuck, do not participate in drafting the constitution, but authorise its enforcement. Since Sieyès did not assign value to referendums, he, for Tuck, falls out of this tradition of modern democracy (Tuck, 2016).

democracy through the people themselves and their immanent struggles for liberation from oppression. Sieyès was an astute observer of this dynamic: through the perspective of labour relations, he saw how the struggle of the Third Estate to become a free people contradicted the existing political system. In contemporary experience, the idea of the people's struggle against oppression is expressed in a variety of critical narratives and social movements – for gender equality, anti-racism, LGBTQ+, etc. On the other hand, there is an idea of the unifying norm of what should constitute a free people. Ideas like 'nation', 'equality', or 'sovereignty' are also guiding ideas which, when being interpreted, give norms as to how a democratic society should be organised. The risk, though, of emphasising these guiding ideas too much is that of delegating their interpretation exclusively to a small group, like Sieyès did with his project of the constitutional jury, which adopts the role of an oracle of the transcendent nation, instead of speaking to and with the people with which it was contemporary.

A reader of Sieyès, Carré de Malberg (see Chapter 10), whose ideas on national sovereignty primarily influenced Belgian discourse, thought of the nation in that transcendent way. He thought, like the late Sieyès, that sovereignty is an attribute of an abstract entity rather than of concrete people with their current grievances and needs. The French Constitution of the Fifth Republic allegedly solved the conflict between the popular and national sovereignty model with the following formulation: "national sovereignty belongs to the people who exercises it through its representatives and through referendums. No section of the people and no individual may purport to exercise it" (Ziller, 2003, p. 267). In contrast, in Belgium today, the debate on the question of popular versus national sovereignty is very much a live one, which is centred on the opposition of direct and representative mechanisms for expressing the national will. In other words, it is centred on *how* the national will is expressed. In my discussion of Sieyès thought in terms of immanent and transcendent paradigms, I pointed out that it is not only *how* the national will is expressed that matters but also *what* is being expressed. Sieyès was never an advocate of direct democracy, always insisting that representation is a modern way of organising politics. However, he pursued two different intuitions as to what (and by which representatives) is being represented as the national will. The early Sieyès highlighted immanent relations within a society that legitimise and inform the act of extraordinary representation and the creation of a new political order that corresponds to these relations. The later Sieyès shifted to the idea of a transcendent nation – its principles need to be discovered and protected by a constitutional jury.

We can think of popular and national sovereignty not only in terms of mechanisms of will expression but also in terms of these immanent and transcendent dimensions. This offers new perspectives on intractable and long-standing political problems. When we talk about Belgium, should we abandon the criticised national sovereignty model? It seems to me that it still holds valuable ideas within itself, i.e. ideas of a society united on the basis of liberal principles, constitutional guarantees, and the separation of powers instead of ethnic ties. Yet, as the early Sieyès reminds us, there is an immanent element in the people that takes the form of critical opposition towards the dominant regime. If the gap between the immanent and the transcendent elements of the people grows too large, the system collapses. This suggests that a combination of the immanent and the transcendent is necessary, especially in cases where more direct participation (i.e. more popular sovereignty) can be a way to conceive of institutionalising the immanent element of the people. Although sketching an institutional model suitable for Belgium is beyond the scope of this chapter, Sieyès' complex negotiation of democracy and representation does suggest ways of moving beyond a dichotomised understanding of popular and national sovereignty.

Bibliography

Arato, A. (2017) *The Adventures of the Constituent Power. Beyond Revolutions?* Cambridge: Cambridge University Press.

Baczko, B. (1988) 'The Social Contract of the French: Sieyès and Rousseau', *The Journal of Modern History*, 60, suppl., pp. 98–125. DOI: 10.1086/243376.

Bastid P. (ed.) (1939) *Les discours de Sieyès en l'an III.* Paris: Hachette.

Bellamy, R. (2007) *Political Constitutionalism. A Republican Defence of the Constitutionality of Democracy.* Cambridge: Cambridge University Press. DOI: 10.1017/cbo9780511490187.

Beaud, O. (1994) *La puissance de l'État.* Paris: Presses universitaires de France.

Carré de Malberg, R. (2003) *Contribution à la théorie générale de l'Etat.* Paris: Dalloz.

Clavreul, C. (1982) *L'influence de la théorie d'Emmanuel Sieyès sur les origines de la représentation en droit public. Sous la dir. de Michel Troper.* Unpublished PhD thesis. Paris: Université de Paris 1 Panthéon-Sorbonne.

Dyzenhaus, D. (2007) 'The Politics of the Question of Constituent Power', in Walker, N. and Loughlin, M. (eds.) *Paradox of Constitutionalism: Constituent Power and Constitutional Form.* Oxford: Oxford University Press, pp. 129–146. DOI: 10.1093/acprof:oso/9780199552207.003.0008.

Forsyth, M. (1981) 'Thomas Hobbes and the Constituent Power of the People', *Political Studies*, 29(2), pp. 191–203. DOI: 10.1111/j.1467-9248.1981.tb00487.x.

Forsyth, M. (1987) *Reason and Revolution: The Political Thought of the Abbe Sieyès.* New York: Leicester University Press.

Gauchet, M. (1995) *La révolution des pouvoirs.* Paris: Gallimard.

Geenens, R. and Sottiaux, S. (2015) 'Sovereignty and Direct Democracy: Lessons from Constant and the Belgian Constitution', *European Constitutional Law Review*, 11(2), pp. 293–320. DOI: 10.1017/s1574019615000188.

Goldoni, M. (2012) 'At the Origins of Constitutional Review: Sieyès' Constitutional Jury and the Taming of Constituent Power', *Oxford Journal of Legal Studies*, 32(2), pp. 211–234. DOI: 10.1093/ojls/gqr034.

Guilhaumou, J. (1997) 'Nation, individu et société chez Sieyès', *Genèses*, Représentations nationales et pouvoirs d'Etat, (26), pp. 4–24. DOI: 10.3406/genes.1997.1430.

Guilhaumou, J. (1999) 'Sieyès et la métaphysique allemande', *Annales Historiques de La Révolution Française*, 317(1), pp. 513–535. DOI: 10.3406/ahrf.1999.2264.

Guilhaumou, J. (2002) *Sieyès et l'ordre de la langue: l'invention de la politique moderne*, Collection Philosophie, Epistémologie. Paris: Kimé.

Hont, I. (1994) 'The Permanent Crisis of a Divided Mankind: "Contemporary Crisis of the Nation State" in Historical Perspective', *Political Studies*, 42(1), pp. 166–231. DOI: 10.1111/j.1467-9248.1994.tb00011.x.

Jaume, L. (1986) *Hobbes et l'état représentatif moderne*. Paris: PUF.

Kalyvas, A. (2005) 'Popular Sovereignty, Democracy, and the Constituent Power', *Constellations*, 12(2), pp. 223–244. DOI: 10.1111/j.1351-0487.2005.00413.x.

Laquièze, A. (2008) 'La réception de Sieyès par la doctrine publiciste française du XIXème et du XXème siècles', in Quiviger, P.-Y., Denis, V., and Salem, J. (eds.) *Figures de Sieyès*. Paris: Publications de la Sorbonne, pp. 83–121. DOI: 10.4000/books.psorbonne.20034.

Leibniz, G.W. (1695) *A Specimen of Dynamics (Specimen Dynamicum)*. Translated in: Ariew, R., Garber, D. (eds.) (1989) *G.W. Leibniz Philosophical Essays*. Indianapolis: Hackett, pp. 117–138.

Locke, J. (1690) *An Essay Concerning Human Understanding*. Reprinted in: Woolhouse, R. (ed.) (1997) *An Essay Concerning Human Understanding*. London, New York: Penguin Books.

Marx, K. (1857) *Grundrisse der Kritik der politischen Ökonomie*. Translated in: Nicolaus, M. (ed.) (1993) *Grundrisse: Foundations of the Critique of Political Economy*. London, New York: Penguin Classics.

Marx, K. (1867) *Das Kapital*. Translated in: Fowkes, B. (ed.) (1981) *Capital: A Critique of Political Economy*. London, New York: Penguin Books in association with New Left Review.

Negri, A. (2009) *Insurgencies: Constituent Power and the Modern State*. Minneapolis: University of Minnesota Press.

Pasquino, P. (1998) *Sieyès et l'invention de la Constitution en France*. Paris: Odile Jacob.

Pasquino, P. (2007) 'Constitution et pouvoir constituant: Le double corps du peuple', in Salem J., Denis V., and Quiviger P.-Y. (eds.) *Figures de Sieyès*. Paris: Presses Universitaires de la Sorbonne, pp. 13–23. DOI: 10.4000/books.psorbonne.20025.

Pasquino P. (2016) 'Constituent Power and Authorization. Anatomy and Failure of a Constitution-Making Process', in Ingimundarson V., Urfalino P., and Erlingsdóttir I. (eds.) *Iceland's Financial Crisis: The Politics of Blame, Protest, and Reconstruction*. London: Routledge, pp. 230–239.

Rubinelli, L. (2016) 'How to Think Beyond Sovereignty: On Sieyès and Constituent Power', *European Journal of Political Theory*, 18(1), pp. 47–67. DOI: 10.1177/1474885116642170.

Archives parlementaires de 1787 à 1860 (Vol. VIII). Paris: Librairie administrative de Paul Dupont.

Sewell, W.H. Jr. (1994) *A Rhetoric of Bourgeois Revolution. The Abbe Sieyès and What Is the Third Estate?* Durham: Duke University Press. DOI: 10.2307/j.ctv11sn152.

Sieyès, E.J. (1789a) *Préliminaire de la Constitution françoise*. Paris: Baudouin.

Sieyès, E.J. (1789b) *Quelques idées de Constitution applicables à la ville de Paris*. Paris: Baudouin.

Sieyès, E.J. (1985) *Ecrits politiques*. Edited by Zapperi, R. Paris: Editions des archives contemporaines.

Sieyès, E.J. (2003) *Political Writings: Including the Debate between Sieyès and Tom Paine in 1791*. Edited by Michael Sonenscher. Indianapolis: Hackett Publishing Company.

Tuck, R. (2016) *The Sleeping Sovereign: The Invention of Modern Democracy*. Cambridge: Cambridge University Press. DOI: 10.1017/CBO9781316417782.

Urbinati, N. (2006) *Representative Democracy. Principles and Genealogy*. Chicago: Chicago University Press. DOI: 10.7208/chicago/9780226842806.001.0001.

Ziller, J. (2003) 'Sovereignty in France: Getting Rid of the Mal de Bodin', in Walker, N. (ed.) *Sovereignty in Transition*. Oxford: Hart Publishing, pp. 261–268. DOI: 10.5040/9781472562883.ch-011.

Part II

1831 – the Belgian moment

5 The liberal and Catholic origins of the Belgian Constitution

From the opposition under the Kingdom of the Netherlands to the constitutional debates of 1830–1831

Stefaan Marteel

In recent years, a strong renewal of interest in the sources and ideas of the Belgian Constitution of 1831 has emerged. This new research is informed by the conviction that many of these ideas have fallen into oblivion, leading to a number of misconceptions about the meaning of certain constitutional articles, primarily those involving the crucial concepts of sovereignty, representation, and participation (Geenens and Sottiaux, 2015; Deseure, 2016b; Deseure and Maes, 2018). Inspired by new theoretical insights in the fields of intellectual and constitutional history, as well as by the exponential growth of studies on the intellectual themes contemporary with the genesis of the Belgian Constitution, this research aims to retrieve the 'lost' meaning of the key concepts as well as to investigate the original intentions of the founding fathers. However, whereas most scholars follow a predominantly synchronic approach, analysing the discourses that were present during constitutional debates in the context of the broader Western European intellectual context, I will use a diachronic perspective in this chapter. Such a perspective reconsiders the political debates and discourses of 1830–1831 in the context of the recent political history of the new country, in particular the emergence and development of liberal and Catholic strands of thinking during the 'United' Kingdom of the Netherlands. In the first two sections, based on the findings of my PhD thesis on the intellectual origins of the Belgian Revolution (Marteel, 2018), I look at the political thought of liberals and Catholics before 1830. The last section considers the way in which the pre-revolutionary ideas were expressed in the Belgian Constitution of 1831 and charts the evolution of the different political strands that emerged after the Revolution.

The liberal opposition: between the question of legitimacy and the political thought of Benjamin Constant

The creators of the Constitution of 1831 drew upon the constitutional examples of their time in an eclectic way (Gilissen, 1968).[1] Where the fundamental

1 John Gilissen established that about 90% of the articles were borrowed from other examples, primarily the French Constitution of 1791, the French *Charte* of 1814/1830, and the

question of sovereignty was concerned, they used the 1815 Constitution of the United Kingdom of the Netherlands as a primarily negative example (Koll, 2012, pp. 491–500; Deseure, 2016b, pp. 96–99). The Constitution of 1815 (*Grondwet voor het Koningrijk der Nederlanden*) came about as a revision of the Dutch Constitution of 1814 (*Grondwet voor de Vereenigde Nederlanden*), which had been drafted with only the territory of the former Republic of the United Provinces in mind. The revision was the work of a commission composed of representatives from the north and the south in equal numbers. In both the 1814 and the 1815 versions, the locus of sovereignty remained unclear. The intellectual father of the Constitution, Gijsbert Karel van Hogendorp, envisaged the new monarchy as an improved version of the 'mixed government' of the Republic of the United Provinces (combining elements of democracy, aristocracy, and monarchy). Nevertheless, as N.C.F. van Sas has pointed out, the circumstances of the time made it clear that Prince William Frederick became king under an "implicit contract", implying that all the powers in the state were derived from the new Constitution (Van Sas, 2004, p. 461). Then again, the text of the Constitution was vague enough to allow for a different interpretation, namely that the sovereign powers of the monarch preceded the Constitution. The 1814 version, for example, declared that that "the Sovereign Power of the United Netherlands *is and remains* transferred to His Royal Highness [...]" (article 1). The Belgian Constitution, on the other hand, would declare unambiguously that "All powers emanate from the Nation" (article 25) as well as that "the king has no other powers than those which the Constitution, and the laws adopted by virtue of the Constitution, formally attribute to him" (article 78).

Even if their determination to distinguish the new Constitution from the Constitution of the United Kingdom of the Netherlands was comprehensible under the circumstances, it is striking that in the preceding 15 years the Belgians had hardly ever explicitly taken issue with the Constitution of 1815. It seems that the only time that the constitutional text was explicitly discussed was the moment of its drafting in 1815 (Marteel, 2018, pp. 53–62). It would be wrong to conclude from this that the ideas that underpinned the Belgian Constitution only emerged as a result of the new revolutionary situation of 1830. The vagueness and incoherence of the 'Fundamental Law' of 1815 had allowed for many different interpretations to be advanced and for many constitutional 'theories' to be projected upon it. Moreover, the liberal opposition was never 'constitutionalist' in *strictu sensu*: the opposition newspapers seldom referred explicitly to constitutional articles or pointed out contradictions between the literal text of the Constitution and the discourse or actions of the government. The opposition always invoked rights and freedom as general principles, not as provisions of the Constitution of 1815, even though it was always argued that the Constitution had somehow adopted these principles. In the north, by contrast, the political debate was to a much

'Dutch' Constitution of 1815.

larger extent informed by the literal text of the Constitution. The dynamics that led to the failure of the United Kingdom of the Netherlands largely originated in these differences in constitutional culture between the north and the south.

Two aspects informed the development of the specific constitutional culture of the Southern Netherlands: firstly, a subdued but resilient criticism of the way in which the Constitution of 1815 was drafted and adopted, and, secondly, the influence of the body of work of one of the major political thinkers of the time, the Swiss-French writer and politician Benjamin Constant.

When the newly drafted Constitution for the United Kingdom of the Netherlands was submitted to an Assembly of Notables in the south in 1815, a majority of its members rejected it. However, the government disregarded the vote and went on to enact the Constitution anyway. From the 1820s onwards, as the liberal opposition obtained momentum and became increasingly determined, it recurrently referred to the initial failure of the government to obtain an endorsement of the Constitution in the southern part of the kingdom. When at the beginning of 1830 the government-sponsored newspaper *La Gazette des Pays-Bas* supported the view that sovereignty lay entirely with the monarch, to whom the people of the Netherlands had in 1813 voluntarily submitted themselves, the liberal daily *Courrier des Pays-Bas* pointed out that the origins of the Dutch Constitution of 1814 were "of no relevance to the South" (*CDPB*, 17 January 1830, no. 17) as the conditions for the establishment of a *united* kingdom had been laid out by the European allied powers in the London Protocol (1815). The newspaper further argued that, with the submission of the Constitution to an assembly (in 1815), the "concurrence of the will of the people" had been "*at least presumed*" (*CDPB*, 17 January 1830; Marteel, 2018, p. 258). In other words, since the voice of the 'Belgians' had not been respected in 1815, there was all the more reason now to honour the principle of popular sovereignty as the foundation of the political order. Another telling example was a pamphlet in the form of an address to the king, written in 1829 by Louis de Potter, one of the spearheads of the liberal-republican opposition in the Southern Netherlands. De Potter wrote that

> the nation only demands from You the total execution of that Fundamental Law [i.e. the Constitution], which You have imposed on her *in disregard of* her wishes, and which she has come to accept, whilst at the same time declaring that she [i.e. the nation] has finally understood it, and that, from now onwards, she will not allow anymore that it is being exploited against her, and made into an instrument of oppression and slavery.
>
> (De Potter, 1829a, p. 6; Marteel, 2018, p. 247)

De Potter therefore invoked the government's choice in 1815 to ignore the rejection of the Constitution in the south to underscore the government's oppressive nature, as well as to contrast the latter with the growing endorsement of *true* constitutionalism by public opinion in the south.

Aside from these rhetorical invocations, the '1815 moment' also had a more substantial impact on the development of constitutional thought in the south. This was in large part due to the efforts of Pierre-François Van Meenen, an influential lawyer, writer, and journalist of *L'Observateur belge*.[2] Van Meenen was the first to take issue with the lack of democratic legitimacy with regard to the way in which the new Constitution was presented to the Belgian people by the provisional government in The Hague. Van Meenen lamented that "the creation, the organisation, the composition and the procedure" of the Assembly of Notables convoked by the government had been prepared in total obscurity (Van Meenen, 1815a, pp. 291–293). Subsequently, after the vote, he wrote critically about the way in which the government dismissed the majority of nays in the assembly and argued that the troubles at the birth of the new state demonstrated the importance of press freedom and strong public debate for keeping the government informed on what went on in the nation (Van Meenen, 1815b, pp. 162–164). In 1816, Van Meenen produced a series of articles on public law with the subtitle "On the projects of subversion of the Belgian civil order" (Marteel, 2018, pp. 77–81). By that time, the government had already initiated a number of policies aimed at the uniformisation or, as it was often dismissively called in the south, "*néerlandisation*" of the country. Around the same time that legislation was enacted to replace French with Dutch as the public language in the south, the government also started the preparatory work to replace the Napoleonic codes of law with new, "national" codes, which stirred up a lot of unrest among the legal professions in the south.

Van Meenen set out to argue that the demise of the French imperial state and the territorial control of the Southern Netherlands by the allied forces had not changed "the legitimacy of the Belgian civil order as it existed on 31 January 1814" (Van Meenen, 1816d). He made the distinction between "civil order" and "political order" to argue that individual rights were always guaranteed by the former, which the latter "has as its foundation and its mission to maintain". Despotism, he further pointed out, always started with the government turning against the civil order, resulting, ultimately, in the violation of individual rights (Van Meenen, 1816c, pp. 193–201, 202–207). Van Meenen proceeded to apply this theory to the analysis of the United Kingdom of the Netherlands as a union of two peoples or nations. The new kingdom could only accomplish a "spontaneous reunion", he pointed out, if the respective (Dutch and Belgian) civil orders were left intact and if the political order was only modified "with regard to those aspects that are irreconcilable with the goals of the reunion" (ibid., pp. 215–216). In other words, Van Meenen argued that the scope for legitimate legislation and decision-making by the new government was, under the circumstances, very limited. "All that has to be positively decided", Van Meenen wrote later in 1816, "will [should] only concern temporary and particular circumstances [...]

2 The newspaper's full title was *L'Observateur politique, administratif, historique et littéraire*.

and will in no sense affect the private relations of citizens among each other, nor their permanent relations with the state" (Van Meenen, 1816a, pp. 150–152).

Therefore, opposition against the government's legislative agenda of uniformisation was not only about preserving the social and legal legacy of the preceding French regime (1794–1814), but it was equally informed by a concern about political legitimacy. On the one hand, as Van Meenen admitted, his ideas about the limited legitimacy of the new power were conservative and based on what he called "the principle of the least possible action" (Van Meenen, 1816c, pp. 202–207). He even acknowledged, on the basis of his interpretation of the constitutional reality, that there existed a power vacuum with regard to "the more intimate parts of the social order" (Van Meenen, 1816a, p. 152). On the other hand, these ideas clearly had a pro-democratic dimension, in the sense that, whenever the government truly wanted to make changes to civil society, it would need to follow, in Van Meenen's words, "the clear, consistent and formal wish of the majority of the people" (Van Meenen, 1816d, p. 361). This brings us to the second aspect that was typical for constitutional culture in the Southern Netherlands in this period: the ideas of Benjamin Constant.

Constant's influence among Belgian liberals was particularly noticeable in the debates on ministerial responsibility, which were essentially concerned with the nature of government and the role of the monarch.[3] While the Fundamental Law of 1815 failed to declare explicitly that ministers were responsible for the acts of government, Belgian pamphleteers, such as lawyer and journalist Antoine Barthélemy, adopted Constant's theory of the inviolability of the king and the individual political responsibility of the ministers. Barthélemy specifically argued that there existed, with regard to the executive branch of power, a difference between the role of the king as the executor of the "general law" and that of the ministers performing discretionary "administrative acts", a distinction which highlighted the necessity of the accountability of the individual ministers towards the elected chambers and public opinion. Barthélemy also borrowed the model of the constitutional monarch as a "neutral power" from Constant. Positioned between the three branches of government, the monarch would not only be able to resolve a possible stand-off between a minister and the parliament (either by dismissing the minister or by calling new elections), but also, ideally, anticipate and prevent such a crisis (Bartélemy, 1815). Van Meenen underscored the need for control and scrutiny of the acts of the government in a similar way by distinguishing between "the law [...] in its general and universal sense of the word [...] rules, written or unwritten, which govern the natural, domestic, civil and political relations of the citizens" and "those momentary wishes, those movements of passion, which are proper to executive agents" (Van Meenen, 1817a, pp. 11–12). Constant's influence became even more visible in 1817 when the government

3 I rely primarily on Constant's discussion of ministerial responsibility in the *Principles of Politics* published in 1815: Constant [1815] (1988, pp. 183–193, 227–250).

instigated a debate on adopting a constitutional provision for ministerial responsibility (Van Velzen, 2005, pp. 120–122; Marteel, 2018, pp. 96–99). The problem with the proposed provision – which outlined by whom a legal procedure against a minister could be initiated, before which institution, and on what grounds – was that it restricted ministerial responsibility to the juridical form. Inspired by Constant, Van Meenen reacted by arguing in *L'Observateur* that if ministers were to be held self-evidently accountable for illegal acts, their proper responsibility involved "faults, prejudicial to the state or to individuals, which were committed in the use of their *legal* power". Consequently, it would have been paradoxical to compose such a list of "constructive offenses [*délits constructifs*]" as a legal basis for the prosecution of ministers. To specify transgressions for which ministers could be held responsible, Van Meenen insisted, was "to destroy responsibility, to consecrate irresponsibility" (Van Meenen, 1817b, p. 72).

The issue of ministerial responsibility remained an object of contention during the 1820s. Moreover, it clearly became a divisive issue between northern and southern opinion makers. While in the Northern Netherlands it was generally accepted, after 1817, that the issue remained unresolved, in the south the press, followed by the southern members of the Second Chamber, increasingly wrote and acted under the presumption that ministers *de facto were* responsible. The issue was again strongly debated in the late 1820s in relation to other debates on judicial reforms, the freedom of the press, and the adoption of a jury system. Defenders of the government directly attacked the southern press for constantly invoking general principles when it remained uncertain if such principles at all applied to the Constitution of the United Kingdom of the Netherlands, while Minister of Justice Cornelis van Maanen equated the principle of ministerial responsibility with the doctrine of the prevalence of the will of the nation over the monarch and flatly denied that either was sanctioned under the law of the country (Van Velzen, 2005, pp. 289–290; Marteel, 2018, p. 205). In reaction, a number of pamphlets appeared in the south defending the existence of ministerial responsibility in the spirit of Benjamin Constant and Pierre-François Van Meenen (Tielemans, 1829; Castiau, 1829).

As a result of the union that was being concluded between the Catholic and liberal opposition movements in the south, the discourse of opposition in the late 1820s also changed. Now that the division between liberals and Catholics had been overcome, so it was argued by the leading pens of the opposition, the country was finally witnessing the emergence of a public spirit. "Some of your ministers cry out that 'the government is lost'", De Potter wrote in the pamphlet he addressed to the king, but "I, Your Majesty, on the contrary, affirm, 'The nation is saved', and the government, to the extent that it becomes prudent and wise, will have gained everything from the fusion of opinions" (De Potter, 1829a, pp. 4–5). The existence of a true opposition, conditioned on the freedom of the press (which itself was under threat), was therefore considered the primary guarantee of the endurance of constitutional, representative government. Accordingly, the guarantee for ministerial responsibility was not to be found in the laws, or even the proper functioning of the institutions, but in the public or patriotic spirit.

"Let us not worry about the [legal] absence of ministerial responsibility", the lawyer Adolphe Castiau wrote, "but let us worry about the absence of patriotism; for the general interests are being compromised if the nation lets itself down" (Castiau, 1829, pp. 27–28).

The trajectory of political Catholicism from the Brabant Revolution to the Belgian Revolution

The liberal ideas discussed in the previous section would probably never have resulted in the crisis of the late 1820s, and the subsequent break-up of the country, if it had not been for the union that was concluded between the liberal opposition and Catholic political forces. It is commonly assumed that the Catholics joined the liberal cause because they believed that, through compromising with moderate liberals, they could obtain an unprecedented level of recognition and autonomy for the Catholic Church, especially compared to the regimes of Napoleon and William I. Secondly, a lot of emphasis has been put on the influence of the ideas of the French priest Félicité de Lamennais who, although initially belonging to the strand of counterrevolutionary and 'ultramontane' Catholicism of Louis de Bonald and Joseph de Maistre, came to believe that the best chance for a revival of political Catholicism lay in wholeheartedly embracing the legacy of the French Revolution, i.e. individual liberties and popular sovereignty. According to his new 'liberal-Catholic' doctrine, only among a Catholic people could these principles be realised without resulting in anarchy, and in an exclusively Catholic country their realisation would inevitably lead to a Catholic revival.

However, the question that has remained absent from most studies on political Catholicism involves the importance of the political culture of the Southern Netherlands, as it was shaped between approximately the 1780s and the 1830s, for the particular trajectory of political Catholicism. There are two different points to make in this respect. The first relates to the idea of *libertas Ecclesiae* developed in Catholic thought, a definition of 'freedom' as a form of institutional freedom reserved in particular (or exclusively) for the Catholic Church. This Catholic preoccupation with institutional freedom first gained urgency in the religiopolitical battles of the eighteenth century in the Southern Netherlands, which, as in other European countries, confronted Catholic (mostly Jansenist) reform movements and regalist political tendencies, on the one hand, with 'devout' or 'ultramontane' Catholic elements, on the other.[4] These fault lines continued to inform the battles over the relation between church and state at the time of the United Kingdom of the Netherlands, which means that the idea of institutional freedom

4 Ultramontanism refers here to the Catholic political movement that emerged in the second half of the eighteenth century in reaction to the increase in attempts to supervise the Church by the worldly powers (often spurred by the Jansenist reform movement), such as the *parlements* in France or the domestic councils (i.e. the Privy Council) in the Southern Netherlands. See Rogiers (1984) and Van Kley (2006).

was primarily rooted in the recent political history of the country. Secondly, a close analysis of the Catholic discourse in pamphlets and journals also shows that the dynamic towards a more liberal-constitutionalist type of discourse is noticeable from the 1810s onwards and was related to how the Catholic involvement in the Brabant Revolution of 1789–1790 (involving the disposal of the Habsburg monarchy and the establishment of a short-lived Belgian republic) had been processed in Catholic political thought.

Catholic and clerical opposition against the Constitution adopted in 1815, accompanied by the refusal of Catholic public servants to take an oath, is commonly considered evidence that Catholics were still in a "nostalgic, traditionalist phase" during the 1810s (e.g. Dagnino, 2018, p. 76). Catholics, according to this view, unequivocally rejected religious freedom and the equal treatment of different religious communities bestowed by the Constitution. However, this reading ignores the fact that the so-called opposition to 'tolerance' was primarily part of a discussion about the authority of the state over the Church. As a number of anonymous pamphlets made clear (*Examen Critique de la lettre de Monseigneur le Comte de Méan*, 1817; *Lettre adressée à un ami sûr une brochure, intitulée Cas de conscience*, 1818a; *Nouvelle théologie à l'usage des assermentés, ou examen d'un cas de conscience proposés et résolu en leur faveur*, 1818b), the main bones of contention were the articles that maintained the Napoleonic system of supervision over, and interference with, the Church. This was a system in which the head of state had the competence to appoint bishops (which the government of William I indeed claimed) and the government had the right to monitor clerical correspondence with Rome, as well as to censor sermons and publications by the clergy. Furthermore, the clergy took issue with the Constitution for potentially providing the government with the right to monopolise public education, as well as to interfere with the 'exterior' (institutional) dimension of the Church. The latter possibility evoked the plans put forward during the 1760s by the Privy Council under the presidency of Patrice François de Neny for a "national church" (Roegiers, 1976). Catholic pamphleteers argued that, in light of the many intrusions into the religious sphere allowed for by the Constitution, the so-called freedom for religion entailed the institutional entrenchment of a doctrine of "official indifferentism" in religious matters, posing a serious challenge to the dogmas of the Catholic Church (*Lettre adressée à un ami sûr une brochure, intitulée Cas de conscience*, 1818a, p. 13; *Nouvelle théologie à l'usage des assermentés, ou examen d'un cas de conscience proposés et résolu en leur faveur*, 1818b, p. 38).

When, in 1821, the oath issue was finally resolved through an agreement between the government and Rome, the adopted solution was in fact indebted to the terminology used by the Catholic opposition: it was agreed that Catholics would take the oath on the basis of the Declaration by Bishop François de Méan,[5]

5 In 1817, Bishop de Méan issued a declaration explaining his understanding of the oath in order to enable his appointment as archbishop.

which stated that Catholics, in abiding by the Constitution, accepted "civil tolerance" but rejected "dogmatic tolerance". However, this solution unintentionally provided a pretext for the opposition to invoke the articles on religious freedom in support of its agenda. If it was no longer possible to interpret the articles in the sense of "official indifferentism" or "dogmatic tolerance", ultramontane Catholics argued, then the articles on religious freedom could only be interpreted as providing a guarantee for the institutional freedom of the Church. Catholics, aside from claiming institutional autonomy on the basis of 'ancient' rights, now *additionally* invoked the freedom of the Belgians under the new law of the land, to establish the Church in accordance with ultramontane, anti-regalist doctrine.

Over the following years, Catholics consistently combined these two lines of argument. This became clear, for example, in an 1827 polemic against the government's plans to step up its control over the Church through the creation of a national council of bishops presided over by a royal commissioner. At this time, Piet van Ghert, secretary to the commission on matters regarding the Catholic faith attached to the Council of State, conjured up a number of so-called ancient legal procedures in church–state relations such as *Placet royal*, *recours au prince* and *appel comme d'abus* (Van Ghert, 1827). The Catholic-ultramontane reaction, in the form of a long pamphlet by seminary priests in Ghent, was predictably one in which the historical legitimacy of such procedures in the Southern Netherlands was disclaimed ("entirely unheard of in our country") (Van Crombrugghe et al., 1827, p. 5). In fact, this all originated in the Jansenist-regalist movement of the eighteenth century when Jansenists, according to the authors, had simply invented an alternative historical tradition "in order to escape the conviction of the errors of their sect" (ibid., pp. 52–54). At the same time, however, complementary to these classical-ultramontane and traditionalist objections, the authors supported their case with the argument of the necessary separation between church and state:

> A government always compromises its power when it makes the rewards and punishments of the law [on the one hand] and the rewards and punishments of religion [on the other] dependent on each other [...] Has experience not made it abundantly clear that, by making use of terror and torture, one does not increase the number of good citizens, but only decreases the number of [good] men?
>
> (Ibid., pp. 66–68)

Depending on the subject, Catholic polemists would easily shift from one type of argumentation to another. In fact, the less a certain issue could be approached from a historical-legitimist perspective (e.g. education), the more the emphasis would tilt towards invoking the civil liberties guaranteed by the Constitution (Marteel, 2018, pp. 176–184).

The second point, about the long-term influence of the Brabant Revolution, relates to the reception of French Catholic counterrevolutionary thought in the Southern Netherlands from the 1790s onwards. In France, Catholicism had always been more accommodating to an absolutist monarchical tradition. The French Revolution, condemned as a conspiracy between Protestant-Jansenist heretics and *philosophes*, resulted in a re-substantiation of the doctrine of divine monarchy in Catholic political thought. An early example of this was a publication from 1791 by the French priest Augustin Barruel, *Question nationale sur l'autorité et sur les droits du peuple dans le gouvernement* (Van Kley, 1996, pp. 364–366). In 1793, the ex-Jesuit François-Xavier de Feller from Liège, who by then had already acquired a reputation for being an ultramontane, anti-Jansenist, and anti-regalist firebrand, and who had played a crucial role in providing clerical support for the revolt of the States of Brabant against Joseph II, published a devastating review of Barruel's book (De Feller, 1793). The core of De Feller's argument was that legitimacy was not something that should be attributed only to monarchical government by divine right, but to all types of government ("democratic, aristocratic, monarchical"). De Feller clearly had the past events of the Brabant Revolution in mind when he argued that when a monarch has entered into a "synallagmatic pact" with the people, and has been made to swear an oath, it could very well be *him* who "troubles a government [...], violates its laws and principles, becomes an enemy of the state" (De Feller, 1793, pp. 90–92). De Feller even took it further, by arguing that there is always a case to be made for resistance against a prince – even a legitimate one – when he is the cause of the "ruin of the nation, of its rights, of its cult, of its customs" (ibid., pp. 100–101). When, almost 30 years later, the French ultramonarchist as well as ultramontane-Catholic writer Joseph de Maistre published *Du Pape* (1819), the work received a remarkably similar negative review in Leo de Foere's *Le Spectateur belge*, the most prominent Catholic, clerical journal in the Southern Netherlands at the time. De Foere rejected the way Maistre made his case for the pope's absolute sovereign authority within the Church: first of all, by purposefully misinterpreting the history of the Gallican Church in France; secondly, by establishing papal authority "through analogies with [the monarchist opposition against] the Estates General, the *parlements* etc." (De Foere, 1821a, pp. 23–28). Furthermore, repeating De Feller's arguments about the multiple forms legitimate government could take, De Foere strongly rejected Maistre's ultra-monarchical views in general, even admitting that he had a slight preference for a republican form of government (if, in an argument reminiscent of Montesquieu, it corresponded with the "mores" of the people) (De Foere, 1821b, pp. 285–287). In a similar manner to De Foere, one of the most important Catholic daily newspapers of the late 1820s, *Le Catholique des Pays-Bas*, rejected in the strongest terms the accusation that Catholics were by nature inclined to support monarchical government. The journal pointed out that in the Middle Ages, when Europe had still been a completely Catholic continent, "there existed more republican states than in our time". And did the Magna Charta not come into existence, it further asked, "when England was an exclusively Catholic country?" (*LCPB*, 23 February 1827, no. 46).

Constitutional legitimacy, or the question of the legitimacy of the new constitutional order, came to play a crucial role in the justification of the intransigent stand of the Catholics (just as it did among the liberals). This becomes clear from reading Leo de Foere's *Le Spectateur belge* at the time of the constitutional crisis in the United Kingdom of the Netherlands' first years. In the debate on tolerance in relation to the matter of the oath, De Foere adhered to the distinction between civil and dogmatic tolerance. In one of his articles on the topic, however, De Foere made an entirely different kind of argument about the Catholic opposition, trying to justify it in relation to the muddled, illegitimate way the Constitution of the kingdom had been adopted in 1815. "When a particular prince", De Foere argued,

> imposed by force and deceit a constitution without the concord of the nation, and when in this constitution tolerance and protection of all religious beliefs found themselves established, then [...] Catholics [...] can by no means concur, with their votes, or, even less, with their oaths, to the establishment, sanctioning, maintenance and protection of the errors condemned by their religion.
>
> (De Foere, 1816, p. 367)

De Foere furthermore expanded the legitimist-constitutionalist argument to include individual rights. This goes to show that liberal ideas developed out of the republican-constitutionalist strand in Catholic political thought, long before Lamennais' liberal turn:

> We, who had to resign ourselves to the forced violation of our *political rights*, we who had to consent to supporting the enormous foreign charges imposed on us [the debt of the Northern Netherlands], do we now also have to abandon the exclusive sphere of our thoughts, consent to despotism and to the enslavement of our conscience?
>
> (Ibid., p. 373)

Furthermore, De Foere pointed out the hypocrisy of those who proclaimed the liberty of conscience but were led by "the intolerance principle that everyone who does not think like [them] will be baffled, injured, slandered etc.", and wrote of the need to "defend liberal ideas against their enemies, but also against their friends" (ibid., pp. 369, 373). He would, in later years, often use a language of rights, and take offence at the notion that Catholics are no friends of the *droits de l'homme*.[6] It seems therefore fair to conclude that the ultimate endorsement by Catholics of liberal political principles resulted at least in part from the earlier political engagement of Catholics with rights and (republican) constitutionalism.

6 In 1819, in an article devoted to human rights, he wrote: "it is not because the intolerant philosophers have treated the rights of man in a horrible fashion, even more so by their actions than by their political theories, that one has to conclude that man has no rights. He has incontestable rights" (De Foere, 1819, pp. 180–181).

'Unionism', the Constitution, and the emergence of a new political landscape

The union concluded in 1828 between Catholic and liberal circles in the Southern Netherlands in order to coordinate their opposition was not primarily informed by strategic reasons, nor was it merely based on a superficial terminological convergence of their political discourses. At the root was an ideological rapprochement of the most prominent oppositional journals on both sides. On the Catholic side, the thrust towards civil liberties also pushed Catholics towards embracing the views of the liberals on the necessity of political freedom and accountability, and therefore, the importance of a free press ("*publicité*"), ministerial accountability, the jury system, etc. On the liberal side, the discourse against nationalisation and uniformisation, which originally concerned the issues of public language and harmonisation of the legal system, was broadened to include the religious issue long before the advent of 'unionism'.[7] Once the union was concluded, moreover, it was described and defended in a liberal language of rights and politics. Louis de Potter, defending the union in *Courrier des Pays-Bas* in 1828,[8] argued that questions of a religious or moral nature should, in a truly free society, no longer be a cause for division as they "strictly belong to the domain of man, of the individual, and society does not have any jurisdiction over it" (De Potter, 1829b, p. 3).[9] Charles Froment, a French refugee who had taken the cause of the opposition to heart, wrote in 1829 that the nation, now that it had finally risen up, would no longer let itself be divided into "pure liberals" and "religious liberals" (Van Herberghen, 1829, p. 18). The anonymous author of a pamphlet defending the Catholic resistance against the new seminary for the education of priests established by the government made the distinction between the government's "official liberalism" and the "true liberalism" of the opposition, arguing that the former taught that "public and religious matters are separated by the text of the constitution", while the latter implied that "our religious freedom is *pleine et entière*", meaning that "our Fundamental Law does not impose any other restrictions to religious freedom than the penal laws of the state" (*Le Collège philosophique en opposition à la Loi fondamentale*, 1829, p. 26). It was the perfect illustration of how the expression of the old Catholic preoccupation with institutional freedom was combined with a liberal language of fundamental rights.

7 Already in 1819, Van Meenen compared the agenda of the government to establish a national legal system and impose a national language with "theologians (creating) a national religion" (Van Meenen, 1819, pp. 327–328).

8 The articles were republished as a pamphlet in 1829: De Potter (1829b).

9 This argument sounds remarkably similar to the one made by Benjamin Constant in his *Principles of Politics Applicable to All Governments* of 1815: "there is a part of human existence which necessarily remains individual and independent, and by right beyond all political jurisdiction. Sovereignty exists only in a limited and relative way. The jurisdiction of this sovereignty stops where independent, individual existence begins" (Constant, 2003, p. 31).

The National Congress, convoked after the Belgian Revolution to finalise the constitutional draft prepared by a constitutional commission, elaborated on the political thought of the 'unionist' opposition.[10] As Raf Geenens and Stefan Sottiaux have pointed out, the constitutional fathers' approach to the question of sovereignty and public power was "primarily negative; they wanted to *restrain* power [...] and not construct a strong state or *empower* the sovereign people" (Geenens and Sottiaux, 2015, p. 312). Having read Montesquieu, they recognised the importance of checks and balances, which in their own time were already associated with the government of the United States of America. At the same time, the constitutional fathers continued to believe that the primary safeguard to restrain the exercise of sovereignty was not to be found in the Constitution as such, but in a political culture characterised by vigilance, publicity, and an active citizenry. With Benjamin Constant, the 'unionists' believed in the importance of "a spirit of inquiry, a habitual interest in the maintenance of the Constitution of the state, a constant participation in public affairs, in a word a vivid sense of political life" (Constant [1815] 1988, p. 239), which underpinned their laws on the freedom of the press, the rights of association, and the adoption of a jury system in criminal cases (to counter the exploitation of the criminal law for political oppression). Bram Delbecke described this as a "two-tier political system", in which "the formal political system would interact with a spontaneous, informal public space" (Delbecke, 2012, p. 94).

The Belgian founding fathers' conception of the separation between church and state and of the place of institutionalised religion in society also resonated with the 'unionist' ideas of the previous years. The Constitution protected religious freedom as a subcategory of the general freedom to express opinions, which was considered an essential attribute of a free and legitimate body politic. However, it also guaranteed the freedom of the public exercise of religion, endorsing the classical ultramontane agenda of the institutional freedom of the church(es) (article 14). Restrictions on activities conducted by religious institutions were limited to criminal law, and the prosecution of transgressions could only target individuals, never the Church as such (article 16). As Vincent Viaene pointed out, the National Congress thereby established "a personal framework for religious liberty", meaning that religions were not conceptualised as communities or corporations that were subject to protections or, for that matter, surveillance: "the dominant sentiment in the National Congress was to arrive at 'church autonomy' by making the churches, as such, legally intangible, rather than by accommodating them" (Viaene, 2007, pp. 122–123).

Of course, if the 'unionist' spirit prevailed in 1830–1831, there were still other, rivalling currents that, in the years to come, would play a role in the unravelling of the Catholic-liberal union. First of all, radical republicans identified, in the wake

10 The questions of how the union of oppositions developed into a Belgian-national movement in the first half of 1830 and how the events in August and September of 1830 were framed as a 'Belgian Revolution' fall outside the scope of this chapter. See Marteel (2018), chapter 9.

of the Belgian Revolution, with the Jacobin phase of the French Revolution. In October 1830, a series of articles appeared in *Courrier des Pays-Bas*, arguing that certain acts in the revolutionary drama had already been played out, but that other acts inevitably were to follow, such as a foreign war or a parliamentary coup in the form of "a new 31 May", the day in 1793 when the National Convention in France had expelled the leaders of the moderate Girondins (*CDPB*, 31 November 1830, no. 304). However, this depiction of events was at odds with the widely supported discourse of 1830, which pitted the Belgians, as a nation or a people, against an oppressive state controlled by (Protestant) Dutchmen. It was largely on the basis of this discourse that the purpose of the Revolution was defined in terms of "Belgium becoming Belgian", i.e. of the Belgians claiming sovereignty as a nation. "Where are the *cris de gueux* supposed to lead us", was one reaction to the voices of republican radicalism, "the Dutch are defeated [...] the remaining inhabitants are Belgians, your brothers!" (*CDPB*, 9 November 1830, no. 313). As Els Witte pointed out, the memory of the Terror and of civil war during the French Revolution still inspired enough fear to put revolutionary republicans on the defensive from the start (Witte, 2018, pp. 93–94; 2020, pp. 34, 65).

Republicanism in this period, however, cannot be reduced to neo-Jacobinism. In fact, Jacobinism presented a diversion from the broad tradition of neoclassical republicanism, with its emphasis on opposition to dependence and domination and on the fertile relation between virtuous citizens and republican institutions. This diversion resulted, on the one hand, from the influence on the French Revolution of the political thought of Jean-Jacques Rousseau[11] and, on the other hand, from the 'transformations' of neoclassical republicanism in the course of the Revolution (Baker, 2001). Moreover, liberalism in the early nineteenth century *was* often still influenced by neoclassical republicanism, and it is now believed (by some) to have partly originated in attempts to adapt republican ideas to modern society. This applied in particular to the political thought of Benjamin Constant (Jaume, 1997, pp. 63–117; Kalyvas and Katznelson, 2008, pp. 146–175) and, largely through his influence, also to the political thought of the liberal opposition in the Southern Netherlands against William I. In this early phase, liberals did not oppose popular sovereignty as the founding principle of government, even when they (along with most republicans) were far from supporting universal suffrage.[12] When it came to the debate on the form of government to be adopted, there was a small group of members who made a principled choice for

11 On how the latter's philosophy of the social contract and the general will stood at odds with the central tenets of neoclassical republicanism, see Spitz (1995) and Pettit (2012, pp. 11–18). For a counter-argument about the place of Rousseau in the history of republicanism, see De Dijn (2018).

12 A liberal strand rejecting popular sovereignty had emerged in France with the group of Doctrinaires around François Guizot and Pierre-Paul Royer-Collard. Although it is often argued that they were very influential in Belgium (e.g. Witte, 2018, p. 94), no evidence of this influence has been provided for the period leading up to the Revolution and the constitutional debates.

the republic. However, the final choice for a constitutional monarchy by a majority in Congress was not indicative of a strong anti-republican sentiment. First of all, many of the reasons for rejecting the republic were circumstantial and did not prevent members from considering the republic as the ideal system of government.[13] Secondly, many did not see republicanism and monarchism as necessarily antinomic, as illustrated by arguments that, under a constitutional monarchy, the Belgians would "enjoy all the advantages of the republican system, without having to fear its instability", and that "the guarantee of the social contract" would not be in the oath of the king, but in the "republican mores [...] the energy, always swift and active, of the citizens". Furthermore, expressions such as "republican monarchy", "a kind of republic with a hereditary head", "the best kind of republic", etc., were used to describe the constitutional monarchy (Deseure, 2016b, pp. 116–117; 2019, pp. 10–14; Witte, 2020, pp. 70–71).

Which were then, regardless of the difficulty of identifying a republican movement, the political extremes in the constitutional debates? On the right side of the political spectrum, some outlets, such as the Catholic newspaper *Courrier de la Meuse*, rejected the idea of popular sovereignty as irreconcilable with the choice for monarchical government (see Chapter 9).[14] Secondly, certain important members of the Congress, such as former president of the constitutional commission Etienne de Gerlache, insisted on a hereditary first chamber according to the English model, and therefore on a separate representation for the nobility in the Belgian government.[15] A more serious challenge was constituted by the radicals or 'democrats', who were hardly represented in the National Congress, but who tried to influence the constitutional debates through political clubs (most famously the *Réunion Centrale* in Brussels), newspapers (*Le Belge*, *L'Emancipation*), and petitions. They were primarily inspired by French egalitarian thinkers like Filippo Buonarroti and Claude Henri de Saint-Simon but, interestingly, also invoked late-medieval charters, such as the *Joyeuse Entrée* of Brabant, which had been a milestone in the political culture of the Southern Netherlands up until the integration of the country into the French Republic (Deseure, 2016a; Witte, 2020, pp. 41–44, 52–59). As Christophe Maes and Brecht Deseure clarify in another chapter of this book, these radicals, in the Jacobin tradition, held on

13 The understanding was that the choice for a republican government would put the recognition of an independent Belgian state by the European powers at risk. Furthermore, it was argued that the virtues and mores required for a republic were no longer strong enough among the Belgian people (De Dijn 2002, p. 236; Witte, 2018, pp. 97–98; 2020, pp. 67–68).

14 This was not very surprising as *Courrier de la Meuse* had, before 1830, represented the opinion of Catholics who sought accommodation with the government of William I, and continued, until it was a lost cause, to defend the legitimacy of the Dutch monarch (Jürgensen, 1963, p. 99).

15 This proposal stood no chance. As Annelien de Dijn has pointed out, "the Belgian founding fathers were of the opinion that modern-day Belgian society was characterised by a state of equality. This was seen to be the result of a (long) historical process of societal change" (De Dijn, 2002, p. 242).

to a "monolithic understanding of national representation: the nation, an abstract and universal entity, had but one indivisible will and, as such, it could only be represented by one elected legislative chamber" (see Chapter 9). Therefore, they opposed any role for the monarch in the legislative branch of government; in fact they considered the hereditary principle as such as completely irreconcilable with the principle of popular sovereignty (on this they were in agreement with *Courrier de la Meuse*). Secondly, they rejected the idea of a first chamber, arguing that either certain interests in society would be given separate representation, which was unacceptable, or the senate would represent the same national will as the chamber, which would make it superfluous (see Chapter 9). Finally, radicals also rejected the very exclusive censitary suffrage adopted by Congress in the electoral law and advanced a different view on the representative function of the vote. Surprisingly, however, none of them advocated universal suffrage, and, like the liberal majority, they emphasised capacity, virtue, and enlightenment as essential attributes of the representatives of the people (see Chapter 9; Witte, 2020, pp. 137–139).

Certain factions within the two political families also took radical positions on the question of the relation between church and state. On the Catholic side, a group of deputies who took up the agenda of the higher clergy, led by the bishop of Liège Cornelis van Bommel, wanted to secure a number of positive arrangements for the Church (notably regarding marriage). On the liberal side, a group of outspoken anticlerical liberals around Eugène Defacqz aimed at maintaining the legal arsenal for state intervention in religious matters inherited from the previous political regimes. Both sides obtained some success, but the core of their agendas remained unfulfilled. A more complicated case was presented by the group of Catholics who, in the autumn of 1830, came under the spell of the particular brand of liberal Catholicism developed by the French writer and priest Félicité de Lamennais and his journal *L'Avenir*.

Lamennais' thought, up until the late 1820s, was very much situated in the counterrevolutionary Catholic tradition of Augustin Barruel, Louis de Bonald, and Joseph de Maistre. Like them, Lamennais was concerned about the restoration of legitimate authority after the years of revolutionary turmoil, and like them he condemned the ('Gallican') submission of the Church to the monarchical state as the central vice in the history of France. However, while the others had remained staunch defenders of monarchical legitimism, albeit in harmony with the spiritual order of an ultramontane Church, Lamennais endorsed an unequivocally theocratic vision of the submission of worldly to spiritual power. As Lucien Jaume has explained, he projected onto the figure of the pope the identification between the king and the people originally made by Jacques Bénigne Bossuet (Jaume, 1997, pp. 201–204). From that perspective, Lamennais increasingly depreciated the sovereignty of the monarchs in the 1820s and, partly inspired by the Catholic-liberal union in the Netherlands, came to the conclusion that embracing civil liberties, and thereby inducing a period of anarchy, might constitute the shortest path to a true Catholic restoration under papal authority; as he wrote in *Des progrès de la révolution et de la guerre contre l'Eglise*: "the tempest purifying the air, the fever saving the patient" (Lamennais [1829] 1839, pp. 259–260, cited in Viaene, 2001, p. 55). Finally, in the wake of the Belgian and French revolutions, Lamennais moved on to a wholehearted embrace of liberal (and republican) principles in the belief that, in a Catholic nation that was intrinsically inhabited by "common sense", the modern liberties and popular sovereignty would be instrumental in ensuring public order (and, ultimately, in establishing papal authority).

Before the Revolution, Lamennais' work had primarily incited enthusiasm among an ultra-Catholic circle of young nobles, including Henri and Félix de Merode, Louis de Robiano-Borsbeek, and Ernest de Beauffort. Initially, they had been influenced by the work of Maistre as well, but, as Vincent Viaene pointed out, they were primarily predisposed to like Lamennais. They were more ambitiously theocratic than Maistre and were ultramontane to the point of believing that "the Pope should have the power to depose a wayward prince" (Viaene, 2001, pp. 51–53). For those men, some of whom had entered into a conversation with Lamennais (Jürgensen, 1963, pp. 110–111), Lamennais' *Des progrès de la révolution* of 1829 became the "charter for a conditional commitment" to the union of oppositions that had emerged in the Southern Netherlands (Viaene, 2001, p. 55). After the Revolution, the new 'liberal' ideas expressed by Lamennais in *L'Avenir*, alongside Jean-Baptiste Lacordaire and Charles de Montalembert, obtained a far broader reception than his earlier work, not only among (some of) the previously theocracy-oriented aristocrats (notably Felix de Merode and Charles Vilain XIIII) but also among seminary priests, primarily in Flanders, and certain bourgeois circles (Lamberts, 1972, p. 34; Viaene, 2001, pp. 64–65; De Smaele, 2016, pp. 69–70). In the National Congress, the influence of Mennaisianism was especially evident in the speeches by some of the young clerical deputies, for example when Désiré de Haerne advanced that the new Constitution came down to the recognition of a "complete independence, leaving to free discussion the future triumph of one system over the other" (Huyttens, 1844, p. 600).

On the other hand, the strong influence of Lamennais on Catholicism in post-revolutionary Belgium seems to have contributed to the unravelling of 'unionism' and the emergence of a bipartisan political system; largely as a result of the condemnation of his ideas in the encyclical *Mirari Vos* (1832) and his subsequent excommunication. In this context, Mennaisianism became increasingly (and exclusively) popular among village priests who endorsed outspoken democratic-republican ideals in defiance of urban-based 'bourgeois' Catholicism (De Smaele, 2016, pp. 64–66).[16] In mainstream Catholicism, however, the papal condemnation of Lamennais and of the Catholic endorsement of the modern liberties

16 Henk de Smaele adds that "Democratic zeal among the young priests was automatically (and probably sometimes mistakenly) attributed to Mennaisist inspiration" (De Smaele, 2016, p. 70).

provoked a conservative turn, meaning that the Catholic engagement with liberal constitutionalism became much more relativist and instrumentalist. The Belgian Constitution was no longer seen as a declaration of absolute principles, but as the fruit of a Belgian tradition of liberties and self-government traceable to the Middle Ages (Viaene, 2001, p. 97). Nevertheless, as Viaene has pointed out, conservative Catholics still remained "children of Maistre and Lamennais" in their continued claim that "only an immutable religion anchored in dogma could provide society with adequate armour against the chaotic human passions unleashed by the French and Industrial Revolution" (Viaene, 2001, p. 83). It seems therefore that, in the wake of the revolutionary events of 1830 and of the (temporarily) strong influence of Lamennais, and in spite of the acceptance of the Belgian constitutional framework by political Catholicism, a paradigmatic shift took place in the political thought of Catholics. Originally anchored in a domestic political culture in which classical, anti-regalist ultramontanism met, at the time of the United Kingdom of the Netherlands, liberal-republican ideas, political Catholicism in Belgium became strongly affiliated to the French tradition of counterrevolutionary Catholic thought.

In reaction to Catholic revivalism, an opposite development took place among liberals, who advocated enhancing the state's role in order to counter the social influence of the Church. On the one hand, this would reconnect liberals with a regalist-Jansenist tradition that saw the state as an essential vehicle for religious reform. On the other hand, they would develop an understanding of the constitutional freedom of religion as a purely individual right and of the sovereign state as the sole guardian of the general interest (Viaene, 2003; 2007, p. 127). It seems, therefore, that the increasingly partisan political culture that emerged in Belgium in the nineteenth century was primarily rooted in ideological developments in the liberal and Catholic camps that moved away from the 'unionist' ideas that inspired the Revolution and the Constitution. Ultimately, this resulted in historical misconceptions about these ideas themselves.

Bibliography

Baker, K.M. (2001) 'Transformations of Classical Republicanism in Eighteenth-Century France', *The Journal of Modern History*, 73(1), pp. 32–53. DOI: 10.1086/319878.

Barthélemy, A. (1815) *Des gouvernements passés et du gouvernement à créer. Suite de l'expose succinct de l'état des Pays-Bas, etc.* Brussels: Adolphe Stapleaux.

Castiau, A. (1829) *De la responsabilité, de la mise en accusation des ministres en Belgique.* Ghent: Vander Schelden.

Constant, B. (1988) 'Principles of Politics Applicable to All Representative Governments' [1815], in Constant, B., *Political Writings.* Edited by Fontana, B. Cambridge: Cambridge University Press, pp. 169–305.

Constant, B. (2003) *Principles of Politics Applicable to All Governments* [1810, unpublished]. Edited by E. Hofmann. Indianapolis: Liberty Fund.

Dagnino, R. (2018) 'Making the Constitution More Catholic? Catholic Adaptation Strategies to the Belgian Constitutional Liberties of 1831', *Journal of Constitutional History/Giornale di Storia Costituzionale*, 35(1), pp. 69–87.

De Dijn, A. (2002) 'A Pragmatic Conservatism. Montesquieu and the Framing of the Belgian Constitution, 1830–1831', *History of European Ideas*, 28(4), pp. 227–245. DOI: 10.1016/s0191-6599(02)00045-1.

De Dijn, A. (2018) 'Rousseau and Republicanism', *Political Theory*, 46(1), pp. 59–80. DOI: 10.1177/0090591715609101.

De Feller, F.-X. (1793) 'Question nationale sur l'autorité et sur les droits du peuple, par M. l'abbé Barruel', *Journal historique et littéraire*. 2, pp. 88–106.

De Foere, L. (1816) 'Tolérance. Objections faites contre le 15me N° du Spectateur belge (Éphém. N° III.)', *Le Spectateur Belge*, 4(8), pp. 363–381.

De Foere, L. (1819) 'Droits de l'homme', *Le Spectateur Belge*, 9(20), pp. 180–181.

De Foere, L. (1821a) 'Du Pape, par le comte de Maistre, ministre plenip. de S.M. le roi de Sardaigne auprès de S.M. l'empereur de Russie. Ier article', *Le Spectateur Belge*, 13(1), pp. 20–31.

De Foere, L. (1821b) 'Du Pape, par le comte de Maistre, ministre plenip. de S.M. le roi de Sardaigne auprès de S.M. l'empereur de Russie. IIe article', *Le Spectateur Belge*, 13(6), pp. 285–293.

De Potter, L. (1829a) *Rapport d'un ministre, ami de sa patrie et de ses concitoyens [...] sur la disposition actuelle des esprits et de la situation des choses en Belgique*. Brussels: Coché-Mommens.

De Potter, L. (1829b) *Union des catholiques et des libéraux*. Brussels: De Greef-Laduron.

De Smaele, H. (2005) 'Eclectisch en toch nieuw. De uitvinding van het Belgisch parlement in 1830–1831', *BMGN—Low Countries Historical Review*, 120(3), pp. 408–416. DOI: 10.18352/bmgn-lchr.6253.

De Smaele, H. (2016) 'Catholic Republicanism Revisited', in De Maeyer, J. and Viaene, V. (eds.), *World Views and Worldly Wisdom. Religion, Ideology and Politics, 1750-2000*. Leuven: Leuven University Press, pp. 57–73. DOI: 10.2307/j.ctt1jktrxq.6.

Delbecke, B. (2012) *De lange schaduw van de grondwetgever. Perswetgeving en persmisdrijven in België, 1831–1914*. Ghent: Academia Press.

Deseure, B. (2016a) 'From Pragmatic Conservatism to Formal Continuity. Nineteenth-Century Views on the Old Regime Origins of the Belgian Constitution', *Journal of Constitutional History/Giornale di Storia Costituzionale*, 32(2), pp. 257–277.

Deseure, B. (2016b) 'National Sovereignty in the Belgian Constitution of 1831. On the Meaning(s) of Article 25', in Müssig, U. (ed.), *Reconsidering Constitutional Formation/National Sovereignty*. Studies in the History of Law and Justice, 6. Cham: Springer, pp. 93–157. DOI: 10.1007/978-3-319-42405-7_2.

Deseure, B. (2019) 'Republican monarchy in the 1830 revolutions. From Lafayette to the Belgian Constitution', *History of European Ideas*, 45(7), pp. 992–1010. DOI: 10.1080/01916599.2019.1628085.

Deseure, B. and Maes, C. (2018) 'Introduction', *Journal of Constitutional History/Giornale di Storia Costituzionale*, 35(1), pp. 7–32.

Geenens, R. and Sottiaux, S. (2015) 'Sovereignty and Direct Democracy. Lessons from Constant and the Belgian Constitution', *European Constitutional Law Review*, 11(2), pp. 293–320. DOI: 10.1017/s1574019615000188.

Gilissen, J. (1968) 'La constitution belge de 1831. Ses sources, son influence', *Res Publica. Politiek-wetenschappelijk tijdschrift van de Lage Landen*, 10, pp. 107–141.

Huyttens, E. (1844) *Discussions du Congrès National de Belgique 1830–1831. Tome premier*. Brussels: Société Typographique Belge.

Jaume, L. (1997) *L'individu effacé ou le paradoxe du libéralisme français*. Paris: Fayard.

Jürgensen, K. (1963) *Lamennais und die Gestaltung des Belgischen Staates. Der liberale Katholizismus in der Verfassungsbewegung des 19. Jahrhunderts*. Wiesbaden: Franz Steiner.

Kalyvas, A. and Katznelson, I. (2008) *Liberal Beginnings. Making a Republic for the Moderns*. Cambridge: Cambridge University Press.

Koll, J. (2012) 'Belgien', in Daum, W. (ed.) *Handbuch der europäischen Verfassungsgeschichte im 19. Jahrhundert. Band 2, 1815–1847*. Bonn: Dietz, pp. 485–542.

Lamberts, E. (1972) *Kerk en liberalisme in het bisdom Gent, 1821–1857. Bijdrage tot de studie van het liberaal- katholicisme en het ultramontanisme*. Leuven: Universiteitsbibliotheek.

Lamennais, F. (1839) 'Des progrès de la révolution et de la guerre contre l'Eglise' [1829] in *Oeuvres complètes de F. De la Mennais. Tome deuxième*. Brussels: Société belge de librairie, pp. 237–322.

Marteel, S. (2018, corrected publication 2020) *The Intellectual Origins of the Belgian Revolution. Political Thought and Disunity in the Kingdom of the Netherlands, 1815–1830*. Basingstoke: Palgrave.

Pettit, P. (2012) *On the People's Terms. A Republican Theory and Model of Democracy*. Cambridge: Cambridge University Press. DOI: 10.1017/cbo9781139017428.

Roegiers, J. (1976) 'De Jansenistische Achtergronden van P.F. de Neny's Streven naar een "Belgische' Kerk"', *BMGN: Low Countries Historical Review*, 91(3), pp. 429–454. DOI: 10.18352/bmgn-lchr.1953.

Roegiers, J. (1984) 'De gedaantewisseling van het Zuidnederlands ultramontanisme, 1750–1830', in Lamberts, E. (ed.) *De Kruistocht tegen het Liberalisme. Facetten van het ultramontanisme in België in de 19e eeuw*. Leuven: Leuven University Press, pp. 11–35.

S.A. (n.d.a.) *Catholique des Pays-Bas, Le* (*LCPB*).

S.A. (n.d.b.) *Courrier des Pays-Bas* (*CDPB*).

S.A. (1817) *Examen Critique de la lettre de Monseigneur le Comte de Méan, ancien Prince- Evêque de Liège, du 3 Juillet 1817, insérée dans le Journal de la Belgique, le Jeudi 24 du même mois*.

S.A. (1818a) *Lettre adressée à un ami sûr une brochure, intitulée Cas de conscience*. Bruges.

S.A. (1818b) *Nouvelle théologie à l'usage des assermentés, ou examen d'un cas de conscience proposés et réso lu en leur faveur*. Bruges.

S.A. (1829) *Le Collège philosophique en opposition à la Loi fondamentale, par un patriote père de famille*. Brussels.

Spitz J.-F. (1995) *La liberté politique. Essai de généalogie conceptuelle*. Paris: Presses universitaires de France.

Tielemans, J.-F. (1829) *Lettre à M. Van Maanen sur la responsabilité ministérielle*. Brussels: Coché-Mommens.

Van Crombrugghe, C. et al. (1827) *Réfutation des Observations sur les libertés de l'Église Belgique*. Aalst: Spitaels.

Van Ghert, P. (1827) *Observations sur les libertés de l'Église Belgique*. Brussels: Lejeune.

Van Herberghen, H. [Charles Froment] (1829) *Coup d'oeuil sur le royaume des Pays-Bas en 1829*. Brussels: Tencé.

Van Kley, D.K. (1996) *The Religious Origins of the French Revolution. From Calvin to the Civil Constitution, 1560–1791*. New Haven: Yale University Press.
Van Kley, D.K. (2006) 'Jansenism and the International Suppression of the Jesuits', in Brown, S.J. and Tackett, T. (eds.) *The Cambridge History of Christianity. Vol. 7: Enlightenment, Reawakening, and Revolution 1660–1815*. Cambridge: Cambridge University Press, pp. 302–328. DOI: 10.1017/chol9780521816052.018.
Van Meenen, P.-F. (1815a) 'Réflexions sur le mode de présentation du projet de constitution à l'assentiment de la nation', *L'Observateur Belge*, 2(45), pp. 287–299.
Van Meenen, P.-F. (1815b) 'Réflexions sur l'intérêt général de tous les Belges en septembre 1815, par un Belge. Bruxelles, 1815', *L'Observateur Belge*, 3(64), pp. 139–170.
Van Meenen, P.-F. (1816a) 'Attributions du pouvoir législative crée par la constitution'. *L'Observateur Belge*, 8(193), pp. 145–207.
Van Meenen, P.-F. (1816b) 'Droit Public. Des projets et des essais de subversion de l'ordre civil Belgique', *L'Observateur Belge*, 5(115), pp. 129–148.
Van Meenen, P.-F. (1816c) 'Droit Public. Des projets et des essais de subversion de l'ordre civil Belgique', *L'Observateur Belge*, 5(119), pp. 193–217.
Van Meenen, P.-F. (1816d) 'Droit Public. Des projets et des essais de subversion de l'ordre civil Belgique', *L'Observateur Belge*, 5(129), pp. 353–379.
Van Meenen, P.-F. (1817a) 'Du pouvoir exécutif. Des arrêtés–Des réglemens–De la responsabilité–De la prise à partie', *L'Observateur Belge*, 9(227), pp. 1–32.
Van Meenen, P.-F. (1817b) 'Ministres justiciables–Responsables–Art. 73 de la Loi Fondamentale', *L'Observateur Belge* 11(285), pp. 60–80.
Van Meenen, P.-F. (1819), 'Discours de M. Kemper, etc. Suite 3. Civilisation. Législation. Codes. Art. 163 de la Loi fondamentale. Nationalité. Uniformité'. *L'Observateur Belge* 17(466), pp. 321–364.
Van Sas, N.C.F. (2004) *De metamorfose van Nederland. Van oude orde naar moderniteit, 1750–1900*. Amsterdam: Amsterdam University Press. DOI: 10.5117/9789053568408.
Van Velzen, P. (2005) *De ongekende ministeriële verantwoordelijkheid. Theorie en praktijk, 1813–1840*. Nijmegen: Wolf Legal Publishers.
Viaene, V. (2001) *Belgium and the Holy See from Gregory XVI to Pius IX (1831–1859). Catholic Revival, Society and Politics in 19th-Century Europe*. Leuven: Leuven University Press.
Viaene, V. (2003) 'Zeger-Bernard van Espen, Liberalism and Religious Reform in 19th-Century Belgium', in Cooman, G., Van Stiphout, M. and Wauters, B. (eds.) *Zeger-Bernard van Espen at the Crossroads of Canon Law, History, Theology and Church-State Relations*. Leuven: Leuven University Press, pp. 361–374.
Viaene, V. (2007) '"La liberté comme en Belgique". The Semantic Stakes of "Separation" Between Church and State in Belgium', in Hölscher, L. (ed.) *Baupläne der sichtbaren Kirche. Sparchliche Konzepte religiöser Vergemeinschaftung in Europa*. Göttingen: Wallstein, pp. 117–135.
Witte, E. (2018) 'Republic and popular sovereignty. The Belgian case: 1830–1831', *Journal of Constitutional History/Giornale di Storia Costituzionale*, 35(1), pp. 89–112.
Witte, E. (2020) *Belgische republikeinen. Radicalen tussen twee revoluties (1830–1850)*. Antwerp: Polis.

Publications without a specific, personal author (such as newspapers and official documents) are listed under S.A.

6 The Coppet Group and the political liberalism of the Belgian founding fathers

Christophe Maes

Introduction[1]

It is well known that, following the violent separation with the United Kingdom of the Netherlands in September 1830, the Belgian revolutionaries advocated 'liberty in everything and for everyone'. Despite several endeavours to elucidate the notion of liberty (De Dijn, 2012; Delbecke, 2010; Demoulin, 1989; De Smaele, 2005; Marteel, 2018), the liberal idiom remains underresearched. This is remarkable, as the concept was extensively used in the Belgian revolutionary discourse (Witte, 2006, p. 236). It is all the more surprising considering that the founding fathers' understanding of liberty was tied to advocacy for specific governmental forms; a connection which equally informed the works of Montesquieu, Germaine de Staël, and Benjamin Constant, the most influential sources for the Belgian founding fathers.[2]

In this chapter, I will argue that the liberal understanding of liberty was mainly informed by a distinction between two forms of liberty: liberty as a means and liberty as an end. In this interpretation, the majority of the Congress was highly influenced by De Staël and Constant's conception of 'liberty'.[3] Moreover, this conception was essential for the Congress' decisive institutional choices. First, I will give a brief overview of the various liberal tendencies towards which the congressmen directed their attention. Secondly, I will analyse De Staël and Constant's insights into 'liberty' and compare them with the views within the Belgian National Congress. Furthermore, this chapter will be limited to De Staël and Constant's works since Montequieu's influence on De Staël and Constant, as

1 This chapter is based on Maes (2018), 'The End Justifies the Means. The Nature of Belgium's 1830 Political Liberalism', Giornale di Storia Constituzionale, 35(1), pp. 129–145. I thank the editors of Giornale di Storia Constitutizionale for their kind permission to (partly) republish the article in this book.

2 For an informed overview of the sources of Belgium's 1831 Constitution, see Gilissen (1968).

3 Note that the concept of liberty does not form an autonomous object in their political philosophical work, but is analysed in a larger framework which connects liberty to the governmental form and the emergence of the 'modern nation' (Krause, 2015; Pasquino, 1998, p. 32).

well as his impact on the Belgian governmental form, has already been established in several articles (e.g. De Dijn, 2012; Illing, 2012).

The influence of French political thought

It is largely accepted in historical scholarship that the Belgian political theorists of 1815–1830 were mainly directed to France in the development of their political theories, in particular to ideas originating from French Restauration liberalism (Lemmens, 2011; Magits, 1977, p. xix). The classical liberal doctrine, which emerged from a reaction against monarchical absolutism and privileges, can generally be understood as the fundamental concern with protecting and encouraging individual liberty. Since decisions in the political sphere have to be taken collectively and bind the community, political liberalism cannot merely be the application of individual liberty (Charvet, 2005, pp. 1262–1263). Political liberalism therefore aspires to find political institutions that enable human liberty to govern itself. It does so by enabling the individual citizens to form voluntary associations to promote their beliefs and ideas in the context of collective decision-making. To ensure this, political liberalism endorses the adoption of procedures for limiting governmental power and making the latter accountable to the citizens (Charvet, 2005, pp. 1262–1263).

In France, liberalism developed in the wake of the French Revolution with the aim of reconciling the legitimacy of the state with the emancipation of society (Jaume, 2012, pp. 36–37).[4] Although all liberals endeavoured to conserve the principles of 1789, French liberalism featured contrasting propensities. The form of French liberalism promoted by the Doctrinaires endeavoured to strengthen the state, as the latter was perceived as the political body that could best express and protect the general interest against private interests. The Doctrinaires aimed to liberalise political institutions, but they simultaneously favoured a strong state with close ties between the middle class and the administration. The state was in the best position to look after the general interest. This entailed that the popular masses should be excluded from any role in the political power. The Doctrinaires' liberalism was thus conceived in support of the state, not against it (Jaume, 2003, pp. 388–389; Rosanvallon, 1989, p. 424 a.f.). A second form of liberalism was mainly promoted by the Coppet Group around Germaine de Staël and Benjamin Constant.[5] It distinguished itself from the Doctrinaires by promoting individualism and more pronounced constitutional and extra-constitutional limitations on political authority (Jaume, 2012, pp. 41–42). Whereas the Doctrinaires (and the liberal Catholics alike) had only a limited consideration for the individual and

4 Political liberalism is to be dissociated from liberal Catholicism. On liberal Catholicism and the distinction with liberalism, see Stefaan Marteel's chapter in this volume (Chapter 5), as well as Dagnino (2018); Jürgensen (1963); Marteel (2018); Viaene (2001, pp. 65–71).

5 The group of intellectuals around De Staël and Constant (also including Necker and Sismondi) has been named after De Staël's family castle in Switzerland where they regularly stayed to discuss their intuitions and theories.

favoured a strong central authority, Coppet liberalism endorsed the importance of the individual's capacity for initiative, the ability to critically evaluate politics and institutional forms, and the belief in human perfectibility (Hoffman, 2009; Jaume, 1997, pp. 91–102).

In Belgium, it was especially Coppet liberalism, and not the Doctrinaires' liberalism, which appealed to the revolutionaries. Several issues made French Doctrinaire liberalism in 1830–1831 Belgium less alluring. First, the Doctrinaires lost a certain amount of credibility due to their political opportunism between 1814 and 1830, blowing hot and cold on the extension of parliamentary and royal prerogatives in the function of their political position (Rosanvallon, 1989, pp. 412–413). At one point, the Doctrinaires even promoted the active participation of the king in governmental policy-making (Selinger, 2019, pp. 136–137), a point of view which was generally rejected in Belgium. Secondly, during the French July Revolution, the Doctrinaires quickly came to advocate a return to the constitutional order of the French Charter of 1814, a Constitution which the king had 'granted' (*octroyée*) to the people (Craiutu, 2003, pp. 174–176). This surely must have been a sensitive issue for the Belgian revolutionaries, who had revolted – among other things – against the governmental reading of the Dutch Fundamental Law as the king's granted document. Finally, the admission of prior censorship for the press – which the Doctrinaires considered to be a governmental instrument aimed at interconnecting government with civil society (Garsten, 2015) – was received with great distrust by the Belgians. After years of de facto censorship and prosecutions, the latter came to consider the freedom of the press to be an (almost) absolute civil right. As such, French Doctrinaire liberalism was mostly considered too "narrow-minded" (Huyttens, 1844b, p. 313, 29 January 1831, Lebeau; Huyttens, 1844b, p. 442, 3 February 1831, De Gerlache with reference to Constant). Some even spoke of a "bastard system of the doctrinaires" (*CDPB*, 16 March 1831, no. 75. See also *CDPB*, 18 March 1831, no. 77; *CDPB*, 28 April 1831, no. 118).

Instead, Belgian liberals turned their heads towards the Coppet Group. Between 1815 and 1830, Constant and De Staël's theories were eagerly discussed by Belgian journalists, lawyers, and public law theorists. Ironically, those men, who would form the liberal vanguard of the Belgian Revolution, had been educated at the new universities of Ghent, Louvain, and Liège, which had been established in the context of William I's unpopular reform of higher education (Delbecke, 2014, p. 450). A key figure in those liberal circles was the constitutional theorist Pierre-François Van Meenen, who was an adept interpreter of Constant. Van Meenen, who was considered to be an intellectual authority in liberal circles, voiced his liberal ideas and opinions in the *Courrier des Pays-Bas*, a newspaper based in Brussels and one of the most influential Belgian journals of the time. Its editorial board also comprised influential liberals such as Charles de Brouckère, Sylvain Van de Weyer, and Jean-Baptiste Nothomb (Witte, 2016, p. 22). Another important circle of liberals that strongly adhered to De Staël and Constant's insights consisted of several Liège-based students of Pierre Destriveaux, a professor of constitutional law: the perspicuous journalist Paul

Devaux; the charming leader of the local revolutionary corps and founder of the provisional government Charles Rogier, who had met Constant personally in Paris in 1827; and the eloquent lawyer and publicist Joseph Lebeau, who had been publishing counterfeit works of Pierre Daunou, Germaine De Staël, and Adolphe Thiers under William I's regime (Royer, 1835, p. 709). Catholics did not remain indifferent to Coppet liberalism either. Even Etienne-Constantin de Gerlache, the president of the National Congress in 1831 and the key figure on the Catholic side, circulated in the orbit of Constant (Viaene, 2001, p. 102). All of these men would eventually get elected to the National Congress, imbuing the debates with their liberal conceptions.[6] Their influence is all the more important as most of them held seats in the Constitutional Commission, which would form the blueprint for the actual Belgian Constitution of 1831 (Van Den Steene, 1963, pp. 12–28).

The problem of the governmental form in the constitutional debates of 1830–1831

Inspired by the bitter recollections of William I's increasingly absolutist rule, the National Congress aimed at limiting the government's autocratic propensities and securing individual freedom against public authority. Royal sovereignty and all forms of privileges prevailing under William I's regime had to be abolished. Simultaneously, and under pressure from the international coalition, there was a tendency to moderate the revolutionary drive. With the excesses of the French Revolution still vividly in mind, the congressmen wished to avoid popular derailment. Hence, liberty and stability became the two topics that dominated the congressional debates as the congressmen sought to set up a state apparatus that was institutionally balanced and adapted to societal nature and needs, providing the necessary guarantees to individual liberty (Van Den Steene, 1963, pp. 60–61). It is therefore no surprise that the governmental form was discussed at the outset of the constitutional debates, especially since the choice of a specific form of government would strongly influence the new state's institutions. Two positions dominated these debates: the call of republicans for a republican state system with an elected head of state, and the appeal of the liberals and the Catholics for a constitutional monarchy. Whereas the broader discussion between republicans and liberals revolved around deep-seated beliefs in the '*res publica*' on the one hand, and the development of individuals on the other, with their respective ramifications concerning the strength of the state, the reliability of the political procedure, the role of public education, etc., in Belgium the discussion quickly focused on the issue of political participation.[7] Although all

6 Constant is the most cited author in the constitutional debates, after Montesquieu: Huyttens, 1844a, pp. 202, 247, 398, 413, 415, 452, 454, 465; ibid., 1844b, pp. 442, 464; ibid., 1844c, p. 520. For De Staël: ibid., 1844a, pp. 415, 425.

7 For an overview of the main republican 'phases' and arguments, see Mouritsen (2006).

congressmen agreed that the people could no longer be excluded entirely from governance (e.g. Huyttens, 1844a, p. 294, 23 November 1830, C. Vilain XIIII; Huyttens, 1844a, p. 471, 15 December 1830, De Gerlache), the issue of participation enabled the liberals and Catholics to frame the republicans and their aspirations for a republic as a call for a radical direct democracy, convincing the hesitant congressmen to opt for a monarchy (Bourgaux, 2015, pp. 536–537; Witte, 2020). Yet, the underlying question was also inherently connected to two fundamental claims that had directed the Revolution, i.e. liberty and equality. The liberal journalist and congressman Paul Devaux perspicuously elucidated the issues at stake:

> what [the republicans] wish for above all else, [...], is not that everything should be done for the greatest wellbeing of the people, but that everything should be done by the people. They make the grave error of placing the forms, the means above the purpose. [...] In the outcome liberty and justice were sacrificed, but in the forms equality was perfectly upheld.
>
> (Huyttens, 1844a, p. 212, 20 November 1830, Devaux)

According to Devaux, the republicans understood liberty as self-governance by the people through the active participation of virtuous citizens in public affairs, the latter committing their efforts entirely to the public good. As the citizens were the ones to make political decisions, they were all equally entitled to elect the head of state from among their midst. Consequently, Devaux argued, the republicans favoured a presidential system with a strong executive power, combined with direct democratic forms or at least a representative system based on universal suffrage. For the moderate liberals, however, the republican reliance on a great number of people who were all equally involved in societal self-regulation would ultimately lead to the self-destruction of society, as the latter would be unable to appease the passions and contain individual self-interests.

The Ancients versus the Moderns

While Devaux's intention was surely to depict the republicans as radical democrats, his intervention equally grasps the core of the two conceptions of liberty that were prevalent at the time. Arguably, his reference to ancient republics as well as his allusion to liberty as a means or as an end was inspired by the works of De Staël and Constant.[8] As the cataclysm of unpredictable forces during the French Revolution had rendered the old constitutional structure inadequate for the post-revolutionary era, both De Staël and Constant had reflected on institutions adapted to the modern age (Fontana, 1994, pp. 137–138). In their search for the causes of the French revolutionary lapse of 1793, they had laid bare the anachronistic error which had

8 For Constant's influence on Devaux, see Demoulin (1989, pp. 32–33).

clouded the minds of the revolutionary leaders. Transposing historical institutions and ancient governmental forms into the modern time frame, the French Jacobins, believing that "all the violations of civil liberty would be redressed by the enjoyment of political liberty in its widest sense", had ended up mixing up the objectives to pursue and the means to reach those objectives (Constant, 2003). The attempts of the French revolutionaries to apply the ancient governmental instruments to the modern context had eventually led to the Terror of '93.

For the Coppet Group, it was clear that the French revolutionaries had misconceived the purpose of liberty by confusing the liberty of the Moderns with the liberty of the Ancients. This idea of a confusion between both the kinds of liberty had appeared in De Staël's *Des circonstances actuelles qui peuvent terminer la Révolution et des principes qui doivent fonder la République en France* and was endorsed by Constant when he corrected De Staël's 1798 manuscript. Constant later systematised De Staël's intuition, which appears most clearly in his 1819 speech *De la liberté des anciens comparée à celles des modernes.*[9] According to De Staël and Constant, in ancient republics liberty was conceived as purely political: the political community acquired its autonomy through the participation of the citizen in public affairs. Simultaneously, the sphere of individual freedom was neglected, which made Constant conclude that if the individual was sovereign in public affairs, he remained a slave in his private relations (Constant, 1819, p. 262). In modern societies, on the contrary, liberty was understood as the citizens' private pursuit of individual goals and the enjoyment of individual rights, protected by and against public authority (De Staël, 1906, pp. 94–95). If 'pure democracy' had its merits in Antiquity, the historical, sociological, economical, and geographical changes had made it obsolete for the Moderns. The ancient institutions of small belligerent city-states, which relied on slaves for much of their economic welfare, were not adapted to large, commercial nations, where the majority of the citizens had to provide for their own needs, leaving them with little or no time to attend to matters of state. Consequently, the preoccupation of the citizens had shifted from political participation and individual self-realisation (the means to a good government) to individual happiness (the result of good government) (De Staël, 1906, pp. 91, 162).

But the French radicals had also erred on the means to establish liberty, by advocating unlimited sovereignty and social levelling. Constant and De Staël disapproved of these inflated abstract theories on inconsiderate self-sacrifice for the public good and egalitarianism, since those theories were too radical, inappropriate to human nature, and practically too difficult to accomplish. On top of that, due to the absolute character of sovereignty, political power became limitless. This legitimated all the decisions taken in the name of the sovereign, as nothing could interfere with the right of the sovereign people to exercise their sovereignty. As a result, unlimited political power became subject to potential usurpation by

9 Note that there are discrepancies between De Staël and Constant (Kalyvas and Katznelson, 2008, pp. 127–128; Ozouf, 1988, p. 773).

individuals who could claim to represent the sovereign and unrestrictedly coerce the members of the community into the so-called 'general will of the community' (Constant, 2003, pp. 13, 17–21, 54, 384. See also Gauchet, 1989, pp. 162–164). Although De Staël and Constant, together with Rousseau, believed that the universality of citizens was the subject of sovereignty, they claimed that the legitimacy of authority should depend on its object (the respect for individual rights) as much as on its subject (the political community). Hence, sovereign power had to be restricted by the respect for individual rights (Constant, 2003, p. 31). For the Coppet Group, this could only be achieved by accepting a property-based political system with limited governmental power, underpinned by political equality.

Political equality and property as the basis of the political system

Political equality meant that the individual rights of citizens were all equally protected by the law. Likewise, it implied that individuals were naturally unequal; as their individual skills and human nature differed, equality could only be legally established. In this respect, hereditary privileges were to be abolished as they reflected a static and rigid conception of status which conflicted with the natural inequality of men.[10] For De Staël and Constant, natural inequality and political equality in society would provide a competitive setting, where only the most capable men would distinguish themselves by acquiring property (De Staël, 1906, pp. 169–170). Since property corresponded with the natural and human differences in character, talents, and industry, both considered property as a key issue. Differences in fortunes might bear defects, but as the French Revolution had shown, these defects could not be adjusted by artificial social levelling. Property fitted perfectly well with the idea of natural inequality and was useful as it established and preserved stable and uniform ties between individuals. It also allowed for the integration of self-interests in the political system, leaving behind abstract theories of virtue and self-sacrifice. It equally allowed for a dynamic and flexible 'open aristocracy', granting political access to the most talented individuals, assuring a 'government of the bests', providing liberty and happiness to the greatest number, and enabling the improvement of the political system through education (De Staël, 1906, pp. 10–11, 46; Constant, 2003, Book X, pp. 163–202. See also Fontana, 1994, pp. 123–124).

This conception of political equality and property was particularly interesting for the Belgian middle class, which was prominently represented in the National Congress. The congressmen repeatedly stressed the importance of individual liberty, conceived as the possibility to act at will and without any constraint in everything that is individual. This individual liberty was the "first need of men"; a

10 De Staël spoke of hereditary aristocracy versus natural aristocracy (De Staël, 1906, pp. 169–170).

need that had "taken root in society" and could not be undone anymore as it was "necessary for man to act freely in his personal sphere" since he was "sovereign in the limits of his attributions" (Huyttens, 1844a, p. 212, 20 November 1830, De Haerne; Huyttens, 1844a, p. 608, 23 December 1830, C. de Brouckère; Huyttens, 1844a, p. 583, 21 December 1830, Defacqz; Huyttens, 1844a, p. 613, 23 December 1830, Verbeke). The choice to enshrine individual rights in a separate title in the Constitution '*Des Belges et de leurs droits*' equally points to this conviction. Yet, these views on liberty did not entail socio-economic equality, nor did they imply the unrestricted participation of citizens in public affairs. If the congressmen dismissed the exclusive access to public affairs on the basis of hereditary privileges (Huyttens, 1844a, p. 407, 13 December 1830, Blargnies), they also warned of inflated abstract political theories and concepts, such as 'equality' and 'unbridled freedom', which had turned the lower classes into an uncontrollable force, steam-rolling the societal order under the false pretence that, through freedom, they had acquired the right to absolute equality (Huyttens, 1844a, p. 200, 19 November 1830, Jacques; Huyttens, 1844a, p. 219, 20 November 1830, De Roo; Huyttens, 1844a, p. 496, 16 December 1830, Goethals). Especially the debates on bicameralism, which at times reveal remarkable resemblances with De Staël and Constant's terminology, provide key insights into the majority view.[11] Abbé De Smet remarked that political equality, which provided stability, should not be confused with absolute equality, since it could lead to democracy as well as to despotism (Huyttens, 1844a, p. 410, 13 December 1830, Abbé De Smet). Helias d'Huddegem assessed that "there does not exist on earth such a thing as absolute equality. There only exists a relative and proportionate equality. [...] As men are equal in liberty, [...] in society, men are unequal in power" (Huyttens, 1844a, p. 444, 14 December 1830, Helias d'Huddegem). Others argued that political equality did not exclude inequalities of fortune, which were inevitable in society and should be considered a "natural form of aristocracy", or an "aristocracy of talents" (Huyttens, 1844a, p. 462, 14 December 1830, Abbé De Haerne; Huyttens, 1844a, pp. 459–460, 14 December 1830, Masbourg). In the same vein, Nothomb endorsed a conditional equality,

> in the sense that the conditions to which the law submits the exercise of political rights are such that everyone would be able to fulfil them, either through the natural course of events, or through the free use of their talents.
> (Huyttens, 1844a, p. 425, 14 December 1830, Nothomb)

For Nothomb, this was exactly the opposite of admitting heredity and personal privileges, which hampered political equality. The previous day, Blargnies had

11 Note that De Staël's *Des circonstances* was published for the first time in 1906. It is nevertheless very likely that the congressmen were acquainted with De Staël's insights, indirectly via Constant's works or more directly through the counterfeit versions of her works.

already claimed that, for this reason, political rights should only be attributed on account of merits and property (Huyttens, 1844a, p. 407, 13 December 1830, Blargnies). Many congressmen considered the existence and the protection of property and the resulting socio-economic differences to be essential conditions for the preservation of stability within society. According to Helias d'Huddegem, men were reunited in society to protect not only their person but also their property. Without property, society could not be sustained. And as property could only be conserved by power, the propertied class should have a right to this power. The propertyless, on the other hand, should be stimulated to follow the natural way of acquiring property in order to access public affairs, instead of usurping it: "the disorder starts when some want to enjoy the rights of others, since they can only enjoy them by usurping them" (Huyttens, 1844a, p. 444, 14 December 1830, Helias d'Huddegem. Compare with Constant, 2003, p. 170).

At the same time, property was considered to be an adequate tool for assessing the capability to participate in power which, in the eyes of the congressmen, was crucial for good governance (see in this sense Huyttens, 1844a, p. 407, 13 December 1830, Blargnies; Huyttens, 1844a, p. 457, 4 February 1831, C. de Brouckère, 4 February 1831, vol. 2, p. 457). The importance of social promotion for the talented citizen was probably most apparent when Lebeau intervened several times during the session of 29 December in favour of capacity representation. "Capacity", as Lebeau saw it, "is the best of possible guarantees". The representatives' capacities would show themselves through their property, as well as during the public discussions of the legislative assemblies. As such, "the representative government is the government of capacities". Lebeau refused to see the representative mandate as a right or a reward, but as the allocation of a function to the most talented men of experience. In this regard, Lebeau believed that political mandates could best be accumulated. The most enlightened men would be found among the members of the legislative chambers. Consequently, the members of the executive power and the administrative councils should be appointed from among the members of the chambers (Huyttens, 1844a, pp. 699–701, 29 December 1830, Lebeau; Huyttens, 1844b, p. 237, 22 January 1831, Lebeau). Others criticised the call for an extensive democratic suffrage on the same grounds. The community members were not entitled to the full trusteeship of society, but to political participation according to their stakes in society (Huyttens, 1844b, p. 532, 16 February 1831, Van Meenen). The Congress eventually endorsed political equality by inserting it formally in article 6 of the Belgian Constitution.[12]

12 "No class distinctions exist in the State. Belgians are equal before the law; they alone are eligible for civil and military service, but for the exceptions that can be created by a law for particular cases". If the competence of the king to attribute nobility titles was maintained in (former) article 75 of the Constitution, it was only as an expression of gratitude to talented and committed citizens for their services rendered to the nation.

Representation

Their distrust of direct democracy as well as their endorsement of political equality had led De Staël and Constant to favour representative government. Both argued that a representative system based on popular elections was perfectly tailored to the modern understanding of liberty, since it was adapted to large nations, allowing for the 'masses' to delegate the protection of their interests to adequate representatives while looking after their own needs (De Staël, 1906, pp. 13, 92; Constant, 1819, p. 281). In line with Sieyès' sociological reasoning, they explained representation as the political application of daily individual operations, where people seek proxies to act in their interest in order to obtain certain results.[13] Simultaneously, public spirit, without which liberty could not last, would be formed through the elective system (Constant, 2003, p. 332).

The best part of the Belgian Congress equally favoured the representative system. Pierre Destriveaux explained his preference for a representative government in terms that were reminiscent of Constant's distinction between Ancients and Moderns:

> For too long have we been accustomed to considering the ancient republics as the true sanctuaries of freedom. [...] abandoning the abstractions of the *pure* forms of government, we know that the forms can be merged, blended, and modified for the benefit of our needs. First of all, the collection of interests and rights, *the public affair*, should be guaranteed in its entirety, as well as in its detail; the political administration should be in function of the community, not the specialty; the state should be *everyone* and never *one* or *several individuals*. This system of community interest does not entail the participation of everyone in the action; it is not in our modern states, in an agricultural and industrial country like ours, that we can conceive the idea to transport all classes of society in one *forum* where they exercise directly the rights of which sovereignty is composed; consequently, there must be particular delegations and institutions to which the masses remain alien.
>
> (Huyttens, 1844a, p. 198, 19 November 1830, emphasis from Destriveaux)[14]

13 The theories of Smith and the Scottish School underpinned Sieyès' arguments against the privileged orders. In his *Essai sur les privilèges* (published in November 1788), Sieyès opposed against the privileges as incompatible with the relations of free trade, making from representation, through the division of labour, the principle which gave to civil society its autonomous existence (Sieyès, 1982, pp. 16–17. Compare with Sieyès' speech of 2 Thermidor Year III, in S.A., 1862, p. 292). For Sieyès' influence on Constant's idea of representation and division of labour, see Pasquino (1998, pp. 31–52).

14 For Van Meenen's endorsement of the representative system as a promise for individual liberty and property, see Van Meenen, '*Droit Public*' in *L'Observateur belge* (D'Elhoungne et al., 1815, pp. 1–7). Observe how he appreciates the impermanence of the ancient institutions and does not rebut them completely.

The republicans also admitted the principle of representation, rejecting an "ultra-liberal" democratic state system (Huyttens, 1844a, pp. 403–404, 13 December 1830, Van Snick. See also Huyttens, 1844a, p. 257, 22 November 1830, Pirson; Huyttens, 1844a, p. 439, 14 December 1830, Fleussu).[15] De Robaulx, Lardinois, and Goffint refuted the idea that the republicans had ever promoted the direct participation of the people in public affairs (Huyttens, 1844a, p. 228, 20 November 1830, De Robaulx; Huyttens, 1844a, p. 197, 22 November 1830, Lardinois; Huyttens, 1844a, pp. 249–250, 22 November 1830, Goffint). For Pirson, contemporary republics and monarchies had nothing to do with those in ancient times (Huyttens, 1844a, p. 257, 22 November 1830, Pirson). And although the committed republican Seron endorsed an extensive form of political liberty, he explicitly abandoned the Greek models of direct democracy, accepting the representative system instead:

> What we ask for is a representative government in accordance with the nature of things, which, establishing happiness for men and protecting the good against the bad, is one where the law is above the will of men, where the will of men is never substituted to the will of the law; [...] Our reasoning has improved since we've read and meditated on Adam Smith and the writers who have walked on the tracks of this renowned economist. I sincerely believe that the more a people is industrious, commercial and rich, the more it is made for liberty, since the more it is well-off, the more it has the means to instruct itself, and the more it is instructed, the more it will love public affairs, or, this is the same, liberty.
>
> (Huyttens, 1844a, pp. 196–197, 19 November 1830, Seron. See also Huyttens, 1844a, pp. 250–253, 22 November 1830, Seron)

Seron's reference to Adam Smith is significant, as it once more reveals the nineteenth-century understanding of representation as the adequate reflection of the social by the political, of which the principal themes were the nature of production and wealth, and the effects of the division of labour.[16]

15 Observe that the republicans repeatedly attempted to subject the Constitution to popular approval by referendum (esp. Huyttens, 1844a, pp. 225–229, session of 20 November 1830). De Robaulx, however, equally motivated his proposal with the statement that republicans were no advocates of direct democracy (Huyttens, 1844a, p. 228, 20 November 1830, De Robaulx).

16 The reflection of the social by the political is equally present in Nothomb's discourse on bicameralism in which he argued that the economic and political interests of labourers and capitalists should be adequately represented in two separate legislative chambers (Huyttens, 1844a, p. 425, 14 December 1830, Nothomb).

Census and mixed government

The endorsement of political equality and property as the basis for the representative system eventually resulted in the acceptance of article 47 of the Constitution, which required that a census restriction on suffrage be determined by electoral law. The article stipulated a high census, between 20 and 100 florins. After a fierce discussion on the electoral law in February 1831, proposals in favour of a lower, 'more democratic' census were rejected (Huyttens, 1844b, pp. 506–508, session of 12 February 1831). With remarkable resemblance to De Staël's insights, Devaux defended the choice of a censitary electoral system:

> Our principle is freedom before everything, and if a certain heredity, a certain aristocracy, a certain electoral census is necessary to the preservation of this freedom, we will go as far as to admit it. The results are everything for us; the forms, the means are almost everything for [the republicans]; we submit the means to the end, they do the opposite. Although in the forms it would be more favourable to equality, we challenge universal suffrage, since it is fatal to liberty in the results.
>
> (Huyttens, 1844a, pp. 212–213, 20 November 1830, Devaux. See also Huyttens, 1844a, p. 658, 26 December 1830, Devaux)

In their search for additional safeguards for the representative system, De Staël and Constant had turned to the idea of mixed government. Democracy in itself was not creative, nor self-sufficient. In its purest form, it was a self-destructive force driven exclusively by the arbitrary and unrestrained passions of the people. It could only end up destroying itself through its own principles (De Staël, 1906, p. 121). Consequently, De Staël argued that democracy could only be salvaged by refuting it partially: "in order to come close to the results of its model, pure democracy, it should move away from it through its forms" (De Staël, 1906, p. 23).

Paradoxically, if one wished to establish solid representative institutions that would guarantee liberty in the long term, aristocratic elements had to be added.[17] As democrats had the ability to break ground and establish social progress, so did the aristocrats know how to conserve these achievements and mitigate the democratic passions. In other words, a modern democratic system could only be realised with the help of non-democratic means (De Staël, 1906, pp. 121, 163. See also Kalyvas and Katznelson, 2008, pp. 126–128). Had the former French democratic representative system, operating through a unicameral legislative assembly, not shown that it was not sufficiently stable to secure liberty in the long term? Hence, De Staël and Constant both endorsed an English-style constitutional monarchy with a representative system consisting of a census-based elected assembly and

17 Note that this does not imply the acceptance of a static aristocratic order.

an aristocratic assembly. The English system successfully blended liberty and stability, while its pragmatism realised a good balance between all social classes and their interests (Craiutu, 2003, pp. 192–193). Yet, in a Montesquieu-esque fashion, both theorists claimed that, since a representative government did not imply a generic state model, it could be established in a variety of possible institutional arrangements and moulded to the specific circumstances and particularities of a country (Fontana, 2016, pp. 167–168).[18]

Likewise, the Belgian congressmen believed that governmental forms could be merged and adapted to time and to specific communities, as long as they provided liberty in their result (Huyttens, 1844a, pp. 212–213, 20 November 1830, Devaux; Huyttens, 1844a, p. 198, 19 November 1830, Destriveaux, vol. 1, p. 198; Huyttens, 1844a, p. 236, 22 November 1830, Blargnies). Consequently, they searched for a suitable combination of political models. History had shown that absolute monarchy sacrificed everything for governmental stability. A republic, on the contrary, stood exclusively for social movement. None of them had resulted in liberty and happiness for the people. Following Coppet's intuition, liberals and Catholics alike contended that a combination of both in the form of an English-fashioned parliamentary constitutional monarchy would form the most natural middle way (Huyttens, 1844a, p. 192, 19 November 1830, Nothomb; Huyttens, 1844a, p. 200, 19 November 1830, C. Vilain XIIII; Huyttens, 1844a, p. 286, 23 November 1830, De Robiano; Huyttens, 1844a, p. 416, 13 December 1830, Lebeau; Huyttens, 1844a, pp. 459–460, 14 December 1830, Masbourg; Huyttens, 1844a, p. 425, 14 December 1830, Nothomb; Huyttens, 1844a, pp. 471–472, 15 December 1830, De Gerlache; Huyttens, 1844a, p. 507, 16 December 1830, Van Meenen; Huyttens, 1844a, p. 545, 18 December 1830, Lebeau). Nothomb spoke in this sense of a 'republican monarchy', stating that, contrary to the Ancients, who had failed to combine republic and monarchy, this governmental form would be more successful. He argued that when a revolution had achieved its objectives, it needed closure. And where a (democratic) republic enabled a revolution, an (aristocratic) monarchy was needed to end it. On a later occasion, he explicitly referred to De Staël and Necker in his plea for an English-style bicameral form (Huyttens, 1844a, p. 193, 19 November 1830, Nothomb). The majority of the Catholics deviated in the same way from Lamennais' support for a republic, advocating a constitutional monarchy "as republican as possible" (Deseure, 2019; Witte, 2020). Both the liberals and Catholics accepted that in order to come closest to the results of democracy, the Belgian governmental system should move away from it through its forms. Devaux crystallised the essence of this point of view very well in his plea for an aristocratic high chamber:

> if one would create a single assembly, it will either be dragged along by a democracy, unimpeded by the limits which the constitution has assigned it

18 See in this regard also Constant's view on the role of aristocracy: Constant (2003, p. note I to Book X, Ch. IV, 465).

to, or it will eventually become aristocratic. If one wants a democratic chamber without inconveniences, vote for the senate.

(Huyttens, 1844a, p. 468, 14 December 1830, Devaux)[19]

This dynamic vision of mixed government combined a democratic tendency or 'fluctuating power' in a lower legislative chamber with an aristocratic tendency or 'persisting power' in a high chamber.[20] The representative institutions were supplemented with an executive power, consisting of a hereditary monarch who acted as '*pouvoir neutre*' and who was supported by responsible ministers who were drawn from the elected parliament. Only this type of government would withstand the test of time as it encompassed societal changes and was adaptable to the emergence of political regimes as well (Raxhon, 1996, pp. 74–75).

Combining individual and political liberty

As various scholars have pointed out, French liberalism has often erroneously been understood as the fundamentally undemocratic counterpart of republicanism (Garsten, 2009, p. 92; Holmes, 1984, pp. 84–87; Jaume, 2003, p. 392, fn. 23). Liberalism and republicanism were actually not part of a binary system of oppositions. French liberalism emerged out of the classical republican language at a moment when, confronted with the crisis of monarchy, republicanism had been incapable of reconciling order and freedom under a stable political structure (Spitz, 2009, p. 25; Vincent, 2015, p. 21, fn. 11). In this sense, it is revealing that Constant did not consider the distinction between ancient and modern freedom as an antagonism. If political freedom remained subsidiary to quasi-unconditional individual liberty, it formed an essential guarantee for the preservation of the latter (Constant, 1819, pp. 278–279). If De Staël believed the political community to be a citizenry of proprietors, her reflections described merely the means through which representative government could function in times of crisis. The 'true depository of power' was not the political elite to which power had been delegated, but civil society at large. If governmental power was to endure in times of crisis, the majority of citizens had to be connected with government and its institutions through the political process (Fontana, 1994, pp. 129–130). Constant, for his part, warned that the seclusion of individuals into their private confines for the enjoyment of their individual rights would leave the public authority with too much power to wield. Vesting all powers in public

19 Devaux considered a second legislative chamber, tailored to the position of the aristocratic elite, to be indispensable to the system's stability as the aristocracy would not be able to "secretly plot for the ruin of liberty" (Huyttens, 1844a, pp. 509–510, 16 December 1830, Devaux).

20 Lebeau additionally argued that a differentiated, higher census for the senate would truly reflect the contrasting roles of the chambers (Huyttens, 1844a, p. 545, 18 December 1830, Lebeau; Huyttens, 1844a, p. 530, 17 December 1830, Lebeau).

authority without any checks to it would eventually lead to the oppression of individuals, even if this authority was primarily exercised by a representative body. An assembly with unrestricted power and extensive prerogatives would be more dangerous than the most absolute despot. In a system of representative government, it was essential for the represented to actively and continuously control and monitor public authority (Constant, 1819, pp. 282–283; 2003, pp. 228, 332. See also Jaume, 2000, p. 156). Moreover, Constant argued that individuals should continuously "judge governmental action" by "examining the source and the content of law" (Constant, 2003, p. 399). Not only was this essential for their own development and progress, but it also formed a strong guarantee for the proper functioning of public authority. Hence, Coppet liberalism searched for a combination of the freedoms of the Ancients and the Moderns, stressing the importance of the participation of the individual citizen in public life and the individual's appreciation and critique of public action (Constant, 1819, p. 285. See also Jainchill, 2012). More specifically, they understood public civic institutions which promoted the formation of a broad public opinion (the press, education, magistrates, juries, municipal powers, elections, etc.) as a reinforcement of the representative system, since they realised the moral education of citizens, while unburdening them from some responsibilities (De Staël, 2008, p. 668; 1906, pp. 93–94; Constant, 1819, p. 285. See also Lacchè, 2000, p. 146).

If in Belgium the congressmen refused to affirm an entirely elitist conception of liberty and political power, much like De Staël and Constant, they believed that political liberty should not be neglected either. With a remarkable resemblance to Constant's argument in favour of political liberty, Van Meenen pointed out during the discussion on the Treaty of the XVIII articles that giving up political liberty and entrusting the protection of civil rights and liberties entirely to public authority would ruin individual liberty (Huyttens, 1844c, p. 556, 9 July 1831, Van Meenen).[21] Hence the importance of the educational system and the need for (extra) constitutional checks like the press, a jury for press and political offences, etc. These institutions would shape a strong public opinion which would react against abuses of any constitutional power (Huyttens, 1844a, p. 656, 26 December 1830, De Foere; Huyttens, 1844b, p. 232, fn. (1), 22 January 1831, De Robaulx; Huyttens, 1844c, p. 651, 3 March 1831, Seron). They would also form an adequate substitute for the oppositional role of the legislative power against the other powers, should the former fail to fulfil its task. Hence, as the congressmen were fully aware that these extra-constitutional checks were the first targets of an oppressive public authority, they embedded as many institutional safeguards as possible (Huyttens, 1844a, p. 429, 14 December 1830,

21 See also his article '*Droit Public.* Article 6. Constitution. (Suite 3.)' in *L'Observateur belge* (D'Elhoungne et al., 1815, pp. 29–40, esp. p. 40): "If political liberty is one of the main guarantees of civil and individual liberty, the latter only exist where there is [political liberty]. [Individual liberty] does not give life to [political liberty]: she receives it from here and perishes with her".

Van Meenen). Since the citizens were not allowed to exercise legislative power directly, they were forced to delegate it. Hence, the necessity of inherent institutional safeties against power concentration by the legislative assembly (Huyttens, 1844a, pp. 408–409, 13 December 1830, Blargnies. See also Huyttens, 1844a, p. 629, 24 December 1830, De Gerlache). To this end, the installation of a bicameral system was crucial.

Conclusion

While strategic considerations and pragmatism certainly motivated the National Congress to opt for a representative system under a constitutional monarchy, this chapter establishes that this choice was not purely instrumental. It equally resulted from a specific understanding of the notion of "liberty", which obviously implied certain beliefs. These beliefs, as well as the congressional choices that stemmed from them, were greatly inspired by the Coppet liberalism of Germaine de Staël and Benjamin Constant. They were the first to distinguish two forms of liberty, entailing two different governmental models. Liberty in its purest form, comprehending direct participation and social equality, was something that naive idealists could only dream of establishing. And this dream was hardly an innocent one, as the Terror had only too well shown them. Political and social reality required a sacrifice in order to achieve and then safeguard the happiness and individual liberty of citizens, which they understood as the core objective of modern society. Giving up the most radical of democratic ideas, while accepting aristocratic forms and maintaining private property as the fundamental connection between the individual and the state, would ensure that this objective would be achieved. Thus, only by disengaging from the means, could the end be secured. This was a position which the majority in the Belgian Congress endorsed.

At the same time, however, Coppet liberalism preserved some important classical republican features that would come to underpin its views on the governmental form. These features followed from the endorsement of political liberty as the safeguard of individual liberty. This demanded a considerable commitment of citizens to public life (in the broad sense of the word), not only to prevent power concentrations within government but also to enable citizens to fully develop their autonomy and their ability for independent reasoning. Like De Staël and Constant, the majority of the Congress understood very well that this could only be achieved by establishing civic institutions which allowed for civic participation and the development of public opinion. By implementing the pivotal thought of the Coppet Group in their constitutional choices, the Belgian liberals effectively inaugurated the passage from a statist tradition of absolutism and enlightened despotism to a politics centred on the autonomy of civil society and the individuals it included. This constituted the core of Belgian constitutional liberalism and would turn the Belgian constitutional edifice into an example of liberalism in Europe.

Bibliography

Bourgaux, A.-E. (2015) 'La consultation populaire régionale: résistance ou résilience de la démocratie représentative belge?', *Administration Publique*, 38(4), pp. 531–583.

Charvet, J. (2005) 'Liberalism', in Horowitz, M.C. (ed.) *New Dictionary of the History of Ideas*. Farmington Hills: Scribner, pp. 1262–1269.

Constant, B. (1819) 'De la liberté des anciens comparée à celle des modernes. Discours prononcé à l'Athénée royal de Paris, 14 avril 1819', in Louandre, C. (ed.) *Œuvres Politiques de Benjamin Constant avec introduction, notes et index*. Paris: Charpentier, pp. 258–286.

Constant, B. (2003) *Principles of Politics Applicable to All Governments*. Indianapolis: Liberty Fund.

Craiutu, A. (2003) *Liberalism under Siege. The Political Thought of the French Doctrinaires*. Lanham: Lexington Books. DOI: 10.1086/ahr/109.4.1320.

Dagnino, R. (2018) 'Making the Constitution more Catholic? Catholic Adaptation Strategies to the Belgian Constitutional Liberties of 1831', *Giornale di Storia Costituzionale*, 35(1), pp. 69–87.

De Dijn, A. (2012) 'A Pragmatic Conservatism. Montesquieu and the Framing of the Belgian Constitution (1830–1831)', *History of European Ideas*, 28(4), pp. 227–245.

De Smaele, H. (2005) 'Eclectisch en toch nieuw. De uitvinding van het Belgisch parlement in 1830–1831', *Bijdragen en Mededelingen betreffende de Geschiedenis der Nederlanden*, 120(3), pp. 408–416. DOI: 10.18352/bmgn-lchr.6253.

De Staël, G. (1906) *Des circonstances actuelles qui peuvent terminer la Révolution et des principes qui doivent fonder la République en France*. Paris: Fischbascher.

De Staël, G. (2008) *Considerations on the Principal Events of the French Revolution*. Indianapolis: Liberty Fund.

Delbecke, B. (2010) *De lange schaduw van de grondwetgever. Perswetgeving en persmisdrijven in België, 1831–1914*. Doctoral thesis in Law. Leuven: KU Leuven.

Delbecke, B. (2014) 'Modern Constitutionalism and Legal Transfer: The Political Offence in the French Charte Constitutionelle (1830) and the Belgian Constitution (1831)', in Duve, T. (ed.) *Modern Constitutionalism and Legal Transfer: The Political Offence in the French Charte Constitutionelle (1830) and the Belgian Constitution (1831)*. Frankfurt am Main: Max Planck Institute for European Legal History, pp. 427–459. DOI: 10.12946/gplh1.

D'Elhoungne, Doncker, and Van Meenen (1815) *L'Observateur politique, administratif, historique et littéraire de la Belgique par une société de jurisconsultes et d'hommes de lettres*. Brussels: De Mat.

Demoulin, R. (1989) 'De liberale stroming tijdens het Koninkrijk der Nederlanden (1815–1830) en de Omwenteling van 1830', in Verhulst, A. and Hasquin, H. (eds.) *Het liberalisme in België. Tweehonderd jaar geschiedenis*. Brussels: Delta, pp. 29–38.

Deseure, B. (2019) 'Republican Monarchy in the 1830 Revolutions: From Lafayette to the Belgian Constitution', *History of European Ideas*, 45(7), pp. 1–19. DOI: 10.1080/01916599.2019.1628085.

Fontana, B. (1994) 'The Thermidorian Republic and its Principles', in Fontana, B. (ed.) *The Invention of the Modern Republic*. Cambridge: Cambridge University Press, pp. 118–138. DOI: 10.1017/cbo9780511558443.007.

Fontana, B. (2016) *Germaine de Stael: A Political Portrait*. Princeton: Princeton University Press.

Garsten, B. (2009) 'Representative Government and Popular Sovereignty', in Shapiro, I., Stokes, S.C., Wood, E.J. and Kirschner, A.S. (eds.) *Political Representation*. Cambridge: Cambridge University Press, pp. 90–110. DOI: 10.1017/cbo978051181314.

Garsten, B. (2015) 'The "Spirit of Independence" in Benjamin Constant's Thoughts on a Free Press', in Kemp, G. (ed.) *Censorship Moments: Reading Texts in the History of Censorship and Freedom of Expression*. London: Bloomsbury Academic, pp. 117–124. DOI: 10.5040/9781472593078.

Gauchet, M. (1989) 'Constant, Staël et la Révolution française', in Furet, F. and Ozouf, M. (eds.) *The French Revolution and the Creation of Modern Political Culture*. Oxford: Pergamon Press, pp. 159–172.

Gilissen, J. (1968) 'La Constitution belge de 1831: ses sources, son influence', *Res Publica*, 10, pp. 107–141.

Hoffman, E. (2009) 'The Theory of the Perfectibility of the Human Race' in Rosenblatt, H. (ed.) *The Cambridge Companion to Constant*. Cambridge: Cambridge University Press, pp. 248–271. DOI: 10.1017/CCOL9780521856461.012.

Holmes, S. (1984) *Benjamin Constant and the Making of Modern Liberalism*. New Haven: Yale University Press.

Huyttens, E. (1844a) *Discussions du Congrès National de Belgique 1830–1831. Tome premier*. Brussels: Société Typographique Belge.

Huyttens, E. (1844b) *Discussions du Congrès National de Belgique 1830–1831. Tome deuxième*. Brussels: Société Typographique Belge.

Huyttens, E. (1844c) *Discussions du Congrès National de Belgique 1830–1831. Tome troisième*. Brussels: Société Typographique Belge.

Illing, P. (2012) 'Montesquieu's Shadow: Debating Reform in the Austrian Netherlands', *History of European Ideas*, 35(3), pp. 330–336. DOI: 10.1016/j.histeuroideas.2008.06.004.

Jainchill, A. (2012) 'The Importance of Republican Liberty in French Liberalism', in Geenens, R. and Rosenblatt, H. (eds.) *French Liberalism. From Montesquieu to the Present Day*. Cambridge: Cambridge University Press, pp. 73–89. DOI: 10.1017/cbo9781139084178.

Jaume, L. (1997) *L'individu effacé, ou, Le paradoxe du libéralisme français*. Paris: Fayard.

Jaume, L. (2000) 'Problèmes du libéralisme. De Mme de Staël à Tocqueville', *Droits* (30), pp. 151–162.

Jaume, L. (2003) 'Le libéralisme français après la Révolution, comparé au libéralisme anglais', *Historia Constitucional*, 4, pp. 383–393.

Jaume, L. (2012) 'The Unity, Diversity and Paradoxes of French Liberalism', in Geenens, R. and Rosenblatt, H. (eds.) *French Liberalism. From Montesquieu to the Present Day*. Cambridge: Cambridge University Press, pp. 36–54. DOI: 10.1017/cbo9781139084178.

Jürgensen, K. (1963) *Lamennais und die Gestaltung des Belgischen Staates. Der liberale Katholizismus in der Verfassungsbewegung des 19. Jahrhunderts*. Wiesbaden: Steiner.

Kalyvas, A. and Katznelson, I. (2008) *Liberal Beginnings: Making a Republic for the Moderns*. Cambridge: Cambridge University Press. DOI: 10.1017/cbo9780511790782.

Krause, S.R. (2015) 'Freedom, Sovereignty, and the General Will in Montesquieu', in Farr, J. and Williams, D.L. (eds.) *The General Will. The Evolution of a Concept.* Cambridge: Cambridge University Press, pp. 147–172. DOI: 10.1017/cbo9781107297982.

Lacchè, L. (2000) 'Coppet et la percée de l'état libéral constitutionnel', in Jaume, L. (ed.) *Coppet, creuset de l'esprit libéral. Les idées politiques et constitutionnelles du groupe de madame de Staël.* Paris: Economica, pp. 135–155.

Lemmens, W. (2011) 'Het onluikend liberalisme: Franse migranten, hun netwerken en journalistieke activiteiten in de Zuidelijke Nederlanden (1815–1820)', *Belgisch Tijdschrift voor Filologie en Geschiedenis*, 89(3–4), pp. 1165–1191. DOI: 10.3406/rbph.2011.8352.

Maes, C. (2018) 'The End Justifies the Means. The Nature of Belgium's 1830 Political Liberalism', *Giornale di Storia Constituzionale*, 35(1), pp. 129–145.

Magits, M. (1977) *De Volksraad en de opstelling van de Belgische Grondwet van 7 februari 1831. Een bijdrage tot de wordingsgeschiedenis van de Belgische Konstitutie.* Unpublished Doctoral thesis, History. Brussels: V.U. Brussel.

Marteel, S. (2018) *The Intellectual Origins of the Belgian Revolution. Political Thought and Disunity in the Kingdom of the Netherlands, 1815–1830.* New York: Springer. DOI: 10.1007/978-3-319-89426-3.

Mouritsen, P. (2006) 'Four Models of Republican Liberty and Self-Government', in Honohan, I. and Jennings, J. (eds.) *Republicanism in Theory and Practice.* London: Routledge, pp. 18–38. DOI: 10.4324/9780203003343.

Ozouf, M. (1988) 'Liberté', in Furet, F. and Ozouf, M. (eds.) *Dictionnaire Critique de la Révolution Française.* Paris: Flammarion, pp. 763–775.

Pasquino, P. (1998) *Sieyès et l'invention de la constitution en France.* Paris: O. Jacob.

Raxhon, P. (1996) 'Mémoire de la Révolution française de 1789 et Congres national belge (1830–31)', *Belgisch Tijdschrift voor Nieuwste Geschiedenis*, 1–2, pp. 33–83.

Rosanvallon, P. (1989) 'Les Doctrinaires et la question du gouvernement représentatif', in Furet, F. and Ozouf, M. (eds.) *The French Revolution and the Creation of Modern Political Culture.* Oxford: Pergamon Press, pp. 411–431.

Royer, A. (1835) 'Les hommes politiques de la Belgique', in Société de la Revue des Deux Mondes (ed.) *Revue des Deux Mondes.* Paris: Fournier, pp. 672–714.

S.A. (1862) *Réimpression de l'ancien Moniteur. Seule histoire authentique et inaltérée de la Révolution Française depuis la réunion des Etats-Généraux jusqu'aux Consulat (Mai 1789 – Novembre 1799) avec notes explicatives.* Paris: Plon Frères.

Selinger, W. (2019) *Parliamentarism. From Burke to Weber.* Cambridge: Cambridge University Press. DOI: 10.1017/9781108585330.

Sieyès, E. (1982) 'Essai sur les privileges', in E. Sieyès (ed.) *Qu'est-ce que le Tiers État.* Paris: PUF.

Spitz, J.-F. (2009) 'Républicanisme et libéralisme dans le moment révolutionnaire', *Annales historiques de la Révolution française*, 385, pp. 21–47. DOI: 10.4000/ahrf.11518.

Van Den Steene, W. (1963) *De Belgische Grondwetscommissie (oktober-november 1830). Tekst van haar notulen en ontstaan van de Belgische Grondwet.* Brussels: Koninklijke Vlaamse academie voor wetenschappen, letteren en schone kunsten van België.

Viaene, V. (2001) *Belgium and the Holy See from Gregory XVI to Pius IX (1831–1859). Catholic Revival, Society and Politics in 19th-Century Europe.* Leuven: Leuven University Press.

Vincent, K.S. (2015) 'Benjamin Constant and Constitutionalism', *Revista de Historia Constitucional*, 16, pp. 19–46. DOI: 10.17811/hc.v0i16.434.

Witte, E. (2005) 'De constructie van België 1828–1847', in Witte, E., Nandrin, J.-P., Gubin, E., and Deneckere, G. (eds.) *Nieuwe geschiedenis van België*. Tielt: Lannoo, pp. 227–235.

Witte, E. (2006) 'Het natiebegrip in het zuidelijke krantendiscours aan de vooravond van de Belgische opstand (augustus 1829-juli 1830)', *Bijdragen en Mededelingen betreffende de Geschiedenis der Nederlanden*, 121(2), pp. 222–239. DOI:10.18352/bmgn-lchr.6395.

Witte, E. (2016) 'De grondwet van het verenigd koninkrijk der Nederlanden (1815) en het ontstaan van de Belgische constitutie (1831)', in Alen, A. et al. (eds.) *De Grondwet van het Verenigd Koninkrijk der Nederlanden van 1815. Staatkundige en historische beschouwingen uit België en Nederland*. The Hague: Boom and Bruges: Die Keure, pp. 15–44.

Witte, E. (2020) *Belgische republikeinen. Radicalen tussen twee revoluties (1830–1850)*. Antwerp: Polis.

Publications without a specific, personal author (such as newspapers and official documents) are listed under S.A.

7 Constituent power in the Belgian National Congress and the 1831 Belgian Constitution

Christophe Maes and Bas Leijssenaar

Introduction

The aim of this part of the book is to get a better grip on the notion of sovereignty in the Belgian Constitution of 1831. In order to refine our understanding of the notion of Belgian sovereignty, an analysis of the framers' conception(s) of constituent power anno 1830–1831 is indispensable. On the one hand, political sovereignty is difficult to comprehend without rules that regulate its exercise and its limits. Legal sovereignty, on the other hand, needs a political power base to establish such rules. In this respect, constituent power forms the starting point of the legal order and its rules, while remaining unrestrained by those rules.

Given article 33 of the Belgian Constitution, which states that all powers stem from the nation, one can ask how exactly the political community (as 'people' or 'nation') could give form to the political structure, which it established during the Belgian Revolution. Did the Belgian Constituent Assembly of 1830–1831 conceive the constituent power as an original, pre-constitutional power? If so, did the assembly understand it as also remaining at all times existent, independently from the constitutional order? In this case, this constituent power would retain all sovereign power and could arise again at any given moment. Or did the assembly rely on another conception of constituent power, e.g. one in which the constituent power would perpetually dissolve? These questions are all the more important as the Belgian congressmen show a certain degree of self-awareness about their status as a constituent power and explicitly engaged with the meaning and implications of the concept, particularly its relation to popular sovereignty.[1] Political actors often invoked the notion of constituent power, not only for the purpose of self-legitimation, but also as a theoretical, normative concept framing the discussion of the new constitutional form and the role of the people in it. The members of the Belgian Constituent Assembly were political actors, indeed, but they were also deeply ingrained in contemporary Francophone political theory. Their thought and action sprung from political theory as much as from empirical

1 This relation was also discussed in the contemporary newspapers. See Deseure (2016, pp. 134–146).

reality (Deseure et al., 2018, p. 18 f.; Marteel, 2018). Nonetheless, their attitudes towards constituent power have never been thoroughly scrutinised. This is regrettable, especially since in Belgian constitutional theory, much of the sovereignty debate hinges on the original intent and the *ratione constitutionis.*

Hence, this chapter examines the role of the constituent power and its relation to sovereignty within the constituent debates. Did the Belgian founding fathers invoke constituent power as a normative category, as a sociological description of reality, or as a metaphysical concept? Furthermore, this chapter will investigate the *locus* of constituent power and its meaning for the Belgian founding fathers.

We will start by briefly looking at the general meaning of the concept of constituent power and its relationship with the concept of sovereignty. We will then look at how the Belgian framers legitimised both the Revolution and their constituent actions, which they enacted through a constituent assembly. Finally, we will investigate how they conceived the notion of constituent power.

The meaning of constituent power

To understand the peculiarity of the notion of constituent power, it is useful to contrast it with traditional conceptions of sovereignty. Whereas sovereignty traditionally refers to persons and institutions within a legal order, constituent power refers to the origins of such orders. They are seen as resulting from the actions of a collective or entity that exists outside of or prior to these orders. These entities, which are the extra-legal sources of legal and political orders, are called 'constituent powers'. Constituent power received its modern articulation when Emmanuel Sieyès, with a daring conceptual innovation, attempted to change the terms of the fierce debate between proponents of monarchical sovereignty and popular sovereignty. In a sweeping move, Sieyès conceptualised the legal-political order as a dichotomy between 'constituent' and 'constituted' powers. *De facto*, this amounted to a reformulation of sovereignty as the 'source' of the constitutional order, implying that the constituent power itself is *sui generis.* Having no legal status, it is understood as the power that constitutes the legal framework and as such precedes any legal determination. Following Sieyès' distinction, constituent power is the power to create authoritative public powers, i.e. constituted powers. Thus, the distinction is between 'powers of shaping the constitution' and 'powers of ordinary legislation within the limits of a constitution'.

Since Sieyès introduced this famous distinction, the concept of constituent power has been a cornerstone of modern constitutionalism. In contemporary usage, constituent power is generally used to emphasise the importance of democratic self-rule and to prevent the reduction of political power to institutions and regimes. In this vein, constituent power refers to the ongoing entitlement of citizens to democratically shape their constitutional order. This is the meaning of popular sovereignty as a constituent power (Geenens, 2016; Tuck, 2016).

Three ideas subtend most conceptions of constituent power. First, although theorists have proposed different subjects as the bearer of constituent power, e.g. the multitude, a people, a nation, a representative body, and so on, the underlying logic is always that constituent power is the power or capacity of a community to determine "the constitutional form, the juridical and political identity, and the governmental structure of a community in its entirety" (Kalyvas, 2005, p. 226). Second, the constitution of a political community should be the object of political autonomy, i.e. there is some (collective) agency behind the fundamental legal and political structures to which people subordinate themselves. Third, there exists a qualitative distinction between ordinary, everyday politics and higher, constitutional politics. Generally, this comes with a commitment to what is called 'double differentiation', i.e. the idea that constituted powers should have no role in the exercise of constituent power and vice versa (Arato, 2016; Klein, 1996; Patberg, 2016). The aim behind this hierarchy between constituent and constituted powers is to ensure that constituted powers have only those competences that have been conferred on them by the constituent power.

Despite many differences between various conceptions of constituent power, all of them seem to presuppose the existence of an entity which is the 'bearer' of political unity and which, through an act of will, 'constitutes' fundamental rules and government.[2] Questions remain, however: who is the constituent power and who should wield it? And what happens to it when it is exercised? Does it burn out, is it absorbed in the constituted order, or does it remain present next to that order?

Constituent power in 1830–1831 Belgium

With these questions in mind, we now turn to the 1830–1831 Belgian constituent debates which established the authority and legitimacy of the new legal order. Like the notion of sovereignty, the interpretation of the concept of constituent power in the Belgian debates is complicated by a basic lack of agreement on the meaning of the concepts around which the debates revolved (Deseure, 2016, p. 147; Witte, 2006). However, by analysing the congressmen's decisions, attitudes, actions, choice of words and concepts, and associations drawn between concepts, we will try to uncover the explicit and implicit meanings which the founding fathers gave to the concept of constituent power.

The Constitution of 1815 and the right of resistance

On 4 October 1830, the provisional government decreed Belgian independence.[3] Having overthrown the Dutch legal order, the Belgian revolutionaries faced a double task. They had to legitimise the newly constituted bodies of the new legal structure and their rejection of the existent governmental institutions.

2 Logically, this suggests a temporal distinction between (the creation of) political unity and the creation of a constitutional contract that establishes the office and competences of government.

3 Decree of 4 October 1830, *Bull. Arr.*, no. 4, p. 3.

The revolutionaries blamed the rupture with the Dutch regime on King William I's non-compliance with the Constitution of 1815, which they interpreted as a reciprocal 'social pact' (*contrat synallagmatique*) between the nation and the king (Huyttens, 1844a, p. 154, 16 November 1830, Comte de Celles; Huyttens, 1844a, p. 166, 17 November 1830, Baron d'Huart and Van de Weyer; Huyttens, 1844a, p. 304, 24 November 1830, De Gerlache; Huyttens, 1844c, p. 173, 30 July 1831, Seron). They were upset not so much with the constitution's contents, but with the king's detrimental interpretation and application of it (Witte, 2016, p. 36). The grievances of the Southern opposition fell on deaf ears. Things worsened when, in 1827, William claimed exclusive royal sovereignty (Bos, 2009, pp. 229–230; Dölle, 2006, pp. 25, 40; Witte, 2016, p. 37). Upset with William's refusal to comply with their requests, the Southern opposition finally asked for an administrative separation (Bauer, 1994, pp. 223, 276; Gaus, 2007, pp. 25–37).

Believing to have faithfully fulfilled every term of their obligations while William unceasingly acted against their rights and interests, the Belgian opposition felt entitled to go beyond a mere suspension of their obligations and to rightfully terminate the social pact at the expense of William. "If the effects of the contract of 1815 are only suspended", congressman Nothomb affirmed, "it falls to the national representation to destroy it forever, by declaring the independence of Belgium and William deposed" (Huyttens, 1844a, p. 157, 16 November 1830, Nothomb). Invoking the principle of popular sovereignty and the right of insurrection, the Belgian nation and its political representatives felt free to dissolve the social contract by revolting, claiming independence, and replacing the Dutch government with one that effectively served the people's interests. The moderate aristocrat Hippolyte Vilain XIIII referred in this regard to Thomas Jefferson's famous formulation:

> the just authority of the governments has to stem from the approval of the governed, every time a form of government becomes destructive for the liberty and happiness of the citizens, the latter have the right to reject or to abolish it.
>
> (Huyttens, 1844a, p. 294, 23 November 1830, H. Vilain XIIII. See also Huyttens, 1844a, p. 157, 23 November 1830, Van Snick; Huyttens, 1844c, p. 163, 21 July 1831, Jottrand; Huyttens, 1844c, p. 432, 4 July 1831, Nothomb; Huyttens, 1844c, p. 514, 7 July 1831, Fleussu; Huyttens, 1844c, p. 557, 9 July 1831, Van Meenen; Huyttens, 1844c, p. 536, 8 July 1831, De Foere)

The right of resistance, originating in the sovereign power of the people to determine the form of their association, pointed to the people's priority and superiority over the constituted forms, including the king. In this context, proposals were made to integrate an individual and a collective right of resistance into the Constitution (resp. Huyttens, 1844b, p. 224, 21 January 1831, De Robaulx;

Huyttens, 1844d, pp. 65–67, pièce just. no. 52, proposal from Thorn). These proposals were, however, discarded out of fear for political instability (see esp. Van Meenen's reaction: Huyttens, 1844b, p. 224, 21 January 1831, Van Meenen).

The first step towards the new legal order: Legitimating the constituent power

Having broken with the Dutch regime, the revolutionaries operated in a juridical vacuum. Initially, the provisional government (acting 'in the name of the Belgian people') became the sovereign decision-making power, combining the legislative, executive, judicial, and (pre-) constituent powers into one single body (Gilissen, 1981, p. 612; Van den Steene, 1963, p. 11). The provisional government legitimised its appropriation of power by declaring that it had 'temporarily' accepted a power which it would hand over to "more worthy hands" as soon as the elements of a 'new authority' were in place.[4] Three weeks later, it officially claimed that the people had attributed power to "its body of representatives, in order to determine the manner of governing itself".[5] The provisional government legitimated its acquisition and exercise of sovereign power by 'necessity' (state of exception) and claimed the people's 'implicit approval'. This seizure of power was legitimated by the fact that it was necessary for regulated society to emerge after the old legal order had been dissolved (Huyttens, 1844a, pp. 117–118, 12 November 1830, De Foere; Huyttens, 1844b, p. 595, 25 February 1831, De Gerlache (president)). By claiming necessity and referring to popular sovereignty and the right of resistance, the provisional government thus engaged in a discourse of self-legitimation. It claimed the people's passive approval as proof of its recognition as the *de facto* and *de iure* government, symbolising the passage of power from action by force to a state of (pre-)legitimacy.

Before long, a struggle broke out regarding the proper legitimation of constituent power. Internally, the provisional government was divided on how to proceed. The republicans Louis de Potter and Jean-François Tielemans endorsed the idea of a temporary, dictatorial regime that would institute a republican government based on universal suffrage (see esp. De Potter's letter of resignation, Huyttens, 1844a, p. 142, 15 November 1830). This entailed that the provisional government had to retain its sovereign power. The majority of the members, on the other hand, was convinced that the provisional government should relinquish its sovereignty to a constituent assembly that should decide on the new form of government (Garsou, 1930, pp. 339–340). Consequently, on 10 November, the provisional government constituted a constituent assembly.[6] Just one day later, the provisional government received notification that the National Congress had

4 Proclamation of 24 September 1830, p. 1.

5 Reply of the provisional government to the proclamation of the Prince of Orange of 16 October 1830 (Huyttens, 1844b, pp. 210–211, fn. 1).

6 Decree of 4 October 1830, *Bull. Arr.*, no. 4, p. 9.

constituted itself. On 12 November, the provisional government formally handed over its power to the National Congress, proclaiming the latter as the legal and regular body of the people (Huyttens, 1844d, p. 5, pièce just. no. 7). The question of whether the constituent assembly was constituted by a preceding power or had constituted itself became crucial.

Louis de Potter refused to consent to the transfer of power. According to him, the provisional government was anterior to, and independent from, the Congress. It should function as a provisional counter-power to the Congress. The latter, he argued, was solely created to finish and consolidate the work of the provisional government (Huyttens, 1844a, p. 101, 10 November 1830, De Potter's speech of instalment of the National Congress). Thus, De Potter considered the provisional government as the 'original' constituent power, whereas the National Congress was only a 'constituted' constituent power.[7] For the republican leadsman and his entourage, the provisional government, deriving its legitimacy from the people as the source of constituent power, was mandated by the people to create a republican state form with universal suffrage in which constituent power belongs, unmediated, to the people.

The other congressmen saw this as an illegitimate imposition of a specific state form. They argued that the people wanted their representatives, in the form of a constituent assembly, to discuss and decide upon a state form and constitutional system. The people should only actively participate in political power within a newly created system. As Brecht Deseure has shown elsewhere, most congressmen denied the existence of another constituent power besides Congress (Deseure, 2016, p. 100 f.). Whereas the provisional government had merely operated on the basis of 'necessity' and had only been 'implicitly' mandated, they conceived of the National Congress as the 'original' constituent power, 'explicitly' mandated by the Belgian people through elections to create a new legal and political system (Huyttens, 1844a, pp. 117–118, 12 November 1830, De Foere; Huyttens, 1844a, p. 142 *in fine*, 15 November 1830; Huyttens, 1844b, p. 13, 3 January 1831, C. Rodenbach). Only when it was "free, uncontested, and without rival", congressman Le Hon observed, would Congress have "the calm of the supreme power" (Huyttens, 1844a, p. 492, 15 December 1830, Le Hon). A rivalry within the constituent power would possibly prevent the establishment of the new legal order, hindering the Revolution altogether.

In terms of understanding the *locus* of constituent power, the republicans seem to have generally endorsed a conception of the actually existing people as the real, inalienable constituent power which should be given a means of expression through universal suffrage (Israel, 2017, pp. 526–528).[8] For the

7 Later, De Potter argued that the National Congress' task should have been limited only to "sanctioning into effect" a Constitution prepared by the provisional revolutionary government (Lehning, 1960, pp. 530, 535–536). Soon after the Revolution, he wholly dismissed the idea of a constituent assembly (De Potter, 1831, pp. 50–52).

8 Some republicans stated, to the contrary, that "the right to regulate and decide on the future fate of Belgium belongs exclusively to the national congress" (Huyttens, 1844a, p. 173,

majority of Congress, however, the people retained no status as constituent power. Congressman Van Hoorbrouck de Mooreghem made this case quite clearly when he argued that "only in you, assembled in congress, resides the constituent power" (Huyttens, 1844c, p. 391, Van Hoorbrouck de Mooreghem, 2 July 1831. See also Huyttens, 1844a, p. 100, 10 November 1830, De Mûelenaere). In such remarks, we see congressmen relying on an understanding of constituent power in which it becomes either 'domesticated' by or 'absorbed' into institutions: the people itself, even if it is symbolically referred to as the source of constituent power, has no actual role in the exercise of constituent power.

Claiming exclusive constituent authority meant that Congress could not admit to having been constituted by another authority. But neither could it completely deny the provisional government's legitimacy. On the one hand, Congress claimed its legitimacy from the explicit consent of the Belgian people, expressed in the general elections organised by the provisional government. Denying the latter's legitimacy would thus be self-undermining. Yet, Congress had to deny that somehow powers had been bestowed on it by the provisional government. The solution was for Congress to acknowledge that, *qua* institutional form, it had been created by the provisional government. It denied, however, that its legitimacy derived from the provisional government. The legitimacy of its powers was derived from 'the nation'. In other words, the Congress existed *de facto* through the provisional government while Congress had constituted itself *de iure* through the verification of powers (e.g. Huyttens, 1844a, p. 681, 28 December 1830, Barthélemy; Huyttens, 1844b, p. 119, 12 January 1831, De Foere; Huyttens, 1844b, p. 47, 7 January 1831, Le Hon; Huyttens, 1844b, p. 201, 18 January 1831, Van Snick). This way, Congress neither admitted being constituted legally by the provisional government nor deriving its powers from the provisional government. Having constituted itself, it then endorsed the provisional government's *de facto* executive acting in a time of necessity by retroactively legitimising its earlier executive actions and granting it *de iure* executive power (Huyttens, 1844a, p. 127, session of 12 November 1830). This solution allowed Congress to depict the provisional government as a constituted power, to strengthen its moral control, and to consolidate its position as the exclusive constituent power.

Conceptions of constituent power

We now turn to the different meanings of constituent power that circulated in these debates. The dominant conception of constituent power that emerged from the constituent debates shows the belief that constituent power resided in the representative body of Congress. Yet, if constituent power resided in Congress, what did this entail? We will see that the congressmen's opinions often changed in accordance with concrete political developments and with the decisions the National Congress made.

---

18 November 1830, Lardinois).

The subject of constituent power

Early 1831, Congress recognised the nation as the ultimate source of all powers, stating that "All powers emanate from the Nation" (Huyttens, 1844b, p. 14, session of 3 January 1831). But if the 'nation' is the source of all powers, how can Congress be the constituent power? This suggests a distinction between the 'source' of constituent power (in this case, the nation or people) and its 'exercise' (by Congress) that most congressmen seemed unwilling to make. This results in a confusion that permeates the debates.

To some extent, all congressmen considered the people as the source of constituent power. Deleeuw, asking, "From whom do we receive our powers?", answered, "From the people". Similarly, Rogier saw Congress as "emerging from the people" (resp. Huyttens, 1844b, p. 298, 29 January 1831, Deleeuw; Huyttens, 1844c, p. 89, 12 April 1831, Rogier. See also Huyttens, 1844a, p. 404, 13 December 1830, Van Snick). Often, this was described in terms of a transfer of constituent power by the people to Congress (Huyttens, 1844a, p. 116, 12 November 1830, De Robaulx; Huyttens, 1844a, p. 118, 12 November 1830, De Foere). On such grounds, most congressmen rejected any interference by the people in the exercise of constituent power. Combined with their refusal of popular participation in the constitutional process, their references to the people as the source of constituent power often appear as merely symbolic.

Other congressmen, however, made arguments which express an understanding of constituent power in which the relation of constituent power with the people or the nation is much more unclear. Republicans regularly stressed the persistent superiority of the people over Congress (e.g. Huyttens, 1844b, p. 324, 30 January 1831, Seron; Huyttens, 1844a, p. 455, 14 December 1830, Wannaar). The democratic-minded priest De Haerne even claimed that he would

> never believe that the representatives of the nation would have a different will than the one of the majority of the nation from which they hold their powers. [...] a representative placed in between his conscience and the opinion of the people that he represents should withdraw, instead of trying to impose his ideas by force.
>
> (Huyttens, 1844c, p. 186, 31 July 1831, De Haerne)

More conservative members also talked about Congress' mandate in terms of "the wish of the people" being "enforced upon" Congress (Huyttens, 1844a, 219, 20 November 1830, De Roo).

The republican congressmen in particular endorsed the enduring presence of the people as the original constituent power, a position over which they repeatedly clashed with their fellow congressmen. When republicans argued that Congress' decision in favour of a monarchical form of state had to be submitted to the judgment of the people by constitutional referendum, they met fierce opposition. Finding support for a decision on the form of the state outside of the constituent assembly, congressman Forgeur argued, would violate the (representative) mandate of the congressmen and, more importantly, would subvert the constituent power of the National Congress. Instigated by liberal congressman Devaux, Congress rejected the idea of direct popular intervention (resp. Huyttens, 1844a, pp. 225–228, 20 November 1830, De Robaulx; Huyttens, 1844a, p. 229, 20 November 1830, Forgeur; Huyttens, 1844a, pp. 253, 260–261, 22 November 1830, Devaux). Congress thus strongly insisted on its exclusive status as the representative of the nation on all occasions.

In the minds of the congressmen then, the National Congress, having emerged from the sovereign people or nation, became the constituent power (e.g. Huyttens, 1844a, p. 367, 6 December 1830, Devaux; Huyttens, 1844b, p. 184, 17 January 1831, Van Snick; Huyttens, 1844b, p. 502, 11 February 1831, De Robaulx; Huyttens, 1844b, p. 577, fn. 1, 23 February 1831, Werbrouck-Pieters; Huyttens, 1844b, p. 590, 24 February 1831, Du Val de Beaulieu; Huyttens, 1844c, p. 87, 12 April 1831, Fallon; Huyttens, 1844c, p. 262, 3 June 1831, Doreye). Yet, as we have seen, they also kept acknowledging the sovereign people to be the source of constituent power. This position is conceptually tense, if not inconsistent. How did the congressmen square this?

Some congressmen understood the National Congress as an *organ* of the Belgian people (e.g. Huyttens, 1844a, p. 193, 19 November 1830, Raikem; Huyttens, 1844a, p. 238, 22 November 1830, Verbeke; Huyttens, 1844a, p. 268, 23 November 1830, A. Rodenbach; Huyttens, 1844b, p. 90, 11 January 1831, Seron; Huyttens, 1844b, p. 589, 24 February 1831, De Gerlache (president); Huyttens, 1844c, p. 88, 12 April 1831, Nothomb). Instead of positing two potentially conflicting entities, one of which (sovereign people) mandates the other (Congress) to exercise power on its behalf, the organ theory recognised only one entity, the Belgian people or nation, and saw Congress as an organ tasked with the exercise of that entity's constituent functions.[9] Yet, most of the congressmen do not seem to have differentiated between the concepts of mandate and organ. We should not forget that the congressmen were both political actors and theorists at the same time. The clashing demands of these two tasks may well explain their espousal of incoherent doctrines.

A sovereign, but substantially limited power

At the outset of the debates in November 1830, according to the majority of liberal congressmen, the constituent power had to be confined within a clear set of rules. This vision of a limitation of power was couched in a conception of natural rights guaranteeing personal freedom. That is, they thought there were natural restrictions to constituent power. Thus, the idea of the regulation and limitation of powers extended both to constituent and constituted powers. In the constitutional debates, this idea led the liberal congressmen to argue that Congress

9 On this 'organic identification', see also Chapter 9.

should, first of all, regulate itself (e.g. Huyttens, 1844a, p. 102, 10 November 1830, De Stassart; Huyttens, 1844a, p. 103, 10 November 1830, Nothomb; Huyttens, 1844a, p. 115, 12 November 1830, Van Meenen). This issue concerned not merely the question of the self-constitution of the constituent power, but equally its auto-limitation, especially since the regulations were considered binding for the members of the Congress.[10]

The National Congress took further steps to limit its power. It refused, for example, to form a congressional diplomatic committee next to the diplomatic committee of the provisional government in order to avoid a confusion of powers (Huyttens, 1844b, p. 144, 13 January 1831. Esp. Huyttens, 1844b, p. 119, 12 January 1831, De Foere). However, the congressmen did not see a problem in the concentration of constituent and legislative power in their hands (Huyttens, 1844c, pp. 120, 124–127, sessions of 21 and 23 July 1831). An exception was the republican Lardinois, who thought that Congress should restrict its legislative work to a small number of matters and delegate legislative power to a legislative body (Huyttens, 1844e, p. 232, pièce just. no. 318). Simultaneously creating and internally organising a legal order was, as the French Revolution had shown, a grave mistake. Constitutional and ordinary politics should be kept strictly separated, Lardinois seemed to suggest. At the outset of the constitutional debates, a considerable number of congressmen agreed with Lardinois that constituent power was essentially limited to the creation of the Constitution (e.g. Huyttens, 1844a, p. 151, 16 November 1830, Van de Weyer; Huyttens, 1844a, p. 154, 16 November 1830, Comte de Celles; Huyttens, 1844b, p. 502, 11 February 1831, Van Meenen).

This commitment to 'double differentiation', i.e. to the idea that constituent and constituted powers have different competences that should remain strictly separated (cf. *supra*), became compromised when the final draft of the Constitution was nearly completed. Around the end of January 1831, having decided on a monarchical governmental form, Congress became increasingly obsessed with the election of the monarch and the implementation of the Constitution. Many liberal and Catholic congressmen held that Congress' mandate would end with the election of the monarch, which would finalise the Constitution and make it legally binding (Huyttens, 1844a, p. 399, 13 December 1830, Van Snick; Huyttens, 1844b, p. 199, 18 January 1831, Le Bègue; Huyttens, 1844b, p. 215, 19 January 1831, De Theux de Meylandt; Huyttens, 1844b, p. 490, 7 February 1831, Gendebien; Huyttens, 1844c, p. 262, 3 June 1831, Doreye). Although the National Congress could activate most of the constituted powers before disbanding (e.g. instituting courts and tribunals, proclaiming elections for the legislative chambers), it could not delegate the election of a king to the ordinary legislative chambers. This was because, under the new Constitution, the king would not

10 When Henri de Brouckère proposed to circumvent an article of the congressional regulation, Van Meenen retorted that the regulation "dictated law" to the Congress (Huyttens, 1844b, pp. 291–292, 28 January 1831, H. de Brouckère and Van Meenen).

only be head of the executive power but also be a part of the legislative body (old article 36 of the Constitution). Moreover, it would entail granting a constituent prerogative to a constituted legislative body. Thus, the congressmen held that Congress, *qua* constituent power, was the only body that could legitimately conclude the agreement in which the king accepted his constitutional role (Huyttens, 1844b, pp. 111–112, 12 January 1831, Du Val de Beaulieu).

Van Meenen dissented. He argued that the Constitution could be promulgated before a king was elected because its contents were independent of a monarch accepting his functional role within the Constitution. The latter only concerned the constitutional mandate the nation conferred upon the king. In stark contrast with the French Charter of 1830, which formed a contract between the nation and the king as two equal parties, the new Belgian monarch was made subordinate to the Constitution and could only function within the system. This constitutional innovation, Van Meenen argued, offered an additional theoretical basis for guaranteeing individual rights against the arbitrary will of a monarch (Huyttens, 1844b, p. 492, 8 February 1831, Van Meenen. See also Huyttens, 1844c, p. 245, 3 June 1831, Destouvelles).[11] Since the promulgation of the Constitution and the confirmation of the monarchy would both appease the international coalition and show the Belgian population the results of the congressional efforts, Van Meenen proposed to promulgate the Constitution and declare it binding before it was finalised with the election of a king (Huyttens, 1844d, p. 132, pièce just. no. 67, 8 February 1831). But this posed a theoretical problem. Congress saw it as its task to give Belgium a completed Constitution. By declaring the election of the monarch integral to the completion of the Constitution, it could not dissolve itself until a king was elected. Accepting Van Meenen's proposal while remaining in session, however, would create the odd situation of a constituent power (Congress) that could no longer amend the constitution.

The republican minority objected to Van Meenen's proposal, arguing that Congress ought to fully retain its constituent power for as long as it was assembled (Huyttens, 1844b, pp. 501–503, 11 February 1831, esp. the interventions from De Robaulx, Delwarde, and Destouvelles). Importantly, however, they also used the occasion to make a more fundamental point about constituent power, arguing that it should never be fully relinquished.[12] In their view, society and political institutions, like all human and natural orders, are subject to permanent change and mutability (Raxhon, 1996, pp. 33, 73–74). This would occasion a regular revision of the constitutional order by the constituent power. Implicitly, they were arguing that Congress should be able to reconvene whenever the people deemed it necessary. Since the people, who existed independently of Congress, were the source of constituent power, they should preserve at all

11 For Van Meenen's insights on the guarantees of individual rights, see Stefaan Marteel's contribution in this book.

12 These interventions were certainly also strategic, as the republicans were mainly concerned with preserving the opportunity to cast off the constitutional monarchy.

times the liberty to reconvene a constituent assembly.[13] The republicans were, however, unable to rally the majority to their conception of constituent power, and Van Meenen's proposal, only slightly amended, prevailed. The Constitution was promulgated on 7 February 1831 but remained unenforceable until a king was elected. Consequently, the National Congress kept constituent power for the time being.

When Congress proved unable to quickly find a willing and suitable candidate to take the Belgian throne, the congressmen considered appointing a regent in anticipation of the election of a king (Huyttens, 1844b, pp. 551–553, 21 February 1831).[14] While this would be a major step forward in finalising the new order, it also introduced additional complications. Congress, for example, had no place in the new order. Yet, nominating a regent and subsequently dissolving Congress would leave the future nomination of a king to the regent, thus making the regent a constituent power. This could destabilise the whole enterprise, as self-interest might drive the regent to delay the nomination of a king (Huyttens, 1844b, p. 579, 23 February 1831, Devaux). Eventually, Congress decided to appoint a regent in order to make the Constitution legally binding,[15] but it kept legislative and constituent power until a king was elected (Huyttens, 1844b, pp. 572–585, 22–23 February 1831). Nevertheless, Nothomb remarked, the congressional mandate to "fix the future of the country" was far from accomplished with the election of a regent (Huyttens, 1844b, p. 581, 23 February 1831, Nothomb). This election was merely a provisional decision, since it was not provided for in the Constitution. Nothomb thus concluded that Congress, still bound by its mandate to fix the future of the country, could not give up constituent power or legislative power. The regent should only have the executive power (Huyttens, 1844b, p. 581, 23 February 1831, Nothomb).[16]

Nothomb confirmed this view in April 1831, when the issue surfaced again. Congressman Fallon had argued that the provisional government's Decree of Independence comprised the limits of the congressional mandate because Congress had been brought into existence by the provisional government. The decree's objective of "establishing the state of Belgium" entailed the drafting and enactment of a constitution but did not mention the election of a king. The latter was therefore merely an "accessory" that fell within the scope of the

13 Noteworthy is De Robaulx's statement that the congressional discussions belonged to the nation, an idea which would grant the nation the right to assist in those debates (Huyttens, 1844b, p. 263, 25 January 1831, De Robaulx).

14 The Congress found a proper candidate in the Duke of Nemours, son of the French king Louis-Philippe, but he was rejected by the international coalition, in particular by England, who feared French domination on the continent.

15 The Constitution was promulgated and formally sanctioned on 7 February. It was declared binding on 25 February, i.e. the day the future regent would assume his function (Huyttens, 1844d, p. 124, pièce just. no. 66, fn. (g)). The Congress elected its president, Surlet de Chokier, as regent.

16 Nothomb erroneously referred to the decree of 6 October 1830 and probably meant to refer to the Decree of Independence. Decree of 4 October 1830, *Bull. Arr.*, no. 4, p. 9.

constituent assembly until a constitution had been finalised. Consequently, now that the Constitution was promulgated and executable, Congress had to disband. Deciding otherwise would amount to the usurpation of power (Huyttens, 1844c, pp. 85–88, 12 April 1831, Fallon). Fallon's conception of constituent power as limited by a strict mandate was received with general disapproval. Comparing Fallon's ideas with De Potter's rejected views on constituent power,[17] Nothomb argued that the decree of 4 October had to be understood *sensu lato*: it did not limit Congress' constituent attributions, because Congress was invested by the citizens with "the plenitude of social powers" (Huyttens, 1844c, pp. 88–89, 12 April 1831, Nothomb).[18] Putting a lid on the discussion, Devaux explained that the mandate expressed in the decree could not have mentioned the election of a king because, at the time, the choice for a constitutional monarchy had not yet been made (Huyttens, 1844c, p. 91, 12 April 1831, Devaux). Congress decided that it would adjourn itself once it had settled several urgent legislative matters (e.g. the electoral law for the constituted legislative chambers) while leaving its president or the regent the right to convoke Congress when necessary (Huyttens, 1844c, pp. 92–97, 12–13 April 1831).

After almost four months of regency, Congress finally found a proper and willing king in the German Prince Leopold I of Saxe-Coburg. It consecrated this choice in article 60 of the Constitution and decreed that it would adjourn itself immediately after the king's pledge on the 21 July 1831. By merely adjourning, Congress would remain in a state of latent existence, with only the king having the right to re-convoke it. Only at this point was Congress' constituent power completely exhausted. On the first day of the reunion of the future legislative chambers, the Congress was legally disbanded.

A sovereign but temporally limited power

What, according to the congressmen, happened with the constituent power after its task had been accomplished? Two positions can be distinguished. The republican congressmen held that the constituent power retreated but did not disappear. Persisting latently, it could at any time return through re-convocation of a constituent assembly. De Robaulx was most clear about this, when he stated in Congress that "We, constituent power, have always the right to come back upon what we have decided [...] we are sovereign judges in the possession of the

17 "[De Potter] also has alleged that our mission is limited to the examination of the Constitution, and in this opinion the provisional government had to exist next to this assembly, and even outlive it to exercise all other powers" (Huyttens, 1844c, pp. 88–89, 12 April 1831, Nothomb).

18 *Qua* understanding of constituent power, Fallon, De Potter, and Nothomb can thus be distinguished: Fallon relied on the decree's temporal anteriority to assert its normative superiority over the National Congress; De Potter gave normative priority to the provisional government due to its reformative efficiency; and Nothomb gave normative priority to the Congress due to its superior representational legitimacy.

power to reform ourselves" (Huyttens, 1844b, pp. 501–503, 11 February 1831, De Robaulx).

The liberal congressmen, on the other hand, believed that the constituent power had to permanently retreat from the constituted legal order (e.g. Huyttens, 1844c, p. 611, 20 July 1831, Fallon). According to Nothomb, the constituent power should not even be absorbed into the constituted legislative power as this would enable the legislative power to change the constituted legal order at will. Such abuse of power had to be prevented at all cost. Hence, Nothomb argued, once its work had ended, the constituent power ought to retreat to "a *nearly* inaccessible sphere" (our emphasis. Huyttens, 1844a, p. 424, 14 December 1830, Nothomb). Having domesticated the constituent power this way, the constituted legislative power would be confined to acting within its constitutional boundaries only.[19]

Nothomb's idea of relegating the now exhausted constituent power to a 'nearly' inaccessible place was a remarkable one. That is, he wished to *banish* constituent power from the constituted order but not to permanently and irrevocably *end* it. Just like a political exile might be called back when a government falls, a banished constituent power reaffirms itself should the legal order fall. This suggests that some *locus* of constituent power remained to the extent that it could potentially be drawn on in future circumstances (for example, if citizens were to revolt and reject the legal order). For the liberals, this did not entail that constituent power remained 'next to' the constituted order as a normatively prior force stimulating the constitutional order to stay true to its purposes. Rather, the liberal congressmen paid lip service to the idea that the people should always be able to overthrow a corrupt power threatening their freedom and security. The idea that constituent power is conditional on the performance of the constituted order is in line with the generally accepted view of the congressmen on the people's right of resistance against an oppressive government (*supra*).

Nevertheless, the congressmen were extraordinarily concerned with preventing any *constituted* powers from seizing constituent power and taking 'extra-constitutional' measures. For this reason, they inserted an article prohibiting the suspension of the Constitution itself (old article 130 of the Constitution, actual article 187). Influenced by the French Restoration liberal Benjamin Constant, Van Snick argued that governments had too often suspended or violated the Constitution under the pretext of the well-being of the people. Van Snick thus proposed the insertion of an article that would prevent the constituted powers from claiming sovereignty in the name of the people. He reasoned that since the constituted powers existed only by means of the Constitution, suspending the latter would immediately invalidate those powers (Huyttens, 1844b, p. 464, 5 February 1831, Van Snick). Article 130 would also prevent the kind of

19 Hence Nothomb's preference for a bicameral system, which enabled one legislative chamber to prevent the other from seizing the constituent power. A similar argument was raised by Lebeau (Huyttens, 1844a, p. 413, 13 December 1830, Lebeau).

ad hoc legislation that had occurred under Charles X in France and William I in the Netherlands (Huyttens, 1844b, p. 465, 5 February 1831, Lebeau).[20] Consequently, the possibility of 'extra-constitutional' politics was fundamentally restricted to cases of popular revolution, i.e. of extra-constitutional dismantlement of the existing legal order.[21] Remarkably, only the republican De Robaulx objected, claiming that such a provision was superfluous because constituent power inalienably resided with the people.[22]

Congress' dominant opinion on the exclusion of constituent power from the constituted order is further demonstrated in its discussion of two important decrees. Congress had decreed Belgian independence on 18 November 1830. Six days later, it had decreed the permanent exclusion of the Orange-Nassau dynasty from the Belgian throne. To his surprise, congressman Devaux discovered in February 1831 that these decisions had not yet been constitutionally enshrined, and he proposed they be immediately constitutionalised. However, Baron Beyts objected that making these decrees part of the constitution would allow future legislatures to amend them in accordance with the procedure of constitutional revision. Constitutionalising the decree of Belgian independence, he argued, could thus potentially lead to the dismantling of the legal order. Consequently, he proposed that Congress proclaim these decrees *qualite qua* (original) constituent power. This would turn them into the immutable base on which the Constitution would rest (by giving them constitutional value), while keeping them outside of the (amendable) Constitution. Congress accepted Beyts' proposal, with even Devaux voting in favour (for the integral discussion, see Huyttens, 1844b, pp. 586–592, 24 February 1831).[23]

Aiming to alleviate the threat of future revolutions caused by the Constitution's 'immutability' once constituent power had retreated, Congress enshrined constitutional flexibility in article 131. According to this article, although amendment entails a constitution-making power, it can only be wielded by the (constituted) legislative body and its exercise is completely delimited by the Constitution. In other words, it can only operate in the constituted order under well-defined conditions and according to a rigid procedure dictated by the Constitution (old article

20 See also article 67 of the Constitution (actual article 108), which prohibited the king from suspending the law.

21 According to early legal doctrine, the nation always retains the right to change, by means of revolution, the constituted order if circumstances compelled it to do so. Revolutions fall outside the scope of legal rules. Therefore, a constitution cannot regulate the original constituent power (De Brouckère and Tielemans, 1834, pp. 50–51, "Abrogation"; Giron, 1895, pp. 10–12, "Actes illégaux"; Orban, 1906, p. 425).

22 For the integral discussion on article 130 of the Constitution, see Huyttens (1844b, pp. 464–465, 5 February 1831).

23 The immutability of those decrees has been confirmed in later legal doctrine. Yet, after the Second World War, probably due to political and diplomatic motives, legal doctrine has evolved, and these decrees are no longer seen as immutable. This seems to be historically inconsistent (Behrendt and Bouhon, 2014, pp. 163–167 with fn. 545–550).

131 of the Constitution, actual article 195). Moreover, any constitutional revision could only target the dispositions in the declaration of the revision made by the three branches of the legislative power. By introducing this 'constituted constituent power', the congressmen further restrained the exercise of original constituent power to the constituent moment, thereby both safeguarding the constituted legal order and providing adaptability in the face of social evolution (Orban, 1906, pp. 413–424).

Conclusion

Looking back at the 1830–1831 Belgian constitutional debates, we see several dominant views emerging that inform the congressmen's understanding of constituent power. Two facts are most striking. First, the strong disagreement between the republican minority, for which constituent power belongs in the hands of the people, and the liberal and Catholic majority, for which constituent power is to be institutionally and constitutionally 'domesticated'. Second, the strong commitment of the majority of congressmen to the limitation of power and the protection of individual rights, particularly among those of liberal conviction and also among republicans. For the former, this entailed keeping constituent power far away from the constituted order, thus preventing groups and governmental bodies from arbitrarily changing the constitutional order. For the latter, the protection of individual rights ought to entail the possibility for the people to re-convoke constituent power. Their conception of constituent power did not, however, convince the liberal and Catholic majority.

With the exception of the republican congressmen, the commitment to the people's ultimate sovereignty, as expressed in the right of revolution, did prevent the congressmen from fully disavowing the enduring existence of constituent power after the Constitution came into effect. But, although they paid lip service to the idea that their powers were *derived* from the people, the majority opinion was that the people should be kept out of constitutional politics. Constituent power was embodied by a single, extraordinary representative body during the constitutional process and relegated to a 'nearly' inaccessible sphere after the Constitution took effect. Except by the republicans, the people were never referred to as an actual popular force that might participate in constitutional politics, but rather as a symbolically normative presence. Although the congressmen recognised the people as the ultimate source of constituent power, this power only 'emerged' from the people. Just like the passive 'emanate' in article 33 suggests that the people's powers need to assume form before they can be exercised, the congressmen saw the people's original constituent power as a formless power. The National Congress provided the form that made constituent power exercisable.

It is furthermore beyond doubt that the majority that dominated the framing of the Constitution did not wish for the constituent power to appear again within the constitutional order. The majority of the congressmen explicitly rejected any role for the 'people as constituent power' in the establishment as well as in the alteration of the constitutional order. They did not conceive of a dynamic relationship between constituent and constituted powers. Far from it: they established a rigid distinction between constituent and constituted powers and bequeathed only the latter with the task of keeping the constitutional arrangement in line with societal developments. In a similar fashion, they institutionalised a bicameral legislative system which they thought would be sufficient to ensure both stability (through the Senate and the king) and collective progress (through the Chamber of Representatives).[24] As such, the congressmen did not presuppose a reflexive interaction between constituent power and the constituted powers, but only between the constituted powers themselves.

Although constituent power and constituted powers could simply not exist simultaneously, the congressmen were nevertheless committed to the people's deep-seated right of resistance against oppressive rule by the constituted powers. They framed this right of resistance in terms of constituent power. The right was, however, not constitutionalised. Nor did it imply a right for the people to assume a constituent role at any given moment. Rather, the congressmen understood it as a conditional right, triggered only when the constituted order displayed serious dysfunction. The distinction between original constituent power and constituted constituent power further reinforces this logic.

The Belgian Constitution, we are forced to conclude, is not based on the active consent of the people. It merely emanates from the people and rests on their passive consent. Nevertheless, an opening towards popular involvement, if deemed desirable, may be found. The congressmen were, after all, adamant that the role of the people could not be entirely dismissed. They reserved participation in the constitution-making effort for extraordinary representatives, yet their references to the people as constituent power were not strictly nominal, as can be seen in the multiple references to a right of resistance that the people possessed by virtue of their being the original constituent power. Although the congressmen dismissed the idea of enshrining this principle constitutionally, they accepted it as a fundamental one. Perhaps, at the back of their minds, the idea of the people as constituent power was more than merely a symbolic reference to the source of sovereignty in the constitutional order. The constituent power of the people equally found its expression in its right to (re-)appear on the political scene whenever the people judged the constituted system to have become deficient. By not limiting this judgment constitutionally, the congressmen have left open a venue for extra-constitutional claims to alter the Constitution.

24 See the oft-invoked interventions of Nothomb and De Gerlache (resp. Huyttens, 1844a, pp. 192–193, 19 November 1830, Nothomb; pp. 471–473, 15 December 1830, De Gerlache).

Bibliography

Arato, A. (2016) *Post Sovereign Constitution Making. Learning and Legitimacy.* Oxford: Oxford University Press. DOI: 10.1093/acprof:oso/9780198755982.001.0001.

Bauer, R. (1994) *De Lage Landen: een geschiedenis in de spiegel van Europa.* Tielt: Lannoo.

Behrendt, C. and Bouhon, F. (2014) *Introduction à la théorie générale de l'Etat.* Brussels: Larcier.

Bos, E. (2009) *Soevereiniteit en religie. Godsdienstvrijheid onder de eerste Oranjevorsten.* Hilversum: Verloren.

De Brouckère, C. and Tielemans, F. (1834) *Répertoire de l'administration et du droit administratif de la Belgique.* Brussels: Weissenbruch.

De Potter, L. (1831) *De la révolution à faire d'après l'expérience des révolutions avortées.* Paris: Ladvocat.

Deseure, B. (2016) 'National Sovereignty in the Belgian Constitution of 1831. On the Meaning(s) of Article 25', in Müßig, U. (ed.) *Reconsidering Constitutional Formation.* Berlin: Springer, pp. 93–156. DOI: 10.1007/978-3-319-42405-7_2.

Deseure, B., Geenens, R., Maes, C., and Sottiaux, S. (2018) 'The Belgian Constitution: Modern Constitutionalism's Greatest Triumph?', *Giornale di Storia Costituzionale*, 35(1), pp. 17–32.

Dölle, A.H.M. (2006) 'De constitutie voor het Koninkrijk Holland van 1806', in Hallebeek, J. and Sirks, A.J.B. (eds.) *Nederland in Franse schaduw. Recht en bestuur in het Koninkrijk Holland (1806–1810).* Hilversum: Verloren, pp. 25–45.

Garsou, J. (1930) *Alexandre Gendebien: sa vie, ses mémoires.* Brussels: Van Sulper.

Gaus, H. (2007) *Alexandre Gendebien en de organisatie van de Belgische revolutie van 1830.* Ghent: Academia Press.

Geenens, R. (2016) 'E pluribus unum? The Manifold Meanings of Sovereignty', *Netherlands Journal of Legal Philosophy*, 45(2), pp. 15–35. DOI: 10.5553/njlp/.000051.

Gilissen, J. (1981) 'Le caractère collegial des premières formes de gouvernement et d'administration de l'état belge (1830–1831)', *Belgisch Tijdschrift voor Nieuwste Geschiedenis*, 12(3), pp. 609–639.

Giron, A. (1895) *Dictionnaire de droit administratif et de droit public.* Brussels: Bruylant-Christophe.

Huyttens, E. (1844a) *Discussions du Congrès National de Belgique 1830–1831. Tome premier.* Brussels: Société Typographique Belge.

Huyttens, E. (1844b) *Discussions du Congrès National de Belgique 1830–1831. Tome deuxième.* Brussels: Société Typographique Belge.

Huyttens, E. (1844c) *Discussions du Congrès National de Belgique 1830–1831. Tome troisième.* Brussels: Société Typographique Belge.

Huyttens, E. (1844d) *Discussions du Congrès National de Belgique 1830–1831. Tome quatrième.* Brussels: Société Typographique Belge.

Huyttens, E. (1844e) *Discussions du Congrès National de Belgique 1830–1831. Tome cinquième.* Brussels: Société Typographique Belge.

Israel, J. (2017) *The Expanding Blaze: How the American Revolution Ignited the World, 1775–1848.* Princeton: Princeton University Press. DOI: 10.1515/9781400888276.

Kalyvas, A. (2005) 'Popular Sovereignty, Democracy, and the Constituent Power', *Constellations*, 12(2), pp. 223–244. DOI: 10.1111/j.1351-0487.2005.00413.x.

Klein, C. (1996) *Théorie et pratique du pouvoir constituant.* Paris: PUF.
Lehning, A. (1960) 'Buonarroti et la révolution belge de 1830', *Annales Historiques de la Révolution Française*, 162 (32), pp. 530–536.
Marteel, S. (2018) *The Intellectual Origins of the Belgian Revolution. Political Thought and Disunity in the Kingdom of the Netherlands, 1815–1830.* New York: Springer. DOI: 10.1007/978-3-319-89426-3.
Orban, O. (1906) *Le droit constitutionnel de la Belgique.* Liège: Dessain.
Patberg, M. (2016) 'Against Democratic Intergovernmentalism: The Case for a Theory of Constituent Power in the Global Realm', *International Journal of Constitutional Law*, 14(3), pp. 622–638. DOI: 10.1093/icon/mow040.
Raxhon, P. (1996) 'Mémoire de la Révolution française de 1789 et Congres national belge (1830–31)', *Belgisch Tijdschrift voor Nieuwste Geschiedenis*, 26 (1–2), pp. 33–83.
S.A. (1831) *Bulletin des arrêtés et actes du Gouvernement provisoire de la Belgique* (Vol. 4). Brussels: Weissenbruch.
Tuck, R. (2016) *The Sleeping Sovereign. The Invention of Modern Democracy.* Cambridge: Cambridge University Press. DOI: 10.1017/cbo9781316417782.
Van den Steene, W. (1963) *De Belgische Grondwetscommissie (oktober-november 1830). Tekst van haar notulen en ontstaan van de Belgische Grondwet.* Brussels: Koninklijke Vlaamse academie voor wetenschappen, letteren en schone kunsten van België.
Witte, E. (2006) 'Het natiebegrip in het zuidelijke krantendiscours aan de vooravond van de Belgische opstand (augustus 1829-juli 1830)', *Bijdragen en Mededelingen betreffende de Geschiedenis der Nederlanden*, 121(2), pp. 222–239. DOI: 10.18352/bmgn-lchr.6395.
Witte, E. (2016) 'De Grondwet van het Verenigd Koninkrijk der Nederlanden (1815) en het ontstaan van de Belgische constitutie (1831)', in Alen, A. et al. (eds.) *De Grondwet van het Verenigd Koninkrijk der Nederlanden van 1815. Staatkundige en historische beschouwingen uit België en Nederland.* The Hague: Boom and Bruges: Die Keure, pp. 15–44.

Publications without a specific, personal author (such as newspapers and official documents) are listed under S.A.

8 'All powers emanate from the Nation'

People, nation, and sovereignty in the Belgian Constitution of 1831

Brecht Deseure and Christophe Maes

Introduction

> The sovereignty question currently draws the attention of many people. We receive many letters on the subject, not to mention the articles which other journals publish every day. We admit that, only a few weeks ago, we would never have imagined the magnitude of the mistakes, nor the ignorance that exist on this subject.
>
> (*CDM*, 15–16 November 1830, no. 276)

In its editions of 15 and 16 November 1830, the Liège-based Catholic newspaper *Courrier de la Meuse* signalled an increased public interest in the issue of (popular) sovereignty. The newspaper deplored the public's lack of enlightenment concerning this fundamental concept and proceeded to discuss it at length in subsequent issues. The *Courrier de la Meuse* was not alone in doing so. Sovereignty was keenly discussed in editorials, opinion pieces, and letters to the editor in the many newspapers that existed in Belgium at the time (Deseure, 2016b).

This is both an obvious and a surprising finding. It is obvious because Belgium was in the process of waging a violent revolution against the United Kingdom of the Netherlands. Independence had been declared on 4 October by a provisional government claiming to represent the insurgent Belgian people. A National Congress was subsequently elected in order to draw up a constitution for the new country.[1] A draft constitution had been prepared beforehand by a Constitutional Commission; its articles were discussed in section meetings and afterwards subjected to plenary debate.[2] Logically, sovereignty and other questions of political theory were the order of the day.[3] All the more since, under the Dutch regime, the nature of sovereignty had sparked a heated debate between government

1 The National Congress counted 200 members. For an overview of the Belgian Revolution: Witte (2005).

2 On the constituent process: Gilissen (1967, pp. 38–69); Magits (1977); Van Den Steene (1963).

3 For the intellectual and ideological background of the Belgian Revolution: Viaene (2001); Marteel (2018).

and opposition (see Chapter 5. See also Van Velzen, 2005, pp. 157 and 267; Deseure, 2016a).

But the explicit newspaper debates about sovereignty are also surprising, since the subject was so rarely discussed by the Belgian founding fathers. Contrary to many other constitutions, the Belgian Constitution does not mention sovereignty. The closest it gets to defining sovereignty is in article 25 (current article 33): "All powers emanate from the Nation. They are exercised in the manner prescribed by the Constitution".[4] Moreover, the article was hardly discussed in the constituent assembly. As both the constitutional text and the founding fathers remained largely silent on the matter, sovereignty has been an underdetermined concept in Belgian public law ever since (see Chapter 1).

In view of the ongoing debate on the nature of sovereignty in the Belgian Constitution, it is of prime importance to clarify the terminology and the theoretical concepts used by the founding fathers. Based on a systematic investigation of the debates in the National Congress and the public debate that took place in the major newspapers of the day, we will elucidate the three key terms of the debate: sovereignty, people, and nation. Our goal is to uncover whether different conceptions of sovereignty were present at the time, and if so, which of these informed the Constitution.

We will argue (1) that the nation was conceived of as a concrete, tangible entity whose opinion was to be faithfully rendered by the representatives; (2) that the founding fathers' conception of sovereignty was nevertheless inherently representative and elitist with regard to political participation; and (3) that the founding fathers, being unacquainted with the theoretical distinction between national and popular sovereignty, recognised the popular origin of all power but avoided using the concept of sovereignty. They did so in a conscious attempt to preclude the concentration of power, as reflected by their profoundly liberal constitutional construction.

The absence of explicit discussion of the concept of sovereignty in the National Congress is one of the reasons for disagreement among scholars of Belgian constitutional history. We will therefore follow a contextual approach and look beyond the constituent debates in the National Congress by analysing the public debate in the most relevant newspapers.[5] The importance of the press as a forum for political discussion in the Belgian Revolution cannot be overestimated. A large number of newspapers, each of them with a particular ideological profile, engaged in political journalism.[6] Some of these journals played an important role in the political opposition against King William I (Breunesse, 2014). Their engagement with political theory had contributed to enlightening the Belgian public on key

4 On the article's origin: Alen (1984, vol. 2, p. 89); Descamps-David (1891); Van Den Steene (1963).

5 The constituent debates have been published in Huyttens (1844a–d).

6 For an in-depth overview of the oppositional newspapers and the ties between their collaborators: Vermeersch (1981).

concepts of public law, which in turn enhanced the revolutionary dynamic. Close ties existed between the revolutionary and political protagonists and the newspapers, allowing for an active interaction between the formal constituent debates and the public forum (Bourgaux, 2013; Stevens, 1981, p. 647).[7] For the purpose of this chapter, eight newspapers' coverage of the period between the outbreak of the Revolution at the end of August 1830 and the inauguration of Leopold I on 21 July 1831 has been systematically analysed, while a number of other newspapers have been selectively read to furnish further context. Their ideological profiles cover the whole range of political positions present at the time.

The leading political newspapers and veterans of the liberal opposition against William I were the Liège-based *Le Politique* and the Brussels-based *Courrier des Pays-Bas* (shortened to *Le Courrier* from 1 January 1831). Their moderate, liberal agenda was mostly in tune with the prevailing opinion in the National Congress, with *Le Courrier* being the more progressive one of the two. Also in the centre was *L'Union belge*, serving as the official newspaper of the new regime. To the left of these were three radical journals: the Brussels-based *L'Émancipation* and *Le Belge* and the Namur-based *Courrier de la Sambre*. *L'Émancipation* served as the mouthpiece of the political club *Réunion centrale*, which was very influential in the early days of the Revolution. Progressive Catholicism was represented by the Ghent-based *Journal des Flanders*, which embraced modern constitutionalism out of a pragmatic concern with safeguarding the position of the Church. To the far right of the political spectrum was the *Courrier de la Meuse*, representing ultramontane and reactionary Catholicism, a position that was particularly popular among members of the Belgian nobility.

Sovereignty from below

Sovereignty as a concept was not a popular subject of discussion in the National Congress. To be sure, the term itself was not absent from the vocabulary of the congressmen; the word was a standard fixture of the political language of the day (Bacot, 1985, p. 9). In the most general terms, it was used to indicate ultimate power, power of last resort, or the origin of power. It was also used as a synonym for the monarch ('the sovereign'), even though it was clear to all that this symbolic term no longer corresponded to political reality. But sovereignty as a concept was rarely explicitly investigated so as to uncover its exact meaning and implications for the constituent work at hand.

It is a well-known fact that article 25 of the Constitution was adopted virtually without debate. Neither the preparatory discussions in the sections nor the plenary debate seems to have caused much of a stir (Huyttens, 1844b, p. 14, session of 3 January 1831; Huyttens, 1844d, p. 68, Raikem's report of 23 December 1830). The formulation of the article proposed in the draft constitution was

7 Men of letters, together with jurists, constituted around 65% of the revolutionary political actors (Witte, 1980, p. 109).

accepted verbatim. Two propositions for minor changes of formulation were made but rejected, and only one congressman confronted the issue head-on. The conservative priest Vander Linden intervened to give a speech in which he "rose against the sovereignty of the people and established that all power comes from God" (Huyttens, 1844b, p. 14, 3 January 1831, Vander Linden. See also Magits, 1977, p. 8). Nonetheless, the meeting records make no mention of any reaction from the benches. If anything, Vander Linden's fruitless intervention indicates a general awareness and acceptance of the fact that article 25 consecrated popular sovereignty (De Smaele, 2005, p. 413; Deseure, 2016b, p. 95).

The term 'popular sovereignty' was widely used both in the constituent debates in the National Congress and in official communication. Nothomb, one of the most influential founding fathers, could hardly have been more explicit on the matter when he discoursed on the inviolability of the head of state: "Opposite these fictions [heredity and inviolability], appears, ever menacing, the sovereignty of the people which, in extreme cases, comes and destroys them. In the end, the country always wins" (Huyttens, 1844a, p. 193, 19 November 1830, Nothomb). In this context, popular sovereignty meant, first and foremost, the predominance of 'the country' over the monarch as constituted power. In other words, it implied the negation of the monarchical principle (Harris, 1955, p. 506).

In this sense, the fact that the term 'popular sovereignty' was used was not surprising.[8] The National Congress' constituent debates took place in the context of a popular revolution against an established government. Although it turned out not to be in itself antimonarchical, the Belgian Revolution consecrated the people's right to rise against, and legitimately depose, a despotic king.[9] This was the premise on which the whole constitutional edifice was constructed.[10] It comes, therefore, as no surprise that the Congress promulgated its laws and decrees "in the name of the Belgian people". Every power held by the provisional government and the National Congress was legitimate only insofar as they represented the interests of the Belgian people.

The introduction of royal inviolability and ministerial responsibility, in combination with the attribution of all residual powers to the Chamber of Representatives, was the keystone of the system (Alen, 1992, p. 4; Clement and Vande Putte, 2018). As a result, the monarch was relegated to a mere constituted power (Deseure, 2016b). The introduction of popular sovereignty in Belgium signalled the end of the monarchical principle (see Chapter 2). The locus of power shifted from the king's government to the representative body, via such constitutional guarantees as royal inviolability, ministerial responsibility, and the

8 Cf. popular sovereignty in the French July Revolution: Barbé (1904); Rosanvallon (1994, p. 175).

9 On the republican movement in the Belgian Revolution: De Mulder (1970); Witte (2020).

10 A preamble to the constitution containing a legitimation of the Belgian Revolution was planned but never realised (Huyttens, 1844b, pp. 590–592, session of 24 February 1831). See also Magits (1977, pp. 398–399); Deseure (2016a, p. 32); Meulebrouck (2017, pp. 777–785).

annual vote on the budget. What is more, the wish of the people became the ultimate ground for legitimate government.[11] Nothomb's quote implied, indeed, that despotic or non-constitutional governments would inevitably meet the same fate as the Dutch regime and perish at the hands of the people. Although it was usually filtered and balanced by the institutions of the constitutional monarchy, the people did retain its natural right of resistance in the extreme case of monarchical despotism. Moderate liberals, liberal Catholics, and 'radical democratic' republicans alike adhered to this principle. Popular sovereignty, therefore, reflected the core characteristics of the Belgian institutional system of 1831 and echoes the terms used by the founding fathers.

The newspapers show a similar picture. Contrary to the congressmen, journalists were rather keen to discuss issues of sovereignty, including the formulation of article 25. Editorial pieces with titles like 'On the sovereignty of the people' or 'Where does sovereignty reside?' were a familiar sight in the newspaper columns of November and December 1830. These discussions were not an exercise in abstract reasoning. They came about in the context of concrete political and institutional questions. The debates on the form of government (monarchy vs. republic) and bicameralism were especially likely to generate reflection on sovereignty. Once these key institutional features were decided upon, the sovereignty discussion lessened in intensity, only to flare up occasionally on a matter such as suffrage or the inauguration of the regency.

In spite of ideological controversy, all newspapers agreed that there was no denying the principle of popular sovereignty in the Belgian Revolution. This was true in two ways. First, it was the popular will, and only that, which legitimised the foundation of the actual (provisional government and National Congress) and future Belgian institutions. They were invested with the people's sovereign powers, on the condition of faithfully executing the people's will. The *Courier des Pays-Bas* wrote "the people alone has won. It has been called, via its representatives, to sovereignly decide on the constitution that will govern it" (*CDPB*, 11 October 1830, no. 284). The people's victory was there to dispel any illusions the monarchs might still have about their claims to divine right. A similar view was defended by *Le Belge*: "Today, sovereignty resides in the people, who exercises it by way of its representatives" (*BEL*, 14 November 1830, no. 287). Anyone who claimed to speak in the name of the people before it had had the chance to pronounce on the question at hand via its representatives violated popular sovereignty. The newspapers insisted that the National Congress wielded sovereign power in the name of the people. The *Courrier des Pays-Bas* declared "The nation has delegated the exercise of its full powers to the Congress; everything

11 The congressmen do not seem to have clearly distinguished between national 'will', 'wish', or 'interest'. We argue that the term 'national wish' – which attributes a certain latitude in the representatives' decisional autonomy, without entirely dissociating the link between their decisions and the will of their constituents – more accurately expresses the founding fathers' view than the 'national will'. On the origin of the distinction, see Grange (1974, pp. 267–272).

emanating from the Congress must be considered to emanate from the nation itself" (*CDPB*, 4 February 1831, no. 35).

Second, the principle of popular sovereignty was understood to be the basis of all future Belgian governments. Following the revolution's popular origins, non-popular sources of power were ruled out. Monarchical sovereignty in particular was disavowed. Monarchy as an instrument of government was not rejected (except by the more radical newspapers) as long as it remained true to its popular origins. As early as 1829, *Le Belge* explained that, according to natural law, sovereignty resided in the nation, a principle which was unanimously accepted by publicists and taught by professors in the state universities of the United Kingdom. A government that ruled by executive decisions going against the national interests could not rightly be believed to uphold the popular principle (*BEL*, 25 September 1829, no. 268). This also meant, according to the expectations of the newspaper, that the balance of powers was to shift towards the representative body. All newspapers agreed that popular sovereignty implied government based on the will of the nation. In practice, this entailed that future governments should govern by the majority principle. A letter to the *Journal des Flandres* expressed it as follows:

> The people has the constitutional right to bind the ministry, to impede the march of the state and to immobilise the government's possibilities for action; in other words, the people is constitutionally entitled to indirectly overturn the government; so ultimately, the people remains the only sovereign.
>
> (*JDF*, 28 November 1830, no. 329)

'Emanating' powers

Although the term 'popular sovereignty' was omnipresent in both the constituent debates of the National Congress and public debates, it is important not to project our contemporary understanding of the concept back in time. As is shown elsewhere in this book, a semantic difference between the terms 'popular' and 'national sovereignty' was not yet present in 1830. Els Witte has pointed out that the political terminology used in the run-up to the Revolution was often vague and semantically underdetermined and that this was true for popular sovereignty as well as for other terms.[12] Like the leading political theorists of their age (including Sieyès, Constant, and Guizot), Belgian congressmen and journalists routinely used the terms interchangeably. This finding explains seeming inconsistencies, such as the National Congress issuing decrees "in the name of the Belgian people" while simultaneously writing into the Constitution that all powers 'emanate from the nation' or the substitution of 'nation' for 'people' in

12 On the eve of the Belgian Revolution, the term 'nation' was central to political discourse in the newspapers. It was bound up with notions of a common language and freedom. It was often liberally connoted, referring to constitutional monarchy, popular sovereignty, and representative government (Witte, 2006).

the constitution's (non-binding) Dutch translation (Witte, 2018; Clement and Vande Putte, 2018). Nevertheless, it does not tell us whether or not the *concept* of national sovereignty informed the founding fathers' deliberations. To find this out, this section looks closely at the debates concerning article 25.

Central to the controversy is the first section of article 25: "All powers emanate from the Nation". Like most of the constitution's articles, it was copied from an older example, in this case, article 2 of the French Constitution of 1791. Given the passage of time and the completely different constitutional context (note the absence of article 1 of the same constitution, which contained an explicit definition of sovereignty), it cannot be supposed that the conception of sovereignty operative in the French Constitution was simply transplanted to Belgium in 1830 (Geenens and Sottiaux, 2015, p. 302; Marteel, 2018, p. 291; cf. Chapter 15). In the absence of explicit debate on the article's formulation in Congress, the newspapers will be our main source of evidence.

Ideological controversy first flared up at the beginning of November 1830, after the publication of the draft constitution by the Constitutional Commission. Across the board, the newspapers took article 6 of the draft constitution (what would first become the constitution's article 25 and is currently article 33) as a recognition of the revolutionary principle of popular sovereignty. The conservative *Courrier de la Meuse* even discerned the spectre of direct democracy in the article, of which it feared the destructive and possibly despotic results (*CDM*, 4 November 1830, no. 266). The progressive Catholic publicists Adrien and Victor Dechamps shared these fears and suggested reformulating the article to read "power must be founded on the general consent of the nation" (*EMP*, 20 November 1830, no. 31). Journals on the far left, on the other hand, applauded the article's radical potential, warning those in power not to sideline the people since it alone was sovereign. *L'Émancipation* underlined the people's position as the source of the National Congress' mandate, over which it kept a watchful eye: "The people has chosen you, your every act must first be submitted to it; remember that it is sovereign, that from it alone emanate all powers" (*EMP*, 2 November 1830, no. 13).

Most newspapers, however, read both popular sovereignty and the need for representation in the article. For *Le Vrai Patriote*, the article meant that the people chose representatives to exercise sovereignty in its name (*VP*, 12 November 1830, no. 272). The *Courrier des Pays-Bas* and *Le Politique* both stressed election and delegation of power as the means to make power emanate from below: "Direct elections, the right of all in the enlightened classes to cast votes, an immense latitude in the choice of deputies: this is how to ascertain the country's real wish. A government that must emanate from the national opinion" (*POL*, 16 October 1830, no. 252).

In a few instances, the difference between 'emanate from' and 'reside in' was explicitly discussed. The anonymous author of a letter published in the Catholic and republican *Journal des Flandres* expected the National Congress to rephrase the article in reaction to the draft's 'aristocratic' character. It judged that 'emanate' was too general and vague a formulation and would probably be found unsatisfactory (*JDF*, 29 November 1830, no. 330). Despite its radical profile, the *Courrier de la Sambre* preferred the first formulation. It agreed with the tacit assumption of the *Courrier des Pays-Bas* and *Le Politique* that 'emanate' implied the necessity of delegation since it was impossible for the whole people to directly exercise its powers. This did not diminish the reality of popular sovereignty in any way, the newspaper asserted: "Sovereign power, which means legislative, executive and juridical power, belongs to the people; its exercise emanates directly from it" (*CDLS*, 17 November 1830, no. 195).

The radical *L'Émancipation* was the only newspaper to outright reject article 6. In an inflammatory article titled 'On the sovereignty of the people', it expressed great concern with the conservative character of the draft constitution, calling it a "gothic and fatal project" (*EMP*, 15 November 1830, no. 26). The newspaper especially objected to the formulation of the 'inane' article 6:

> This proposal has perfidiously been thrown in the draft, in the hope that we would be simple enough to believe that it equalled declaring that sovereignty essentially resides in the nation. However, the difference is immense, especially in its consequences.
>
> (*EMP*, 15 November 1830, no. 26)

The newspaper maintained that this formulation could serve as a cover for any kind of restorative or reactionary regime because of the vagueness it introduced into the relationship between the origin and the execution of power: "If necessary, even Mr. Metternich himself, the champion of European despotism, could agree to this declaration" (*EMP*, 15 November 1830, no. 26). To really declare popular sovereignty, 'emanate' needed to be changed to 'reside'.[13] That said, the journal did not object to the use of the term 'nation', indicating that there was no particular sensitivity concerning this term.

The republican newspaper was nevertheless careful to explain that it did not condemn representation per se. In a response to accusations made by the reactionary *Courrier de la Meuse*, it denied that the popular sovereignty it defended equalled the tyranny of the masses. On the contrary, the newspaper explained, its adversary made the mistake of confounding the origin and the execution of sovereign power:

> they imagine that, when we ask that the people be sovereign, we ask that it be magistrate and judge at the same time, or in other words, that it must itself execute the general will or the law, at the risk of staying in a perpetual state of anarchy.
>
> (*EMP*, 15 November 1830, no. 26)

13 Afterwards, the newspaper changed its stance and recognised the article as an incarnation of popular sovereignty: *EMP* (2 November 1830, no. 13).

Division of power, political representation, and the rule of law were in no way precluded by a regime of popular sovereignty, the newspaper argued. The sovereign people only disposed of the legislative power, which was nothing more than the expression of the indivisible general will: "the sovereign has no other power than the legislative one, which is simply the general will, and evidently the general will can only exist in the generality, i.e., in the universality of the nation" (*EMP*, 15 November 1830, no. 26). According to this reading, popular sovereignty implied self-government by means of the elected representatives of the nation, not mob rule.

Nation and people

In short, all newspapers interpreted the formulation of article 6 of the draft constitution as a recognition of popular sovereignty. Moreover, most newspapers understood it to imply the principle of representation. But whereas the wording 'emanate' elicited debate between the newspapers, the term 'nation' did not. The meaning assigned to the terms 'nation' and 'people' was never an object of debate. A year prior to the Revolution, *Le Belge* had designated "all the citizens of the same country that live by the same laws" as a people, and it went on to assert that "In the same sense we have claimed that, according to natural law, sovereignty resides in the people or, if you prefer, the nation" (*BEL*, 3 October 1829, no. 276). All in all, like *Le Belge*, the other newspapers offer no indication that these terms designated conceptually different, let alone opposite, beings.

What can be ascertained, nevertheless, is that 'nation' and 'people' had different connotations. For instance, the *Courrier des Pays-Bas* wrote:

> two beings which were essentially the same, under two different forms of existence: the nation, in other words, the people, and the national representation, in other words, the people again, but acting in an agreed-upon form to facilitate the exercise of its will.
>
> (*CDPB*, 17 November 1830, no. 321 – see Chapter 9 for a detailed discussion)

After defining 'the people' thus, the newspaper, tending towards progressive liberalism, did not need to shy away from using the word continuously. *Le Politique* mocked *L'Émancipation* for its overabundant use of the word 'people' – it was said to use the word every second sentence – and claimed that it did so in a conscious attempt to stimulate the acceptance of a republican discourse (*POL*, 7 January 1831, no. 6). Like the other radical newspapers, *L'Émancipation* indeed capitalised on the double meaning of the word. When moderate newspapers referenced 'the people', they usually meant the population at large or, in other words, the nation, but the republican newspapers simultaneously hinted at 'the common people'. For example, a noteworthy article in *Le Belge* argued that

> neither the rich merchants nor the great landowners have made our glorious revolution; it was the people who did it; it was the middle classes who

prevailed; therefore, the people has to be awarded a bigger part of the fruits of victory.

(*BEL*, 15 October 1830, no. 288)

The conservative *Courrier de la Meuse* used 'people' in the same sense when interpreting popular sovereignty as "that monstrous sovereignty which runs the streets with torch in hand, living off disorder alone" (*CDM*, 15 July 1831, no. 169). *Le Politique* was clearly uneasy about this double connotation. Hardly a week after the declaration of Belgian independence, it wrote that the Revolution was over and that the people needed to retreat from direct intervention in politics in an editorial that displayed typical liberal fears of popular despotism: "The people's day is [...] over in Belgium; decisions on the last difficulties must now be left to cabinet men and to the new deputies about to be elected by the people" (*POL*, 13 October 1830, no. 249).

With the Terror in mind, the bourgeoisie were fearful of popular despotism; a sensitivity reflected in the different connotations of the terms 'people' and 'nation'. Although it was used continuously in both the public and constituent debates, 'people' was substituted for 'nation' in legal discourse. Possibly, the Constitutional Commission preferred to use the term 'nation' in article 25 because it had a less active and direct ring to it, precluding any suggestions of mass democracy. Or it may have preferred, for reasons of time and space, to simply copy the sentence from the French Constitution of 1791 and leave discussion over the finer terminological points to the National Congress. Nonetheless, the difference was anything but absolute, as the common synonymous usage of both terms in the debates illustrates.

What was clearly absent, however, was any sort of reference to the nation as an abstract or transgenerational being distinct from the set of citizens that composed it at that point in time. In fact, the congressmen showed abundant consciousness of acting according to the will of the concrete nation, which they identified with the insurgent Belgian population. The institution of the National Congress was indeed the immediate result of the nation manifesting its wishes in its revolt against the Dutch regime. Charles de Brouckère explained that

as an insurgent people we demand the territory on which we exist; as a new people we need no antecedent in order to exist and to have a nationality as long as those who compose it agree to form a nation.

(Huyttens, 1844c, p. 532, 8 July 1831, C. de Brouckère)

The nation was conceived as a natural collective (i.e. preceding institutional organisation), consisting of all the individuals in a particular territory, who, while occupying different positions in society, shared the same national identity, past, and traditions and longed for the same thing: liberty and stability.[14]

14 On the characteristics of the Belgian nation as perceived by the congressmen: Gilissen (1952, pp. 82–90); De Dijn (2012).

A direct relationship was, moreover, supposed between the people or nation and the opinion of its representatives (see in detail Chapter 9). The national will expressed by the representatives was none other than the will of the Belgian population. The representatives did not 'find' the will nor 'create' it. Although they were expected to discuss and deliberate on the interests of the country so as to make the best choice, their decisions needed to reflect the majority view present in contemporary society. The *Courrier des Pays-Bas* wrote about the Congress: "its wisdom complies with the expectations of the people and the wish of the immense majority of the nation, of whom it is the exponent" (*CDPB*, 21 November 1830, no. 325). The constituent debates of the National Congress clearly indicate that any regime that did not do this was in immediate danger of being overthrown by the people. As congressman D'Elhounge put it, "Next to the laudable desire to close the revolution by a decree, sits the danger of starting new storms by going against the will of the people who authored it [the Revolution] and by deceiving the country's interests" (Huyttens, 1844c, p. 198, 31 May 1831, D'Elhounge).

This did not mean, however, that the whole population was to participate in the decision-making process (see Chapter 9). The necessity of limiting political participation to society's upper layers was self-evident in mainstream opinion. The exercise of political power by means of direct participation was something that could not be achieved in large modern nations, hence the need for a representative system based on 'direct and popular' elections (Maes, 2018). But although only the elite was called upon to represent the nation, that elite was expected to act in accordance with the will of Belgian society as a whole. *Le Politique* maintained that 'the real will of the people' could only be determined by calling on 'all the enlightened classes of society' so that the government might truly 'emanate from national opinion' (*POL*, 16 October 1830, no. 252). The limitation of political participation was not argued for on the basis of the nation's supposedly abstract or transgenerational character. Rather, an evolutionary perspective was present. In the long run, it could be imagined that the entire adult (male) population was to contribute to the election of its representatives. The difference between voters and non-voters was a gradual and not an essential one. The more society progressed, the more citizens would gain the necessary capacities to qualify as voters. This idea is succinctly expressed by the *Courrier*:

> it is obvious that future legislators, living in a morally and politically progressive society, will successively widen the circle of electoral and elective capacity, and the day will come when the popular masses will be enlightened enough to concur, without exception and without danger, to the election of the deputies.
>
> (*LC*, 28 April 1831, no. 118)[15]

15 On 1 January 1831, the *Courrier des Pays-Bas* changed its title to *Le Courrier*.

The right to vote depended purely on financial and thus moral capacity. In an ideal scenario, the represented nation would coincide almost perfectly with the actual nation.

Dividing power

Despite the newspapers' collective recognition of popular sovereignty, the ideological controversy concerning the nature of that principle and its realisation in practice raged at regular intervals. The moderate or majority view was challenged from the far left as well as the far right. The confrontation between these views reveals an essential characteristic of the majority view, namely its belief in the necessity of limiting sovereignty by dividing it.

The republican movement grew disenchanted with the work of the National Congress as a result of the latter's choice for a monarchical form of government and the introduction of a Senate and a high census restriction on suffrage. In the eyes of the radicals, to restrict suffrage to the social elite was to sap popular sovereignty. *L'Émancipation* bitterly reproached the provisional government for having excluded from political power that part of the population which had actually made the Revolution possible: "you have feared to call to the formation of this Congress precisely that part of the nation which today is in power and speaks as sovereign master" (*EMP*, 30 October 1830, no. 10). More than their moderate liberal counterparts, the radical newspapers identified the people of popular sovereignty with the concrete part of the population which had actively waged the Revolution (Witte, 2020, pp. 138–139). Logically, they expected a widening of the franchise to include at least part of 'the common people'.

For the radicals, the general will was an indivisible whole, as the debate over bicameralism illustrates. This will was to be represented in a unique legislative chamber, which held absolute primacy over the executive and the judicial powers. Consequently, the radical newspapers opposed the introduction of a Senate. Not only was it a mainstay against the popular will, but to entrust the national will to several chambers was to divide that will and thus to alienate it. The *Courrier de la Sambre* wrote, "Sovereignty is divided, or it is partly alienated, and the Congress does not seem to understand that if it had the right to alienate, it can alienate it entirely" (*CDLS*, 8 January 1831, no. 238). Like Rousseau and Sieyès, the radicals were keen to introduce 'unity of action': in order to express the uniform wish of the people, it was essential for the representatives to reach their decision as one single body (Maes, 2020, p. 191–195).

Paradoxically, the radicals' opponents on the far-right side of the spectrum shared this monolithic conception of sovereignty (Deseure, 2016b; Witte, 2018). The reactionary newspaper *Courrier de la Meuse* filled column after column with arguments demonstrating the logical impossibility of popular sovereignty as a principle of government. The newspaper identified sovereignty with ultimate executive power, the origin of which it considered to be divine. Since sovereignty signified ultimate power, it was *a priori* indivisible, the newspaper held. Claiming that sovereignty belonged to the people was an absurdity because it required dividing sovereign power by an infinite number of people. In the end, everyone and no one was sovereign, and chaos would ensue:

> Because all sovereignty is absolute, in the sense that it decides in the last resort and that no one resists it. [...] Sovereignty is here or it is there, but it cannot be in two places at the same time; it cannot be partitioned, it cannot be divided. You can divide it in theory, like Montesquieu does, you can even divide it in our Constitution, but in practice, in the facts, it is indivisible.
> (*CDM*, 3 March 1831, no. 58)[16]

The newspaper directed its critique at the *Courrier*. The centrist newspaper consistently pretended that society could be organised without the institution of a "sovereign and superior power [...], an absolute power who decides in the last resort" (*CDM*, 10 March 1831, no. 59). It even promoted this absence of ultimate power as a guarantee against the kind of power abuse which the Belgians had known under the authoritarian rule of sovereign kings. But according to the *Courrier de la Meuse*, this was a chimera. As long as there was an ultimate sovereign, and this was an inevitable principle of human society, that sovereign would be able to abuse its power.

The *Courrier* reacted by clearly affirming its belief in the divisibility of power as a guarantee against power concentration. Sovereignty meant omnipotent power, but only in its origin. In its execution, it needed to be parcelled out and distributed among the constituted powers. Liberty from oppression was guaranteed by the counterbalancing of these powers. Despotism was precluded by the division of power over a number of institutional players, whose tasks and jurisdiction were carefully set out in the Constitution:

> The limitation of powers lies not in the dependence of powers, as our confrère seems to suppose [...]. It lies in their ponderation, in the partitioning of the power charged with the government of the state. In that system, every power remains independent within the circle provided for it by the constitution; outside of that circle it encounters the action of another power.
> (*LC*, 5 March 1831, no. 64)

At the same time, following Montesquieu's and Constant's socio-historical relativism,[17] the divisibility of state power was to reflect the sociological reality of Belgian society. A separate representation for the aristocracy and the bourgeoisie would bring stability by balancing their respective social interests (De Dijn, 2012; Geenens and Sottiaux, 2015, pp. 312–314).

16 The newspaper even explicitly acknowledged the radicals' viewpoints on this matter: *CDM* (25 November 1830, no. 284) with reference to *L'Émancipation*.
17 See on this relativism e.g. Todorov (1999, pp. 63–64).

It was the question of divisibility, more than any other, that created a fault line within the Belgian sovereignty debate. All political camps shared a concern for liberty and a desire to place limits on the executive as a guarantee against despotism. For the radicals, that guarantee was to be attained by firmly establishing power in the hands of the people. A correct representation of the popular wish through a unicameral system with a large electoral base was the best means of preventing the executive from turning against the people's interests. The conservatives judged that such guarantees and limitations were illusory since sovereign power automatically meant power concentration. The people was just as prone to abusing its power as any other holder of sovereignty (and maybe even more so).

For the moderate liberals, on the other hand, the best guarantee against the abuse of sovereign power was to divide it. *Le Politique* and *Le Courrier des Pays-Bas* demonstrated a distrust of power concentration at any level. Although the centre of gravity in the new state clearly needed to shift to the people's representatives, the popular will was not to reign freely. In response to the idea of introducing a Senate, the *Courrier des Pays-Bas* wrote:

> The existence of a Senate is useful, indispensable even, not in order to resist the wishes of the people's deputies but in order to weaken the dangers of demagogy and to preserve the head of state against the effervescence of parties.
>
> (*CDPB*, 2 December 1830, no. 336)

The moderate liberal newspapers recognised the principle of popular sovereignty, but they distrusted the concept because of its connotation of omnipotence. To ensure the institutional entrenchment of liberty, it was necessary to prevent any group within society from reaching a position that enabled them to seize power. The way to do so was to divide power between rival institutional bodies, which would result in their mutual balance.

Earlier research has shown the founding fathers' fundamental indebtedness to Benjamin Constant's liberal theory of power (Alen, 1992, p. 7; De Smaele, 2005; Van Velzen, 2005; Delbecke, 2010; Marteel, 2011; Maes, 2018). Alongside Montesquieu, Constant was the political philosopher whose authority was most often cited in the National Congress (Barbé, 1904, p. 139; Gilissen, 1967, p. 59). Contrary to Doctrinaire thinkers like Guizot, whose view of sovereignty was entirely negative, Constant stayed true to the notion of popular sovereignty (Geenens and Sottiaux, 2015, p. 308). Nevertheless, he fundamentally mistrusted the concentration of power suggested by the term 'sovereignty' (Brunet, 2004, p. 33). His solution was not to locate sovereign power in any specific group or institution, but instead to divide it over multiple players. Furthermore, he insisted on the population's engagement with the common good and its active surveillance of the constituted powers. Constant's constitutional solutions to this effect are clearly present in the Belgian Constitution (Geenens and Sottiaux, 2015; Marteel, 2018, p. 293).

Conclusion

It is well known that the moderate liberal view won the day in the Belgian constituent debate. The Constitution became a model for continental liberal constitutions for decades to come (Gilissen, 1968, pp. 135–140). Its attractiveness lay in its combination of personal liberties with a government that was politically and legally responsible to the representative body. Typically liberal was the far-reaching division of powers. Although the origin of sovereignty was located in the nation, its execution was divided over several state branches, which were so designed to keep each other in check. Active political involvement was limited to the national elite. High census requirements for suffrage prevented the population at large from intervening in politics.

Political and individual liberty under a stable form of government was the founding fathers' main concern for the regime under construction. In trying to attain it, they needed to navigate between the cliffs of royal despotism on the one hand and popular tyranny on the other. Yet, despite the clearness of their constitutional agenda, they have remained conspicuously silent about key theoretical concepts. Who is the nation? Where is sovereignty located? How does the source of sovereignty relate to its execution? As a result, competing theoretical claims have been made on the meaning of sovereignty in the Belgian Constitution. We hypothesise with André Alen that the Belgian drafters, working against the clock in the middle of a popular revolution, hardly engaged with the abstract and juridical aspects of sovereignty.[18] The liberal opposition was not concerned with the locus of sovereignty. What counted for them was the preservation of individual liberty and the limitation of political power: "Holding your rights from the sovereignty of the people", congressman Destouvelles exclaimed, "you [congressmen] will only conserve them to make [the people] happy, and to let it enjoy this liberty, this wellbeing, for which it has given its blood" (Huyttens, 1844a, p. 308, 24 November 1830, Destouvelles. See also Marteel, 2018, p. 291).

In this contribution, we have tried to elucidate the question by paying renewed attention to the terms and concepts used in the constituent and public debates. Moreover, we have argued that the silences in the constituent debate can be overcome by analysing the newspapers of the day, which often had close ties with the political protagonists. The newspapers treated the same issues as the National Congress but often in more explicit political-theoretical terms.

The debates reveal that a number of rival conceptions of sovereignty existed simultaneously. All recognised that the people henceforward counted as the only source of sovereignty and that the Constitution was based upon that principle. Even those groups which did not support this principle in theory, such as the

18 See e.g. Nothomb's argumentation against abstract theories revolving around the form of state (Huyttens, 1844a, pp. 192, 19 November 1830, Nothomb). See also Alen (1984, vol. 1, p. 207); Geenens and Sottiaux (2015, p. 308); Deseure (2016b, p. 147).

ultramontane Catholics, admitted that it was realised in practice. The main fault line was between a divisible and an indivisible conception of sovereignty.

Mainstream opinion adhered to the former option, allowing for a liberal conception of state power. Inherent to this conception were the representative principle and the restriction of political participation to the competent elite. These restrictions on political freedom were attained without recourse to a conceptual distinction between people and nation. A systematic reading of the constituent and public debates does not allow for a definition of the nation as abstract and transgenerational. Instead, the congressmen acted upon the will of the actual Belgian population, expressed by the representatives elected by its competent elite. Only later was this system legitimated by the theoretical differentiation of nation and people (see Chapter 11). Whereas the contemporary framework of national sovereignty is different from the original conceptualisation of sovereignty, it is largely identical in its results.

In light of the specifically Belgian reception of the concept of sovereignty, it is hardly surprising that the term does not figure in the Constitution or that 'emanate' was preferred over 'reside in'. The Belgian drafters did not view sovereignty positively since they associated it with the misfortunes brought about by omnipotent power. The term's omnipresence in the newspaper debates suggests that its omission from the constitution was a conscious choice by the drafters. The congressmen did not overlook sovereignty but avoided giving it too much prominence.

Bibliography

Alen, A. (1984) *Rechter en bestuur in het Belgische publiekrecht: de grondslagen van de rechterlijke wettigheidskontrole* (2 vols). Antwerp: Kluwer Rechtswetenschappen.

Alen, A. (1992) *Treatise on Belgian Constitutional Law*. Deventer: Kluwer. DOI: 10.1093/iclqaj/42.4.990.

Bacot, G. (1985) *Carré de Malberg et l'origine de la distinction entre souveraineté du peuple et souveraineté nationale*. Paris: CNRS.

Barbé, M. (1904) *Étude historique des idées sur la souveraineté en France de 1815 à 1848*. Paris: Librairie générale de droit et de jurisprudence.

Bourgaux, A.-E. (2013) *La démocratisation du gouvernement représentatif en Belgique: une promesse oubliée* (vol. 1). Unpublished doctoral thesis. Law. Brussels: Université Libre de Bruxelles.

Breunesse, C.J.M. (2014) *'Losgemaakt uit de verdrukking'. Opiniejournalistiek rond de scheiding van Noord en Zuid 1828–1832*. Unpublished doctoral thesis, History. Amsterdam: University of Amsterdam.

Brunet, P. (2004) *Vouloir pour la nation. Le concept de représentation dans la théorie de l'Etat*. Paris: L.G.D.J.

Clement, J. and Vande Putte, M. (2018) 'The Constitution of the Belgian people. The Nation as legitimisation', *Giornale di Storia Costituzionale*, 35(1), pp. 113–128.

De Dijn, A. (2012) 'A Pragmatic Conservatism. Montesquieu and the Framing of the Belgian Constitution (1830–1831)', *History of European Ideas*, 28(4), pp. 227–245.

De Mulder, C. (1970) *De republikeinse beweging in de peiode 1830–1831: haar leiders, haar verenigingen.* Ghent: Rijksuniversiteit Gent.

De Smaele, H. (2005) 'Eclectisch en toch nieuw. De uitvinding van het Belgisch parlement in 1830–1831', *Bijdragen en Mededelingen betreffende de Geschiedenis der Nederlanden*, 120(3), pp. 408–416. DOI: 10.18352/bmgn-lchr.6253.

Delbecke, B. (2010) *De lange schaduw van de grondwetgever. Perswetgeving en persmisdrijven in België, 1831–1914.* Published doctoral thesis, Law. Leuven: KU Leuven.

Descamps-David, E.-D. (1891) *La mosaïque constitutionnelle. Essai sur les sources du texte de la Constitution Belge.* Leuven: Peeters.

Deseure, B. (2016a) 'Constitutional Precedence and the Genesis of the Belgian Constitution of 1831', in Müßig, U. (ed.) *Reconsidering Constitutional Formation.* Berlin: Springer, pp. 211–256. DOI: 10.1007/978-3-319-73037-0_5.

Deseure, B. (2016b) 'National Sovereignty in the Belgian Constitution of 1831. On the Meaning(s) of Article 25', in Müßig, U. (ed.) *Reconsidering Constitutional Formation.* Berlin: Springer, pp. 93–156. DOI: 10.1007/978-3-319-42405-7_2.

Geenens, R. and Sottiaux, S. (2015) 'Sovereignty and Direct Democracy: Lessons from Constant and the Belgian Constitution', *European Constitutional Law Review*, 11, pp. 293–320. DOI: 10.1017/s1574019615000188.

Gilissen, J. (1952) *Le régime représentatif avant 1790 en Belgique.* Brussels: La Renaissance du livre.

Gilissen, J. (1967) 'Die belgische Verfassung von 1831. Ihr Ursprung und ihr Einfluss' in Conze, W. (ed.) *Beiträge zur deutschen und belgischen Verfassungsgeschichte im 19. Jahrhundert.* Stuttgart: E. Klett, pp. 38–69.

Gilissen, J. (1968) 'La Constitution belge de 1831: ses sources, son influence', *Res Publica*, 10, pp. 107–141.

Grange, H. (1974) *Les idées de Necker.* Paris: C. Klincksieck.

Harris, D. (1955) 'European Liberalism in the Nineteenth Century', *The American Historical Review*, 60(3), pp. 501–526.

Huyttens, E. (1844a) *Discussions du Congrès National de Belgique 1830–1831. Tome premier.* Brussels: Société Typographique Belge.

Huyttens, E. (1844b) *Discussions du Congrès National de Belgique 1830–1831. Tome deuxième.* Brussels: Société Typographique Belge.

Huyttens, E. (1844c) *Discussions du Congrès National de Belgique 1830–1831. Tome troisième.* Brussels: Société Typographique Belge.

Huyttens, E. (1844d) *Discussions du Congrès National de Belgique 1830–1831. Tome quatrième.* Brussels: Société Typographique Belge.

Maes, C. (2018) 'The End Justifies the Means. The Nature of Belgium's 1830 Political Liberalism', *Giornale di Storia Costituzionale*, 35(1), pp. 129–145.

Maes, C. (2020) *Het soevereiniteitsbegrip in de Belgische Grondwet van 1831. Een rechtshistorisch onderzoek naar de betekenis van soevereiniteit voor de organisatie van de Belgische staatsmacht.* Unpublished doctoral thesis. Law. Leuven: KU Leuven.

Magits, M. (1977) *De Volksraad en de opstelling van de Belgische Grondwet van 7 februari 1831. Een bijdrage tot de wordingsgeschiedenis van de Belgische Konstitutie.* Brussels: V.U. Brussel.

Marteel, S. (2011) 'Polemieken over natievorming in het Verenigd Koninkrijk der Nederlanden. Een blik op de intellectuele wortels van het Belgisch nationalisme', in Vosters, R. and Weijermars, J. (eds.) *Taal, cultuurbeleid en natievorming onder Willem I.* Brussels: KVAB, pp. 35–59.

Marteel, S. (2018) *The Intellectual Origins of the Belgian Revolution. Political Thought and Disunity in the Kingdom of the Netherlands*, 1815–1830. New York: Springer. DOI: 10.1007/978-3-319-89426-3.

Meulebrouck, M. (2017) 'Een preambule voor de Belgische Grondwet. Constitutionele spitstechnologie of nil novi sub sole?', *Jura Falconis*, 54(4), pp. 757–878.

Rosanvallon, P. (1994) *La monarchie impossible. Les chartes de 1814 et de 1830*. Paris: Fayard.

S.A. (n.d.a.) *Belge, Le* (BEL).

S.A. (n.d.b.) *Courrier, Le* (LC).

S.A. (n.d.c.) *Courrier de la Meuse, Le* (CDM).

S.A. (n.d.d.) *Courrier de la Sambre, Le* (CDLS).

S.A. (n.d.e.) *Courrier des Pays-Bas, Le* (CDPB).

S.A. (n.d.f.) *Émancipation, L'* (EMP).

S.A. (n.d.g.) *Journal des Flandres* (JDF).

S.A. (n.d.h.) *Politique, Le* (POL).

S.A. (n.d.i.) *Vrai Patriote, Le* (VP).

Stevens, F. (1981) 'Een belangrijke faze in de wordingsgeschiedenis van de Belgische grondwet: de optie voor een tweekamerstelsel', *Belgisch Tijdschrift voor Nieuwste Geschiedenis*, 12(3), pp. 641–662.

Todorov, T. (1999) *A Passion for Democracy. Benjamin Constant*. New York: Algora Publishers.

Van Den Steene, W. (1963) *De Belgische Grondwetscommissie (oktober-november 1830). Tekst van haar notulen en ontstaan van de Belgische Grondwet*. Brussels: Koninklijke Vlaamse academie voor wetenschappen, letteren en schone kunsten van België.

Van Velzen, P.L.G. (2005) *De ongekende ministeriële verantwoordelijkheid, theorie en praktijk 1813–1840*. Nijmegen: Wolf Legal Publishers.

Vermeersch, A.J. (1981) *Ontstaan, personele en structurele ontwikkeling van de Brusselse opiniepers en haar verhouding tot de regering van het Verenigde Koninkrijk der Nederlanden : 1814–1830*. Unpublished doctoral thesis, History. Ghent: UGent.

Viaene, V. (2001) *Belgium and the Holy See from Gregory XVI to Pius IX (1831–1859). Catholic Revival, Society and Politics in 19th-Century Europe*. Leuven: Leuven University Press.

Witte, E. (1980) 'Changes in the Belgian Elite in 1830. A Provisional Study', in Jansen, H.P.H. et al. (eds.) *The Low Countries History Yearbook. Acta Historiae Neerlandicae*. The Hague: Nijhoff, pp. 90–113. DOI: 10.1007/978-94-009-8358-8_6.

Witte, E. (2005) 'La Construction de la Belgique. 1828–1847', in Witte, E., Gubin, E., Nandrin, J.-P., and Deneckere, G. (eds.) *Nouvelle Histoire de Belgique*. Brussels: Editions Complexe.

Witte, E. (2006) 'Het natiebegrip in het zuidelijke krantendiscours aan de vooravond van de Belgische opstand (augustus 1829-juli 1830)', *Bijdragen en Mededelingen betreffende de Geschiedenis der Nederlanden*, 121(2), pp. 222–239. DOI: 10.18352/bmgn-lchr.6395.

Witte, E. (2018) 'Republic and Popular Sovereignty. The Belgian Case: 1830–1831', *Giornale di Storia Costituzionale*, 35(1), pp. 89–112.

Witte, E. (2020) *Belgische republikeinen. Radicalen tussen twee revoluties (1830–1850)*. Antwerp: Polis.

Publications without a specific, personal author (such as newspapers and official documents) are listed under S.A.

9 Belgium's 1831 representative system

Making representation national again[1]

Christophe Maes and Brecht Deseure

Introduction

In Chapter 8, we argued that sovereignty in the Belgian Constitution did not conform to the definition of national sovereignty set forth by Raymond Carré de Malberg. In a nutshell, this view of national sovereignty presupposes exclusive representation by political representatives and excludes the direct involvement of non-elected citizens in the political decision-making process. Yet, as is argued in Chapters 10 and 11 of this book, this definition of national sovereignty had not been formulated in 1830 and was therefore unknown to the founding fathers. Since national sovereignty implies a specific concept of representation, this finding has important implications for the understanding of representative government in Belgium.[2] Questions arise regarding the soundness of the historical reading of the (intellectual) origins of Belgium's representative government. Was the choice for representation generally accepted, and did it necessarily entail elections? Did the model of representative government presuppose the existence of a will to be represented? Or did the representative bodies exclusively create the national will? Furthermore, to what extent were the representatives independent in the exercise of their 'representative mandate'?

In this chapter, we address these questions by re-evaluating the representative system elaborated by the Belgian founding fathers between November 1830 and July 1831. The constituent debates in the National Congress will be our main source. When the constituent debates remain silent, as they do on certain aspects of the representative system and almost completely on the understanding of

1 This chapter is based on C. Maes and B. Deseure (2020), '"The Nation will always prevail". Representation, participation and contestation in the Belgian Constitution of 1831', *Tijdschrift voor Rechtsgeschiedenis - Legal History Review*, 88 (3-4), pp. 495–531. DOI: 10.1163/15718190-00880A10. We are grateful to the editors of *Tijdschrift voor Rechtsgeschiedenis - Legal History Review* for their kind permission to (partly) republish the article in this book.

2 For the contrast between Carré de Malberg's understanding of the representative government and the Doctrinaires' understanding: Rosanvallon (1989); Krulic (2007).

sovereignty, we turn to the press of the day for further evidence (see Chapter 8 for an overview of the consulted newspapers).

In the first section, we will argue that the founding fathers strove to make representation 'national', i.e. reflective of the whole of the Belgian community. In doing so, they subscribed to an understanding of representation that was close to, but not identical with, the modern one (cf. *infra*). This probably explains why the Belgian doctrine later resorted to Carré de Malberg's definition of represented sovereignty, which was based on his analysis of the French Constitution of 1791. We will examine the scope of the representative mandate and question whether representation necessarily entailed elections. In the second section, we will argue that the founding fathers furthermore aimed to make the representative institutions 'genuinely' national. They were concerned that the wishes and the interests of the actual nation, i.e. the population at large, should not be substituted for the wishes of the representatives or the government. In the third section, we will investigate the participation channels that enabled the existence of a reflexive relation between the legal order and the public sphere. The representative institutions were embedded within a specific framework that allowed for participation and permanent contestation by public opinion, an aspect of Belgium's representative system which has largely been overlooked by the Belgian doctrine and which we aim to foreground again with this chapter.

As we have seen in Chapter 8, not only did the Belgian founding fathers recognise popular sovereignty, but most of them also understood it to imply representation. In order to operationalise the exercise of sovereignty, they advocated a model of representative government that expressed the national wish in a continuous way, thereby substantiating the principles of reason, justice, and liberty.[3] For many congressmen, a representative system based on 'direct and popular' elections was a *conditio sine qua non* for the new legal order (Maes, 2018). The people's direct participation in public affairs (known from the republics of antiquity) had become obsolete in the modern age. The congressmen agreed that, in modern times, delegation of power and representative institutions were key (Huyttens, 1844a, p. 198, 19 November 1830, Destriveaux; Huyttens, 1844a, p. 212, 20 November 1830, Devaux; Huyttens, 1844b, p. 28, 6 January 1831, Defacqz). Even the radical and republican members admitted that no state system was feasible without representation (Huyttens, 1844a, pp. 249–250, 22 November 1830, Goffint; Huyttens, 1844a, p. 197, 22 November 1830, Lardinois; Huyttens 1844a, pp. 196–197, 19 November 1830, Seron; Huyttens, 1844a, p. 253, 22 November 1830, Seron; Huyttens, 1844a, p. 228,

3 The congressmen do not seem to have clearly distinguished between national 'will', 'wish', or 'interest'. We argue that the term national wish – which attributes a certain latitude in the representatives' decisional autonomy, without entirely dissociating the link between their decisions and the will of their constituents – more accurately expresses the founding fathers' view than the 'national will'. On the origin of the distinction, see Grange (1974, pp. 267–272)

20 November 1830, De Robaulx). The influential moderate liberal newspaper *Courrier des Pays-Bas* characterised representation in striking terms:

> two beings which were essentially the same, under two different forms of existence: the nation, in other words the people, and the national representation, in other words, the people again, but acting in an agreed-upon form, to facilitate the exercise of its will.
>
> (*CDPB*, 17 November 1830, no. 321)

This conception of representation clearly indicates an organic identification between the people and its representatives. At the same time, it shows that this identification was not complete: representation facilitated the exercise of the will. In other words, it was a means to channel the nation's will, thereby effectively constituting the nation internally.[4] Although the people continued to be the original holders of sovereign power, it delegated the execution to its ordinary (legislative assembly) or extraordinary (National Congress) representatives. In principle, the nation could directly intervene in its affairs, but from a practical and normative point of view this was undesirable.

A modern understanding of representation

The new institutions of the Belgian state were conceived as a true national representation, based on the liberal ideals of liberty and political equality. This was a conscious reaction against the perceived 'corruption' of representation under the previous regime, which was marked by the absence of ministerial responsibility, indirect elections, and separate representation for the nobility.[5] In order for representation to be national, social orders and privileges were eliminated, and every citizen (theoretically) obtained access to public positions. However, the exclusion of corporate interests and social orders necessitated a redefinition of representation. In carrying out this task, the Belgian founding fathers were influenced by the modern understanding of representation inherent to the French Constitution of 1791 and subsequently elaborated by French Doctrinaire thinkers (Foriers, 1981, pp. 16–17; Velu, 1997, pp. 599–600). Nevertheless, as we will show, a number of important differences existed.

4 "The Belgians, freed from the odious domination of the Nassaus, have constituted themselves as a nation" (Huyttens, 1844b, p. 138, 13 January 1831, Masbourg). In a letter to *Courrier des Pays-Bas*, Lebeau asserted that the country was internally constituted, since the moment of the election of the Congress, which functioned as national representation. Letter of Lebeau of 14 May 1831, published in *CDPB* (16 May 1831, no. 136).

5 Lebeau spoke of a "bastard system of representative government" (Huyttens, 1844a, p. 518, 16 December 1830, Lebeau). See also Huyttens (1844a, p. 661, 27 December 1830, Le Hon). *Le Belge* and *Le Politique* spoke of a "denaturation" of the constitutional regime (*BEL*, 29 November 1829, no. 333; *POL*, 10 February 1831, no. 35).

Legal scholars and historians have argued that the 1791 Constitution disconnected the representative function from elections (Alen, 1984, pp. 482–484; Bacot, 1985, pp. 85–87; Rosanvallon, 1989, pp. 415–416; Velu, 1997, p. 600; Brunet, 2012, pp. 625–631). This meant that it was no longer a matter of knowing *who* was to be represented (individuals, social groups, professions), but rather *what* was to be represented (the common good or interests).[6] The essential criterion of the new understanding of representation thus became the selection procedure that guaranteed that representatives would act in conformity with the nation's interests. The manner in which the representatives were appointed, i.e. through elections, consequently became less important than the function that they performed, which consisted of discerning the nation's interests and acting accordingly. Deputies were national representatives because they represented the nation's interests, not necessarily because they were elected (Rosanvallon, 1989, pp. 415–420; Gueniffey, 1993, p. 17). This 'virtual representation' was further established with the abolition of the imperative mandate, which had previously tied the representatives to the (often divergent) instructions of their constituents and thereby impeded the political unification of the nation. The elimination of binding instructions from the electorate enabled the representatives to grasp the general interest via mutual deliberation and, in turn, to speak for the collective.[7] Through this representative action the nation was politically constituted and gained its legal personality.

In Belgium, such a conception of representation had already been in circulation in the decade prior to the 1830 Revolution.[8] The dissociation of representation from elections then reappeared in the 1831 constitutional system.[9] Unquestionably, elections were by far preferred over heredity or divine origin as the essential legitimating principle on which the formation and the working of public authority hinged.[10] In addition, elections provided for a procedure of selection and even purification, while at the same time symbolising the idea of the consent to power as well as equality and participation (Rosanvallon, 1989, p. 417). Thought to generate a sense of obligation and commitment towards the elected officeholders, elections also had the advantage, from the point of

6 The distinction had already appeared during the American Revolution in the debates between the federalists and anti-federalists (Brunet, 2012, pp. 625–627).

7 Thus, the abolition of the imperative mandate had a practical purpose and was not the direct or mechanical consequence of the "choice for a one and indivisible sovereignty of the nation" (Troper, 1996, pp. 179–192; Brunet, 2012, p. 628).

8 Referring to the French revolutionary politician Pierre Daunou, the newspaper *l'Observateur Belge* mentioned that the representatives had to be "designated or chosen in such a way that they would have by themselves and within themselves the interest, the opinions, the wills of the represented" (*OB*, 1819, vol. 18, p. 407).

9 Old articles 47 and 53 of the Constitution.

10 The Congress voted with a great majority for an elected Senate (130 votes against 40). The Congress even considered the 'election' of the monarch as a crucial legitimating factor: "That he may be our king, not merely by the grace of God [...] but by the election of the representatives of a nation that has conquered its independence" (Huyttens, 1844b, p. 301, 29 January 1831, De Langhe).

view of the represented, of limiting the representatives' power to their term of office (Manin, 1997; for the Belgian case see Bourgaux, 2013, pp. 214–220). For all these reasons, the choice for elections seemed almost self-evident to the founding fathers. Moreover, they wished to replace the 'cascade system' of indirect elections that had prevailed in the United Kingdom of the Netherlands, in which provincial representatives elected the national representatives, with a 'fair' and direct electoral system.[11] A cascade system concentrated power in the hands of the few, discarding the nation's true wish (Lebeau, 1830, p. 70), and it weakened the representative link between the electorate – "the backbone of the nation" – and the representatives (*CDPB*, 2 September 1830, no. 245; *CDPB*, 4 September 1830, no. 247).[12] The congressmen, in contrast, grounded their representative system in directly elected legislative assemblies, expected to act in accordance with the national interest (Huyttens, 1844b, p. 77, 10 January 1831, Van Meenen; Huyttens, 1844d, pp. 72–74, pièce just. no. 54, report Raikem of 24 December 1830; ibid., pièces just. no. 55–56, reports Devaux of 4 December and 11 December 1830). Congressman Charles Le Hon could not have voiced this idea more strongly than when he stated that "the source of all powers resides in the elections" (Huyttens, 1844a, p. 208, 20 November 1830, Lebeau; Huyttens, 1844b, p. 29, 6 January 1831, Le Hon).

But although elections were direct and representation was characterised as 'national', suffrage was far from universal. Census suffrage enfranchised less than 1% of the population (Witte, 2005b, pp. 90–91). The governing representatives in the chambers could not claim to represent the nation on the basis of election, as only a slight fraction of the population had participated in it. If sovereignty had exclusively depended on elections, the congressmen should have opted for universal suffrage instead of census-based suffrage. Instead, the electors themselves exercised a representative function since they were supposed to speak for the nation at large when electing national representatives (Huyttens, 1844b, pp. 532–533, 16 February 1831, Van Meenen).

Radical deputies criticised the very exclusive version of censitary suffrage promoted by moderate liberal and Catholic deputies. The democratic radicals denounced the provisional government – which had organised the constituent elections – for having excluded the part of the population which had most actively engaged in the Revolution (Huyttens, 1844b, p. 532, 16 February 1831, A. Rodenbach. See also *EMP*, 30 October 1830, no. 10). Republican congressman De Robaulx virulently attacked the advocates of the high census restriction on suffrage, accusing them of intentionally substituting the people's will with their own (Huyttens, 1844b, p. 640, 2 March 1831, De Robaulx).

11 See the discussion on the nomination of the senators (Huyttens, 1844a, pp. 508–523, session of 16 December 1830; Huyttens, 1844b, p. 28, 6 January 1831, Defacqz).

12 See also *Handelingen van de regering* (1842, pp. 437–439); Bourgaux (2013, p. 307 with fn. 1412). French Doctrinaire thought, on the other hand, repudiated indirect elections for a different reason, namely the non-transferability of electoral capacity from a secondary electorate to a primary one (Roels, 1982, pp. 163–164).

Radicals like De Robaulx firmly rejected the idea that the electorate exercised a function. Following their claim that the constitutional principle of equality before the law also entailed social equality, they considered representative agency as the exercise of a collective right of the nation (Huyttens, 1844b, p. 533, 16 February 1831, De Robaulx). Accordingly, they conceived the relation between the representatives and their constituents as a contractual one.[13]

Nevertheless, none of the radicals advocated universal suffrage. They saw suffrage restrictions as a necessary evil that made representation effective and enabled the expression of the national wish in practice. Consequently, the limitation of suffrage was considered legitimate on the condition that it be liberal enough to include a substantial part of the population (Huyttens, 1844b, p. 533, 16 February 1831, De Robaulx).[14] Although only the enlightened social elite was called upon to represent the nation, most revolutionaries believed that the ensuing concentration of intelligence would ensure that government acted in accordance with the will of Belgian society as a whole.[15] It was thought that an uneven distribution of intelligence over the nation meant that not everyone had the capacity to participate in public affairs.[16] Financial and moral independence, and a certain degree of enlightenment, were deemed indispensable prerequisites for the accurate representation of the nation's interests.[17] The discrimination between voters and non-voters was not written in stone, however. Leading liberal publicist and founding father Joseph Lebeau asserted that the more society advanced, the more the census suffrage restrictions would be lowered (Huyttens,

13 Anne-Emmanuelle Bourgaux has deduced from these and other interventions in Congress, as well as from former political practice in Belgium, that the congressmen generally understood their representative function in a contractual fashion, resulting in an ambiguous representative link (Bourgaux, 2013, pp. 293–320).

14 At the same time, the republicans maintained that the representative institutions should concentrate the most enlightened and virtuous citizens in their midst; e.g. congressman Lardinois rejoiced over the fact that the Congress was "composed of the elite of the nation, that it is filled with enlightenment, pure intentions and insight into the public good" (Huyttens, 1844b, p. 91, 11 January 1831, Lardinois). For De Robaulx, see the closing words in his plea for a republic: "I vote for the republic because it is the triumph of capacity and of virtue" (Huyttens, 1844a, p. 255, 22 November 1830, De Robaulx).

15 "Governments belong to capacity, to intelligence" (Huyttens, 1844a, p. 263, 23 November 1830, C. Rodenbach); "it is within the legislative power that you will find the best capacity" (Huyttens, 1844a, p. 702, 29 December 1830, C. de Brouckère); "The representative government is the government of capacity. One must take it wherever one finds it" (Huyttens, 1844a, p. 700, 29 December 1830, Lebeau).

16 The discussion over the uneven distribution of intelligence and capacity among the population confirms that the revolutionaries conceived of the nation as a heterogeneous, hierarchical entity, in contrast to Carré de Malberg's understanding.

17 "Property is the basis of the census; the payment of the census concerns the prosperity of the country: the census must be paid in order to exercise the citizen's most precious right" (Huyttens, 1844b, p. 30, 6 January 1831, Le Hon).

1844b, p. 535, 17 February 1831, Lebeau).[18] Ideally, the congressmen believed, society would advance to a point where suffrage restrictions were abolished.[19]

Old article 32 of the Constitution provides another indicator of the Congressmen's modern understanding of national representation (i.e. detached from elections). The article, which implies the rejection of the imperative mandate, states that "The members of the two Chambers represent the Nation, and not only the province or the subdivision of the province which appointed them".[20] The Congressmen's resistance against insistent expressions of popular will in the course of the Revolution makes clear that the representatives alone – taken from the most intelligent among the people and continuously deliberating in conformity with the nation's interests – were supposed to express the nation's wish.[21]

Finally, the idea that representation did not presuppose elections surfaced in the congressional debates regarding the role of the monarch. A large majority of congressmen endorsed a model of mixed government that combined the elective (the legislative chambers) and hereditary principles (the monarch) in the legislative decision-making process (old article 26). In the case of the French Constitution of 1791, the National Constituent Assembly had refused to admit the king as a co-legislator. Gradually, and out of conceptual necessity, the French revolutionaries attributed a representative role to the king.[22] Yet, his participation in the legislative power and his representative function were explained in a merely mechanical fashion and he remained entirely subordinate to the *Corps Législatif*. The Belgian congressmen went further than this by accepting the king as a genuine national representative who acted on the same representative level as the other two organs of the legislative branch (Chamber and Senate). Since the monarch disposed of the right of legislative initiative (old article 27), the absolute legislative veto (old article 69), and the right to disband the legislative chambers (old article 71), he could effectively steer the national wish in a certain direction when he believed that the representative chambers neglected their representative task:

18 It was generally recognised that many aspects of the governmental form were to be built upon principles that were accommodated to the 'needs of the era' (Huyttens, 1844a, p. 192, 19 November 1830, Nothomb).

19 "the day will come when the popular masses will be enlightened enough to participate without any exception, and without danger, to the election of the representatives" (*CDPB*, 28 April 1831, no. 118).

20 Actual article 42.

21 See esp. the discussion between Constantin Rodenbach and Lucien Jottrand (Huyttens, 1844a, p. 268, 23 November 1830, Rodenbach; compare with Huyttens, 1844a, pp. 280–281, 23 November 1830, Jottrand).

22 In order to defend himself against the *Corps Législatif*, the monarch was offered a place in the legislative power. Afterwards, when the question of whether to grant him veto-power arose, the only way to account for his place in the legislative power was to admit him as a representative. Note that Carré de Malberg's analysis does not withhold a representative function for the monarch, which has been criticised in French legal scholarship (Brunet, 2002, pp. 41–45; Maulin, 2002).

> Should, hypothetically, a conflict emerge between the two Chambers, the Head of the State will end it the moment he finds it suitable, either by pronouncing the dissolution of a Chamber that is not representing the country's opinion any longer or by breaking the majority of a Senate that is blind enough to remain in rebellion against the wishes of the country.
>
> (Huyttens, 1844a, p. 397, 13 December 1830, De Baillet)[23]

This view was shared by the majority of congressmen. Writing in the context of the Dutch representative system one year earlier, Lebeau had advanced that the monarch's position as national representative entailed a right to dissolve the chambers (Lebeau, 1830, pp. 65 and 67). To this end, the monarch had "the right to know if the opinion of the chambers is the opinion of the voters. If the nation, represented by the voters, thinks like its representatives [députés], the king must yield" (Lebeau, 1830, p. 65). Clearly, Lebeau considered the monarch to be a national representative. At the same time, these passages in Lebeau's work indicate that the representatives did not have a monopoly on the creation of the national wish and that Lebeau did not dissociate the representatives from the electorate's wishes. The monarch, by examining the need for the parliament's dissolution, could indeed determine whether the wish of the electorate *effectively* corroborated the position of the representatives. If that were the case, he had to give way to parliament.[24]

The radical democrats persistently opposed the idea of non-elected representatives. They were convinced that political representation should find its legitimation exclusively in elections and in the indivisibility of the people's power. In short, only elections could provide a government based on popular will. Positioning the monarch next to the people was highly problematic from this perspective (Huyttens, 1844a, pp. 216–217, 20 November 1830, De Haerne; Huyttens, 1844a, p. 226, 20 November 1830, De Robaulx). How could the indivisible sovereign people, personified by the elected representative body, possibly

23 Nothomb equally identified the right of dissolution as "an extreme right to call upon the country". Van Meenen expressed a similar view when he stated that the monarch could never use the right of dissolution against the "manifest wish of the country" (Resp. Huyttens, 1844a, p. 425, 14 December 1830, Nothomb; Huyttens, 1844a, p. 538, 17 December 1830, Van Meenen).

24 Rodenbach affirmed that the monarch could only act as sovereign if he identified himself with the nation by taking the wishes of the people into account. De Mûelenaere shared Rodenbach's mindset when he argued that the royal heir should automatically be made senator. Admitting the future monarch in the Senate would not only get him acquainted with the national institutions but also inform him of "the true interests of the nation". See also Le Hon's intervention, where he argued for a Senate, "established in a fashion that, should there emerge a systematic or hostile resistance against the national wishes or interests, this resistance can be legally stopped or overcome" (Resp. Huyttens, 1844a, p. 549, 18 December 1830, De Mûelenaere; Huyttens, 1844a, p. 492, 15 December 1830, Le Hon; Huyttens, 1844c, p. 138, 25 May 1831, C. Rodenbach).

share its sovereign power with a hereditary monarch? The republicans' key belief was that representation should remain one and indivisible, a belief which they clearly manifested in Congress: "the social unity calls for, commands, even, the unity of representation; one single nation, one unique representation to deliberate about the laws, one single entity to guarantee its execution" (Huyttens, 1844a, p. 493, 15 December 1830, J.-F. Gendebien; Huyttens 1844a, p. 404, 13 December 1830, Van Snick; Huyttens, 1844a, p. 431, 14 December 1830, Seron; Huyttens, 1844a, pp. 439–440, 14 December 1830, Fleussu). Republican congressmen argued that to create another representative alongside parliament was to deprive the nation of its indivisible sovereignty as well as to introduce a logical absurdity: if the people aimed to overthrow the monarch, it would be acting against a representative of the nation – and thus against its own will. Since the interests of both representative actors correlated, why create a third actor in order to defuse a problem that could (at least theoretically) not arise (Huyttens, 1844a, p. 487, 15 December 1830, De Robaulx)?

These arguments illustrate the republicans' monolithic understanding of national representation: the nation, an abstract and universal entity, had but one indivisible will and, as such, it could only be represented by one elected legislative chamber.[25] The radicals' objections were intensely debated in the press, but they were almost completely ignored by the congressmen, who adopted constitutional monarchy with a bicameral legislature by a large majority. The resulting system displayed characteristics of modern representative government: a multiplication of elected or non-elected representative actors with a certain degree of independence in the exercise of their function.

However, neither the choice for a representative form of government, based on an electorate defined by functional criteria nor the rejection of the imperative mandate, stemmed from a preference for 'national sovereignty'. The discussion on the binding nature of the representative mandate was motivated by practical considerations and by fear of popular demagogy in the context of specific debates (such as the exclusion of the Nassau dynasty). The same was true for the choice for a representative government, which was practically uncontested. And in the same vein, the preference for census suffrage was motivated by the idea of capacity and not in any way related to the idea of a holistic, abstract nation.

A genuine representation of the nation

As shown above, the modern understanding of representation clearly influenced the Belgian founding fathers. There are, however, important differences. In the modern conception of representation, where the nature of representation is

25 Jottrand described the monocameralist understanding of the nation as "a homogenous whole without sharp division of caste or interest" (Huyttens, 1844a, p. 508, 16 December 1830, Jottrand). Note that the majority of the unicameralists were republicans (see esp. Huyttens, 1844a, p. 501, session of 15 December 1830).

virtual, representatives no longer depend on their constituents: since the representatives are constitutionally appointed to represent the nation, their power is almost automatically justified. Yet, as we have seen, the Belgian revolutionaries did not believe that the representation of the nation came down to an unlimited and unaccountable exercise of political power in the name of the sovereign people. Indeed, those who exercised sovereignty did not have any actual rights to sovereignty itself. In the Belgian Revolution, this was not merely a theoretical consideration.

The Belgian founding fathers were concerned that the representative system would not effectively represent the actual nation and its collective interest. This concern was the logical outcome of a long advocacy under Dutch rule for proportionate representation, that is, for representation corresponding to the actual distribution of the population.[26] This confirms yet again that they did not understand the nation as an abstract being that was conceptually distinct from the contemporary population (De Smaele, 2002, p. 20). If such were the case, the exact composition of the National Congress would have mattered less than it did. As it was, public debate regularly ensued over supposed flaws in the national representation caused by an inaccurate repartition of votes.[27]

Furthermore, the revolutionaries did not perceive the representative institutions in the constituted order as fully autonomous 'producers' of a national wish.[28] Unquestionably, the agency of the nation was achieved through its representatives, who 'filtered' and exteriorised the people's wishes and interests. But representation did not mean that the representatives expressed their own will in the name of an abstract and timeless nation. Although they were expected to discuss and deliberate about the interests of the country in order to make the best choices, their decisions still needed to reflect the majority view present in contemporary society.

In other words, the representatives did not construct the popular will *ex nihilo*. The nation – a substantial yet rudimentary and collective entity composed of

26 The underrepresentation of Belgians in the Estates-General was an important point of contention. Although the Southern population was numerically superior to the North, both parts of the country had the same number of representatives. The Southern claim for proportionate representation met with consistent refusal from King William I, who feared a Southern and Catholic majority in the Estates (Bos, 2009, pp. 145–146; Van Nifterik, 2011, pp. 30–31).

27 In the run-up to the congressional elections, newspapers debated whether the inhabitants of those parts of the territory that had joined the revolt, but which were still partly under Dutch occupation, should have the right to vote. The newspaper *Le Belge*, for example, argued to the negative, stating that those inhabitants were not actually free and that their votes would subsequently reflect the force of military occupation rather than popular opinion. This situation would result in a distortion of the national representation (*BEL*, 28 October 1830, no. 301, *Élections au Congrès National*).

28 Le Hon, for example, stated in Congress, "until the decisive moment, we cannot alienate our right to vote. It is not even ours; it belongs to the fatherland" (Huyttens, 1844b, p. 418, 2 February 1831, Le Hon).

a myriad of persons with diverse ideas – certainly had a will of its own, but it could not express these shared intentions by itself.[29] In order to express its will, it needed to create institutions that would distil all the individual interests into a common interest. In this way, a 'national wish' could be produced. The idea was succinctly formulated by congressman Leclerq in the debate on representative monarchy:

> Under this form of government [i.e. representative monarchy], the nation also intervenes in its affairs, but this intervention is merely indirect; it starts from the nation, but it passes through the hands of the elected; it is concentrated, purified, if I may say so, in the hands of those most worthy and most interested in the general wellbeing.
>
> (Huyttens, 1844a, pp. 188–189, 19 November 1830, Leclercq)

In short, the genuine articulation of the national wish was an important topic in the debates of the day. Even if this may, on certain occasions, have been the stuff of rhetorical argument more than anything else, the fact remains that the instituted powers could not simply replace the existent national wish with their own. This was all the more logical considering the Congressmen's awareness of public opinion both within and outside of the Congress.[30] Their words provoked a reaction in the public gallery of the assembly room and were copied in the press and responded to by petitions. Also, the congressmen knew they would be judged by their peers after their return to civil society.[31] Moreover, they understood that

29 For references of the congressmen to their introspective as 'translators of the national wish': Huyttens (1844a, p. 118, 12 November 1830, De Foere); Huyttens (1844a, p. 178, 18 November 1830, Masbourg); Huyttens (1844a, p. 228, 20 November 1830, De Robaulx); Huyttens (1844a, p. 238, 22 November 1830, Abbé Verbeke); Huyttens (1844a, p. 245, 22 November 1830, De Mûelenaere); Huyttens (1844a, p. 259, 22 November 1830, Masbourg [in footnote]); Huyttens (1844a, p. 219, 20 November 1830, De Roo); Huyttens (1844a, p. 436, 14 November 1830, Fleussu); Huyttens (1844b, pp. 98–99, 11 January 1831, De Liedel de Well); Huyttens (1844c, p. 248, 3 June 1831, Boucqueau de Villeraie); Huyttens (1844c, p. 260, 3 June 1831, Doreye); Huyttens (1844c, p. 333, 25 June 1831, Seron); Huyttens (1844c, p. 444, 4 July 1831, De Pélichy van Huerne); Huyttens (1844c, p. 496, 7 July 1831, De Mûelenaere).

30 Several incidents in the Congress reveal the physical and mental proximity between the representatives and the represented as well as the representatives' recognition of the latter. See e.g. Huyttens (1844b, p. 318, 29 January 1831, Surlet de Chokier, 1844a, pp. 572–573, session of 21 December 1830).

31 See e.g. Huyttens (1844a, p. 187, 19 November 1830, Leclercq). See in the same vein De Gerlache's intervention concerning the members of the provisional government (Huyttens, 1844b, p. 595, 25 February 1831, De Gerlache). See also Van Snick's request to act his vote in the congressional minutes, "because I cannot bear the responsibility of the assembly's decision vis-à-vis my constituents" (Huyttens, 1844a, p. 639, 24 December 1830, Van Snick).

inadequate choices on their part entailed the risk of occasioning a new popular revolution.[32]

The constituent debates indicate that direct interference by the nation was not completely excluded. Resorting to the nation's immediate agency was sometimes inevitable (see Chapter 8). This was the case, for instance, when the instituted powers stopped legitimately exercising their authority in conformity with the national wish. When the political order was distracted and committed to issues that were unrelated to the preoccupations of the people, when it refused to engage with the nation's interests, or when it violated the constitutional limits imposed by the nation, the latter had the exceptional right to manifest itself and to reclaim its sovereignty through resistance and insurgency.[33]

This Lockean idea of resistance brings us to a final element underpinning the Belgian revolutionaries' conception of representation, which was anchored in the republican tradition: the idea of control and contestation.[34] The people, which had entrusted the public authorities with governmental power, was entitled to continuously evaluate how these authorities exercised their tasks and, potentially, challenge them. This vision of representation relied not so much on the mechanism of popular authorisation of governmental power as on contestation and resistance (Pettit, 1997, p. 202).

Press and congressmen alike insisted that the system instated by the Constitution could only work on the condition that the population actively surveyed the political class. Involvement in politics was imperative for all citizens, not only for the limited group of qualified voters. Without continuous control, the nation would effectively renounce its sovereign rights. Hence, the nation's intervention was not strictly limited to periodic elections. The sovereignty of the nation only became true when public opinion – "the queen of the world" – permanently judged and guided governmental action (Huyttens, 1844a, p. 217, 20 November 1830, De Haerne; Huyttens, 1844b, p. 340, 31 January 1831, Van Snick).

This belief was clearly expressed when the National Congress was instituted. The Revolution had shown that the population at large was ready to sacrifice its own private interests for the well-being of society. After the active phase of the Revolution, it was up to the National Congress to decide the nation's destiny and

32 "who has made the revolution? The masses [...] but these masses, [...], if you will not give them the amount of happiness which they have a right to expect, they might compare their actual fate with their former conditions! And then our revolution will be in peril" (Huyttens, 1844b, p. 446, 3 January 1831, Forgeur). See also Huyttens (1844a, p. 176, 18 November 1830, Lardinois); Huyttens (1844a, p. 236, 22 November 1830, Blargnies); Huyttens (1844c, p. 198, 31 May 1831, D'Elhounge).

33 *Courrier des Pays-Bas* wrote that a violation of the constitutional limits by the government constituted in fact not so much a rebellion of the nation, as of the constituted powers. Inevitably, it entailed a struggle between the nation and the government, which could result either in national liberty or in absolute domination of the government over the nation (*CDPB*, 5 March 1831, no. 64. See also Chapter 7).

34 For the contestatory element in the republican tradition: Pettit (1997, pp. 200–202).

to establish a new order. *Courrier des Pays-Bas* reminded its readers that it was nevertheless essential for the population to continue its active engagement with the public cause:

> religious men and those who are attached to the principles of order and legitimacy should not withdraw from [public] affairs; from now on [...] they have the rigorous obligation to take care of it. The dearest interests of the homeland will be debated, a new order of things, on which our future and that of our children and cousins depends, will be established. Woe to the man who withdraws! Woe to him who prefers personal tranquillity over the general well-being! In the crisis which befalls us, prosperity will only be accomplished thanks to the efforts of obliging men.
>
> (*CDPB*, 29 October 1830, no. 292)

According to this view, involvement should not be limited to the constituent moment, when momentous choices were made. If the law was made in the name of the nation, the nation needed to keep a close watch on the lawmakers (*CDM*, 9 December 1830, no. 296). For *Courrier des Pays-Bas*, the real national wish could only be discovered by consulting public opinion. It was therefore essential for the citizens to publicly debate politics.

This political eclecticism was the only way to sustain a political regime upholding the unionist polity of the liberals and the Catholics. Still, the insistence on public debate has a republican flavour. Debate in the public sphere was essential for enlightening the people's representatives on the will of the nation. Debate needed to be moderate and reasonable, but nevertheless thorough (e.g. *BEL*, 11 November 1830, no. 315).

Participation channels

Several channels of participation stood at the public's disposal to contribute to the formation of public opinion and to communicate it to the representatives. First among these channels was, quite evidently, the press. For the revolutionaries, the freedom of the press constituted by far the most important of political liberties.[35] It was the very incarnation of liberty and reason. In the constituent debate, Nothomb proposed inserting an additional sentence aimed at prohibiting any preventive measure against criticism of the public authorities (Huyttens, 1844a, p. 643, 24 December 1830, Nothomb). The press was there not only to

35 "after having assured yourselves of the guarantee of the omnipotence of the opinion through the press, and of the press through the jury, can you still fear for liberty?" (Huyttens, 1844a, p. 471, 15 December 1830, De Gerlache). De Haerne approvingly described the press as "the great lever by which, today, one directs the world"; Verduyn as "the safeguard and the palladium of all the others [liberties]"; and Devaux as "the most important of our liberties" (Resp. Huyttens, 1844a, p. 660, 27 December 1830, De Haerne; Huyttens, 1844a, p. 653, 26 December 1830, Verduyn; Huyttens, 1844a, p. 643, 24 December 1830, Devaux).

inform its readers but equally to critically evaluate governmental action and to denounce judicial abuses or legislative problems.[36]

Yet, the press not only disclosed abuses but also facilitated the reciprocal circulation of ideas horizontally between the citizens as well as vertically between them and the constituted powers. It was the newspapers' task to debate politics and thus to help the representatives and the government understand the national wish (Delbecke, 2010, pp. 50–61). In a modern state, composed of a multitude of individuals, only the press could enable the exchange of ideas and the formation of a common public opinion important enough to weigh on governmental decision-making. It was the medium par excellence for bringing together the multiplicity of opinions into a 'national' public opinion, simultaneously creating a connection between the citizens and the government (Delbecke, 2010, p. 56). At the same time, the press had an educative role to play at the political level: in order to create a stable institutional system, it was essential to inform the citizens about political affairs and the working of their national institutions (Delbecke, 2010, p. 56).

The "sacred right of petition" (Huyttens, 1844b, p. 278, 27 January 1831, De Robaulx) and the right of association were understood in the same way.[37] The massive petition waves against the Dutch government in the late 1820s had been an essential stepping stone in the creation of an oppositional public spirit. Not only were the revolutionaries aware that petitions were an instrument of complaint, but they also saw them as a participation channel and even as a right of initiative (Faider, 1882, pp. 2 and 6; Errera, 1909, p. 179; Witte, 2005a, p. 70). In this regard, *Courrier des Pays-Bas* argued that the right of petition was a part of the legislative power that belonged to every Belgian. Staging petition campaigns among the non-enfranchised population was a way of enabling citizens to take part in the legislative process. As such, the right of petition was seen as "a legal expression of the public opinion" (*CDPB*, 27 July 1829, no. 208). It constituted an excellent complement to the press in developing an efficient public opinion that could not only inform but also control the government (*CDPB*, 27 July 1829, no. 208). But the greatest advantage of the petition right was that it could ultimately constitute an instrument of collective action and responsiveness, especially when the community's grievances were being ignored (De Keyser, 2000, pp. 596–599).

The right to assemble and the freedom of association were also considered essential for the formation of public spirit. Associations were yet another form

36 "Do you want more guarantees still? You will find them in the press, that tireless sentinel, that mighty organ of opinion, which reports and exposes abuses from wherever they proceed, and in the right and judicious sense of the nation, which will quickly denounce the false measures for which its own interest would serve as a pretext" (Huyttens, 1844a, p. 423, 14 December 1830, Defacqz). See also Huyttens (1844a, p. 627, 24 December 1830, Morel-Blanneel); Huyttens (1844a, p. 656, 24 December 1830, de Foere); Huyttens (1844b, p. 502, 11 February 1831, Destouvelles). See also Marteel (2010, p. 90).

37 There was almost no discussion on the right of petition, whereas the discussion relating to the right of association focused primarily on the religious congregations (Huyttens, 1844a, p. 666, session of 27 December 1830; Huyttens, 1844b, pp. 472–478, session of 5 February 1831). See also Bourgaux (2013, pp. 254–264).

of bottom-up organisation intended to influence the public sphere. They had proven very effective in the run-up to the Revolution, so obviously the revolutionaries did not fail to provide them with constitutional protection.[38] *Le Belge* defined their mission as follows: "1° to enlighten the government about its mistakes, 2° to indicate the useful measures to take in the difficult circumstances we are facing, and 3° to form and to develop the public spirit as much as possible" (*BEL*, 20 October 1830, no. 293).

Lastly, a popular jury was established for press delicts and political crimes as well as for the worst criminal offences. The main purpose of the jury was to provide a guarantee against despotic tendencies in the government, which might be tempted to muzzle public opinion through judicial power (Delbecke, 2013). Hence the attribution of press delicts and political crimes to lay judges, who were considered to represent public opinion[39] and to be more independent and objective than official authorities.[40] The jury was especially useful as it could deviate from the government's potentially despotic points of view and undo illegitimate prosecutions (Huyttens, 1844b, p. 232 in fn. 1, 22 January 1831, De Robaulx). Additionally, it was argued that the jury contributed to the formation of a public spirit by fostering a shared interest in the public cause as well as a shared form of participation and that it would enable a 'moral fusion' of the citizens, necessary for the stability of the representative government (*BEL*, 31 March 1829, no. 90).[41] These effects also played a pivotal supportive role for public opinion, making it a resilient bulwark against any abuse of the constituted powers.

These participation channels contributed to expressing the national wish, but they did not dictate political decisions.[42] Only the representative institutions were able to materialise this wish, and they did this through deliberation. The relation between the representative institutions and public opinion was a responsive and dialectic one: "In this government, when it is well organized, the law is the result of the enlightened public opinion, expressed by the people, by the press, by the petitions", Blargnies asserted in Congress (Huyttens, 1844a, p. 238, 22 November 1830, Blargnies). Similarly optimistic, De Roo thought that the combination of direct and popular elections with modern guarantees

38 Old articles 19 and 20 of the Constitution.

39 Future congressman and representative in the Dutch States-General Théophile Fallon described the jury in the Second Chamber as "a sort of national representation, which, in a way, associates public opinion to the force of res judicata". Another future congressman, Baron De Sécus, defined its decisions as "the judgement of the country [...] proper to representative governments, by which it can be truly the judgement of society" (Resp. *BEL*, 16 April 1829, no. 106; *BEL*, 11 April 1829, no. 101). See also Huyttens (1844c, pp. 576–577, 18 July 1831, Raikem).

40 See the speeches of Charles Le Hon and De Gerlache in the Second Chamber of the States-General (Resp. *CDPB*, 25 April 1829, no. 115; *CDPB*, 19 April 1830, no. 97).

41 See also the earlier speeches from Goswin de Stassart and Charles Le Hon of 13 April 1829 in the Second Chamber of the Estates-General (*BEL*, 15 April 1829, no. 105).

42 E.g. Lebeau on petitions: "Since they are non-binding, the referrals of petitions [to the bureau of petitions] have never been considered decisions in either of the deliberative chambers" (Huyttens, 1844b, p. 501, 11 February 1831, Lebeau).

of governmental responsibility (freedom of education and the press as well as a well-functioning jury, judicial order, and civic militia) meant that "you will simply have the will of the entire nation" (Huyttens, 1844a, p. 220, 20 November 1830, De Roo).

The above goes to show that a republican concern for public involvement in politics was very present in the debates of the period. The active development of public spirit was counted as an essential component of constitutional monarchy, and the extent of popular involvement in that public opinion clearly went beyond that of the electorate so as to include all enlightened spirits. All of this reflects a conception of the nation in which the political involvement of society at large belonged to the core of the political system. The permeability of the representative system ensured that the exercise of sovereignty not only became 'national' but also remained the 'genuine' expression of the nation's will.

Conclusion

The primary goal of the Belgian founding fathers was to prevent individuals or particular groups from usurping governmental power at the expense of the community and the individual rights of citizens. The constitution of a national representative system, based on the sovereignty of the Belgian people, was imperative. Performing their constituent work under the pressure of time and revolutionary circumstances, the drafters borrowed useful elements from different contexts and from various political theories (Descamps-David, 1891; Gilissen, 1967; De Smaele, 2005). Although they constructed an internally coherent political system, the Constitution was based less on abstract principles than on ad hoc procedure (Descamps-David, 1891, p. 51; Van Den Steene, 1963, p. 60). This eclecticism in intellectual sources may have contributed to the later confusion in the Belgian doctrine, resulting in an explanation of representative government which is not supported by the spirit of the original debates.

We have argued that the Belgian founding fathers understood popular sovereignty as power from below but simultaneously considered representation and direct elections as necessary conditions for the realisation of sovereignty. Their understanding of the representative system was certainly indebted to the modern idea of representation, which was introduced to the continent by the French Constitution of 1791. As explained above, this entailed virtual representation, the multiplication of representative actors, and suffrage restrictions, while the binding nature of the representative mandate was ruled out. But even though the representatives were supposed to materialise and canalise the national wish, the Belgian congressmen did not understand this wish as an arbitrary creation. It was clear to all that the representation of the nation was not merely a legal function. Parliament did not artificially construct the national wish *ad libitum*. Nor were its decisions considered to be the irrefutable expression of the nation's wishes and interests. The nation had a will of its own. Through various participation channels, public opinion constantly evaluated the representatives' decisions.

The Belgian Constitution of 1831 is often described as a turning point in the history of constitutional monarchy: its limitation of royal power, introduction of ministerial responsibility, and strong representative structures opened the way to parliamentary regimes (Mirkine-Guetzevitch, 1931; Gilissen, 1968, pp. 135–141; Dippel, 2005). However, the republican and contestatory elements of the new state system, which ensured effective control of the government by the entire enlightened population, were certainly just as innovative in light of contemporary European state theory. In France, Doctrinaire thinking increasingly loosened the ties between national representation and the living population, substituting national sovereignty with the sovereignty of reason and justice (Bacot, 1985, p. 119; Brunet, 2004, p. 33). In the Kingdom of the Netherlands, on the other hand, a resurgence of national feeling in defence of king and constitution following the Belgian Revolution stifled the evolution towards a more national representation for about 20 years (Van Sas, 1992, p. 181; Koch, 2015, p. 50).

The aforementioned elements have largely been overlooked in the Belgian doctrine, which has mainly focused on the lack or the rejection of (direct) participative elements. In the original spirit of the Constitution, public opinion articulated its assessment of representative government not only through the press but also through petitions and associations. And when public opinion stirred, parliament was expected to respond. When it failed to do justice to the grievances, other representatives were qualified to address the issue: the king could dissolve parliament or pronounce his veto when he believed that the assembly's actions did not serve the national interest. The electorate would then indirectly speak up again by sending new representatives. The jury, for its part, corrected oppressive governmental action by assessing press offences and political crimes. The king's action was subject to parliamentary control and necessitated ministerial countersign. If all this failed, and only then, the nation could ultimately resist. Taking matters directly into its own hands, it could realise the words of Charles de Brouckère: "public opinion, namely the nation, will always prevail" (Huyttens, 1844a, p. 427, 14 December 1830, C. de Brouckère).

Bibliography

Alen, A. (1984) *Rechter en bestuur in het Belgische publiekrecht: de grondslagen van de rechterlijke wettigheidskontrole* (2 vols). Antwerp: Kluwer rechtswetenschappen.

Bacot, G. (1985) *Carré de Malberg et l'origine de la distinction entre souveraineté du peuple et souveraineté nationale*. Paris: CNRS.

Bos, E. (2009) *Soevereiniteit en religie. Godsdienstvrijheid onder de eerste Oranjevorsten*. Hilversum: Verloren.

Bourgaux, A.-E. (2013) *La démocratisation du gouvernement représentatif en Belgique: une promesse oubliée* (1 vol). Unpublished doctoral thesis. Law. Brussels: Université Libre de Bruxelles.

Brunet, P. (2002) 'La notion de représentation sous la Révolution française', *Annales historiques de la Révolution française* (328), pp. 27–45. DOI: 10.3406/ahrf.2002.2578.

Brunet, P. (2004) *Vouloir pour la nation. Le concept de représentation dans la théorie de l'Etat*. Paris: L.G.D.J.

Brunet, P. (2012) 'La représentation', in Troper, M. and Chagnollaud, D. (eds.) *Traité international de droit constitutionnel*. Paris: Dalloz, pp. 607–641.

De Keyser, P. (2000) 'Het petitierecht afgestoft', *Tijdschrift voor Bestuurswetenschappen en Publiekrecht* (8), pp. 596–618.

De Smaele, H. (2002) *Omdat we uwe vrienden zijn: religie en partijidentificatie, 1884–1914*. Unpublished doctoral thesis. History. Leuven: KU Leuven.

De Smaele, H. (2005) 'Eclectisch en toch nieuw. De uitvinding van het Belgisch parlement in 1830–1831', *Bijdragen en Mededelingen betreffende de Geschiedenis der Nederlanden*, 120(3), pp. 408–416. DOI: 10.18352/bmgn-lchr.6253.

Delbecke, B. (2010) *De lange schaduw van de grondwetgever. Perswetgeving en persmisdrijven in België, 1831–1914*. Published doctoral thesis. Law. Leuven: KU Leuven.

Delbecke, B. (2013) 'La prédominance de l'opinion publique sur le sens privé du magistrat. De volksjury volgens de Belgische grondwetgever (1830–31)', in De Ruysscher, D. (ed.) *Rechtspreken en lekenparticipatie. Noodzaak of traditie?* Antwerp: Maklu, pp. 39–66.

D'Elhoungne, Doncker, and Van Meenen (1819) *L'Observateur politique, administratif, historique et littéraire de la Belgique par une société de jurisconsultes et d'hommes de lettres* (18 vols). Brussels: De Mat.

Descamps-David, E.-D. (1891) *La mosaïque constitutionnelle. Essai sur les sources du texte de la Constitution Belge*. Leuven: Peeters.

Dippel, H. (2005) 'Modern Constitutionalism, an Introduction to a History in Need of Writing', *Tijdschrift voor Rechtsgeschiedenis – Legal History Review*, 1(73), pp. 153–169. DOI:10.1163/1571819054088670.

Errera, P. (1909) *Traité de droit public belge*. Paris: Giard et Brière.

Faider, C. (1882) *Le droit de pétition*. Discours prononcé à l'audience solennelle de rentrée de la Cour de cassation de Belgique le 16 octobre 1882.

Foriers, P. (1981) 'Le droit investi par la politique', in S.A. (ed.) *Dialogues Multiples. Hommage à Paul Foriers*. Brussels: Editions de l'Université de Bruxelles, pp. 13–33.

Gilissen, J. (1967) 'Die belgische Verfassung von 1831. Ihr Ursprung und ihr Einfluss', in Conze, W. (ed.) *Beiträge zur deutschen und belgischen Verfassungsgeschichte im 19. Jahrhundert*. Stuttgart: E. Klett, pp. 38–69.

Gilissen, J. (1968) 'La Constitution belge de 1831: ses sources, son influence', *Res Publica* 10, pp. 107–141.

Grange, H. (1974) *Les idées de Necker*. Paris: C. Klincksieck.

Gueniffey, P. (1993) *Le nombre et la raison. La Révolution française et les élections*. Paris: EHESS.

Huyttens, E. (1844a) *Discussions du Congrès National de Belgique 1830–1831. Tome premier*. Brussels: Société Typographique Belge.

Huyttens, E. (1844b) *Discussions du Congrès National de Belgique 1830–1831. Tome deuxième*. Brussels: Société Typographique Belge.

Huyttens, E. (1844c) *Discussions du Congrès National de Belgique 1830–1831. Tome troisième*. Brussels: Société Typographique Belge.

Huyttens, E. (1844d) *Discussions du Congrès National de Belgique 1830–1831. Tome quatrième*. Brussels: Société Typographique Belge.

Koch, J. (2015) 'Le roi décide seul/De Koning alleen besluit. Het «systeem Willem I »', in Aerts, R. and Deneckere, G. (eds.) *Het (on)verenigd Koninkrijk*

1815–1830-2015. Een politiek experiment in de Lage Landen. Rekkem: Ons Erfdeel, pp. 49–58.

Krulic, J. (2007) 'L'idée de peuple dans la tradition constitutionnelle française', *Sens Public*, 2, pp. 1–19.

Lebeau, J. (1830) *Observations sur le Pouvoir Royal ou Examen de quelques questions relatives aux droits de la couronne dans les Pays-Bas*. Liège: Lebeau-Ouwerx.

Maes, C. (2018) 'The End Justifies the Means. The Nature of Belgium's 1830 Political Liberalism', *Giornale di Storia Costituzionale*, 35(1), pp. 129–145.

Maes, C. and Deseure, B. (forthcoming) '"The Nation Will Always Prevail". Sovereignty, Representation and Participation in 1830 Belgium', *Tijdschrift voor Rechtsgeschiedenis - Legal History Review*, 88 (3–4), pp. 495–531. DOI: 10.1163/15718190-00880A10.

Manin, B. (1997) *The Principles of Representative Government*. Cambridge: Cambridge University Press. DOI: 10.1017/CBO9780511659935.

Marteel, S. (2010) 'Constitutional Thought Under the Union of the Netherlands: The 'Fundamental Law' of 1814–15 in the Political and Intellectual Context of the Restoration', *Parliaments, Estates and Representation*, 27(1), p. 7794. DOI: 10.1080/02606755.2007.9522254.

Maulin, E. (2002) 'Carré de Malberg et le droit constitutionnel de la Révolution française', *Annales historiques de la Révolution française* (328), pp. 5–25. DOI: 10.3406/ahrf.2002.2577.

Mirkine-Guetzevitch, B. (1931) 'Mille huit cent trente dans l'évolution constitutionnelle de l'europe', *Revue d'Histoire Moderne et Contemporaine*, 34(6), pp. 241–256. DOI: 10.3406/rhmc.1931.3662.

Pettit, P. (1997) *Republicanism: A Theory of Freedom and Government*. Oxford: Clarendon Press. DOI: 10.1093/0198296428.001.0001.

Roels, J. (1982) 'La théorie doctrinaire du régime représentatif: les discours parlementaires de Royer-Collard', *Parliaments, Estates and Representation*, 2(2), pp. 155–172. DOI: 10.1080/02606755.1982.9525610.

Rosanvallon, P. (1989) 'Les Doctrinaires et la question du gouvernement représentatif', in Furet, F. and Ozouf, M. (eds.) *The French Revolution and the Creation of Modern Political Culture*. Oxford: Pergamon Press, pp. 411–431.

S.A. (n.d.a.) *Belge, Le* (BEL).

S.A. (n.d.b.) *Courrier de la Meuse, Le* (CDM).

S.A. (n.d.c.) *Courrier des Pays-Bas, Le* (CDPB).

S.A. (n.d.d.) *Observateur Belge, L'* (OB).

S.A. (n.d.e.) *Politique, Le* (POL).

S.A. (1842) *Handelingen van de regering en de Staten-Generaal over de herziening der Grondwet*. The Hague: Belinfante.

Troper, M. (1996) 'La Constitution de l'an III ou la continuité : la souveraineté populaire sous la Convention', in Dupuy, R. and Morabito, M. (eds.) *1795, Pour une République sans Révolution*. Rennes: Presses universitaires de Rennes, pp. 179–192.

Van Den Steene, W. (1963) *De Belgische Grondwetscommissie (oktober-november 1830). Tekst van haar notulen en ontstaan van de Belgische Grondwet*. Brussels: KVAB.

Van Nifterik, G. (2011) 'On the Idea of Democracy in the Dutch Constitution Committees of 1814 and 1815', *Parliaments, Estates and Representation*, 31(1), pp. 17–32. DOI: 10.1080/02606755.2011.560750.

Van Sas, N.C.F. (1992) 'Het Grote Nederland van Willem I: een schone slaapster die niet wakker wilde worden', in Tamse, C.A. and Witte, E. (eds.) *Staats- en natievorming in Willem I's koninkrijk (1815–1830)*. Brussels: VUB press, pp. 171–185.

Velu, J. (1997) 'Vertegenwoordiging en rechterlijke macht (eerste deel)', *Rechtskundig Weekblad*, 18, pp. 585–620.

Witte, E. (2005a) 'De constructie van België 1828–1847', in Witte, E., Nandrin, J.-P., Gubin, E. and Deneckere, G. (eds.) *Nieuwe geschiedenis van België*. Tielt: Lannoo, pp. 27–235.

Witte, E. (2005b) 'La construction de la Belgique. 1828–1847', in Witte, E., Gubin, E., Nandrin, J.-P. and Deneckere, G. (eds.) *Nouvelle Histoire de Belgique*. Brussels: Editions Complexe, pp. 7–207.

Publications without a specific, personal author (such as newspapers and official documents) are listed under S.A.

Part III

Sovereignty and civic participation

10 The monist nation and the general will

Raymond Carré de Malberg on sovereignty

Olga Bashkina

Introduction

Article 33 of the Constitution of Belgium proclaims that "All powers emanate from the Nation". The ubiquitous interpretation of this formula attributes sovereignty to the Belgian *nation* as opposed to the Belgian *people*. While the people are believed to comprehend all presently living citizens, it is claimed that the nation signifies an entity encompassing past, current, and future generations of Belgian citizens. The consequence of such a distinction between the people and the nation is accordingly a contrast between popular and national sovereignty. On the one hand, popular sovereignty is believed to refer to a regime making extensive use of direct forms of citizen participation. National sovereignty, on the other hand, expresses the primacy of representative government and excludes direct citizen influence over representatives, be it in the form of imperative mandate or referendums.

This distinction was most prominently introduced into the Belgian context by a legal scholar from Ghent, André Mast. First editions of his influential textbook *Overview of the Constitutional Law* appeared in 1950 and 1952 and attributed to the Belgian founding fathers the intention of opting for the model of national sovereignty rather than that of popular sovereignty (Mast, 1950). Mast did not claim the invention of the distinction between the two models. He adopted the distinction from the constitutional theory of the French Third Republic, his major reference being a legal scholar from Strasbourg, Raymond Carré de Malberg (1861–1935). In this chapter, I suggest looking at the origins of the distinction between popular and national sovereignty in the theory of Carré de Malberg.

Carré de Malberg's work belongs to the genre of the general theory of the state developed at the end of the nineteenth century. Represented by several prominent figures (Carré de Malberg, Jellinek, Kelsen, etc.), this short-lived genre perished after the Second World War with the rise of political science (Jouanjan and Maulin, 2012). While in Germany, the general theory of the state appeared as a contribution to the ongoing state-building process, in France it took the form of a response to the tendencies of democratisation. Expanding suffrage and an increase in social conflicts led to a questioning of the validity of representative claims and of the correspondence between the legal will of the government and the real will of the people (ibid.). Carré de Malberg is one of four canonical theorists of French constitutional thought (together with Adhémar Esmein, Léon Duguit, and Maurice Hauriou). While the distinction between the people and the nation as subjects of sovereignty, which is the focus of my analysis below, does not originate with Carré de Malberg (Bacot, 2001),[1] he brought it to its full theoretical explication.

This chapter does three things. First, it situates Carré de Malberg's project vis-à-vis German state theory. Second, it explains the meaning of the popular versus national sovereignty distinction for Carré de Malberg's vision of the constitutional state. And finally, it traces a change in his thought on and his argument for referendums. This last step allows for a critical view of the doctrine of national sovereignty and its future in Belgium.

Carré de Malberg and the project of constitutional theory in dialogue with German state theory

A native of Strasbourg, Carré de Malberg to a large extent incorporated his national feelings into his theory. The Franco-Prussian War, "a great trauma" (Beaud, 1997, p. 222) in Carré de Malberg's childhood, left its mark on his thought: his reception of German legal thought stamped by rivalry and competition and his conception of the French constitutional state imprinted with his appreciation of its uniqueness. Carré de Malberg developed his political and legal views under the influence of discussion of the Alsace-Lorraine region (ibid., p. 232–233). From his earlier articles, devoted to the status of Alsace-Lorraine under the German Empire and to the legal basis of the reparation payments, until his later programmatic work on the state, he depicted Germany as an imperialist aggressor enforcing domination and causing unrest on the continent. He juxtaposed the French state built around "the national sentiment" to the German state constructed around the *Herrscher*, the figure of the monarch – the one uniting the many. While Carré de Malberg's intention is to demonstrate how the French state is deeply rooted in the revolutionary tradition and finds its legitimacy in the French nation, he is at the same time attempting to pass between the Scylla and Charybdis of French post-revolutionary politics, namely the threat of Jacobinism and the excesses of the Napoleonic dictatorship. Consequently, while on the one hand devising an alternative theory to the German monarchic state, on the other hand, Carré de Malberg distances himself from exaggerated resort to democratic method and from positing sovereignty in the people. To this

1 Bacot argues not only that the distinction between popular and national sovereignty was not Carré de Malberg's invention, but also that he had misidentified the source of this distinction. Carré de Malberg associates the doctrine of popular sovereignty with the theory of Rousseau, and national sovereignty with the constitutional thought of the French Revolution, while Bacot claims that the distinction comes about later, most significantly with the counter-revolutionary tendencies during the Bourbon Restoration and the political thought of the Doctrinaires.

end, he counterposes the concepts of the people and the nation and establishes a distinction between popular and national sovereignty on the basis of their ability to constitute a lasting and stable state. In other words, even though Carré de Malberg criticises the German domination model of the state, the alternative that he wants to see in the French state model needs to be equally strong in order to qualify it as an adversary. This agenda led to Carré de Malberg's conception of the state as the personification of the nation and his substitution of the allegedly excessively democratic concept of the sovereign people with a more unitary and consolidated concept of the nation.

Many researchers emphasise that the originality of Carré de Malberg's project consists in his combination of the French constitutional tradition and German *Staatslehre*[2] (Maulin, 2003). The spirit and essential components of late nineteenth- and early twentieth-century theories of sovereignty and state can already be found in Hegel. In his *Philosophy of Right*, he defined sovereignty in the following way:

> Since sovereignty is the ideality of every particular authority, it is easy to fall into the very common misunderstanding of regarding this ideality as mere power and empty arbitrariness, and of equating sovereignty with despotism. But despotism signifies the condition of lawlessness in general, in which the particular will as such, whether of a monarch or of the people (ochlocracy), counts as law (or rather replaces law), whereas sovereignty is to be found specifically under lawful and constitutional conditions as the moment of ideality of the particular spheres and functions within the state.
>
> (Hegel, 1820/2003, pp. 315–316)

Hegel emphasises sovereignty's ideal character rather than associating it with factual power, which grounds subsequent explorations of sovereignty with regard to the idea of the constitutional state. It is only a matter of defining how this ideal function of sovereignty operates. Hegel himself observed that sovereignty as 'ideality' is only possible if it is grounded in subjectivity, which in Hegel's case means the concrete individual subjectivity of the monarch (ibid., p. 317). This, Hegel argued, is necessary in order to give legitimation and concrete representation to a complex system of separated powers and forces. This observation reveals that 'sovereignty', a concept correlated in modern philosophy with the idea of subjectivity, although ideal, cannot, in Hegel's terms, remain abstract. In order to function concretely, it needs a concrete embodied representation – the monarch. In one way or another, this idea that sovereignty needs a concrete embodiment has pervaded German thought up until Schmitt's version of this argument. While agreeing with the ideal function of sovereignty, Carré de Malberg stood opposed to monarchy as its sole expression. In

2 Éric Maulin, "Raymond Carré de Malberg, le légiste de la République", in *R. Carré de Malberg, Contribution à la théorie générale de l'Etat* (Dalloz, 2003); Brunet (1977).

contemporary constitutional theory, the transformation of the modern understanding of sovereignty is narrated as the shift from personal power of command to an abstract signifier that "symbolizes the unity of ordering" (Loughlin, 2003, p. 48), where, in the name of separation of powers, sovereignty is refused to a ruler, an office of government, or even to the people as a concrete entity. Instead, in this modern liberal understanding, the people may be understood as a purely legal denominator, as a very general and 'thin' expression of a unitary sovereign subject. Carré de Malberg pursued a similar project. He juxtaposed the French tradition, built around the principles of representation and constitutionalism, to the German tradition's conception of the power of the state as *Herrschaftsgewalt.* For Carré de Malberg, the German doctrine took the state as a *Herrscher*, a dominating instance, and theorised the state as positioned above the people, who remain sheer subjects of state power. The goal of French thought, as Carré de Malberg saw it, was to establish a theory of the people and their sovereignty that would allow the people to be thought of not as being dominated and governed but as self-governing (Carré de Malberg, 2003, p. xix).

Éric Maulin notes that the idea of the combination of German and French traditions is, at first glance, controversial. On the one hand, the legitimacy of the German Reich was founded on the right of force, which allowed German jurists to formulate their positivist project as a theory of public law sanctioned by state power. On the other hand, French constitutionalism inherited its core from the French Revolution, which grounded legitimacy in the principles of equality, individual rights, and separation of powers (Maulin, 2003, pp. 2–3). Carré de Malberg borrows his essential terminology from German positivists: legal person of the state and organs of the state are concepts that were developed systematically by C.F. Gerber, P. Laband, G. Jellinek et al. However, German state theory is inseparably connected with the principle of monarchy: it is this principle that allows one to think of the state, in the first place, as having a legal personality. The monarch is considered to be the highest organ of state power, embodying and representing the state. The monarch, who has the ultimate power to sanction all laws proposed by the legislative assembly, performs the act of auto-limitation by submitting himself to the laws that he sanctions. The person of the state in the German version of *Rechtsstaat* is unthinkable without the person of the monarch (ibid., p. 4). Pierre Brunet remarks that Carré de Malberg's reason for marrying the German principle of the legal personality of the state with a principle of national sovereignty that he ascribes uniquely to the French legal tradition is double. On the one hand, Carré de Malberg thinks of the idea of legal personality and its organs as the best way to give a juridical explanation of collective subjectivity. On the other hand, he strives to demonstrate that organ theory did not originate with German jurists. Instead, its origins can be found in the French revolutionary tradition (Brunet, 1997, pp. 256–259). Thus, by adopting the heritage of the German tradition, Carré de Malberg aims to preserve its ontology of unity while conceiving of the people not only as standing in submission to the sovereign state but also as the subject of sovereignty itself.

The monist system and the search for unity: Sovereignty and the constitutional state

A crucial question in Carré de Malberg's conception of the state concerns who should be deemed the subject of sovereignty – the concrete and tangible people or the more abstract nation, devoid of the dangerous excesses of power. More importantly, however, is that the distinction drawn by Carré de Malberg between the people and the nation allows him to argue for a monist theory of sovereignty and the state. The failure of German state theory, for Carré de Malberg, lies in trying to think of the unity of a sovereign state by initially positing two substances – the state and the people. German dualism of this sort ultimately leads to an oppressive conception of the state when it exerts power over the people. As opposed to that, a monist system would only posit one foundation – the nation. It is in defending the nation as the subject of sovereignty that can guarantee its stable unwavering character that Carré de Malberg first repudiates the people as a potential sovereign. His analysis of popular sovereignty and the people revolves around a critique of Rousseau's theory of popular sovereignty, which, according to him, posits the people, considered as a concrete assemblage of individuals, as the source of absolute and indivisible sovereignty. Carré de Malberg sees Rousseau's theory of sovereignty as representative of a wide variety of theories, such as those of the monarchomachs and that of Hobbes. It is also this theory that he sees as standing behind the American Constitution as well as the French Constitution of 1793.

Carré de Malberg on the origins of French constitutionalism

That key distinction in French legal thought between popular and national sovereignty is seen by Carré de Malberg as epitomising the process of sovereignty's modernisation from concrete power to abstract legal framework. The transformation from people to nation happens, so his story goes, when an earlier conception of direct popular sovereignty formulated by Jean-Jacques Rousseau is replaced by a new one, born during the French Revolution. A more progressive version of sovereignty, in line with developing liberal and constitutional values, is then theorised over the course of the French Revolution, specifically exemplified by Abbé Sieyès' theory of representation. The new theory places sovereignty in the hands of the nation, a constructed symbolic community, where sovereignty ceases to be exercised directly by the entire citizenry and instead stands for the combination of all powers exercised in the name of this community.

Carré de Malberg's account of popular sovereignty is formed around a series of critiques that he directs at Rousseau's theory. The first one pertains to Carré de Malberg's claim that popular sovereignty is born as a result of the combination of the individual sovereignty of citizens. He understands Rousseau's idea of the social contract to rely on the premise that there exist atomised individuals who are sovereign in their own will, which allows them to participate equally in contracting and thus creating a new sovereign power out of their individual sovereignties. Although Carré de Malberg's exaggeratedly arithmetical reading of popular sovereignty misses Rousseau's central distinction between *volonté de tous* and *volonté générale*, it illustrates how in this discourse the non-constituted people are conceived as monadic individuals incapable of forming a state organisation of their own. The idea of the social contract, or individuals creating collective sovereignty, appears to Carré de Malberg as containing a logical contradiction. He believes that if individual sovereignty is posited, it can hardly be combined with the general will as total collective control, for one cannot submit oneself to the rule of others without losing one's own sovereignty: "sovereignty and subjection to the will of the other are two incompatible things" (Carré de Malberg, 2003, II, p. 156). At the same time, this formulation also illustrates Carré de Malberg's fear that if people are actually endowed with sovereignty, they will not submit to the domination of the state. Thus, the logical contradiction of popular sovereignty manifests itself in the troubled relationship between the one and the many. The many, Carré de Malberg argues, are logically incapable of forming the one, where the one is posited to be the state with centralised power.

The second criticism of Rousseau and popular sovereignty, following from the first, is based on an analogy Carré de Malberg draws between popular sovereignty and the confederation of states. If a confederation of states does not form a new sovereign state, a confederation of citizens does not form a state properly speaking either:

> If it were true that the democratic state, in accordance with Rousseau's ideas, was analysed as a pure association or confederation of sovereign citizens, it must be immediately inferred that the democratic state is not a true state; for a confederation of individuals is no more able than a confederation of states to form a state. [...] The doctrine of Rousseau, far from founding the state and sovereignty, implies denial of the one and the other.
>
> (Ibid., p. 165)

Just as he claims that if the state in the Rousseauian vision were to be founded on popular sovereignty, it could not be a real state, Carré de Malberg also invokes Rousseau's theory of popular sovereignty to undermine the idea of the democratic state. He argues that 'democracy' and 'state' are fundamentally incompatible since democracy is a system with an institutional structure that is completely dependent on the unstable will of the people, while a proper state is defined by its durable organisation. Whereas the states forming a confederation are free to leave any time they please, the same does not apply to the people forming a state. But if individual persons are granted sovereignty, then the association they form – the state – is vulnerable to their decision to remain part of it or to destroy it (ibid., p. 166), rendering the dominating power of the state "*impuissant*" (impotent) (ibid., p. 165).

This results in a third and final criticism. Carré de Malberg points out that, in fact, democracy and popular sovereignty are not synonymous for Rousseau, since they are separated by Rousseau's major distinction between sovereignty and government. While advocating popular sovereignty, Rousseau theorises democracy as a type of government which is not co-original with popular sovereignty. Nevertheless, while Rousseau never defended democracy and did not envision democracy as a universally applicable form of government, Carré de Malberg's equivalence of popular sovereignty and the democratic state allows him to further elaborate on his point that the people cannot be the source of sovereignty properly speaking. He calls this a 'political' argument and concludes that it is impractical to describe the outcomes of the decisions of those in power as made in the name of the people since, in that case, people would be able to question those decisions and potentially challenge the whole system that leads to their production (ibid., p. 166). This argument amounts to the rejection of what some today call 'strong popular sovereignty', that is, of popular sovereignty as constituent power pre-existing the constitution as opposed to "the outcomes of a democratic process governed by constitutional law" (Vinx, 2013, p. 102), except that popular sovereignty for Carré de Malberg is always 'strong' and so always potentially destructive for the state.

Rejecting Rousseau's conception of sovereignty, Carré de Malberg traces an alternative tradition. He finds the roots of the French national sovereignty doctrine in Abbé Sieyès' theory of representation. When Carré de Malberg approaches Sieyès' thought, he interprets it in connection with the parliamentary debates that took place in the National Assembly in 1789. First and foremost, separating the ideas of king and state, previously so tightly conjoined ('*L'État, c'est moi*'), French revolutionaries set the ground for a new way of conceiving of state and sovereignty, where the sovereignty of the monarch is replaced by the sovereignty of the French nation. As the French Constitution of 1791 proclaimed: "Sovereignty [...] belongs to the Nation; no section of the people, no individual, can usurp its exercise. The Nation, from which all the powers emanate, can exercise them only by delegation".[3] Although the participants of the debate about the novel organisation of public powers are numerous, for Carré de Malberg, it was Sieyès who "defined the representative government, at the beginning of the new era of public law, with an accuracy and precision that has not been exceeded since then" (Carré de Malberg, 2003, II, p. 257). Carré de Malberg is particularly interested in Sieyès' position on representation and the role of the imperative mandate. In Carré de Malberg's view, the originality of Sieyès lies in his distinguishing representative government from democracy and proclaiming the indivisible anti-federalist character of the French nation (ibid., II, pp. 254–259). This comes to fruition when, according to Carré de Malberg, Sieyès proposes the theory of national sovereignty. Carré de Malberg quotes Sieyès:

> I know that because of various distinctions and confusion we have come to consider the national will as if it could be something else than the will of the

3 Available at: https://www.conseil-constitutionnel.fr/les-constitutions-dans-l-histoire/constitution-de-1791

> representatives of the nation, as if the nation could speak other than through its representatives. Here false principles become extremely dangerous. They are meant only to fragment, to tear France into an infinite number of small democracies which would then unite only by the ties of a general confederation. France is not an assemblage of states, it is a unique whole composed of integral parts.
>
> (Ibid., II, p. 254)

For Carré de Malberg, this emphatically anti-federalist intention is key to understanding Sieyès' conception as well as the overall conception of the nation that predominated among constituents in 1789. From this definition, Carré de Malberg concludes that the nation as the indivisible and united body is where "exclusively resides sovereignty" and that "the general will that forms the expression of sovereignty cannot be understood as the sum of particular wills coming from each of the districts, but this general will is itself part of the unity and indivisibility of the nation" (ibid., II, p. 255).

In explaining the principle of national sovereignty, Carré de Malberg transforms Sieyès' idea of representation into the idea of the personification of the nation by the state. The personhood of the state, as Carré de Malberg emphasises, is not a fiction, not a metaphor, nor a comparison. It is a juridical reality which is prerequisite to the conception of the unity of the legal space within the state and the legitimate existence of other associations (ibid., I, p. 40).

> The personality of any association or establishment which will be formed within the state [...] depends on the superior will of the state to grant permission or not to exist to groups that claim to be created within it and exercise their rights under it.
>
> (Ibid., I, p. 42)

Together with the exclusive power to authorise the existence of other associations, the idea of the state *qua* legal person permits the continuity of the state's existence to be imagined through time.

In order to distance his theory of personification from its German influences, specifically from Georg Jellinek's theory of the state, Carré de Malberg emphasises that the state is neither a person capable of legitimising itself nor is it bound together by the person of the monarch. Rather, the state acquires its legitimacy through being the personification of the nation:

> The state is nothing else but the nation itself. The nation has no powers, it is not a subject of law, it does not appear as sovereign unless it is legally organized and follows the laws of its organization. In other words, the nation becomes a person only by the fact of its state organization, that is by the fact of being constituted as a state.
>
> (Carré de Malberg, 2003, I, p. 15)

The double-bind of the state and the nation is a way, on the one hand, to rule out any prior, non-instituted manifestation of the people (an ultimate rejection of constituent power) and, on the other hand, to legitimise the actions of state organs by the claim that they are made in the name of the nation.

Carré de Malberg emphasises that 'sovereignty' is a term that was originally coined in French legal and political thought and that later made its way into other traditions. In French terminological practice, '*souveraineté*' designates the supreme power essentially characteristic of the state (ibid., I, p. 70). Not only in French theory but also in French constitutional texts, sovereignty is synonymous with state power ("la puissance de commander avec une force irrésistible ou – selon la terminologie française – la 'souveraineté'" [ibid., I, p. 255])[4]. For Carré de Malberg, all types of sovereignty – monarchic, popular, and eventually national – are ways of describing how the state functions. Carré de Malberg holds an ultimately state-centric point of view: in his opinion, the only starting point for any discussion on sovereignty is the state, while the only difference between various regimes consists in the way that state power, or sovereignty, is established and exercised. He is convinced that this primacy of the state, and the coincidence of the nation with the state in particular, is something that was actively promoted by the legislators of the French Revolution. Carré de Malberg sees the drastic shift from the Constitution of 1791 with its precept that "all powers come from the nation" and the constitutions of 1793 and of the year III where sovereignty is ascribed to "the universality of French citizens" (ibid., I, p. 84).

In this respect, Carré de Malberg juxtaposes the French legal experience to that of Germany, Great Britain, and the United States. Sovereignty of the monarch, sovereignty of parliament, or popular sovereignty have something in common that is absent from French discourse, namely the figure of the original holder of supreme power who has full right to exercise it whenever he pleases. In the model of monarchic sovereignty, the king is granted supreme authority, which he holds due to his divine right. Monarchic power is unlimited and is exercised according to the principle "*si veut le roi, si veut la loi*", as it used to be in the France of the *Ancien Régime*. In Germany, although the power of the monarch is limited by the Constitution, the Constitution itself is nothing but an act of auto-limitation by the sovereign, who remains the personal guarantor of the constitutional regime. The British tradition ascribes sovereignty to parliament, while the American and Swiss traditions rely on the idea of the sovereignty of the people. Next to France, Carré de Malberg sees only two other cases of national

4 Olivier Beaud (1994) explains how Carré de Malberg attempts to make a distinction between state power and sovereignty. In this attempted distinction, he is influenced by the school of *Isolierung* and its founder, a German jurist Hans Gerber, who defined state power (*Staatsgewalt*) as the power of domination and commandment, and sovereignty (*Souveränität*) as independence from any other power. Beaud explains that this distinction is specific to the German context as it was supposed to ideologically prove that member states of the Second Reich, although dominated by Prussia, still remain independent sovereign states. Although Carré de Malberg is aware of this context, he insists on the distinction, claiming that what is termed state power in Germany is called sovereignty in France. However, he keeps using these terms interchangeably throughout the text (ibid., pp. 1256–1264).

sovereignty, namely the constitutions of Belgium (1831) and Greece (1864), which also ascribed sovereignty to the nation under the influence of the French experience in the aftermath of the July Revolution (ibid., II, p. 169).

Originally directed against royal power, the idea of national sovereignty as formulated by the authors of the Declaration of the Rights of Man and of the Citizen of 1789 and the Constitution of 1791 implies several elements. The nation, personified by the state, obtains a reality that is totally differentiated from the people insofar as it is legally organised. National subjectivity is intrinsically connected with the notion of the state and state constitution. Both the very existence of the nation-state as a collective subject and its essential attribute – sovereign power – find its origins in the legal order that is established by the constitution of the state. Carré de Malberg's adherence to the written constitution as the only source and guarantee of sovereignty and subjectivity is so strong that he refuses to take into account any other forms of legal practice, including constituent power or customary law (Dumont, 2013).[5] In an ultimately positivist fashion, Carré de Malberg refuses to recognise any other form of constitutionality except the rigid written constitution and thus literally merges the state, the constitution, and the nation. Because of Carré de Malberg's inflexibility in this respect, Olivier Beaud calls his position "the fetishism of the written constitution" (Beaud, 2003, p. 263).

Challenging monist national sovereignty by plural popular sovereignty

Carré de Malberg's theory of national sovereignty is his attempt to distance the idea of sovereignty from connotations of domination. Absolute undivided power, in its Bodinian and Hobbesian versions, sovereignty is epitomised in the figure of the ruler that governs over its subjects. Debunking Rousseau's doctrine, Carré de Malberg observed that the French Revolution posited the principle of representation at the foundation of the newly emerged republic. The Constitution of 1791 transferred the eradicated sovereignty of the monarch not to the French people but to the French nation. This transference was manifested by the first act of representation whereby representatives of the Third Estate

5 Dumont (2013, p. 585) explains that Carré de Malberg advocates the rigidity of the constitution in France and leaves no place for constituent power or non-written constitutional norms. Some of his contemporaries or disciples attempted to amend this rigid view of the constitution. Léon Duguit and René Capitant, for example, neglect a purely positivist view on constitutional norms and make room for other forms of constitutionality. R. Capitant (Dumont 2013, p. 585): "la force constituante de la coutume n'est qu'un aspect de la souveraineté nationale. [...] Lors même qu'elle [la nation] n'a pas le droit de manifester par écrit sa volonté, elle a néanmoins une volonté et qui s'impose. Elle reste au moins maîtresse de son obéissance, et par conséquent détient la positivité du droit [...]. Le droit peut bien recevoir son contenu du législateur, c'est de la nation qu'il tiendra toujours sa vigueur". But starting in the 1970s, the rigid Malbergian view on constitutionality returns. It is also dominant in Belgium.

announced themselves as the National Assembly. Carré de Malberg thus makes a point of distinguishing between the nation and the people as two subjects of sovereignty. 'The people' refers to an immanent principle of organisation that Carré de Malberg denies. Popular sovereignty always remains an impossible idea because the people stay a multitude, unable to organise and cooperate. 'The nation', on the contrary, is an entity that manifests itself solely through representation, an idea succinctly expressed by Sieyès when he trumpeted that "the people cannot act, cannot speak, other than by means of their representatives" (Sieyès, 1789). 'The nation' thus points to the inescapable transcendence of the people who can never be fully presented to themselves. Carré de Malberg calls attention to another aspect of the concept: it is only by reference to something that by definition can never be fully expressed that those claiming to represent it can be granted with temporary power.

A way to escape the dualism of the state and the people engrained in German theory, for Carré de Malberg, is to think of the state and the people (the nation) as co-original. The state should not be thought of as something separate from the people that it governs and imposes norms as commands over. Rather, the people and the state appear at the same time as organised by the founding document – the constitution. This way, the state is not framed as the subject above the law that creates the norm at will and that is somehow separate from the people that form it. Instead, it is by virtue of the founding norm that the nation (organised people) and the state emerge as one and the same thing:

> The state is the result of a certain organization of the national collectivity [...] If one now wonders wherefrom the holders of power, whoever they are, rulers or assembly of the citizens, draw their quality of organs of the State, and by virtue of which right they have been able to acquire this quality, it is necessary to answer, from the legal point of view, that they hold this title and that they have received their vocation from the legal order established in this respect in each state. This legal order is contained in the Constitution. They derive their vocation from the Constitution, and it is by virtue of this Constitution that they exercise their competence.
>
> (Carré de Malberg, 2003, II, p. 144)

Positing a founding norm as the factual basis of the legal order, Carré de Malberg attempts to remove the element of force from the original moment of foundation and substitute it with a transcendent principle. We cannot find anybody at the moment of foundation who imposed their will on others because the governing and the governed emerge simultaneously. Yet, postulating *the transcendent principle*, Carré de Malberg distinguishes himself from another brand of legal positivism and another monist system – that of Hans Kelsen. In *Confrontation de la théorie de la formation du droit par degrés avec les idées et les institutions consacrées par le droit positif français relativement à sa formation* (1933), Carré de Malberg scrutinises the legal theory of the Viennese school. He claims that the *Stufentheorie* developed by Hans Kelsen and Adolf Merkl is mistaken about the original source of the norm or that at least this theory does not match the French practice. For Kelsen, the validity of a norm does not come from force (might does not make right). Kelsen argues that every norm is valid only in so far as it is made according to another higher norm which leads him to postulating a basic norm (*Grundnorm*) that is a transcendent foundation to any normative order (Kelsen, 2005). According to Carré de Malberg, this conclusion is misguided since norms are human made and the infinite regress of norms presupposed by Kelsen does not lead us to an understanding of their legitimacy. Instead, the original norm has a concrete source: it is made by a constituent representative assembly. What distinguishes, however, the act of this assembly from an act of enforcement of law is that the assembly does not impose its own will, but it makes a claim to speak in the name of something else than itself: the nation.[6] This original act of representation is what founds the legitimacy of the subsequent legal order.

The primary act of representation, a reference to something that cannot express itself directly, reveals that the concept of representation encompasses more than the appointment of delegates. In fact, the delegation model of representation is rejected by Carré de Malberg because it assumes the pre-existing organisation of the people who entrust their power to representatives. This is the American model of popular sovereignty for Carré de Malberg (Carré de Malberg, 2003, II, p. 169). The foundational act of representation, on the contrary, shows that no one speaking in the name of the people or exercising power does so because they received this power directly from the people. The nation that is being represented remains entirely transcendent and only in this capacity can it be the foundation of legitimacy and sovereignty. The formulation of national sovereignty proposed by Carré de Malberg throws popular sovereignty overboard in its entirety. It is opposed to national sovereignty as immanence is opposed to transcendence. The principle of popular sovereignty (immanent causation, unorganised multitude) excludes the principle of national sovereignty (the people as a political unity, organised and represented by the constitution). As we have seen, Carré de Malberg believed Sieyès to be the founder of this specifically French theory of representation and national sovereignty.[7] Yet, it is precisely Sieyès' conception of

6 "La souveraineté ne se crée pas par voie de prescription juridique, pas plus qu'elle n'est susceptible d'être transférée par aucune règle de droit; elle est un fait, et non le produit consécutif d'une règle de celte sorte. En posant en principe que le Parlement exprime législativement la volonté nationale, et en traitant ainsi le Corps législatif comme l'égal du souverain, la Constitution de 1791 ne prétendait pas non plus lui conférer sa souveraineté: elle se bornait à la reconnaître, non point comme la conséquence d'une délégation constitutionnelle, mais comme une réalité antérieure à elle-même et fondée sur tes rapports spéciaux qui, selon la conception révolutionnaire, unissent entre elles, au point de les identifier l'une avec l'autre, l'assemblée élective des députés et l'universalité des citoyens composant la nation souveraine" (Raymond Carré De Malberg, *Confrontation de la théorie de la formation du droit par degrés: avec les idées et les institutions consacrées par le droit positif français relativement à sa formation* (Paris: Dalloz, 2008, p. 64).

7 Carré de Malberg claims that Sieyès "defined the representative government, at the beginning of the new era of public law, with an accuracy and precision that has not been exceeded since

constituent power that is deemed by Carré de Malberg to be inconsistent with the representative nature of national sovereignty and the rest of Sieyès' doctrine since it is formulated in terms of delegation (ibid., II, pp. 487–488). Trying to avoid the immanence of the people at any cost, Carré de Malberg thus draws a clear conceptual distinction between national sovereignty, on the one hand, and popular sovereignty and constituent power, on the other hand. In the process, he has to leave most of Sieyès' ideas out of the picture.

A turn towards referendums

In the concluding remarks to the *Contribution*, Carré de Malberg discusses the political situation of contemporary France. He acknowledges that many voice the opinion that the Constitution of the Third Republic of 1875 does not uphold the principle of national sovereignty. The parliamentary regime of the Third Republic allegedly compromises the precept of national sovereignty in two ways: it does not regulate the legislative process of the parliament and it leaves constituent power in the hands of ordinary representatives. This purportedly results in the substitution of national sovereignty by sovereignty of the parliament and in the submission of the French people to a regime of parliamentary oligarchy (ibid., II, pp. 616–618). Although recognising these criticisms, Carré de Malberg concludes that the rule of the French parliament is still sufficiently limited by a specific power that the French people possess, namely the power of re-election. He maintains that this is the only "truly effective limitation" on parliamentary power and rules out the possibility of referendums as an additional form of popular participation (ibid., II, pp. 618–620).

However, in his work *La loi, expression de la volonté générale* (1931b) and in the article '*Considérations théoriques sur la question de la combinaison du referendum avec le parlementarisme*' (1931b), both from a decade later than *Contribution*, Carré de Malberg suggests that the idea of the organ of the national will is nothing but a juridical fiction ("une fiction de représentation exclut toute participation populaire autre que celle réduite a l'électorat" [Carré de Malberg, 1931a, p. 15]), used in order to mask the fact that parliament usurps the totality of state power (ibid.). What is more, Carré de Malberg now writes that the regime of representation produced by the French Revolution was aimed at ensuring the domination of the bourgeoisie over the popular masses (ibid., p. 16). In Carré de Malberg's view, this became possible because of the original assumption, which was established by the French Revolution and inherited by the later French constitutional tradition, that the idea of the general will and the idea of representation could be combined. Merging Rousseau's idea of the general will as initially attributed to the people and the principle of representation, the revolutionaries set up for a dead end, which eventually led to parliamentary authoritarianism. Parliament can hardly be an apt body for

then" (Carré de Malberg, 2003, II, p. 257).

appropriately expressing the general will as it is not consolidated within itself: there is no general will in the parliament, just dispersed wills of various parties (ibid., p. 23).

According to the Carré de Malberg of these later works, two alternatives present themselves to remedy the situation. The first one is to preserve the idea of the general will, or the 'sovereignty of the general will', and keep associating the law with the expression of the general will of the people. In this case, referendums are a necessary addition to the parliamentary regime because only referendums allow the general will to be expressed in its most direct way (ibid., p. 22). The second alternative is to abandon the idea of the general will altogether and to renounce any potential democratic justification of the parliamentary regime. In this case, referendums are not necessary as parliament is legitimised solely by the constitution and not by reference to the people (Carré de Malberg, 1931b, pp. 221–222; Carré de Malberg, 1931a, pp. 22–23). Considering emerging democratic tendencies and the increased activity of social movements, Carré de Malberg is inclined towards the first alternative. Additionally, he sees several upsides to introducing referendums, such as drawing a sharper line between ordinary and constitutional lawmaking, creating a better balance between the legislative and the executive powers, and limiting the role of parties. All in all, he concludes that referendums are a necessary part of a democratic politics of the general will.

Conclusion

Allegedly, a compromise was achieved in France between national and popular sovereignty in the Constitution of the Fifth Republic adopted in 1958. It stated that "national sovereignty belongs to the people who exercises it through its representatives and through referendums. No section of the people and no individual may purport to exercise it" (Ziller, 2003, p. 267). The adoption of the distinction between national and popular sovereignty in Belgium in the early 1950s was accompanied by an additional ideological layer which potentially complicated a similar resolution. André Mast not only understood the distinction as one between representative and direct government but also read it as an opposition between the Western, liberal-constitutional state and proletarian, revolutionary dictatorships. Mast grouped sovereignty theories into two types. Classical democracy ('*klassieke democratie*') is based on national sovereignty and implies a constitutional regime with limitation of powers, individual rights, and the rule of law. In contrast, popular democracy ('*volksdemocratie*') and popular sovereignty, which uphold the revolutionary role of the proletariat, inevitably lead to the dictatorship of the party and a totalitarian communist regime, developments Mast had observed in the 1950s. For Mast, Belgium, as a constitutional state, should remain founded on the idea of national sovereignty as the regime of a classless society (based on popular sovereignty) is incompatible with Western democracies.

Thinking about the future of the national sovereignty interpretation in Belgium, it might be useful to keep this additional layer in mind. Perhaps this Cold War opposition between the Marxist and liberal projects still informs today's animosity towards popular sovereignty in Belgium. The author of the national sovereignty doctrine, Carré de Malberg, eventually became disenchanted with his own model and made attempts to reimagine the content of the idea of popular sovereignty. A similar exercise, informed by contemporary advances in democratic theory and practice, is to be welcomed in Belgium.

Bibliography

Bacot, G. (2001) *Carré de Malberg et l'origine de la distinction entre souveraineté du peuple et souveraineté nationale.* Paris: CNRS.

Beaud, O. (1994) 'La souveraineté dans la "Contribution à la théorie générale de l'État" de Carré de Malberg', *Revue du Droit Public et de la Science Politique*, 5, pp. 1251–1301.

Beaud, O. (1997) 'Carré de Malberg, juriste alsacien. La biographie comme élément d'explication d'une doctrine constitutionnelle', in Beaud, O., Wachsmann, P. (eds.) *La science juridique française et la science juridique allemande de 1870 à 1918.* Strasbourg: Presses universitaires de Strasbourg.

Beaud, O. (2003) 'Constitution et droit constitutionnel', in Alland, D., Rials, S. (eds.) *Dictionnaire de la culture juridique.* Paris: Presses Universitaires de France, pp. 257–266.

Brunet, P. (1997) 'Entre représentation et nation: Le concept d'organe chez Carré de Malberg', in Beaud, O. et al. (eds.) *La science juridique française et la science juridique allemande de 1870 à 1918.* Annales de la Faculté de Droit de Strasbourg, Strasbourg: Presses Universitaires de Strasbourg.

Carré de Malberg, R. (1931a) 'Considérations théoriques sur la question de la combinaison du referendum avec le parlementarisme', *Revue du Droit Public et de la Science Politique en France et à l'Étranger*, pp. 6–24.

Carré de Malberg, R. (1931b) *La loi, expression de la volonté générale. Étude sur le concept de la loi dans la Constitution de 1875.* Paris: Librairie du Recueil Sirey.

Carré de Malberg, R. (2003) *Contribution à la théorie générale de l'Etat.* Paris: Dalloz.

Carré de Malberg, R. (2008) *Confrontation de la théorie de la formation du droit par degrés: avec les idées et les institutions consacrées par le droit positif français relativement à sa formation.* Paris: Dalloz.

Dumont, H. (2013) 'Les coutumes constitutionnelle, une source de droit et de controverses', in Hachez, I., Cartuyvels, Y., Gérard, P., Ost, F., van de Kerchove, M., Dumont, H. (eds.) *Les sources du droit revisitées, Vol. 1: Normes internationales et constitutionnelles.* Brussels: Presses de l'Université Saint-Louis, pp. 581–634. DOI: 10.4000/books.pusl.1851.

Hegel, G.W.F. (1820) *Grundlinien der Philosophie des Rechts.* Translated in: Wood, A. (ed.) (2003) *Elements of the Philosophy of Right.* Cambridge: Cambridge University Press.

Jouanjan, O. and Maulin, E. (2012) 'Introduction: La théorie de l'État entre passé et avenir. Journées en l'honneur de Carré de Malberg', *Jus Politicum*, 8 [online]. Available at: http://juspoliticum.com/article/Introduction-La-theorie-de-l-Etat-entre-passe-et-avenir-Journees-en-l-honneur-de-Carres-de-Malberg-549.html. (Accessed: 03 August 2020)

Kelsen, H. (2005) *Pure Theory of Law.* Clark, NJ: Lawbook Exchange.

Loughlin, M. (2003) 'Why Sovereignty?' in Rawlings, R., Leyland, P., Young, A. (eds.) *Sovereignty and the Law: Domestic, European and International Perspectives.* Oxford: Oxford University Press, pp. 34–49. DOI: 10.1093/acprof:oso/9780199684069.003.0003.

Mast, A. (1950) *Overzicht van het grondwettelijk recht* (Vol. 1). Ghent: Standaard Boekhandel.

Maulin, É. (2003) 'Raymond Carré de Malberg, le légiste de la République', in R. Carré de Malberg (ed.), *Contribution à la théorie générale de l'Etat.* Paris: Dalloz.

Sieyès, E.J. (1789) *Dire de l'abbé Sieyès sur la question du veto royal, à la séance du 7 septembre 1789.* Versailles: Baudouin.

Vinx, L. (2013) 'The Incoherence of Strong Popular Sovereignty', *International Journal of Constitutional Law*, 11(1), pp. 101–124. DOI: 10.1093/icon/mos049.

Ziller, J. (2003) 'Sovereignty in France: Getting Rid of the Mal de Bodin' in Walker, N. (ed.) *Sovereignty in Transition.* Oxford: Hart Publishing, pp. 261–268. DOI: 10.5040/9781472562883.ch-011.

11 Pulling the curtain on the national sovereignty myth

Sovereignty and referendums in Belgian constitutional doctrine

Christophe Maes, Brecht Deseure, and Ronald Van Crombrugge

Introduction

The dominant interpretation of sovereignty in the Belgian Constitution holds that the National Congress consciously opted for national sovereignty as opposed to popular sovereignty. Followers of this interpretation argue that direct consultation of the people – most notably through referendums – is unconstitutional. Giving voice to the nation through legal decision-making is reserved exclusively for political representatives. Yet, it has been shown elsewhere that the national sovereignty interpretation is an anachronism (De Smaele, 2005; Deseure, 2016b; Geenens and Sottiaux, 2015). This chapter traces the development of the closely related subjects of sovereignty and referendums in Belgian constitutional doctrine from 1831 onwards. We will chart the different points of view on sovereignty from the nineteenth century until the definite breakthrough of the national sovereignty interpretation between 1893 and 1950, as well as the implications this development had for the perceived (un)constitutionality of referendums. We will also briefly address the more recent (post-2000) debates on citizen participation and their connection to the issue of sovereignty.

Our central claim is that there is not one well-defined, stable sovereignty interpretation which undergirds the Belgian Constitution. Instead, sovereignty has been defined and redefined on several occasions under the influence of societal circumstances and in service to political goals. Three major fields of conflict have subsequently shaped Belgian constitutional doctrine on sovereignty: (1) the rivalry between Catholics and liberals; (2) the rise of – and resistance to – emancipatory movements, including socialism; and (3) the post–Second World War reaction against communism. The cumulative effect of these reinterpretations has been to promote a conservative understanding of sovereignty, enabling the establishment to preserve the political status quo for its own benefit. The national sovereignty theory is the culmination point of this evolution. This theory is a myth, however, which denies historical contingency by projecting one specific conception of sovereignty back in time. Not only is the result historically and juridically inaccurate but it also obscures the rich and nuanced debates on sovereignty in Belgian constitutional doctrine as they developed over almost two centuries. We conclude by reconnecting our understanding of sovereignty to these historical struggles, and by asking what lessons we can draw from them in light of modern concerns about democracy such as the rise of populism and the demand for more active citizen involvement.

The early Belgian era (1831–1839)

The early Belgian period was characterised by political unionism: the two major political factions of liberals and Catholics – which later developed into regular political parties – continued the political alliance forged during the Belgian Revolution. The threat of an external enemy endured, as the Dutch king did not accept the peace treaty with Belgium until 1839. Despite mounting ideological tension between both factions, this resulted in internal political cohesion. A conservative tendency was clearly present in Belgian politics: in both the Catholic and liberal movements, the progressive wings lost prominence in favour of their more 'social-conservative' counterparts. Radical democrats, who had not wavered in their claims for a republican and more democratic government, were gradually sidelined (Witte, 2020). This tendency was reinforced by the policies of King Leopold I, who held restrictive views on political participation and defended a strong royal power, as well as by the ambitions of the Church to regain its grip on the clergy (Velaers, 2019, pp. 443–444; Viaene, 2001, pp. 148–149; Witte, 2020, pp. 180, 224–232, 344–345).

Given the prevalent political unionism, there was little need for explicit doctrinal statements on sovereignty. The early constitutional handbooks and commentaries remain very brief on the subject. They mainly point to a negative definition of sovereignty, interpreting article 25 of the Constitution (now article 33) as the negation of royal or divine sovereignty. There are no traces of an identification of article 25 with (representative) national sovereignty as opposed to (direct) popular sovereignty. The oldest existing handbooks trace the article back to the notion of sovereignty in the French Constitution of 1791, which they explained as popular sovereignty in a represented form (S.A., 1831, p. 40; Plaisant, 1832, p. vi; Rogron, 1836, p. i). There did seem to be agreement, however, on the fact that the National Congress had opted for a representative regime rather than direct democracy, though no link was made between this choice and the issue of sovereignty (see Chapter 9 on the relation between representation and sovereignty).

The era of national consolidation and the confessional feuds (1839–1893)

The political struggle between liberals and Catholics

As the Belgian state gained stability after the peace treaty with Holland in 1839, internal political conflicts resurfaced. The end of unionism signalled a return to the liberal versus Catholic opposition which had dominated the period prior to the Belgian Revolution. A second major line of ideological division surfaced in 1850–1860 with the rise of socialism, which was pitted against both liberals and

Catholics. In the context of these evolutions, a wide array of interpretations concerning sovereignty emerged – though conservative understandings remained dominant. What is clear, however, is that today's conceptual differentiation between national and popular sovereignty was not yet present during this period.

To be sure, a few individual authors differentiated national and popular sovereignty. In France, the political economist Simonde de Sismondi was the first to introduce a differentiation in his *Études sur les constitutions des peuples libres* of 1836 (Simonde de Sismondi, 1836). Concerned with the idea of an absolute 'general will' upon which political power rested, Sismondi believed unrestrained popular sovereignty to be illegitimate. The general will resulted from a conciliation of, or transaction between, the individual wills. Thus, Sismondi came to affirm that sovereignty did not belong to the absolute and indivisible people, but to the nation as "plural totality" (Simonde de Sismondi, 1836, p. 66 f. On this theme in Sismondi's work, see also Paulet-Grandguillot, 2010). In Belgium, Heinrich Ahrens was the first to make the distinction in his *Cours de droit naturel ou de philosophie du droit* (Ahrens, 1892, orig. 1838). Ahrens, a native German, was a follower of Karl Krause's organ theory. He saw the nation as a holistic entity spanning generations. National sovereignty implied that the unified and internally organised nation acted through its constituted organs. Popular sovereignty, on the other hand, was a product of social atomism. Based on the imperative mandate and on the universal franchise, it came down to a 'sovereignty of the number'. Ahrens theory, however, had little influence on Belgian doctrine.[1]

The lack of consensus and the discourse of the ancient constitutions

A uniform vision on sovereignty did not develop before the end of the nineteenth century, as the diversity of opinions during this time period shows. Article 25 continued to be explained as the negation of royal or divine sovereignty. Furthermore, most scholars explained sovereignty as omnipotence (Britz, 1865, pp. 57–58; Destriveaux, 1849, pp. 30–34, 40–46; Stecher, 1851, pp. 18–19; Thonissen, 1844, pp. 103–104; Van Hoorebeke, 1848, p. 16; Wyvekens, 1854, p. 9).[2] Others still associated article 25 with the idea of mixed government (Docquier, 1856, p. 10; Masson and Wiliquet, 1885, p. 39; Wyvekens, 1854, pp. 11, 14–15). Despite the divergence of interpretations, a specific narrative pertaining to the Constitution dominated in the middle of the nineteenth century: that of the ancient constitutions (Deseure, 2016a; Marteel, 2006). It was generally believed that the ancient constitutions of the former Southern Netherlands had their origin in a reciprocal social contract with the monarch. Depicting the

1 The limited influence of Ahrens's theory can be found in the writings of his student and successor at the philosophy chair of the University of Brussels, Guillaume Tiberghien (Tiberghien, 1844; 1875).

2 A more Rousseauian version of inalienable yet unrestricted sovereignty was given in De Fooz (1859, pp. 30–31, 49–50, 57–58).

Constitution as a 'national product' was politically useful, since the emphasis on authenticity and continuity was a way to legitimise the country's independence (Delbecke, 2007, pp. 373, 389; Deseure, 2016a; Raxhon, 1989, pp. 32–35).

At the same time, this discourse was deployed as a propaganda tool by the different political parties. Liberals stressed that popular sovereignty underlaid the social contract, as well as individual liberties (Faider, 1842, pp. 146, 155; Kupfferschlaeger, 1871, pp. 1524–1541; Waille, 1838, pp. 150–151). They focused on the history of the cities which had functioned as liberal bastions against Catholic hegemony (Polain, 1844, p. 286; Vandenpeereboom, 1873, pp. 256–257). For Catholic writers, meanwhile, the ancient constitutions allowed them to deny that the origin of the modern liberties lay in the French Revolution. Especially after the revolutions of 1848, they argued that the constitutional liberties were of national origin and derived from the liberties guaranteed under the ancient constitutions by stable, traditional, and Catholic institutions. In the same move, the ancient constitutions served to disavow popular sovereignty, social equality, and universal suffrage. The Belgian Revolution, and the Constitution it produced, was not based on the principle of popular sovereignty, nor on the modern liberties of the French Revolution. It resulted from William I's breach of Catholic values and traditions, which the ancient constitutions embodied (De Gerlache, 1852, pp. 65–73; Van Den Broeck, 1859, pp. 4–5). Prompted by French expansionism under Napoleon III, this narrative of ancient constitutionalism enjoyed a renewed wave of popularity in the 1870s. Although it became less prominent afterwards, it remained an important element in constitutional law handbooks well into the twentieth century.

The elitist liberal interpretation of sovereignty and the rise of the democratic movement

Aside from the discourse of the ancient constitution, the middle of the nineteenth century was marked by the struggle between the democratic emancipatory movement and the socially conservative establishment. Despite the disagreement on the details of the concept of sovereignty in Belgian doctrine, there did exist a consensus that it was to be interpreted in a social-conservative and elitist manner. Catholics and liberals alike made sure to consolidate their political position in response to the challenge coming from the new democratic movements. Whereas the Catholics openly attacked the idea of popular sovereignty and the belief that it entailed universal suffrage, this was much more difficult for the liberals, for whom this principle continued to be the source of state legitimacy. However, from 1850 on, French Doctrinaire ideas slowly made their way into liberal circles. The liberal politician Ernest Vandenpeereboom was the first to explicitly promote Doctrinaire liberalism in the Belgian context. In a typically Doctrinaire manner, he explained article 25 as an expression of the sovereignty of reason. Referring to the French Doctrinaire frontman François Guizot, he argued that capacity was the basis upon which suffrage restrictions were reasonably permitted. Vandenpeereboom believed that the Belgian constituent assembly of 1830–1831 had followed this point of view "in the name of reason, as well as in the name of doctrine" (Vandenpeereboom, 1856, pp. 25–26 with reference to Guizot, *Histoire*, II, lesson XV, pp. 301–304). However, he did not yet differentiate popular from national sovereignty.

In contrast to the ideas of these Doctrinaires, who disconnected the will of the electors from the will of the representatives, a number of liberals and liberal Catholics stressed the importance of a 'reflexive' relationship between the constituted powers and the people or the electors. According to these scholars, the legislative chambers were certainly not alone in the exercise of sovereignty. Despite the rejection of the imperative mandate, the electorate was always in a position to judge the actions of the legislator (Bivort, 1849, pp. 29, 34; Thonissen, 1844, p. 167; Verhaegen, 1859, pp. 100–102). Alongside this, a minority of progressive liberals promoted the idea of enlarging the censitary suffrage to a suffrage based on capacity. Rejecting the elitism of French Doctrinaire liberalism, they supported the idea of a gradual democratisation of the political system as human reason progressed. Education was the obvious road towards enlightenment and, as a result, political emancipation (Stecher, 1851, pp. 17, 31; Tempels, 1873, pp. 440–441; Voituron, 1876; 1878, pp. 1–4). Around the same time, a new movement emerged in Catholic circles which tried to strike a connection with the social movements. Competing with liberal and social democratic movements and driven to a certain extent by strategic considerations, this Christian-democratic movement tried to reconvert and to redirect a part of the masses to its cause (Witte, 2007, p. 10; 2003).

The call for democratic reform and the emergence of the national sovereignty doctrine (1893–1921)

The constitutional reform of 1893

The elitist theories that eventually came to dominate the Belgian understanding of sovereignty first appeared in the debates on the reform and improvement of the representative system that took place at the end of the nineteenth century (François, 1985, pp. 573–574). Movements for democratic emancipation prompted anxiety about the preservation of the parliamentary system (De Smaele, 2002, pp. 114–121), while the diversity of the social body – which was not reflected in parliament – increasingly became an object of attention for reformers and politicians (De Smaele, 1999, pp. 345–346).

The Belgian Workers' Party (BWP), founded in 1885, quickly became a powerful voice in the struggle for the social betterment and political representation of the working class. The introduction of universal suffrage was its single most important demand (Puissant, 2007, pp. 98–99; 2004; Reynebeau, 2009, pp. 94–95; Stengers, 2004, p. 253). The BWP saw universal suffrage as a means to defend the interests of the groups it represented, as opposed to the general interest. Such a definition of the representative mandate ran counter to the 'functional' definition of election defended by the majority of interpreters of the Belgian doctrine, according to whom the vote is not an individual right but rather a function to appoint those best placed to reveal the will of the nation as a whole.

A combination of social unrest, mass demonstrations, and general strikes finally convinced the established powers that constitutional reform, including an extension of suffrage of some kind, was no longer avoidable. The public debate in the early 1890s on constitutional reform focused on three issues, notably: the representation of interests, proportional representation, and the introduction of the referendum (De Smaele, 1999; Röttger, 2005; Velaers, 2007). It is in these debates – and those on the referendum in particular – that a novel conception of national sovereignty surfaced for the first time.

Universal suffrage, as demanded by the social democratic movement, quickly proved to be unattainable. Since the social democrats were not yet represented in parliament, a compromise needed to be found between Catholics and liberals and between the various tendencies within these parties. Different forms of censitary suffrage, capacitary suffrage, and corporative representation were considered. A compromise was finally found around the proposal of Albert Nyssens, a professor of law at the Catholic University of Leuven and later minister of industry. Nyssens came up with 'multiple universal suffrage': one vote for each adult male, supplemented with one or two additional votes depending on wealth and capacity. Nyssens' proposal was not purely informed by strategic considerations. He believed the gradual enlargement of suffrage to be a logical and inevitable outcome of the constitution's choice for a representative regime based on popular sovereignty (Nyssens, 1890, p. 8).

The reform of voting rights was only one of several avenues which were explored in order to improve the representative system. Another one was the introduction of the referendum. The initiative in this regard was taken by King Leopold II. Just like the Catholic establishment, the king had consented to open the procedure for constitutional reform in order to avoid serious social upheaval.[3] He expected the enlargement of suffrage to result in a reinforcement of parliamentary authority at the expense of the executive power. At the same time, he feared the breakthrough of socialism in parliament. As he described his own role as that of the "truthful guardian and protector" of the interest of the state,[4] he sought to strengthen the royal powers as a way to guarantee the stability of the state institutions (Senelle et al., 2004, p. 30). His preferred option for doing so was the introduction of a referendum on royal initiative, which would have enabled the king to bypass and overrule a parliamentary majority if necessary (Orban, 1908, p. 514; Witte et al., 2003, p. 399).

The proponents of this proposal (e.g. the Catholic prime minister Auguste Beernaert, doctrinal liberals like Emile Banning, and progressive liberals like Emile de Laveleye and Paul Janson) argued that the balance between the different state

3 For a more detailed discussion of this procedure and its connection to the issue of constituent power, see Chapter 9.

4 See Leopold II's letter of 31 December 1891 (Van der Smissen, 1920, pp. 101–102).

powers had been thrown out of whack by the increase in parliamentary authority. According to them, parliamentary omnipotence was not what the framers had envisaged. Such a regime reduced all the guarantees for the protection of individual rights and undermined the institutions which the framers had set up to this end, e.g. the monarch as neutral power, the balance of the constituted powers, ministerial responsibility, etc. (e.g. Banning, 1899, pp. 11, 20–27, 32–40, 50; De Laveleye, 1897, p. 394). So, a new balance had to be achieved. A consultative referendum was considered useful in this respect since it would allow the electorate to settle conflicts between the chambers or between the chambers and the king. For the progressive liberal De Laveleye, this would allow the king to truly become a neutral power, as originally intended. The royal referendum would reactivate the royal veto, which had fallen into disuse. By consulting the nation, the king would be in a position to make sure that legislation reflected the real interests and opinion of the country:

> Or the project of law, against which popular manifestations have arisen, will be ratified by *referendum* by a majority of voters. Then the advocates of the sovereignty of the people will have to bend before the clearly expressed will of the people; or the majority rejects the project, which would prove that it was genuinely unpopular. In this case, it would be good that the constituted powers would acknowledge the opposition of the real country.
>
> (emphasis from the original author. De Laveleye, 1897, p. 402)

For Prime Minister Beernaert, the referendum was a way to moderate the democratic powers and integrate them into the political system. Although the nation had delegated its powers under the Constitution, he claimed that it retained the right to be consulted on important matters.[5] Beernaert anticipated the argument of the referendum's unconstitutionality by stressing its consultative nature. Additionally, he argued that the referendum would act as a useful corrective on the (at that time) majoritarian electoral system, where alternating liberal and Catholic governments were systematically reversing the measures taken by their predecessor. This kind of immobilisation could be prevented by consulting the nation in a referendum. Others, such as Catholic member of parliament Frans Schollaert, argued that the parliamentary right of investigation (old article 40 of the Constitution) provided a constitutional basis for the introduction of a consultative referendum. This right followed from parliament's legislative initiative and principally admitted that the legislative assembly could inform itself through consultation with the electorate. Similar arguments were formulated by Émile Dupont and Eugène Goblet d'Alviella.[6]

5 *Hand.* Kamer 1891–1892, p. 507, 2 February 1892, Beernaert.

6 *Hand.* Kamer 1892–1893, p. 1904, 13 July 1893, Schollaert; *Hand.* Senaat, 1892–1893, p. 498, 3 August 1893, Dupont; *Hand.* Senaat, 1892–1893, p. 499, 3 August 1893, Goblet d'Alviella.

The opponents of the referendum, in turn, argued – somewhat unsurprisingly – that it was not compatible with the representative regime established by the Belgian Constitution. Fierce opposition to the proposal was voiced in parliament by the Catholic leader Charles Woeste and Doctrinaire liberals such as Walthère Frère-Orban and Jules Bara. They rejected the referendum because it risked disfiguring the parliamentary system by locating power directly with the people.[7] Leopold II, meanwhile, was accused of using the referendum as an instrument to realise his ideal of Caesarism and royal despotism. For the first time, the idea that Belgian government was exclusively representative in nature was explicitly stated. Frère-Orban argued in parliament that sovereignty in Belgium was therefore not reconcilable with plebiscites.[8] Moreover, he explicitly differentiated representative sovereignty from the direct, popular sovereignty desired by the progressives and radicals:

> The Constitution [...] formally condemns the sovereignty of the people, which you affirm. The Constitution says it is true that the Belgians are equal before the law and that all the powers emanate from the nation, i.e. it does not recognize the regime which has been called "of divine origin". Yet, [the Constitution] adds [...] that these powers are exercised in a manner that it determines. In which manner are the origin of the powers and the powers themselves determined? This is what the Constitution says in explicit terms. [...] Furthermore, she defines the powers and the manner of their exercise, which excludes in the most absolute way your interpretation of the sovereignty of the people.
>
> (*Hand.* Kamer 1892–1893, p. 1032, 23 March 1893, Frère-Orban)

This passage shows that Doctrinaire liberals now clearly made a distinction between a mediated form of sovereignty, on the one hand, and an unmediated one on the other. Showing a remarkable affinity with the French Doctrinaires, Frère-Orban identified the first form with the "theory of the numbers", according to which the referendum and universal suffrage followed. He rejected this form in favour of "the insights of reason", which were to be found in the representative regime.[9]

The ideological entente between Catholics and Doctrinaire liberals against direct democracy seemed complete (De Smaele, 1998, pp. 29–31; Raxhon, 2007, pp. 37–38). Jules Van den Heuvel, a professor of public law at the Catholic University of Leuven and later Catholic minister of justice, published an extensive refutation of the referendum and of universal suffrage. He argued against

7 *Hand.* Kamer 1892–1893, p. 1036, 23 March 1893, Frère-Orban.

8 "*Le régime* [représentatif] *sous lequel nous vivons exclut la législation directe par le corps électoral.* [...] *L'application d'une telle mesure renverserait toute l'économie du régime représentatif et parlementaire*" (Letter of Frère-Orban of 23 December 1891, published in *L'Indépendance belge*, 'Le referendum royal. Une lettre de M. Frère-Orban', 30 December 1891, no. 363).

9 *Hand.* Kamer 1892–1893, pp. 1033–1034, 23 March 1893, Frère-Orban.

the total uprooting of the constitutional system by the introduction of these measures, the risk of personal government by the king based on plebiscites, the loss of prestige and authority for the constituted powers, and the impossibility of consistent policy-making due to the whims of the electorate (Van Den Heuvel, 1892; 1898). Similar arguments were advanced by the Catholic aristocrat and communal politician Fernand de Zerezo de Téjada (Zerezo de Téjada, 1891, esp. pp. 1–3, 20, 23).

It is obvious, however, that this rejection by the established parties of direct citizen participation was not purely based on principle, but also on strategy. Woeste indicated as much when he stated that the proposed reforms went against the tradition and principles of the existing systems as well as against the interests of the conservative party.[10] The more moderate Van den Heuvel joined this position, fearing that universal suffrage and the referendum would allow social democrats and republicans to attack the parliamentary system (Van Den Heuvel, 1892, pp. 24–25, 161). Further government initiatives towards the introduction of referendums failed due to this broad opposition (Lejeune and Regnier, 1985, pp. 23 with references in n. 33–35; Orban, 1906, pp. 123–124).

Fruitless attempts at further democratisation

Several additional attempts to introduce referendums were made in the decades following the constitutional revision of 1893. In 1899, social democrats and progressive liberals proposed to organise a national referendum on the subject of the introduction of proportional representation.[11] Two years later, the progressive liberal Paul Janson filed a similar proposal for a national referendum on the introduction of universal single suffrage and proportional representation.[12] In both cases, the progressive opposition tried to organise a referendum as a way to bypass the parliamentary majority blocking their proposals to change the political system. The arguments of the 1893 debate were largely repeated, and both proposals were subsequently defeated in parliament.[13]

The situation was different in 1919–1921, when a government of national unity sought to revise the Constitution as part of the country's post-war modernisation. In 1919, the government single-handedly introduced universal male suffrage in the face of communist agitation and massive social disruption (and in direct contravention of the written Constitution). This radical move was justified by liberal minister Henri Jaspar (backed by the liberal constitutional scholar Paul Errera) through the argument that the circumstances of the war, which among other things prevented regular elections, had already created an unconstitutional political situation. Errera's Catholic counterpart Léon Dupriez added that the

10 *Hand.* Kamer 1892–1893, p. 1336, 20 May 1892, Woeste.
11 *Parl. St.* Kamer 1898–1899, p. 229.
12 *Parl. St.* Kamer 1900–1901, p. 192.
13 *Hand.* Kamer 1898–1899, p. 2847; *Hand.* Kamer 1900–1901, p. 1669.

parliamentary majority of the time could no longer be said to reflect the true national opinion, since it had been elected before the war (Haag, 1976, p. 172). This debate is interesting because it suggests that, at least for some constitutional scholars, elections alone do not legitimise parliament. Both its composition and its decisions need to express the will of the nation as it exists at that moment. Among the measures proposed by the government of national unity was the introduction of a so-called *référendum de partage*. Under this proposal, referendums could be called in cases of disagreement between the chambers, when a legislative proposal was contested by a significant minority and when the king deemed it necessary.[14] The proposal concerned both referendums on ordinary legislation and on constitutional revisions. Articles 26 and 39 of the Constitution would be amended to make the change possible. Remarkably article 25 (at least the first paragraph) remained out of the picture. This suggests that the connection between national sovereignty and the representative regime on the one hand, and the principle that "all the powers emanate from the nation", on the other, was still not present. The government's proposal, as well as four additional proposals for the revision of article 26, was nevertheless defeated in parliament: they (narrowly) failed to reach the two-thirds majority required for constitutional amendments.[15]

After this period, and with the introduction of universal male suffrage, interest in the introduction of referendums waned. Particularly in social democratic circles, the referendum had primarily been conceived as a corrective of the existing representative system and its exclusive nature. With the introduction of universal suffrage (and the earlier adoption of proportional representation in 1899), the socialist party was able to obtain a landslide victory in the 1919 elections. Now constituting a regular political party, it became less concerned with direct political participation than it had been before, which shows once more the intimate connection between political strategic motives and positions on matters of constitutional principle.

The post-war era (1950–1985)

The Royal Question and Belgium's first and only referendum

As we have seen, the modern conceptual differentiation between national sovereignty and popular sovereignty only came about in 1893 in the context of the debates on constitutional reform and the introduction of the referendum on the royal initiative in particular. It is important to note that for the time being, this conceptual opposition occupied a minority position. In most cases, the terms national and popular sovereignty continued to be used interchangeably. A sizeable number of handbooks still explained article 25 as a manifestation of popular sovereignty (Boon, 1940; Brants, 1937; De Hoon, 1927; De Putter,

14 *Parl. St.* Kamer 1918–1919, no. 329, p. 2.

15 *Parl. St.* Kamer 1920–1921, p. 207, 6 April 1921; *Hand.* Kamer 1920–1921, p. 1400, 31 May 1921.

1944; Noterdaeme, 1956; Vauthier, 1931). The national sovereignty interpretation, however, gradually gained support over the course of the first half of the twentieth century (e.g. Dor and Braas, 1935, pp. 161, 157 with reference to Raymond Carré de Malberg; Errera, 1909, pp. 117–119; Orban, 1906, p. 276, with reference to Frère-Orban, 1908, pp. 3–8, 26–27; Speyer, 1927, pp. 30–33, 45–46; Vanden Bossche, 1925, pp. 547–550), until finally becoming the dominant doctrine in the aftermath of the referendum on the Royal Question which was held in 1950.

The post-war period in Belgian politics was characterised by attempts at political normalisation, as well as by a revival of Belgian patriotism. The collective experience of the war became embodied in the abstract 'nation' and the idea of a 'Belgian community', terms which became omnipresent in political discourse (Conway, 2012, p. 246). The interbellum scepticism towards parliamentary institutions now made way for a wholehearted celebration of democratic representative institutions. "Outside of parliamentary democracy", Prime Minister Achiel Van Acker declared in 1945, "there only exists escapades, misery and perils".[16] It is somewhat surprising therefore that Belgium's first – and to date, only – national referendum was held in this context.

The political crisis which led to the organisation of this referendum erupted in 1945 with a power struggle between parliament, which was dominated at the time by the social democrats, and King Leopold III, who was supported by the right-wing Catholics. When the king surrendered to Germany in May 1940 (becoming a German prisoner of war for the remainder of the conflict), the government declared him unable to govern. Shortly after Leopold III's liberation, discussion arose about his return to power. The revelation of his sympathies for Hitler as well as his stubbornness and autocratic attitude only worsened his relations with the social democrats, who promptly passed legislation to make sure that the decision on the king's return remained exclusively with parliament (Gérard-Libois and Gotovitch, 1983, p. 25). In response, Leopold toyed with the idea of a referendum in order to circumvent parliament. Intent on electoral gain, the Catholics publicly supported this idea. Their strategy paid off, and having attained a parliamentary majority, they could now impose the organisation of a referendum (Theunissen, 1984, pp. 27–28). A majority now considered the organization of a referendum without altering the Constitution possible, but on the conditions that it would remain an exceptional, one-time event and that the result of the referendum could not bind parliament. One month later, on 12 March 1950, the electorate was asked whether "King Leopold III should retake the exercise of his constitutional powers". The referendum revealed deep linguistic and regional disagreements within the country.[17] The king and the Catholic majority in parliament nevertheless interpreted the result as the 'will of the majority', and thereby

16 As cited in Conway (2012, p. 251).

17 Of the Flemish population, 72% voted for the king's return, whereas in Wallonia and in Brussels the return only received 42% and 48% of the votes, respectively.

as the national will. However, when they made preparations for the king's return, deadly riots broke out. Revolution and civil war now threatened the government, and the king was compelled to step down on 16 July 1951 in favour of his son, Baudouin (Senelle et al., 2004, pp. 120–121).

Very quickly, the impact of the Royal Question became apparent in Belgian legal scholarship. Leopold III's inclination towards autocratic governance, if need be with the direct support of the electorate, urged several constitutional scholars to reach back to the 1891–1893 arguments against the plebiscitary monarchy. However, whereas they were initially concerned with the limitation of royal power, their attention would shift in the light of the emergent communist threat. Gradually, the legal scholarship would come to associate national sovereignty with Western democracies, which they contrasted with the popular sovereignty defended by Marxist regimes (cf. *infra*).

The main protagonists in this shift were the professors of constitutional law André Mast (at the University of Ghent) and Pierre Wigny (at the Catholic universities of Leuven and Namur). The impact of the crisis on constitutional thought was already noticeable a few months after the referendum, when Mast published his 'Overview of constitutional law'. In this handbook, Mast made a sharp distinction between national and popular sovereignty, which he associated with representative and direct democracy, respectively (Mast, 1950, pp. 66–67). According to him, the Belgian National Congress had deliberately opted for national sovereignty. This meant that sovereignty resided in the complex, intangible, and transgenerational nation. For Mast, it was precisely this abstraction that enabled a democratic regime to impose limits on, and to prevent abuses by, accidental majorities. The counter-image to this view of democracy was provided by what Mast termed 'Rousseauian' democracy, that is, popular sovereignty, where sovereignty belonged to the mass of individuals. Surprisingly, Mast concluded that this regime did not exclude representation. Nor did national sovereignty necessarily entail representative government (Mast, 1950, p. 69; 1953, p. 74). For Mast, popular sovereignty rather meant that sovereignty became personified in the representative assembly and more specifically in the momentary parliamentary majority. Since the parliamentary majority represented the people's will, no checks or balances could limit its powers (Mast, 1950, pp. 66–67). This was Mast's main critique of popular sovereignty. Consequently, for Mast, popular sovereignty was not so much a problem of direct democracy as a problem of unchecked parliamentary power. In fact, Mast's critique seems to have been directed mainly against any governmental institution – whether it be the king or parliament – which tried to impose its will through the direct intervention of the electorate. The fear of a plebiscitary monarchy, in particular, seems to have been a concern for Mast.[18]

18 Especially Mast's reference to Charles Woeste's views on sovereignty (instead of references to the constitutional debates of 1830–1831) catch the eye, as they were explicitly directed against the possibility of a plebiscitary monarchy (Mast, 1950, pp. 82, 84).

Mast's contemporary colleague Wigny further developed the national sovereignty doctrine. Just like Mast, Wigny dismissed popular sovereignty. In his view, a Rousseauian interpretation of popular sovereignty attributed a fraction of the highest power to all citizens. As a result, popular sovereignty entailed direct or semi-direct democracy with an imperative mandate for the representatives (Wigny, 1952, p. 224). Wigny contrasted this with national sovereignty, where power lies with the nation, "considered in its indivisible and global consistence" (Wigny, 1952, p. 225). Wigny found support for the Belgian case in Carré de Malberg's organ theory, which asserted that "far from presupposing a pre-existing will, the organ establishes this will and this juridical person [the nation]" (Carré de Malberg, 1922, p. 228). This was the system Wigny recognised in the Belgian Constitution's sovereignty clause, and which he attributed to the framers.

Anticommunism and the shift in the conception of sovereignty

After the Royal Question, the views of both men gradually shifted in response to changing political circumstances. As Olga Bashkina recently observed, the Belgian sovereignty debate became influenced by growing international tensions as the world stage became divided between the two geo-political spheres of Western democracies and the communist Soviet Union (Bashkina, 2018, pp. 162–163). The outbreak of the Korean War in June 1950 resulted in a national anti-communist campaign in Belgium, led by the Catholic party (Gerard, 2016, p. 59). This Cold War context also affected the understanding of sovereignty as legal scholars increasingly sharpened the contrast between national and popular sovereignty, eventually resulting in two antagonistic conceptions of sovereignty. Carré de Malberg's binary conception of national and popular sovereignty proved particularly useful to this end (Bashkina, 2018, p. 163).

While Mast had first identified popular sovereignty with unconstrained parliamentary power, during the 1960s he gradually came to associate the term with the totalitarian pseudo-democracies of the Soviet regime (Bashkina, 2018, p. 163). According to Mast, a "classical democracy" built on national sovereignty entailed respect for individual rights and constitutional limitations to the exercise of state power. On the other hand, a "popular democracy", based on a Rousseauian understanding of popular sovereignty and on the Marxist ideal of a classless society, paid exclusive homage to the absolute authority of "the People". The latter knew no limits and inevitably led to the usurpation of state power and eventually to dictatorship (Mast, 1981, pp. 22–24; 1967, pp. 21–22).

Similarly, Pierre Wigny gradually complemented his distinction between national and popular sovereignty with an anti-communist interpretation of these concepts. Using a comparable terminology to Mast, Wigny opposed Western "classical democracies" to communist "popular democracies" (Wigny, 1956, pp. 11–13). Only the former provided true government by the people and for the people, thereby securing the plurality of opinions under permanent control of the nation (Wigny, 1969, pp. 44–46). Stalinist regimes, on the other hand, established dictatorship in French Jacobin fashion and on the basis of Rousseauian principles (Wigny, 1973, p. 41). Just like Mast, Wigny now wielded national sovereignty as an instrument to denounce the theoretical legitimation of communist regimes.[19]

Even though these eminent constitutional scholars managed to set the standard in Belgium on the notion of sovereignty for the second half of the twentieth century, it took quite some time before their views achieved the status of a majority consensus. Several legal scholars continued to use national and popular sovereignty interchangeably, or refused to distinguish between both interpretations (De Meyer, 1982; Vliebergh, 1973). In time, however, these viewpoints became a minority. The discussion came to a decisive end with a 1985 opinion issued by the Council of State, which settled the national sovereignty doctrine as the standard for the next decades.[20] Additionally, it also permanently settled the question of the constitutionality of referendums. From that point on, a large consensus existed among legal scholars that referendums were incompatible with the existing constitutional structure and that in order to introduce them a constitutional revision was required. Importantly, however, while the opinion became one of the most important legal sources in support of the national sovereignty doctrine, it omitted any reference to the circumstances (the Royal Question and anti-communist sentiment) which had helped to shape it. Later handbooks too omitted this aspect of history, further decontextualising the concept of national sovereignty and (wrongly) attributing it to the framers.

The contemporary debate (the 2000s onwards)

The 1985 opinion handed down by the Council of State thus temporarily closed the legal debate on sovereignty and referendums. Contemporary legal doctrine acknowledged the Council's point of view (Alen, 2000, p. 73; Delpérée, 2000, p. 163; Geudens, 2000; Rimanque, 1999, pp. 100–101; Uyttendaele, 1994; Velaers, 2001, p. 165; Velu, 1986). This did not mean, however, that the question of the referendum disappeared from the political agenda. On numerous occasions over the decades following the Council's decision, new efforts were made to introduce referendums. In the meantime, a series of state reforms transformed Belgium from a unitary state into a federal one, consisting of three territorial regions and three linguistic communities. Most often, the proposals for the introduction of referendums were not intended to alter the democratic system in a durable way, but rather concerned *ad hoc* specific issues that were politically contentious at that time, such as European integration or Belgian federalism (Velaers, 2019). Several of these proposals gave the Council of State the

19 This corresponded with contemporary actions of his political party, which tried to silence the national communist movements through legal channels. See e.g. Kwanten (2001, pp. 424–427).

20 R.v.St., afd. Wetgeving, adviezen van 15 mei 1985, *Parl. St.* Kamer, 1983–1984, 783/2. See Chapter 1 on this milestone opinion.

opportunity to repeat its jurisprudence: there exists a tension between the representative nature of the Belgian Constitution and the direct democratic nature of referendums; and in any case, the referendum cannot be introduced without explicit constitutional basis.

Perhaps the most serious attempt (apart from the post–First World War debates) to incorporate referendums into the Belgian Constitution came in the early 2000s, with the formation of a government coalition between liberal, social democratic, and green parties. A notable aspect of this coalition's programme was the stated aim of renewing and deepening Belgian democracy, most obviously through 'direct democratic' instruments such as referendums or popular initiatives. While this proposal generated much discussion and disagreement, there was a widespread consensus among legislators and experts alike that introducing referendums necessitated a constitutional amendment, thus cementing even further the Council of State's position. Disagreement nevertheless existed as to whether non-binding referendums also required an explicit constitutional basis. Part of the legal profession, especially scholars upholding a living constitutionalism approach to the interpretation of the sovereignty clause, took a sceptical stance (e.g. Bourgaux, 2015; De Witte, 2003, pp. 352–353; Lejeune and Regnier, 1985, pp. 31–32; Popelier, 2004, pp. 118–123; Vande Lanotte et al., 2015, pp. 208–212). In the end, however, this effort to introduce referendums – like all the ones before it – failed.

The next important development occurred in 2014, when democratic reform was one of the topics of Belgium's Sixth State Reform. As part of the eventual compromise, a new article 39 bis was inserted into the Constitution. This article created a constitutional basis for non-binding referendums, though exclusively at the level of the regions. The possibility of also holding referendums at the federal level was considered a step too far as it continued to evoke strong fears that this would pit Belgium's different linguistic communities against each other. Thus, the referendum on the Royal Question, as well as the memory of the conflicts it generated, continued to cast their shadow on constitutional debates. Yet, for the sovereignty debate, the adoption of article 39 bis nonetheless constituted an important evolution, since the inclusion of this provision in the Constitution shows that parliament did not consider the national sovereignty doctrine – which continues to be the majority position in legal thought – a sufficient reason to refrain from giving referendums a place within the Belgian Constitution. Unlike during the pre-war constitutional debates, in 2014, the sovereignty issue did not feature in the parliamentary discussions, which focused mostly on technical issues – such as which policy issues should be placed beyond the reach of the referendum.[21] But the impact of article 39 bis should not be overstated either. The article as such has little in the way of specific legal consequences, since it merely provides the *possibility* for the regions to start using referendums. It is up to each region to decide whether or not to make use of this possibility. So far, only the

21 *Parl. St.* Kamer, 2010–2014, 2966/003; *Parl. St.* Senaat 2010–2014, 2372/3.

region of Wallonia has adopted the necessary enabling legislation to do so, but as of yet no referendums have taken place under this law.[22]

The value of sovereignty today

While the practical impact of the national sovereignty doctrine may have somewhat lessened in light of these constitutional developments, it continues to hold a strong influence over the legal thinking on democracy in Belgium. In general, legal scholars and practitioners remain hostile to active citizen involvement and see participation and representation as polar opposites. Contemporary legal handbooks continue to present the choice as one between national and popular sovereignty, the former synonymous with representation and the latter with participation, with the Belgian Constitution clearly falling on the side of the former (e.g. De Schepper, 2018, pp. 14–18; Keunen and Bijnens, 2017; Schram, 2015, p. 110). As the previous discussion has shown, to present these concepts in this way is highly misleading and strips them of their historical context. Throughout the constitutional history of Belgium, the concept of sovereignty has been used to highlight different distinctions, often in service of the political needs of that specific moment: reason versus mob rule, parliamentarism versus monarchical plebiscitarianism, liberal versus Marxist democracy. By stripping the national sovereignty doctrine of this context and the historical struggles in which it arose, its elitist consequences are legitimised. It presents the theory as an objective, originalist reading of the Constitution rather than as a political instrument which was used at several stages in Belgium's political history to deny new democratic rights. Strangely, even legal scholars and practitioners who now question the historicity of the classic distinction still refuse to dismiss it entirely and eventually revert back to it by arguing that constitutional practice has corroborated the national sovereignty doctrine – thus switching between originalism and living constitutionalism (e.g. Alen, 2015, pp. 7, 44; Velaers, 2019, pp. 6–7).

These elitist consequences become especially obvious when we contrast the Council of State's view on representation with recent theories of representation. An important argument used by the Council to defend the incompatibility between direct participation and representation is the fact that referendums could possibly generate discordance between the will of the population as expressed directly in a referendum and the will of the population as expressed in parliament. However, in contrast to what is argued by the Council of State, a representative system does not require the "complete conformity between the will of the citizens and their representatives".[23] Contemporary theorists of representation, such as Nadia Urbinati, have emphasised how the unbridgeable distance between representatives and citizens is crucial for democracy's proper functioning. It is this distance which creates the space for critical reflection on the part of citizens and

22 See Chapter 12 for a more detailed discussion of the Walloon referendum legislation.
23 R.v.St., afd. Wetgeving, adviezen van 15 mei 1985, *Parl. St.* Kamer, 1983–1984, 783/2.

enables them to exercise democratic control on the use of state power (Urbinati, 2006). Members of parliament should therefore not be presumed "*iuris et de iure*" to represent the will of the people, as the Council of State argues. Rather, the opposite is true. Michael Saward rightly states that the possibility to contest any claim to represent someone or something is the essence of democratic representation (Saward, 2010). A representative's authority is best protected, not by hiding the disagreements between elected representatives and their constituents behind juridical abstractions such as the idea of the 'nation', but rather by recognising the inevitable gap that separates representatives from the represented. One way to recognise this gap is by providing citizens with tools that allow them to enter into a dialogue with representatives and which give them the feeling that their perspective has been taken into account.

From a cursory glance, this looks like a conflict between a strictly trustee-based view of representation and more contemporary approaches to representation. However, when seen in light of the historical struggles which shaped the sovereignty debate in Belgium, it becomes clear that these tensions were part of the debate since the beginning. The idea that representation cannot exist in isolation but needs to be connected to the broader realm of public opinion has always been present in Belgian constitutional doctrine. By incorporating the lessons of these struggles in our understanding of sovereignty, it thus becomes possible to gain a richer, more nuanced understanding of this concept which is fit for modern times and transcends the stale distinction between popular and national sovereignty.

Before concluding, we would like to highlight two particular lessons which appear especially instructive in light of current concerns about democracy. The first is that sovereignty entails a negative aspect. The negative aspect of sovereignty implies that no political actor, be it in the person of the king or even parliament itself, can legitimately claim to embody the nation or the people as a whole. This, as we saw, was one of the purposes attributed to the sovereignty clause by the framers of the Belgian Constitution. Yet, it is a lesson worth relearning given the rise – in several Western democracies – of populism, the core premise of which is precisely its claim to embody the 'will of the people' (Mudde, 2017; Rummens, 2017). Though the national sovereignty doctrine and populism hold different conceptions of state power, legitimacy, and representation, they are aligned on one crucial point which makes the national sovereignty doctrine vulnerable to being instrumentalised by a populist majority in parliament: they both deny the gap that exists between representatives and the represented. In populism, the will of the people is said to exist independently from its representation in politics. However, since the people is conceptualised as a homogeneous whole speaking with one voice, its will can be embodied by the populist party or leader itself, which is therefore seen as the only legitimate representative of the people (Arditi, 2003; Urbinati, 2014, p. 113). In contrast, the national sovereignty doctrine denies that there is any sort of pre-existing will of the people. Rather, this will is constructed by parliament itself. Yet, there exists an irrefutable presumption ("*iuris et de iure*" in the words of the Council of State) that the will of parliament is indeed the will of the people; which is why any challenge through referendums must be avoided. While the national sovereignty doctrine is conscious of the fact that the equation between the will of the people and the will of parliament is a legal fiction, this matters little in practical terms: it still renders the collective will of the representatives incontestable for the represented. As a result, in the hands of a populist majority, the national sovereignty doctrine is likely to become just another tool to foreclose any contestation of their claims to represent the will of the people. In contrast, re-incorporating the negative aspect of sovereignty in our understanding of this concept would provide the necessary conceptual tools to deflect these populist claims: while a majority in parliament may exercise power in the name of the people, it cannot claim to constitute or embody the people itself, the exact meaning of which remains forever beyond the grasp of state institutions.

A second lesson concerns the communicative aspect of sovereignty. As we saw, the choice for a representative system of government never implied that representatives had to perform their representative role in isolation and unconnected from public opinion. While it is the task of representatives to legislate, they are free to consult the public when performing this task. Nor was the outcome of the representative process presumed to be infallible (as the national sovereignty doctrine assumes). As the lengthy debates around the turn of the nineteenth century show, the idea that the representative system sometimes needs correcting was very much alive. While we certainly do not have to adopt the solutions contemplated at that time to address failures of representation, such as the referendum on royal initiative, the concerns expressed in those debates remain relevant today. Especially in times of growing popular dissatisfaction with how democracy operates, it is not a far stretch to argue that a conception of sovereignty which emphasises the right of citizens to criticise, contest, and if need be correct the judgements of representatives is better suited to respond to these popular concerns than a conception of sovereignty based on the presumption that the will of parliament is the correct and irrefutable interpretation of the popular will.

Conclusion

This chapter explored the historical development of the concept of sovereignty in Belgian constitutional doctrine. It became clear that the theory of national sovereignty did not exist in 1830–1831 but only developed from the late nineteenth century on. Nor can we speak of a unified and consistent theory, since national sovereignty came in different forms and varieties which gradually developed in response to specific political conflicts. We saw that popular sovereignty was treated with hostility out of a conservative fear for social-emancipatory movements and 'mob rule', although a systematic differentiation with the concept of national sovereignty was initially absent. Early formulations of national sovereignty appeared from 1893 onward, in response to the threat of personal rule by the king occasioned by Leopold II's aspirations to extend his power via plebiscite. Both concerns continued to inform the sovereignty debate in the twentieth century. Belgium's one-time experience with a referendum in the post-war Royal Question provided the final catalyst for establishing the doctrinal dichotomy between national sovereignty and popular sovereignty, between representative government and direct democracy. Not long afterwards, Cold War polarisation between Western and communist societies contributed to grafting the opposition between constitutional liberalism and popular totalitarianism onto the same divide. The Council of State's momentous 1985 opinion thus canonised an interpretation which was fairly recent and certainly did not originate in the constituent moment.

In a sense, the intellectual shifts and the appropriation of specific intellectual frameworks (e.g. the Doctrinaires' sovereignty of reason versus sovereignty of numbers, or Carré de Malberg's national sovereignty versus popular sovereignty) are the natural consequence of the essentially contested nature of the concept of sovereignty. Yet, as the national sovereignty doctrine solidified into the majority position, the contested nature of the concept – and the historical conflicts which shaped it – became obscured. This evolution was not innocent, since it helped legitimise the elitist consequences of the national sovereignty doctrine (such as the unconstitutionality of referendums) by dressing them up as the original intention of the framers. By pulling the curtain on the national sovereignty myth and laying bare its political roots, this chapter aimed to re-establish the contestable nature of sovereignty. In particular, we showed how this context-sensitive, historical approach provides a much more versatile understanding of sovereignty. This reading of sovereignty not only abandons the elitist view on representation inherited from bygone days but is also more receptive to the introduction of participatory elements, which we think are better adapted to deal with today's democratic challenges.

Bibliography

Ahrens, H. (1892, orig. 1838) *Cours de droit naturel ou de philosophie du droit.* Leipzig: Brockhaus.

Alen, A. (2000) *Compendium van het Belgisch staatsrecht.* Diegem: Kluwer.

Alen, A. (2015) *Hoe "Belgisch" is het "Belgisch Staatsrecht" nog?* Antwerp: Intersentia.

Arditi, B. (2003) 'Populism, or, Politics at the Edges of Democracy', *Contemporary Politics*, 9(1), pp. 17–31. DOI: 10.1080/1356977032000072486.

Banning, E. (1899) *Réflexions, morales et politiques.* Brussels: Spineux.

Bashkina, O. (2018) 'Raymond Carré de Malberg and the Interpretation of Sovereignty in the Belgian Constitution', *Giornale di Storia Costituzionale*, 35(3), pp. 149–166.

Bivort, J.-B. (1849) *Code constitutionnel de la Belgique ou commentaire sur la constitution, la loi électorale, la loi communale et la loi provinciale.* Brussels: Deprez-Parent.

Boon, V. (1940) *Het Belgisch staatsrecht.* Lier: Van In.

Bourgaux, A.-E. (2015) 'La consultation populaire régionale: résistance ou résilience de la démocratie représentative belge?', *Administration Publique*, 38(4), pp. 531–583.

Brants, K. (1937) *De staatsinrichting van België. Beginselen van grondwettelijk recht en van administratief recht.* Brussels: Standaard Boekhandel.

Britz, J. (1865) *La Constitution belge et les lois organiques.* Brussels: Bruylant-Christophe.

Carré de Malberg, R. (1922) *Contribution à la théorie générale de l'Etat: spécialement d'après les données fournies par le droit constitutionnel français.* Paris: Sirey.
Conway, M. (2012) *The Sorrows of Belgium. Liberation and Political Reconstruction, 1944–1947.* Oxford: Oxford University Press. DOI: 10.1093/acprof:oso/9780199694341.001.0001.
De Fooz, J.H.N. (1859) *Le droit administratif belge.* Tournai: Casterman.
De Gerlache, E.-C. (1852) *Essai sur le mouvement des partis en Belgique depuis 1830 jusqu'à ce jour, suivi de quelques réflexions sur ce qu'on appelle les grands principes de 1789.* Librairie Polytechnique d'Aug. Brussels: Decq.
De Hoon, H. (1927) *De Belgische Grondwet.* Brussels: Lebègue.
De Laveleye, E. (1897) *Essais et études.* Ghent: Vuylsteke.
De Meyer, J. (1982) 'A propos du référendum', *Journal des Tribunaux*, p. 218.
De Putter, J. (1944) *La Constitution de la libre Belgique.* Brussels: Les Éditions Libres.
De Schepper, V. (2018) 'Art. 33', in Dalle, B., Keyaerts, D., Pas, W., Theunis, J., Verrijdt, W. (eds.) *Duiding: Federale staatsstructuur.* Brussels: Larcier, pp. 14–18.
De Smaele, H. (1998) 'Het Belgische politieke discours en de "eigenheid" van de vrouw aan het einde van de negentiende eeuw', *Tijdschrift voor Genderstudies*, 4, pp. 27–38.
De Smaele, H. (1999) 'Politiek als hanengevecht of cerebraal systeem. Ideeën over politieke representatie en de invoering van de evenredige vertegenwoordiging in Belgie (1899)', *Bijdragen en Mededelingen betreffende de Geschiedenis der Nederlanden*, 114(3), pp. 328–357. DOI: 10.18352/bmgn-lchr.4999.
De Smaele, H. (2002) 'De beroepspoliticus. Waarom de "aristocratie" onvermijdelijk is', in Tollebeek, J., De Smaele, H.D. (eds.) *Politieke representatie.* Leuven: Universitaire Pers Leuven, pp. 109–122. DOI: 10.18352/tseg.730.
De Smaele, H. (2005) 'Eclectisch en toch nieuw. De uitvinding van het Belgisch parlement in 1830–1831', *Bijdragen en Mededelingen betreffende de Geschiedenis der Nederlanden*, 120(3), pp. 408–416. DOI: 10.18352/bmgn-lchr.6253.
De Witte, B. (2003) 'Do Not Mention the Word: Sovereignty in Two Europhile Countries: Belgium and the Netherlands', in Walker, N. (ed.) *Sovereignty in Transition.* Oxford: Hart Publishing, pp. 351–366. DOI: 10.5040/9781472562883.ch-015.
Delbecke, B. (2007) 'Gerechtelijke nationale cultuur en haar blinde vlek: de mercuriales en gelegenheidsredes van Charles Faider als procureur-generaal bij het Hof van Cassatie (1871–1885)', *Tijdschrift voor Rechtsgeschiedenis*, 75, pp. 363–394. DOI: 10.1163/157181907782912435.
Delpérée, F. (2000) *Le droit constitutionnel de la Belgique.* Brussels: Bruylant.
Deseure, B. (2016a) 'From Pragmatic Conservatism to Formal Continuity. Nineteenth-Century Views on the Old Regime Origins of the Belgian Constitution', *Giornale di Storia Costituzionale*, 32(3), pp. 257–272.
Deseure, B. (2016b) 'National Sovereignty in the Belgian Constitution of 1831. On the Meaning(s) of Article 25', in Müßig, U. (ed.) *Reconsidering Constitutional Formation.* Berlin: Springer, pp. 93–156. DOI: 10.1007/978-3-319-42405-7_2.
Destriveaux, P. (1849) *Traité de droit public.* Brussels: Tircher.
Docquier, A. (1856) *Manuel des institutions constitutionnelles & administratives, des droits & des devoirs des belges.* Mons: H. Manceaux.
Dor, G., Braas, A. (1935) 'La Constitution', in Goddyn, A. (ed.) *Les Novelles. Corpus Juris Belgici.* Brussels: Ferdinand Larcier.

Errera, P. (1909) *Traité de droit public belge*. Paris: Giard et Brière.

Faider, C. (1842) *Études sur les constitutions nationales (Pays Bas autrichiens et Pays de Liege)*. Brussels: Gregoir.

François, L. (1985) 'Theorievorming als machtsfactor: politieke elites en hun legitimatie 1830–1914', *Res Publica XXVII*, 4, pp. 567–587.

Geenens, R., Sottiaux, S. (2015) 'Sovereignty and Direct Democracy: Lessons from Constant and the Belgian Constitution', *European Constitutional Law Review*, 11(2), pp. 293–320. DOI: 10.1017/s1574019615000188.

Gerard, E. (2016) 'The Murder of Julien Lahaut (1950) and the Anti-Communist Campaign in Belgium', *Dutch Crossing*, 40, pp. 54–67. DOI: 10.1080/03096564.2016.1129193.

Gérard-Libois, J., Gotovitch, J. (1983) 'Léopold III: le non-retour', *Courrier hebdomadaire du CRISP*, 1010, pp. 1–28. DOI: 10.3917/cris.1010.0001.

Geudens, G. (2000) 'Het gemeentelijk referendum en volksinitiatief in België en Nederland. Een rechtsvergelijkende benadering', *Tijdschrift voor Bestuurswetenschappen en Publiekrecht*, 8, pp. 619–631.

Haag, H. (1976) 'Le choix du roi Albert à Loppem', in Wyffels, C. (ed.) *Handelingen van het colloquium Koning Albert. 26–29 Mei 1975*. Brussels: Algemeen Rijksarchief, pp. 169–191.

Keunen, S., Bijnens, D. (2017) 'Ceci est une fiction. Grondwetgevende referenda in de Belgische rechtsorde', *Tijdschrift voor Bestuurswetenschappen en Publiekrecht*, pp. 248–260.

Kupfferschlaeger, J. (1871) 'Les origines nationales de la Constitution belge', *La Belgique Judiciaire*, XXIX, pp. 1521–1542.

Kwanten, G. (2001) *August-Edmond De Schryver. 1898–1991*. Leuven: Universitaire Pers Leuven.

Lejeune, Y., Regnier, J. (1985) 'Belgique', in Delpérée, F. (ed.) *Référendums*. Brussels: CRISP.

Marteel, S. (2006) 'Van "oude constitutie" tot liberale grondwet. Het Belgische politieke natiebesef tussen 1815 en 1830', in Rietbergen, P.J.A.N., Verschaffel, T. (eds.) *De erfenis van 1830*. Leuven: Acco, pp. 35–51.

Masson, F., Wiliquet, C. (1885) *Manuel de droit constitutionnel*. Mons: Hector Manceaux.

Mast, A. (1950) *Overzicht van het grondwettelijk recht*. Ghent: Standaard Boekhandel.

Mast, A. (1953) *Overzicht van het grondwettelijk recht*. Antwerp: Standaard Boekhandel.

Mast, A. (1967) *Overzicht van het Belgisch grondwettelijk recht*. Ghent: Story-Scientia.

Mast, A. (1981) *Overzicht van het Belgisch grondwettelijk recht*. Leuven: Story-Scientia.

Mudde, C. (2017) *Populism. An Ideational Approach*. Oxford: Oxford University Press.

Noterdaeme (1956) *De Belgische Grondwet. Tekst en uitleg met vragen en antwoorden*. Antwerp: Standaard Boekhandel.

Nyssens, A. (1890) *Le suffrage universel tempéré*. Brussels: Société Belge de Librairie.

Orban, O. (1906) *Le droit constitutionnel de la Belgique* (Vol. 1). Liège: Dessain.

Orban, O. (1908) *Le droit constitutionnel de la Belgique* (Vol. 2). Liège: Dessain.

Paulet-Grandguillot, E. (2010) *Libéralisme et démocratie. De Sismondi à Constant, à partir du Contrat Social (1801–1806)*. Genève: Slatkine.

Plaisant, I. (1832) *Constitution belge annotée*. Brussels: A la librairie de jurisprudence.

Polain, M.-L. (1844) *Histoire de l'ancien pays de Liège*. Liège: Ledoux.

Popelier, P. (2004) 'Democratie in de Belgische Grondwet', in Popelier, P., Adams, M. (eds.) *Recht en democratie. De democratische verbeelding in het recht*. Antwerp: Intersentia, pp. 103–127.

Puissant, J. (2004) 'Le socialisme en Belgique et la question du suffrage', *Les Cahiers de la Fonderie*, 31, pp. 18–23.

Puissant, J. (2007) 'Le POB entre contestation et intégration 1890–1920', in Witte, E., Kurgan-Van Hentenryk, G., Lamberts, E., Balthazar, H., Deneckere, G., Raxhon, P., Wynants, P., Beyen, M., Verdoodt, F.-J. (eds.) *Natie en democratie. 1890–1921. Acta van het interuniversitair colloquium, Brussel, 8–9 Juni 2006*. Brussels: Koninklijke Academie voor Wetenschappen, Letteren en Schone Kunsten van België, pp. 97–105.

Raxhon, P. (1989) *La révolution liégeoise de 1789 vue par les historiens belges*. Brussels: Editions de l'Université de Bruxelles.

Raxhon, P. (2007) 'La démocratie contre la nation', in Witte, E., Kurgan-Van Hentenryk, G., Lamberts, E., Balthazar, H., Deneckere, G., Raxhon, P., Wynants, P., Beyen, M., Verdoodt, F.-J. (eds.) *Natie En Democratie. 1890–1921. Acta van het interuniversitair colloquium, Brussel, 8–9 Juni 2006*. Brussels: Koninklijke Academie voor Wetenschappen, Letteren en Schone Kunsten van België, pp. 32–38.

Reynebeau, M. (2009) *Een geschiedenis van België*. Tielt: Lannoo.

Rimanque, K. (1999) *De grondwet toegelicht, gewikt en gewogen*. Antwerp: Kluwer.

Rogron, J. A. (1836) *Code constitutionnel de la Belgique expliqué par ses motifs et par ses exemples*. Brussels: Tarlier.

Röttger, R. (2005) 'Een rode draad voor een blauw verhaal. De links-liberale uitwerking van mimetische representatie en de opvattingen over democratisch burgerschap in België, 1893–1900', *Bijdragen en Mededelingen betreffende de Geschiedenis der Nederlanden*, 120, pp. 435–465. DOI: 10.18352/bmgn-lchr.6255.

Rummens, S. (2017) 'Populism as a Threat to Liberal Democracy', in Ochoa Espejo, P., Ostiguy, P., Roviara Kaltwasser, C., Taggart, P. (eds.) *The Oxford Handbook of Populism*. Oxford: Oxford University Press, pp. 554–570. DOI: 10.1093/oxfordhb/9780198803560.013.27.

S.A. (n.d.a.) *Handelingen van de Kamer van Volksvertegenwoordigers* (Parliamentary debates in the Chamber of Representatives) [*Hand.* Kamer].

S.A. (n.d.b.) *Handelingen van de Senaat* (Parliamentary debates in the Senate) [*Hand.* Senaat].

S.A. (n.d.c.) *Parlementaire Stukken Kamer van Volksvertegenwoordigers* (Parliamentary documents of the Chamber of Representatives) [*Parl. St.* Kamer].

S.A. (n.d.d.) *Parlementaire Stukken Senaat* (Parliamentary documents of the Senate) [*Parl. St.* Senaat].

S.A. (1831) *Manuel constitutionnel de la Belgique, contenant: le portrait, la vie et la nomination de M. le Régent; la Constitution et la loi électorale de la Belgique, expliquées et conférées avec l'ancienne loi fondamentale, et les lois françaises sur cette matière; les lois sur l'institution et la mobilisation de la Garde civique; le réglement d'ordre du Congrès national; le Traité de Londres de 1814 et celui de Vienne de 1815*. Brussels: De Mat.

Saward, M. (2010) *The Representative Claim*. Oxford: Oxford University Press. DOI: 10.1093/acprof:oso/9780199579389.001.0001.

Schram, F. (2015) *België: een handleiding. België na de 6de staatshervorming.* Brussels: Politeia.

Senelle, R., Clement, M., Van De Velde, E. (2004) *Handboek voor de Koning.* Tielt: Lannoo.

Simonde de Sismondi, J. C. L. (1836) *Études sur les constitutions des peuples libres.* Brussels: Dumont.

Speyer, H. (1927) *La Réforme de l'Etat en Belgique.* Brussels: Bruylant.

Stecher, J. (1851) *Onpartydige volkshistorie der Belgische Grondwet.* Ghent: Bivort-Crowie.

Stengers, J. (2004) 'Histoire de la législation électorale en Belgique', *Revue belge de philologie et d'histoire*, 82, pp. 247–270. DOI: 10.3406/rbph.2004.4826.

Tempels, P. (1873) 'Droit constitutionnel', in Van Bemmel, E. (ed.) *Patria Belgica. Encyclopédie nationale ou Exposé méthodique de toutes les connaissances relatives à la Belgique physique, sociale et intellectuelle.* Brussels: Bruylant-Christophe, pp. 439–472.

Theunissen, P. (1984) *1950: ontknoping van de koningskwestie.* Antwerp: De Nederlandsche Boekhandel.

Thonissen, J.-J. (1844) *La Constitution Belge annotée offrant sous chaque article l'état de la doctrine, de la jurisprudence et de la législation.* Hasselt: Milis.

Tiberghien, G. (1844) *Essai théorique et historique sur la génération des connaissances humaines dans ses rapports avec la morale, la politique et la religion.* Brussels: Librairie encyclopédique de Périchon.

Tiberghien, G. (1875) *Enseignement et philosophie.* Brussels: Gustave Mayolez.

Urbinati, N. (2006) *Representative Democracy: Principles and Genealogy.* Chicago: University of Chicago Press. DOI: 10.7208/chicago/9780226842806.001.0001.

Urbinati, N. (2014) *Democracy Disfigured*: Opinion, *Truth, and the People.* Cambridge: Harvard University Press. DOI: 10.4159/harvard.9780674726383.

Uyttendaele, M. (1994) 'Le référendum constitutionnel en Belgique ou une réponse inadaptée à une question pertinente', *Administration publique trimestrielle*, pp. 109–114.

Van Den Broeck, V. (1859) *La Constitution et l'unionisme en Belgique, leurs racines dans notre passé antérieurement à la Révolution française de 1789.* Brussels: K. Verbruggen.

Van Den Heuvel, J. (1892) *De la révision de la Constitution Belge.* Brussels: Société Belge de Librairie.

Van Den Heuvel, J. (1898) 'A Letter on the Referendum in Belgium', in Deploigne, S. (ed.) *The Referendum in Switzerland.* London: Longmans, Green & Co., pp. 39–69.

Van Der Smissen, E. (1920) *Léopold II et Beernaert d'après leur correspondance inédite de 1884 à 1894.* Brussels: Goemaere.

Van Hoorebeke, E. (1848) *Manuel du droit public interne en Belgique.* Ghent: H. Hoste.

Vande Lanotte, J., Goedertier, G., Haeck, Y., Goossens, J., De Pelsmaeker, T. (2015) *Belgisch publiekrecht.* Bruges: Die Keure.

Vanden Bossche, G. (1925) 'Le Régime parlementaire en Belgique. Discours prononcé à la séance solennelle de rentrée de l'Université de Gand, le 20 octobre 1925', *La Belgique Judiciaire*, 83, pp. 545–557.

Vandenpeereboom, E. (1856) *Du gouvernement représentatif en Belgique (1831–1848).* Brussels: Librairie Polytechnique d'Aug. Decq.

Vandenpeereboom, A. (1873) 'Gildes, corps de métiers, serments', in Van Bemmel, E. (ed.) *Patria Belgica. Encyclopédie nationale ou Exposé méthodique de toutes les connaissances relatives à la Belgique physique, sociale et intellectuelle*. Brussels: Bruylant-Christophe, pp. 243–278.

Vauthier, M. (1931) 'La Constitution et le régime politique (Eléments de droit constitutionnel)', in Levy-Ullman, H., Mirkine-Guetzevitch, B. (eds.) *Belgique*. Paris: Delagrave, pp. 11–21.

Velaers, J. (2001) 'Het referendum en de volksraadpleging in grondwettelijk perspectief', in Fleerackers, F. (ed.) *De referenda. Een meta-juridische conflictanalyse van het referendum*. Ghent: Larcier, pp. 145–197.

Velaers, J. (2007) 'Leopold II en de versterking van de democratie en de monarchie', in Witte, E., Kurgan-Van Hentenryk, G., Lamberts, E., Balthazar, H., Deneckere, G., Raxhon, P., Wynants, P., Beyen, M., Verdoodt, F.-J. (eds.) *Natie En Democratie. 1890–1921. Acta van het interuniversitair colloquium, Brussel, 8–9 June 2006*. Brussels: Koninklijke Academie voor Wetenschappen, Letteren en Schone Kunsten van België, pp. 146–155.

Velaers, J. (2019) *De Grondwet. Een artikelsgewijze commentaar*. Bruges: Die Keure.

Velu, J. (1986) *Droit public*. Brussels: Bruylant.

Verhaegen, E. (1859) *Études de droit public*. Brussels: Claassen.

Viaene, V. (2001) *Belgium and the Holy See from Gregory XVI to Pius IX (1831–1859). Catholic Revival, Society and Politics in 19th-Century Europe*. Leuven: Leuven University Press.

Vliebergh, H. (1973) *De Belgische Grondwet*. Antwerp: Standaard Wetenschappelijke Uitgeverij.

Voituron, M. (1878) *Manuel du libéralisme belge*. Brussels: C. Muquardt.

Voituron, P. (1876) 'Le droit du suffrage', *Revue de Belgique*, VIII, pp. 375–395.

Waille, V.-A. (1838) *Essai sur l'histoire politique et constitutionnelle de la Belgique*. Brussels: De Mat.

Wigny, P. (1952) *Droit constitutionnel: principes et droit positif*. Brussels: Bruylant.

Wigny, P. (1956) 'Le fonctionnement du régime parlementaire en Belgique', in Ciselet, G., Fayat, H., Ganshof Van Der Meersch, W.J., Gérard, M.-L., Grégoire, M., Harmel, P., Rolin, H., Wigny, P. (eds.) *Aspects du régime parlementaire belge*. Brussels: Librairie Encyclopédique, pp. 9–26.

Wigny, P. (1969) *Comprendre la Belgique. Connaître ses structures pour mieux participer à sa vie politique*. Verviers: Gérard.

Wigny, P. (1973) *Cours de droit constitutionnel*. Brussels: Emile Bruylant.

Witte, E. (2003) 'The Battle for Monasteries, Cemeteries and Schools: Belgium', in Clark, C., Kaiser, W. (eds.) *Culture Wars. Secular-Catholic Conflict in Nineteenth-Century Europe*. Cambridge: Cambridge University Press, pp. 102–128. DOI: 10.1017/cbo9780511496714.005.

Witte, E. (2007) 'Natie en democratie, 1890–1921: de probleemstelling', in Witte, E., Kurgan-Van Hentenryk, G., Lamberts, E., Balthazar, H., Deneckere, G., Raxhon, P., Wynants, P., Beyen, M., Verddodt, F.-J. (eds.) *Natie en democratie. 1890–1921. Acta van het interuniversitair colloquium, Brussel 8–9 June 2006*. Brussels: Koninklijke Academie voor Wetenschappen, Letteren en Schone Kunsten van België, pp. 7–18.

Witte, E. (2020) *Belgische republikeinen. Radicalen tussen twee revoluties (1830–1850)*. Antwerp: Polis.

Witte, E., Gubin, E., Gerard, E., Nandrin, J.-P. (2003) 'De Kamer van Volksvertegenwoordigers (1830–2002). Constanten en verschuivingen', in Gerard, E., Witte, E., Gubin, E., Nandrin, J.-P. (eds.) *Geschiedenis van de Belgische Kamer van Volksvertegenwoordigers. 1830–2002*. Brussels: Kamer van Volksvertegenwoordigers, pp. 385–418.
Wyvekens, H. (1854) *Notions élémentaires sur la Constitution belge et les lois politiques et administratives*. Brussels: Deprez-Parent.
Zerezo de Téjada, F. de (1891) *La révision de la Constitution en Belgique*. Brussels: Lebègue.

Publications without a specific, personal author (such as newspapers and official documents) are listed under S.A.

12 Laboratories for democracy

Democratic renewal in the Belgian federation

Ronald Van Crombrugge

Introduction

The question of democratic renewal has long been on the political agenda in Belgium. Since the early 2000s in particular, politicians from all persuasions have continually lamented the 'gap' that exists between citizens and representatives. The way to close this gap, it was argued, was to involve the citizen more closely in the decision-making process. However, at the federal level, little has actually been achieved in terms of democratic reform. As has become clear throughout this book, the hurdles for democratic reform have been numerous, and perhaps one of the most important obstacles has been the national sovereignty doctrine which continues to dominate the thinking in Belgian constitutional law on democracy. Several of the chapters in this book are devoted to staking out in great detail the intellectual basis and historical development of the national sovereignty doctrine; and ultimately, to dismantling 'the national sovereignty myth'. With this particular stumbling block for democratic reform out of the way, the question remains: what should this reform actually look like? If we want to strengthen the opportunities for citizens to participate in politics, what forms could this participation take? It is these questions that this chapter seeks to answer.

Fortunately, recent years have seen increasing experimentation with new types of citizen participation around the globe. These have been collectively termed democratic innovations, that is, innovations which "have been specifically designed to increase and deepen citizen participation in the political decision-making process" (Smith, 2009). These experiments can form a valuable source of inspiration when seeking to renew Belgian democracy. Somewhat surprisingly perhaps, rather than having to look far afield for inspiration, Belgium itself has recently become a trailblazer when it comes to democratic innovation (OECD, 2020). Yet, so far, this openness to experiment with new forms of participation has remained restricted to Belgium's federated entities, the communities and regions. Thus, the aim of this chapter is to ask what lessons democracy at the federal level can learn from these developments at the sub-state level. To answer this question, I proceed in three steps. In the first step, I discuss the relation between federalism and democracy in Belgium. Why has democratic reform been so much more successful at the sub-state level? What are the additional hurdles that democratic reform at the federal level needs to overcome? In the second step, I examine these developments in more detail. Examples of democratic innovation happening in the four main federated entities which together make up the Belgian federation: Flanders, Wallonia, Brussels, and Ostbelgien, are discussed.[1] In the third and final step, I ask whether – and, if so, how – these experiences can be transposed to the federal level.

Federalism and democracy in Belgium, an ambiguous relation

At its most basic, the Belgian form of state can be defined as 'consociational federalism' (Caluwaerts and Reuchamps, 2015). Federalism and consociationalism are the two main institutional strategies employed to deal with the deeply divided nature of Belgian society. Federalism, for its part, seeks to defuse the tensions between the different linguistic groups by granting them a large degree of self-rule. It does so by establishing a constitutionally entrenched division of competences between the federal level of government and a number of autonomous federated entities (Elazar, 1987; Watts, 1999), which in Belgium are defined on the basis of the majority-spoken language of the area in question (the so-called 'language areas', or '*taalgebieden*').[2] While the exact principles which govern this division of competences may differ between federal states, the most important thing to note is that federalism reserves certain competences to be exclusively exercised by federated entities who are not subject to administrative oversight from the federal government (thus differentiating federalism from other types of decentralised government).

Consociationalism complements this federal arrangement by establishing a regime of power-sharing at the federal level. All competences at the federal level are thus exercised jointly by the country's two large language communities. In its original formulation by Lijphart, consociationalism has four main characteristics: proportional representation, grand coalitions, minority veto, and segmental autonomy (Lijphart, 1977; 1984). All these characteristics can be seen – in some shape or form – in the Belgian constitutional system. Proportional representation is intended to ensure that all different groups are adequately represented on the national level, and was introduced in Belgium in the late nineteenth century to accommodate (socialist) calls for more inclusive democratic representation. Aside from representation, the requirement of grand coalition governments and the provision of a minority veto ensure that, in a consociationalist system, numerically superior groups cannot ride roughshod over the concerns of minorities.

1 This list has a pedagogical purpose and is intended to simplify the complex structure of the Belgian federation. Rather than being comprised of four federated entities, in reality the Belgian federation is comprised of two distinct types of federated entities – the communities and the regions – with overlapping territories. Since the Belgian state structure as such is not the main subject of this chapter, I have opted not to delve into this.

2 Article 4 of the Constitution.

In Belgium, the grand coalition principle is institutionalised in the form of a required parity within the federal government between Flemish-speaking and French-speaking ministers.[3] Moreover, though it is not written down in the formal Constitution, customary law dictates that governments decide by consensus. As a result, all major decisions taken by the government require the consent of representatives of both language communities. Importantly, the requirement of parity only applies to the government, not to parliament. There is thus no constitutional obligation for governments to be supported by a majority of both language groups in parliament. However, parliamentary minorities are protected through the so-called 'alarm bell procedure', which allows a super-majority within one of the two language groups to adopt a motion stating that it considers a particular legislative proposal harmful to the relations between the two communities. If successful, parliamentary debates on the proposal are suspended and the issue is sent to the government to be resolved.[4] Though technically the alarm bell procedure merely suspends parliamentary debate, in practice it acts as a minority veto. If the government does not manage to find a compromise, its political existence is threatened and it will most likely resign (Sinardet, 2010). Given all this, it is no wonder that Lijphart considered Belgium to be "the most perfect, most convincing and most impressive example of a consociation" (Lijphart, 1981, p. 8).

Lijphart's assessment, however, appears to have been overly optimistic. Since Lijphart made his evaluation back in 1981, when Belgium was only just starting out on its path towards becoming a federation, the country has gone through a number of institutional and political crises; and some have argued that while the combination of an increasingly far-reaching federalisation of the country with consociational decision-making at the federal level might have been able to buy the peace for a while, it has now become a source of instability and conflict in the long term (Caluwaerts and Reuchamps, 2015; Deschouwer, 2005; Sinardet, 2010). For the purpose of this chapter, I want to zoom in on one particular aspect of this debate on the negative side-effect of consociationalism, namely how this development towards consociational federalism has contracted the space for a democratic engagement at the federal level.

Consociationalism is – pretty much by definition – a highly top-down and elite-led process. It is built on the premise that the best way to avoid conflict in a deeply divided society is to have well-meaning elites from the different groups govern society together, and has thus also been described by Lijphart as "government by elite cartel" (Lijphart, 1969). In order for this to work, however, the leaders in question have to be able to exert control over their own group's members and ensure that compromises are actually implemented. This explains why consociationalism tends to go together with strong executives, weak parliaments, and highly centralised political parties (Luther and Deschouwer, 1999). Not surprisingly, all of these characteristics apply to the Belgian democratic

3 Article 99 of the Constitution.
4 Article 54 of the Constitution.

system which has also been called a 'particracy' as a result (Dewachter, 2014). Aside from exerting control over parliament and rank-and-file party members, consociationalism requires a deferent attitude from society as a whole towards its leaders (Caluwaerts and Reuchamps, 2014). From this perspective, active citizen participation is considered generally unhelpful, as it might interfere with the compromise-finding process engaged in by elites. Even more strikingly, consociationalists tend to consider a politically active population a risk factor for the peaceful governance of society rather than a democratic good, since mass participation might arouse 'passions' in the population which could hurt the coexistence between the different groups.[5] Instead, consociationalism tries to shepherd political communication by ordinary citizens into within-bloc channels where it can do little damage (Dryzek, 2005, p. 222). Consociationalism thus seeks to provide a framework for democracy in deeply divided societies by sacrificing much of what makes a democracy 'democratic' in the first place.

Federalism lessens this loss in democracy somewhat, however. In line with the principle of 'segmental autonomy', consensual decision-making is only to be used to deal with issues which do not allow for a differentiated solution. All matters that can be dealt with separately by the different segments are to be decided at the lower state level (this is sometimes also called the 'subsidiarity' principle). At this level, the fear of inter-group conflict does not arise; hence there is (at least in principle) no need to restrict democratic engagement. At the same time, the autonomy granted to the federated entities is not limited to substantive policy decisions, but also covers competences to shape the democratic process itself. In Belgium, these procedural competences are grouped under the name 'constitutive autonomy' (Elst and Van Nieuwenhove, 2016). As a result, not only is there no fear for inter-group conflict at the regional level which acts as a 'sociological barrier' to strengthening the democratic role of citizens, but federalism also provides the institutional architecture which enables lower-level governments to provide new avenues for democratic participation. It is this dynamic in particular which explains the diverging situation between the federal and regional levels in Belgium when it comes to deepening democratic engagement. Whereas the federal level is locked in a rigid consociational framework that is distrustful towards active citizen involvement, the regional governments are free to experiment with new types of citizen participation.

Democratic experimentation at the regional level

Wallonia: Direct decision-making through referendum

As has become clear in this book, the debate on referendums has a long and heated history in Belgium. The traumatic memory of the referendum on the Royal Question continues to shape this debate, giving strength to the argument

5 This was one of the arguments of the Council of State against referendums.

that referendums in a divided society invariably end up pitting communities against each other and are a recipe for disaster (I question this accepted truth in the next section). Even so, the idea of introducing some form of referendum never completely disappeared from the political stage, especially as elected representatives became more and more concerned about the growing divide between politics and the broader public. The eventual compromise was to provide an explicit constitutional basis for (non-binding) referendums on the regional level.[6]

Wallonia was the first (and so far only) region to make use of this possibility. The necessary enabling legislation which sets out the modalities under which referendums are to be organised, was passed in 2018 and entered into force after the general election of 2019, though no referendums have taken place as of yet.[7] This legislation establishes who gets to initiate the referendum process and what conditions have to be met in order for the referendum result to be considered valid, and more generally governs how the referendum campaign is to be run – in particular regarding campaign finance.

The right to initiate a referendum is granted to both the Walloon parliament and members of the broader public. If the initiative derives from parliament, it has to be supported by a simple majority of its members. In the case of a popular initiative, it has to be supported by at least 60,000 signatures which have to represent at least 2% of the inhabitants of a majority of the region's electoral districts.[8] In that case, while the subject of the referendum is determined by the public, parliament may still decide to reformulate the proposed referendum questions if it deems this necessary to ensure their intelligibility (it is supported in this endeavour by a commission of experts).[9] Moreover, before a request to organise a referendum can be granted, the Constitutional Court has to attest that the subject of the vote does not go against fundamental or human rights, does not exceed the regional competences, and more generally respects the conditions laid down in article 39bis of the Constitution – which among other things excludes referendums on the budget.[10] After the vote there are a number of additional requirements in order for the result of a referendum to be valid. Two measures stand out. First of all, the law imposes a moderate turnout requirement. At least 10% of the region's inhabitants entitled to vote need to have participated in order for the referendum to be valid. If this threshold is not met, the votes will not even be counted and no result will be made public.[11] Secondly, the law foresees the possibility for parliament to decide to annul the vote if it is shown that campaign

6 Article 39bis of the Constitution.

7 *Décret spécial instituant la consultation populaire*, 2018. Hereafter simply 'the decree'.

8 Article 2 of the decree.

9 Article 7 of the decree.

10 Article 30ter of the *Bijzondere wet op het Grondwettelijk Hof*, 1989. Also see article 4 § 4 of the decree.

11 Article 17 of the decree.

finance law has been violated, and that this violation is likely to have had a determinative impact on the outcome of the vote.[12]

The campaign finance regime put in place by the Walloon legislation is particularly far-reaching, and easily positions it as one of the most stringent regulatory frameworks for referendums around the world.[13] The basic idea behind these campaign finance provisions is to try and channel all campaign activities into two umbrella committees, one for each side, which enjoy roughly the same financial resources. The objective of this legislation is therefore to ensure an equality of arms between the yes- and no-side of the campaign. It does so by imposing an equal spending limit of €750,000 on both committees, and by enacting strict rules on their sources of income. The law foresees that both committees will be able to enjoy a public subsidy, the exact amount of which is determined anew during each legislative session. Aside from this, the committees' activities are to be funded through donations, subject of course to the law's regulations which give pride of place to political parties public subsidy. Whereas political parties can decide to transfer up to 10% of the party's yearly public subsidy to the treasury of the referendum committee, individual citizens are limited to donating up to €500, and no provision is made for other civil society organisations to contribute to a campaign.[14] This is particularly important since the law makes it a criminal offence (punishable by up to one month in prison) for anyone not associated with one of the committees to spend money for campaigning purposes.[15]

While the egalitarian rationale behind these rules is understandable, their impact on the democratic right of free speech can hardly be overstated. They stifle independent political action unconnected from formal political institutions. Given the committees' funding rules, political parties are likely to play a dominant role in their internal decision-making and campaign strategising. Particracy with a direct democratic twist if you will. The rules are particularly harsh on those wishing to support a position not covered by the committees such as abstention, or those who for some other reason cannot join one of the committees. These voices are effectively barred from any meaningful participation in a referendum campaign.

It is questionable whether these rules would survive judicial scrutiny. It is noteworthy, for example, that the Canadian Supreme Court invalidated a similar provision in the Quebec Referendum Act which prohibited independent campaign expenditures.[16] In the case of *Libman v. Quebec*, the Court argued that while strict limitations on third-party expenditures could be justified as a

12 Article 20 § 3 of the decree.

13 For an overview of referendum campaign regulation and the various possibilities, see IDEA (2008).

14 Article 13 of the decree.

15 Article 20 of the decree.

16 Parliamentary discussions within the Walloon parliament reveal that the campaign finance regime in Quebec served as an important inspiration. It is striking therefore that parliament did not appear to have taken the *Libman* judgment into account when drafting the Walloon referendum legislation. See: Parlement Wallon, Compte rendu integral. Séance pub-

necessary measure in order to ensure the effectiveness of the legislation's overall system of spending limits and umbrella committees, a complete ban constitutes a violation of the freedoms of speech and association.[17] Perhaps more important, the European Court for Human Rights (ECtHR) too has generally been critical of legislation which bans independent expenditures in electoral contests. In the case of *Bowman v. UK*, the Court concluded that while the United Kingdom was entitled to take measures in order to safeguard the equality between candidates and more generally the fairness of elections, the legislation in question constituted a near total ban on independent political expenditures and could not be considered necessary in a democratic society, and thus violated article 10 of the convention.[18] While the *Bowman* case dealt with elections rather than referendums, it is easy to see how the same reasoning applies to referendum regulation (especially considering the similarities between the ECtHR's decision in *Bowman* and the Canadian Supreme Court's *Libman* judgment).

While the Walloon campaign finance regime can be (rightfully) criticised for being overly strict, it does reveal an important truth about referendums and their place in the broader system of democracy: namely that they are not intended to facilitate an open-ended discussion, but are geared towards making a collective decision on a very specific issue. Yes, or no? While this has often been lamented as one of the referendum's weaknesses, since there is no possibility to discuss, to search for consensus, or to look for a compromise (Chambers, 2001, p. 232), this misconstrues the finality of the referendum device. All these functions need to be performed elsewhere in the democratic system, most notably in representative institutions, since it is quite simply impossible to draft legislation with millions of people. Yet, it is precisely because referendums give an equal vote to every full citizen, and because the barriers to participate in a referendum are so low, that they are uniquely suited to legitimate a collective decision (Parkinson, 2012, p. 162). In fact, the so-called 'simplicity' of a referendum campaign – revolving as it does around a simple 'yes-or-no' question – might prove crucial in order for a referendum to actually fulfil its legitimating role. Just imagine the difficulty for ordinary citizens to gain a good understanding of the choice before them when ballot options could change, or new options added, during a referendum campaign. It is impossible to debate everything at once, and public debate – especially in a mass democratic setting – needs to be structured so as to be readily understandable by the broader audience. One can therefore hardly blame referendum campaigns for doing what every democratic system needs: enabling collective decision-making by narrowing down the discussion to a manageable number of options, and presenting this choice to voters in a way that makes sense to them.

lique de commission spéciale relative au renouveau démocratique du 28 Juin 2018, C.R.I.C. No. 170.

17 *Libman v. Quebec (AG)*, 1997.

18 *Bowman v. the United Kingdom*, 1998, para. 47.

Ostbelgien and Brussels: Deepening democracy through randomly selected citizen' assemblies

While referendums have for a long time been the main focus of the debate on democratic renewal in Belgium, recent years have seen somewhat of a shift away from so-called 'direct democratic' instruments towards a more deliberative democratic approach. Of particular note here is the idea of mini-publics, an instrument of citizen participation where a diverse group of randomly selected citizens – with some claim of being representative of the broader population – is given the opportunity to reason together about an issue of public concern under circumstances specifically designed to enable high-quality deliberation (Goodin and Dryzek, 2006; Smith and Setälä, 2018).

The catalyst for the growing popularity of mini-publics in Belgium was the G1000, a grassroots mini-public which took place in Belgium in 2011 in the midst of a political crisis gripping the country. The G1000 and the media attention it received offered politicians an interesting exemplar of democratic innovation. As was noted elsewhere, after the G1000, deliberative mini-publics suddenly became an important element of the discourse of many Belgian political parties (Jacquet et al., 2016). Not only do democratic innovations now feature explicitly in the election party manifestos of several political parties (while the manifestos of others include a general call for more citizen participation), but over the years numerous ideas have been launched – and continue to be launched – by different parties would incorporate some form of deliberative mini-publics in political decision-making.

For most of this time, the debate on deliberative democracy remained just that: a debate, with little in the way of actions intended to actually bring these ideas into practice. This changed in 2019, when two of Belgium's federated entities – Ostbelgien and Brussels – introduced legislation which gives a durable place to randomly selected citizens' assemblies in the decision-making process. This is not only an important development within the specific Belgian context, but internationally as well.[19] Most deliberative mini-publics continue to be organised on an ad hoc basis and on the sole initiative of the relevant policy-makers when – and importantly, *only* when – *they* experience a need for this type of citizen engagement. As ad hoc democratic experiments, mini-publics risk being 'co-opted', where the mini-public's agenda, procedural rules, and even outcomes are shaped specifically to fit the purpose of the organiser (Böker, 2017; Lafont, 2015). The move towards the institutionalisation of mini-publics in Ostbelgien and Brussels guards against this danger by investing them with a certain degree of stability and autonomy, and thus constitutes an important next step in the development of mini-publics. Moreover, Ostbelgien and Brussels offer two very

19 It is noteworthy, for example, that in the OECD's report on the development of deliberative practices, both the Ostbelgien and Brussels model were included as "best practice" (OECD, 2020).

different examples of just *how* mini-publics could become integrated in the workings of representative democracy. Whereas Ostbelgien opted for a system which could be called 'bicameralism light', Brussels chose to incorporate the random selection of citizens into a new type of hybrid select committee, composed of both elected representatives and ordinary citizens.

The system established in the German-speaking community – which has become known as the 'Ostbelgien model' – relies on two types of mini-public, the citizen council (*Bürgerrat*) on the one hand, and the citizens' assemblies (*Bürgerversammlungen*) on the other.[20] The citizens' assemblies form the heart of the process. It is here that topics are discussed and recommendations to parliament are formulated by random samples of 25–50 randomly selected inhabitants of the community. Up to three of these assemblies can take place every year on any topic belonging to the competencies of the German-speaking community. These assemblies therefore have a temporary mandate and are reconvened with different people for each topic.[21] The citizen council, on the other hand, is a more permanent institution, composed of 24 people who serve for 18 months and who are selected by lot from a list of citizens who have already participated in one of the assemblies. This council decides at the beginning of every parliamentary session how many assemblies will be organised and on which topics. Throughout the year, the council convenes regularly to prepare, organise, and follow-up on the individual assemblies.[22]

In the first instance, the assemblies and the council decide by consensus. If no consensus can be found, decisions require a supermajority of two-thirds of the votes for the council, and an exceptionally high four-fifths of the votes for decisions by the assemblies.[23] This choice represents a particular strand in deliberative democratic theory which stresses the search for consensus as the primary goal of deliberation. Where consensus is not possible, the requirement of a supermajority is intended to incentivise cooperative behaviour and a willingness to compromise among the participants. However, these requirements come with their own deliberative downsides. Consensus has long been criticised as the primary aim of deliberation (Bächtiger et al., 2018). Critics have – among other things – warned of the practical dangers inherent in trying to translate a theoretical ideal of consensus (properly understood as a regulative ideal) into a practical rule for decision-making. Not only is it highly implausible that consensus is actually reached in the real world, but greater agreement between participants simply does not have to be the result of rational persuasion or respectful cooperation and may instead be caused by group-think or social pressures to conform (Sanders, 1996; Sunstein, 2002).

20 *Dekret zur Eubführung eines Permanenten Bürgerdialogs in der Deutssprachigen Gemeinschaft*, 2019 (Decree on the introduction of a permanent citizen dialogue in the German-speaking community).

21 Article 3.

22 Articles 4 and 7.

23 Article 3 § 5; Article 4 § 3.

Brussels, meanwhile, took a very different approach. In December 2019, the Brussels parliament amended its rules of procedure to create a new type of hybrid parliamentary committee. These committees consist of 15 elected representatives and 45 randomly selected citizens (though this number may be increased or lowered if necessary). The elected representatives are those members of the Brussels parliament who normally take part in the standing committee responsible for the policy issue in question.[24] The rules of procedure specify how deliberations are to proceed and distinguish three phases. In the first 'preparatory information' phase, the members of the committee are invited to learn about the issue. The materials to be used in this phase are prepared by an expert support committee ('*comité d'accompagnement*'). The second phase takes place in smaller groups to enable effective face-to-face deliberation between the elected representatives and selected citizens. The third, plenary phase starts with the presentation and discussion of the results and recommendations of the smaller group-deliberations, followed by the actual decision-making which occurs by secret majority vote.[25] However, only the votes of the elected members of parliament are binding. While the randomly selected citizens can take part in the voting process, their votes are merely consultative – since it is legally impossible to give non-elected citizens the right to vote in parliament (Minsart and Jacquet, 2020).[26]

Even though both Ostbelgien and Brussels utilise random selection to involve citizens more directly in the parliamentary process, they represent two very different approaches. Whereas the Ostbelgien model seeks to maximise the autonomy of citizens in their deliberations, the Brussels model emphasises cooperation between the elected representatives and randomly selected citizens. The Ostbelgien model creates a space where citizens can deliberate among each other and formulate policy recommendations. It is only after the deliberative process has been concluded that the members of the citizens' assemblies interact with elected representatives, namely in a special parliamentary hearing where the assembly's recommendations are discussed by the relevant parliamentary committee and the competent ministers together with the members of the assembly.[27] Moreover, by including a permanent citizen council in the process, citizens remain in control of the entire process – even in between the citizens' assemblies; most importantly by deciding on the agenda of future assemblies and following up on the implementation of recommendations from previous assemblies.

In contrast, in Brussels, elected representatives are involved in every step of the process. Parliament establishes the deliberative committees and sets their agenda. The mixed composition of the committee, moreover, prevents a disconnect between the citizens' assembly and traditional representative institutions.

24 Article 25/1 .5 of the *Règlement Du Parlement de La Région de Bruxelles-Capitale et l'Assemblée Réunie de La Commission Communautaire Commune*. Hereafter simply 'the Règlement'.

25 Article 25/1 .12 of the Règlement.

26 Article 25/1 .13 of the Règlement.

27 Article 9.

This increases the chances that the committee's recommendations are taken up in the parliamentary decision-making process down the line (Hendriks, 2016). This connection is strengthened by the fact that the elected representatives who take part in the deliberative committee also constitute the standing committee for these policy matters, and are therefore directly responsible for translating the deliberative committee's proposals into law. Strong coupling is generally seen as positive, but it also carries with it certain risks, namely that the proceedings of the mini-public become dominated by the voices of professional politicians (Mansbridge et al., 2012). This risk is particularly relevant in Brussels, since the votes of citizens are merely consultative, so that the only way for citizens to influence the outcome of the process is indirectly through the debate itself. Whether this risk manifests itself will, to a large extent, depend on how deliberations are moderated, and whether moderators take active steps to secure the equal voice of citizens.

Flanders: Institutionalised popular agenda-setting

A last example of democratic innovation at the regional level is a proposal to introduce a system of citizen-initiated citizens' assemblies that was discussed – but eventually voted down – in the Flemish parliament.[28] Even so, it forms an interesting case study. If adopted, the bill would have made it possible for 80,000 citizens to demand a citizens' assembly on any topic belonging to the competencies of Flanders.[29] This would have transformed mini-publics into a powerful instrument for popular agenda-setting. While the Flemish bill shares this agenda-setting feature with the Ostbelgien model – where the citizen council is responsible for deciding the agenda of the citizens' assemblies – there is an important difference in how it institutionalises this agenda-setting role. While the citizen-initiated citizens' assembly as a whole would serve an agenda-setting role by transmitting new issues, ideas, and recommendations to parliament, the original initiative comes from *outside* the citizens' assembly, through the petition device. In this regard, the Flemish citizen-initiated citizens' assemblies would have operated very differently from the Ostbelgien model which endowed deliberative mini-publics with an autonomous agenda-setting power independent from the outside public.

There are several reasons why this connection to the outside public is preferable over an autonomous agenda-setting role for the citizens' assembly itself. While mini-publics can play useful roles within a democratic system, one should always take care not to conflate the random sample of citizens a mini-public consists

28 *Voorstel van decreet betreffende de invoering van een procedure voor het geven van toegang aan burgers tot de parlementaire besluitvorming via een adviserend deliberatief proces*, 2017. (Bill concerning the introduction of a procedure to give citizens access to parliamentary decision-making via a consultative deliberative process.) Hereinafter simply 'the bill'.

29 Article 4 of the bill.

of with the people as a whole (Lafont, 2020). Even the best selection methods cannot guarantee that a random sample will include (equally) *all* the ideas and perspectives that make up society. This is particularly true for Ostbelgien's citizen council, where citizens have to serve an 18-month term which makes some form of self-selection bias more likely. The Flemish Citizens' Assembly Bill would have avoided this particular bias by opening the agenda-setting stage up to the entire public, and by creating a right for *every* citizen to gather signatures and place *their* issues on the assembly's agenda. To be sure, whether citizens – individually or (more likely) in cooperation with others – would be able to make use of this right would largely depend on the macro-deliberative qualities of the public sphere and how inclusive it is; yet, at face value, the requirement of 80,000 signatures does not seem excessively high within the Flemish context.[30]

Of course, simply because a group of citizens can claim a right – through the petition device – to be listened to, does not mean that its proposals should be treated as the law of the land without any further notice. At the agenda-setting stage, we should avoid treating as decisive what are unavoidably "fragmented, pieces-of-the-jigsaw claims on public attention, resources, and coercive powers" (Bachtiger and Parkinson, 2019, p. 99). What is needed then is an additional filter, one that is not based on numbers or signatures but allows the widest possible range of perspectives and viewpoints to be represented, before these are structured and narrowed down in a discursive process. It is precisely this role which the citizen-initiated citizens' assembly would be able to fulfil. It would act as something of a 'discursive filter' by passing calls for political action through a deliberative 'sluice'.

The gathering of signatures forms a first test, where the initiative's sponsors need to be able to show that their proposal addresses a felt need among a significant part of the citizenry. This is important since a deliberative system's capacity to respond to these calls for action is necessarily limited – both in terms of time as well as the financial means available. There is thus a need for a procedure through which we can distinguish between those claims, ideas, and proposals which enjoy a degree of support in society that warrants that they be taken seriously by the formal institutions of the state, and those which do not. The signature threshold is such a 'claim-laundering' process (Cheneval and el-Wakil, 2018). This is then followed by a second, deliberative test: does the proposal hold up after being scrutinised by a diverse group of citizens over several days of deliberation? Only those proposals which are able to pass both tests would be submitted to parliament.

30 By way of example, in 2009 – in the context of a local referendum in the Flemish city of Antwerp – a group of citizens called Ademloos ('without breath') was able to gather 66,158 signatures to demand a referendum on the city's plans to build a new highway bridge close to the city centre (https://www.demorgen.be/nieuws/66-158-handtekeningen-voor-referendum-oosterweel~baf24a78/, last accessed on 14 January 2020). It is difficult to provide examples for the region of Flanders as a whole since there exists no comparable right to referendum or petition on the Flemish level.

This idea of the deliberative assembly acting as an additional discursive filter on top of the signature threshold can be seen in the institutional specifics of the Citizens' Assembly Bill, and most clearly in the composition of the assembly and the special role given to the sponsors of the initiative. According to the bill, the assembly would include one to five of the initiative's sponsors in addition to the other participants.[31] This last addition is specific to the citizen-initiated nature of this deliberative assembly. Most deliberative processes, in contrast, limit the role of a proposal's proponents to testifying before the citizen sample. The special status these sponsors get in the citizen-initiated deliberative assembly can be explained as a way to accommodate the distinct representative claim the assembly's initiative-takers can boast: they claim to represent the public voice on the basis of having received the support of at least 80,000 of their fellow citizens (Saward, 2010). In light of this representative claim, the initiative's sponsors are given the right not only to address the deliberative assembly – as other interest or activist groups – but also to actively participate in its deliberative work. However, while the automatic inclusion of the initiative's sponsors in the deliberative assembly ensures that this representative claim is taken up in the process, the fact that they are given only five (at most) seats out of more than a hundred shows that in the end, this claim alone will be of little avail if they fail to persuade the other members of the assembly.

If they succeed in this endeavour, however, the fact that the initiative-takers are supported in their demands by a statistically representative sample of the population would give more credence to their claim to represent the public voice, and not just a vocal minority. The government would, therefore, be in a better position to assess calls for political action. Yet, it is particularly for the broader public that this information would be revealing. If the government were still to refuse to take action, it would no longer be able to simply dismiss these demands as unrepresentative or misguided. The citizen-initiated citizens' assembly therefore not only forces petitioners to appeal to mutually acceptable reasons as to why collective action needs to be undertaken (Gutmann and Thompson, 1997, p. 55), but once these demands have passed through the discursive filter of the deliberative forum, it also forces governments to provide the same kind of reasons – not just excuses – why such action is not taken. Deliberative assemblies can thus strengthen democratic control over the public agenda through what Cristina Lafont has called the 'vigilant' use of deliberative mini-publics: they draw the attention of the public to instances where existing policy clashes with the considered opinion of a diverse group of their fellow citizens, signalling that on these issues the political system is most likely insufficiently responsive (Lafont, 2020).

31 Article 12 of the bill.

Lessons for federal Belgium?

While all the examples discussed above constitute valuable lessons in institutional design, this does not mean that these experiences can be easily transposed to the Belgian federal level. After all, there were very good reasons why Belgium developed the consociational structure it has today. This institutional context, along with the multilingual nature of Belgian society, surely has to be taken into account when designing new forms of citizen participation. It would be wrong, however, to presume that these factors would make a more active involvement of citizens impossible by definition.

This assumption is most clearly visible in the debate on referendums, where it is often argued that a referendum would invariably pit the different communities against each other. There are reasons to doubt this, however. For one thing, Switzerland, one of the world's leaders in the number of referendums being held every year, is a consosciational multilingual country, much like Belgium (Stojanović, 2009). The argument here is not that Belgium should evolve to become a Swiss-style democracy, but rather that we should not treat as a law of nature what are in the end political considerations. Even more instructive perhaps, is the example of the 1998 referendum in Northern Ireland on the Belfast Agreement. There, the referendum was able to play an important unifying and legitimating role. Yet, what was crucial for the referendum to be successful was a cross-community agreement on the very question of whether to hold the referendum. If such an agreement exists, this has the potential to generate the trust and mutual respect that is necessary to overcome divisiveness during the referendum campaign. Where this is not the case, increased conflict is likely. The negotiators of the Good Friday Agreement had learned this lesson personally after the failure of an earlier referendum in 1973. The question in this referendum had been unilaterally fixed by the Unionist majority and the government in London, and was therefore boycotted by the Republican minority. The 1973 referendum not only failed to resolve the Northern Irish conflict but even resulted in further polarisation and violence. Rather than seeing this negative experience as a reason to avoid future referendums, the whole Belfast process was aimed at avoiding the same mistakes and ensuring that the referendum in this case would be able to involve both communities on an equal footing.

One way of increasing the chances of such cross-community agreement is to adopt what Stephen Tierney has called a 'consociational referendum', that is, a referendum where the proposal only carries the day if it is approved by a majority of citizens *in each of the relevant communities* (Tierney, 2012, p. 282). What a solution like this does is it replaces the standard interpretation of political equality that usually underpins the idea of referendums – an idea of political equality as *undifferentiated equality* – with a differentiated approach: the consociational referendum confers equal respect to every citizen *qualitate qua* – or in their capacity as – a member of a particular community (Tierney, 2012, p. 265). The downside of this approach, however, is that it would 'communautarise' policy issues which have nothing to do with the political divide between Flemings and French speakers. One of the arguments for a repeated recourse to direct decision-making through referendum in the context of a multilingual and divided country like Belgium is that it could contribute to the emergence of a common '*demos*'. By discussing issues of common concern and deciding them together through referendum, the fact of belonging to the same political community would be visibly enacted on a regular basis (Stojanović, 2009, p. 14; Van Parijs, 2018). However, if every one of these referendums were to demand a double majority, the exact opposite effect is created: the existence of a common *demos* would be denied, since the only relevant majorities are regionally defined. The referendum would then serve to deepen these divisions rather than help to bridge them. There is no easy answer to this dilemma, however, and where a community cannot agree whether – or under what conditions – the referendum amounts to a fair procedure, it might simply not be a very good idea to decide contentious issues in this way.

As the recent developments on the regional level have shown, however, the referendum is no longer the only game in town. Increasingly, governments around the world are experimenting with new forms of popular consultation, most often through the use of random selection. Ostbelgien and Brussels are at the forefront of this "deliberative wave" (OECD, 2020). Of course, applying these lessons to the federal level is not without its own distinct set of challenges. Most obviously, the sort of face-to-face dialogue deliberative consultation processes try to stimulate is complicated by the multilingual nature of the Belgian state, since language differences pose a barrier to mutual understanding. That deliberation is more difficult in multilingual settings does not render it impossible, however. Of particular note in this respect is the Europolis project – a mini-public organised by the European Union in 2009 – which managed to facilitate discussions between European citizens despite huge linguistic diversity (Fishkin, 2018). Within Belgium itself, the G1000 constitutes a successful example of multilingual deliberation. Not only did this event overcome the linguistic barrier, but research has shown that participants to the event held a more positive view of the other community afterwards (Caluwaerts and Reuchamps, 2014). This experience with the G1000 shows that deliberation in a multilingual setting not only is practically feasible but can also manage to cut across the political divisions which characterise Belgian consociationalism.[32]

Giving such forms of citizen deliberation a more profound place within the Belgian democratic system – for example by transforming the now largely defunct Senate into a randomly selected citizens' assembly, an idea that has been floated repeatedly by a number of elected representatives and academics alike (Vandamme et al., 2019) – would serve an important function that is now missing from its institutional architecture. It would act as a counterweight to the centrifugal and particratic tendencies of Belgian federalism. Not only would this restore a degree

32 A deliberative mini-public organised in Northern Ireland in 2007 found similar effects (Fishkin, 2009, p. 166).

of popular control over federal decision-making, but, if successful, it could also positively affect the epistemic quality of the democratic system as a whole. The dominance of political parties in parliamentary proceedings has a number of negative deliberative effects. The iron law of party discipline – which, to a large extent, defines the internal working of parliament – reduces the prospect of high-quality deliberation. Most obviously, this party discipline denies elected representatives the freedom to vote according to their own judgment. Aside from these internal disincentives, the fact that the parliamentary agenda is defined by electoral cycles discourages representatives from engaging in longer-term reflection and from putting forward policies that will only bear fruit in the long run, because such policies do not help their re-election effort. While regular elections are crucial for keeping representatives accountable, and for allowing citizens to reject and actively contest representative claims (Saward, 2010), the overall short-termism of electoral democracy is an important side-effect which negatively undermines the capacity of elected parliaments to deal with issues which require sustained legislative effort to tackle successfully – such as climate change. This problem is compounded in the Belgian context by the fact that elected representatives are only accountable to their own language group, so that elected representatives are discouraged from taking into consideration the opinion and beliefs of citizens who do not belong to their own community (Caluwaerts and Reuchamps, 2014; Sinardet, 2010).

A randomly selected citizens' assembly would not be subject to the same incentive structure. Citizens selected through sortition only represent themselves and are not accountable to anyone. While this is a reason to limit the sorted assembly to an advisory role, it does mean that these citizens are free to deliberate. They can listen to experts and their peers and change their mind if they so choose, without having to worry about re-election or having to fear negative repercussions for breaking party ranks or crossing community lines. Moreover, in their deliberations, these citizens are more likely to adopt a wider temporal perspective which reaches far beyond the next election date, so that a randomly selected Senate could be seen as a means to represent the interests of future generations in collective decision-making.[33] In all these ways, a randomly selected Senate could act both as a useful deliberative input in the democratic system – by including un- or under-represented perspectives in the decision-making process – and as a necessary corrective against some of the weaknesses of elective representation. In both cases, however, its role is merely to supplement, not to replace. Due to the democratic limitations sortition suffers from, the last word should continue to lie with the elected chamber, or with the population as a whole through referendum.

33 It should be recalled that the idea that citizen participation favours the existing generation over future generations was one of the elements of the 'national sovereignty myth', according to which the concept of the nation encompasses past, present, and future generations (Geenens and Sottiaux, 2015).

Conclusion

This chapter explored the complex relation between federalism and democracy in Belgium. In a strange twist, federalism appeared as both the villain and the hero in this story. Belgium's particular brand of federalism characterised by consociational decision-making at the federal level was identified as the underlying reason for the elite-driven nature of Belgian democracy, and its aversion to active citizen involvement. At the same time, however, federalism creates room for the sub-state levels to start experimenting with new forms of citizen participation.

Over the past few years, every federated entity in Belgium has in some way or form engaged with the question of democratic renewal. Whereas Wallonia introduced legislation allowing its citizens to initiate referendums, Brussels and Ostbelgien turned to the theory of deliberative democracy for inspiration. Although in both cases random selection was used to involve citizens in the decision-making process, the underlying rationale is different. While the Ostbelgien model emphasises citizen autonomy and sets its citizens' assemblies up as a *de facto* second chamber, the deliberative committees in Brussels take a different approach and act as a venue where a group of randomly selected citizens can enter into a dialogue with their elected representatives. Lastly, the experience in Flanders with the failed Citizens' Assembly Bill shows that democratic renewal – even at the regional level – cannot be taken for granted. Even so, the citizen-initiated citizens' assemblies it promoted constitute a valuable example in institutional design.

These developments at the regional level could serve as an impetus to reinvigorate the debate on the role of citizens in federal decision-making as well. Though it is often presented as if the divided nature of Belgium renders active citizen involvement ill-advised at best and outright dangerous at worst, this chapter presented a number of arguments to question this assumption. Under the right conditions, citizen participation can serve as a counterweight to the elitist and particratic aspects of Belgium's consociationalist institutions without endangering the coexistence between its communities. Whether these opportunities will be taken advantage of is an altogether different matter, however. The story is not over yet.

Bibliography

Bächtiger, A., Parkinson, J. (2019) *Mapping and Measuring Deliberation: Towards a New Deliberative Quality*. New York: Oxford University Press.

Bächtiger, A., Dryzek, J.S., Mansbridge, J., Warren, M. (2018) 'Deliberative Democracy: An Introduction', in Bächtiger, A., Dryzek, J.S., Mansbridge, J., Warren, M. (eds.), *The Oxford Handbook of Deliberative Democracy*. Oxford: Oxford University Press, pp. 22–32. DOI: 10.1093/oxfordhb/9780198747369.013.50.

Böker, M. (2017) 'Justification, Critique and Deliberative Legitimacy: The Limits of Mini-Publics', *Contemporary Political Theory*, 16, pp. 19–40. DOI: 10.1057/cpt.2016.11.

Caluwaerts, D., Reuchamps, M. (2014) 'Deliberative Stress in Linguistically Divided Belgium' in Ugarriza, J.E., Caluwaerts, D. (eds.) *Democratic Deliberation in Deeply Divided Societies: From Conflict to Common Ground*. London: Palgrave Macmillan, pp. 35–52.

Caluwaerts, D., Reuchamps, M. (2015) 'Combining Federalism with Consociationalism: Is Belgian Consociational Federalism Digging its Own Grave?', *Ethnopolitics*, 14(3), pp. 277–295. DOI: 10.1080/17449057.2014.986866.

Chambers, S. (2001) 'Constitutional Referendums and Democratic Deliberation', in Mendelsohn, M., Parkin, A. (eds.) *Referendum Democracy : Citizens, Elites and Deliberation in Referendum Campaigns*. Basingstoke: Palgrave Macmillan, pp. 231–255.

Cheneval, F., el-Wakil, A. (2018) 'The Institutional Design of Referendums: Bottom-Up and Binding', *Swiss Political Science Review*, 24(3), pp. 294–304. DOI: 10.1111/spsr.12319.

Deschouwer, K. (2005) 'The Unintended Consequences of Consociational Federalism: The Case of Belgium', in O'Flynn, I., Russel, D. (eds.) *Power Sharing, New Challenges for Divided Societies*. London: Pluto Press, pp. 92–106.

Dewachter, W. (2014) *De trukendoos van de Belgische particratie*. Kalmthout: Pelckmans.

Dryzek, J.S. (2005) 'Deliberative Democracy in Divided Societies: Alternatives to Agonism and Analgesia', *Political Theory*, 33(2), pp. 218–242. DOI: 10.1177/0090591704268372.

Elazar, D.J. (1987) *Exploring Federalism*. Birmingham: University of Alabama Press.

Elst, M., Nieuwenhove, J. van (2016) *De zelfinrichtingsbevoegdheden van de deelstaten*. Bruges: Die Keure.

Fishkin, J.S. (2009) *When the People Speak. Deliberative Democracy and Public Consultation*. Oxford: Oxford University Press.

Fishkin, J.S. (2018) *Democracy When the People Are Thinking*. Oxford: Oxford University Press. DOI: 10.1093/oso/9780198820291.001.0001.

Geenens, R., Sottiaux, S. (2015) 'Sovereignty and Direct Democracy: Lessons from Constant and the Belgian Constitution', *European Constitutional Law Review*, 11(2), pp. 293–320. DOI: 10.1017/S1574019615000188.

Goodin, R.E., Dryzek, J.S. (2006) 'Deliberative Impacts: The Macro-Political Uptake of Mini-Publics', *Politics & Society*, 34(2), pp. 219–244. DOI: 10.1177/0032329206288152.

Gutmann, A., Thompson, D. (1997) *Democracy and Disagreement*. Cambridge, MA: Harvard University Press.

Hendriks, C.M. (2016) 'Coupling Citizens and Elites in Deliberative Systems: The role of Institutional Design', *European Journal of Political Research*, 55(1), pp. 43–60. DOI: 10.1111/1475-6765.12123.

IDEA (Institute for Democracy and Electoral Assistance) (2008) *Direct Democracy: The International IDEA Handbook*. Stockholm: International Institute for Democracy and Electoral Assistance.

Jacquet, V., Moskovic, J., Caluwaerts, D., Reuchamps, M. (2016) 'The Macro Political Uptake of the G1000 in Belgium', in Reuchamps, M., Suiter, J. (eds.) *Constitutional Deliberative Democracy in Europe*. Colchester: ECPR Press, pp. 53–74.

Lafont, C. (2015) 'Deliberation, Participation, and Democratic Legitimacy: Should Deliberative Mini-publics Shape Public Policy?', *Journal of Political Philosophy*, 23(1), pp. 40–63. DOI: 10.1111/jopp.12031.

Lafont, C. (2020) *Democracy Without Shortcuts.* Oxford, New York: Oxford University Press.
Lijphart, A. (1969) 'Consociational Democracy', *World Politics*, 21(2), pp. 207–225. DOI: 10.2307/2009820.
Lijphart, A. (1977) *Democracy in Plural Societies: A Comparative Exploration.* New Haven, CT: Yale University Press.
Lijphart, A. (ed.) (1981) *Conflict and Coexistence in Belgium: The Dynamics of a Culturally Divided Society.* Berkeley, CA: Institute of International Studies, University of California.
Lijphart, A. (1984) *Patterns of Majoritarian and Consensus Government in Twenty-One Countries.* New Haven, CT: Yale University Press.
Luther, K.R., Deschouwer, K. (eds.) (1999) *Party Elites in Divided Societies: Political Parties in Consociational Democracy.* Routledge/ECPR Studies in European Political Science. London, New York: Routledge.
Mansbridge, J., et al. (2012) 'A Systemic Approach to Deliberative Democracy', in Mansbridge, J., Parkinson, J. (eds.) *Deliberative Systems.* Cambridge: Cambridge University Press, pp. 1–26.
Minsart, E., Jacquet, V. (2020) 'Permanent Joint Committees in Belgium: Involving Citizens in Parliamentary Debate', Constitution Unit [online]. Available at: https://constitution-unit.com/2020/05/28/permanent-joint-committees-in-belgium-involving-citizens-in-parliamentary-debate/ (Accessed: 17 June 2020).
OECD (Organisation for Economic Cooperation and Development) (2020) *Innovative Citizen Participation and New Democratic Institutions: Catching the Deliberative Wave.* Paris: OECD. DOI: 10.1787/339306da-en.
Parkinson, J. (2012) 'Democratizing Deliberative Systems', in Parkinson, J., Mansbridge, J. (eds.) *Deliberative Systems.* Cambridge: Cambridge University Press, pp. 151–172.
S.A. (1989) Bijzondere wet van 26/01/1989 op het Grondwettelijk Hof, Parl. St. Kamer 483.
S.A. (1997) Canadian Supreme Court, Libman v. Quebec (AG), 1997, 3 S.C.R. 569.
S.A. (1998) ECtHR, Bowman v. the United Kingdom, 1998, 26 EHRR 1.
S.A. (2017) Voorstel van decreet betreffende de invoering van een procedure voor het geven van toegang aan burgers tot de parlementaire besluitvorming via een adviserend deliberatief proces, Parl. St. Vlaams Parlement 917/1.
S.A. (2018a) Décret spécial du 19/07/2018 instituant la consultation populaire. Documents du Parlement Wallon 559.
S.A. (2018b) Parlement Wallon, Compte rendu intégral de la séance publique de commission spéciale relative au renouveau démocratique du 28 Juin 2018, C.R.I.C. N° 170.
S.A. (2019a) Dekret von 25/02/2019 fur Einführung eines Permanenten Bürgerdialogs in der Deutssprachigen Gemeinschaft. Dokument 284.
S.A. (2019b) Règlement du Parlement de la Région de Bruxelles-Capitale et l'Assemblée Réunie de la Commission Communautaire Commune.
Sanders, L. (1996) 'Against Deliberation', *Political Theory*, 25(3), pp. 347–376.
Saward, M. (2010) *The Representative Claim.* Oxford: Oxford University Press. DOI: 10.1093/acprof:oso/9780199579389.001.0001.
Sinardet, D. (2010) 'From Consociational Consciousness to Majoritarian Myth: Consociational Democracy, Multi-Level Politics and the Belgian case of

Brussels-Halle-Vilvoorde', *Acta Politica: International Journal of Political Science*, 45(3), pp. 346–369.

Smith, G. (2009) *Democratic Innovations: Designing Institutions for Citizen Participation*. Cambridge: Cambridge University Press. DOI: 10.1017/CBO9780511609848.

Smith, G., Setälä, M. (2018) 'Mini-Publics and Deliberative Democracy', in Bächtiger, A., Dryzek, J.S., Mansbridge, J., Warren, M. (eds.) *The Oxford Handbook of Deliberative Democracy*. Oxford: Oxford University Press, pp. 299–314. DOI: 10.1093/oxfordhb/9780198747369.013.27.

Stojanović, N. (2009) 'Is Democracy Possible in a Multilingual Country? The Swiss Experience and the Paradox of Direct Democracy', in Sinardet, D., Hooghe, M. (eds.) *Is Democracy Viable without a Unified Public Opinion?* Brussel: Re-Bel e-book, pp. 10–18.

Sunstein, C.R. (2002) 'The Law of Group Polarization', *Journal of Political Philosophy*, 10(2), pp. 175–195. DOI: 10.1111/1467-9760.00148.

Tierney, S. (2012) *Constitutional Referendums: The Theory and Practice of Republican Deliberation*. Oxford: Oxford University Press.

Van Parijs, P. (2018) *Belgium. Une Utopie pour notre temps*. Brussels: Académie royale de Belgique.

Vandamme, P.-E., Jacquet, V., Niessen, C., Pitseys, J., Reuchamps, M. (2019) 'Intercameral Relations in a Bicameral Elected and Sortition Legislature', in Gastil, J., Wright, E.O. (eds.) *Legislature by Lot. Transformative Designs for Deliberative Governance*. London and New York: Verso, pp. 123–144.

Watts, R.L. (1999) *Comparing Federal Systems*. Kingston: McGill-Queen's University Press.

Publications without a specific, personal author (such as newspapers and official documents) are listed under S.A.

13 A non-populist direct democracy for Belgium

Nenad Stojanović

Introduction

Belgium and Switzerland are the only *deeply* multilingual countries in Europe. By 'deeply multilingual', I mean polities where there are two or more official languages but where most citizens are predominantly monolingual and there is no lingua franca, unlike Spanish in Spain or English in Ireland (see Stojanović and Bonotti, 2020). From the point of view of institutional design, both Switzerland and Belgium are federations and have been considered prime examples of consociational democracy (Lijphart, 1977).[1] Clearly, there are also many differences between them, but the most important one from the institutional point of view is the role of direct democracy, which is crucial in the political system of Switzerland but next to inexistent in Belgium, at the national level at least.[2]

Direct democracy is a truly popular institution in Switzerland. A large majority of the Swiss see it as an important element of their national identity,[3] and no Swiss political party is against direct democratic tools such as popular initiatives and referendums.[4]

1 While I have argued elsewhere that Switzerland is not an example of linguistic consociation (Stojanović, 2020), this is not a matter of concern in the context of the present chapter.

2 The only exception is the 1950 referendum on the Royal Question, if we don't count the 1793 referendum on becoming a part of France, and the 1920 local referendums in Eupen and Malmedy on whether their residents wanted to be a part of Germany or of Belgium (source: c2d.ch.). In more recent years, Belgium's Constitution was amended in 1997 in order to allow for the possibility of local referendums, and then in 1998 to extend the possibility to the provincial level (Reuchamps, 2011). A further change to the Constitution (article 39bis, since 2013) created the possibility of introducing referendums at the regional level too. However, such referendums are not binding, and until now the option has been used only rarely and only at the local level.

3 See Garessus (2016).

4 A *popular initiative* can be launched by any group of citizens, who then have 18 months to collect 100,000 valid signatures (approximately 2% of the electorate). It can be on any topic (e.g. unconditional basic income and the ban on dehorning cows were recent topics). Parliament can declare it invalid if it violates *jus cogens* (e.g. prohibition of slavery and torture); this happened only once, in 1996, when an initiative of the extreme right violated the 'principle of *non-refoulement*' of refugees and asylum-seekers. If the initiative is declared valid, parlia-

The situation is quite different outside of Switzerland. Surveys show that citizens of other countries also want more direct participation in political decisions (Donovan and Karp, 2006, p. 677). But this has hardly led to an upsurge in direct democracy in the respective countries. The reason, in my view, is that their political, economic, and academic elites fear that referendums and popular initiatives might open the door to populist policies and end up undermining democracy itself (Offe, 2017).

Scepticism towards direct democracy is further nourished by the fact that populists themselves are actually calling for more direct democracy. In 2014, for example, parties such as the UK Independence Party (UKIP), the Swedish Democrats, and Alternative for Germany (AfD) founded the 'Alliance for Direct Democracy in Europe'. It is telling that an AfD politician declared that his goal was to promote the "*Verschweizerung Deutschlands*", that is, the Helvetisation of Germany (Theile, 2017).

In Belgium too, populism is considered a disruptive force (see e.g. De Cleen and Van Aelst, 2016) and, in addition, there is the risk that direct democracy would only accelerate the linguistic division of the country (see e.g. Hooghe and Sinardet, 2009). Nevertheless, its political system is slowly opening up to referendums at the sub-national level (see fn. 2). Hence, it makes sense to discuss its possible effects.

Against that background, the aim of this chapter is twofold. First, I want to show that scepticism towards direct democracy rests on shaky ground. In fact, I will try to argue that frequent use of direct democracy could structurally undermine populism. In this regard, the Swiss experience with direct democracy may serve as a source of inspiration, rather than as a model. Second, I want to use that inspiration to discuss the case of Belgium and the potential effects of direct democracy on that country.

The chapter is structured as follows. I first show how direct democracy challenges the populist fiction of a unified 'people'. I then explore its 'valve function', which allows citizens to peacefully express their frustrations with political elites and the outcomes of representative democracy. The chapter proceeds by presenting the main arguments underlying the scepticism towards direct democracy, before turning to the rationale for possible use of direct democratic instruments

---

ment can accept it, reject it, or make a counterproposal. In any event, a popular vote must be held (unless the initiative is accepted by parliament or its committee decides to withdraw it). If the majority of the voters and the majority of the cantons accept the initiative, it enters the Constitution (either as a new article or as an amendment of an existing one). In most cases, parliament is then called to implement it by emending an existing law or by writing a new law. Often, however, parliament does not fully implement the content of the initiative (e.g. in 5 out of 12 cases since 1994; see Kley, 2015). Such decisions by parliament cannot be sanctioned as there is no judicial review. The *referendum* can be either mandatory (e.g. when a constitutional emendment is triggered by parliament) or facultative. Facultative referendums can veto any law approved by parliament. They can be launched within 100 days and require 50,000 valid signatures. If successful, a popular vote must be held and the majority of the voters decides.

in the context of a deeply multilingual Belgium and an overview of practical recommendations. I conclude by stressing the problem of availability heuristics that haunts debates on direct democracy in academia and beyond.

The unified people?

An essential characteristic of populists is that they are not only anti-elitist but also anti-pluralist. "Their claim is always 'We – and only we – represent the true people'" (Müller, 2016a, p. 129).[5] The 'true people' is thereby represented as a unitary, homogeneous community. Müller further outlines that "[t]he populist always operates with the following contrast: on the one hand the morally immaculate, homogeneous people, on the other the corrupt or at least incompetent elites" (Müller, 2016b).

Now, it is relatively easy, I argue, to spread this fiction in countries where you never actually ask voters what they think about a particular political issue. Take, for example, the following quote typical of the politician Marine Le Pen (of France's '*Rassemblement national*' party): "The people no longer want immigrants" (Ginori, 2015). Or, in the words of Tom Van Grieken, the leader of the Belgian '*Vlaams Belang*' party: "Immigration is really the topic that keeps people awake [and thus] we need the migration [to] stop".[6] Yet neither we nor the populists themselves know how 'the people' – the French people, the Flemish people – would actually vote on this particular issue.

A key insight, here, is that *frequent and regular* use of direct democracy *structurally* undermines populist ideology based on 'the people's will' and a unified, non-pluralist conception of the people. Of course, we know that this conception is fiction (Chollet, 2011, p. 109; Müller, 2016a) but it is, or so I will argue, easier to unmask in a political system in which direct democracy is commonly used.

To see this, it is of crucial importance to underline that frequent use of direct democratic tools creates a context of unstable and ever-changing majorities and minorities. While mainstream theorists of democracy consider this fact as a significant *disadvantage* of direct democracy (Schmidt, 2010, p. 188), it is crucial to my non-populist account as it increases the likelihood that members of minorities will be parts of political majorities on some issues (Rothchild and Roeder, 2005, p. 17). This insight also contributes to relativising the charge that direct democracy can exacerbate the danger of majority tyranny and the twin problem of persistent minorities. I argue that the opposite is actually true: it is in purely representative democracies, especially if the representatives are elected according to majoritarian rules, that minority groups can be systematically outnumbered by the majority. In a system of frequently employed direct democracy – where

5 My translation from the German. The remark applies to all other quotes in this chapter of which the source is not English.

6 "omdat immigratie echt het tema is waar de mensen van wakker liggen [...] dan heb je de migratiestop nodig" (Van Grieken, 2019).

people can vote on ordinary policy issues such as pension reform, healthcare, a new motorway tunnel, or environmental regulations – the chances are high that a citizen belonging to a minority group will quite often be on the winning side, that is, in the *majority* (cf. Stojanović, 2011, pp. 104–105). This effect of direct democracy confers legitimacy on the political system and allows it to counter the populist rhetoric of real or potential ethnonationalist leaders and movements.

Consider the fact that the Swiss populists have often tried to launch popular initiatives with the aim of limiting immigration. And yet, with one exception since 1970, all such proposals have failed because the majority of the people were against them.[7] The sole exception is the popular initiative 'against mass immigration' that was narrowly accepted (by 50.3%) on 9 February 2014. (Actually, the majority of the voters were not in favour of the initiative; if we count the blank ballots, 49.8% were 'yes' votes.) Is this one vote a reason to reject direct democracy as an institution? Of course not. We should not judge democracy only on the basis of its outcomes. After all, hardly anyone has proposed to abolish free elections and representative democracy on the grounds that a considerable number of citizens of France, Italy, and the United States voted for populists such as Le Pen, Salvini, and Trump. Thus, leaving aside the narrowly successful outcome of 9 February 2014 – which, by the way, has never been implemented by parliament, nor has that decision of parliament been challenged by a successful referendum – we can say that, contrary to populist slogans, the majority of Swiss do not want to stop (or even simply limit) immigration. Indeed, in spite of direct democracy, after Luxembourg, Switzerland is the European country with the second highest rate of immigrants – 25.3% (as of March 2020). Do, say, citizens of France, Germany, the United Kingdom, or Belgium want to stop or limit immigration? We simply do not know, because they have never been allowed to vote on this issue. In such institutional contexts it is easier for populists to claim to speak 'on behalf of the people'.

The valve function of popular initiatives

The instruments of direct democracy, especially the popular initiative, fulfil several functions in the political system. One of them is the so-called 'valve function' (*Ventilfunktion*; Linder, 2012, p. 287). Thanks to the popular initiative, dissatisfied citizens can "let off steam by protesting against the system" (Caroni and Vatter, 2016, p. 192).

Let us take the rise of Islamophobia as an example. In Germany, it is at the heart of 'Pegida', a populist movement.[8] Its name – 'Patriotic Europeans against the Islamisation of the West' – is a perfect summary of its cause (Korsch, 2016,

7 See the Schwarzenbach initiatives in the 1970s, the '18 percent initiative' in 2000, the initiative 'against abuse of asylum rights' in 2002, and the 'Ecopop' initiative, which was rejected by 74% of voters on 30 November 2014.

8 See www.islamophobiaeurope.com.

p. 112). Despite several attempts, Pegida has never succeeded in setting foot in Switzerland. Violent attacks against asylum centres have also been virtually non-existent in Switzerland. One hypothesis is that direct democracy allows (potentially or actually) Islamophobic Swiss citizens to 'let off steam' and express their frustration by voting 'yes' or 'no' on certain popular initiatives, for example in the federal vote against the construction of minarets in 2009 or in popular votes that took place in the cantons of Ticino in 2013 and St Gallen in 2018 on a burka ban. On these three occasions, a majority of voters approved the respective populists' proposals.

While we may regret the outcome of these popular votes,[9] a far-right movement like Pegida seems far more frightening to me. According to Bühlmann, "it would be worth investigating if protest phenomena such as Pegida or Podemos are not getting through in Switzerland because the critical debate is constantly being fuelled by direct democracy" (Bühlmann, 2015, p. 582, fn. 14). In other words, people who have a direct say in decisions do not need to raise tensions and to provoke (potentially or actually) violent conflicts on the streets.

Clearly, empirical analysis is required in order to test this thesis. At this stage, let me stress that, according to Caroni and Vatter (2016, p. 205), 12 out of 137 popular initiatives launched between 1987 and 2015 in Switzerland can be considered as having had a valve function.

An example is the initiative 'against rip-off salaries', which proposed to increase the decision-making power of the shareholders of Swiss companies listed on the stock exchange. Its valve function is attested to by the fact that it was launched in October 2006, in a context of widespread popular anger against the hubris of well-known executives. By February 2008, it had gathered over 114,000 valid signatures and was put before parliament. It was rejected by parliament; however, in March 2013, a popular vote was held and the initiative won a landslide victory: 68% of Swiss voters and a majority in each canton voted in favour of it.[10]

Nowadays, it is likely that populist proposals such as the burka ban can gain a majority at the ballot box. But, again, we can ask if the situation is different in purely representative democracies? By June 2017, countries such as France, Belgium, and Austria had already adopted a burka ban.

9 I emphasise that we *may* regret such outcomes because I do not expect that all readers will agree that the burka ban, for example, is actually a decision that we should regret. In a different context, the burka ban might be considered necessary for gender equality and a certain idea of what it means to 'live together'. Indeed, it was upheld by the French and the Belgian constitutional courts, as well as by the European Court of Human Rights. (I thank Stefan Sottiaux for this remark.) But in the Swiss context – where hardly any woman, except for a limited number of tourists, wears a niqab or a burka – the popular initiatives demanding a burka ban have clearly been populist and had a discriminatory intent. According to the president of the Swiss Federal Commission against Racism, it is "a pretext to attack Islam" (Swissinfo, 30 August 2016; https://www.swissinfo.ch/eng/controversial-initiative_anti-racism-official-burka-ban-is-excuse-to-attack-islam/42408780).

10 https://www.bk.admin.ch/ch/d/pore/va/20130303/index.html.

Beyond populism: Other reasons to be sceptical about direct democracy

In the previous two sections, I have presented tentative arguments defending direct democracy from the charge that it is prone (or more prone than representative democracy) to populist manipulations. Let me now take a step back and ask why many scholars and practitioners alike think that direct democracy encourages populism? The most important reason is the supposed ignorance or political incompetence of citizens. Giovanni Sartori (1987, p. 120), for one, argues that the "cognitive incompetence" of the electorate allows populist proposals to win majorities in direct democratic popular votes.

Of course, voters can make highly controversial decisions. However, this is not a distinctive feature of direct democracy alone. The risk also exists in representative democracy. After all, a plurality of Germans – 37% in July and 33% in November 1932 – voted for the Nazis. And in Bosnia, 75% of voters supported the ethnonationalist parties in November 1990 (Stojanović, 2014).

A second reason for scepticism is that less than half – about 46% – of Switzerland's enfranchised citizens take part in popular votes, with the better educated and wealthier social classes being over-represented. It is important to address the issue of turnout and to see who makes use of their political rights and who does not (see Kriesi, 1993). But it is wrong, I think, to take this as a benchmark for supporting or refusing direct democracy. We know very well that even in a representative democracy certain societal groups are greatly over- or under-represented. Lawyers and men, for example, are clearly over-represented. Women, on the other hand, are typically under-represented, and it is almost impossible to find working-class people in parliaments (Mansbridge, 2015). But is that a reason to reject representative democracy as a form of government? If not, then logically, one should refrain from using similar arguments against direct democracy.[11]

A third reason for scepticism towards direct democracy is the 'tyranny of the majority'. If the majority (of at least 50% plus one) always wins, then even strong minorities are always defeated. In my view, and on the basis of the Swiss experience, this risk is highly exaggerated. Notwithstanding its majoritarian logic, Swiss direct democracy has not created problems for the linguistic minorities. On the contrary, it has significantly contributed to forging national cohesion and the perception that the Swiss form a single 'people' (Stojanović, 2011; see also the

11 That being said, we can still do a lot to address the problems related to low turnout. Italy, for example, has a quorum of 50% for referendums. In the canton of Schaffhausen, Switzerland, voters pay a fine of 6 Swiss francs if they fail to vote without a valid excuse. This alone has already produced turnouts that are 15–20 percentage points above the Swiss average. This said, I am much less critical of the low turnout problem and do not favour quorums, because they produce perverse effects (e.g. people who are against a proposal put to referendum might abstain from voting), as shown by the recent, short-lived experience with direct democracy in the Netherlands. I am also not in favour of compulsory voting. For reasons of space, I cannot further elaborate on these two points. Rather, my objective has simply been to stress that *if* we think the low turnout is a problem, then we can find ways to mitigate it.

next section of this chapter). Paradoxically perhaps, direct democracy is used as if Switzerland were a centralised and unitary state *à la* France: the majority decides. It is true that constitutional amendments – via popular initiatives or referendums triggered by parliament – also require a majority of the cantons (see fn. 4), and this is certainly a federal element in the direct democratic procedure. But this tool does not protect the linguistic minorities (i.e. French, Italian, and Romansh speakers) whatsoever, since the vast majority of the cantons are German speaking.

A viable proposal for a deeply multilingual Belgium?

The Belgian political philosopher Philippe Van Parijs has recently arrived at the conclusion that carefully designed direct democratic tools such as referendums have great potential, especially in divided societies such as Belgium, where linguistic diversity has created a fragmented public space (Van Parijs, 2018, p. 85). He looks for inspiration to Switzerland and reports a 2011 conversation with the then president of the Swiss Confederation Micheline Calmy-Rey (p. 86). According to Ms Calmy-Rey, there are three reasons why Swiss democracy 'functions better' than its Belgian counterpart in spite of the 'similar challenges' that the two countries face: (1) conflict management is easier when there are 26 cantons instead of only two linguistic blocs; (2) the existence of national parties and a single voting space in Switzerland; and (3) the Swiss have the idea of forming a single 'people'.

The reasons put forward by Ms Calmy-Rey to explain why Switzerland 'functions better' than Belgium were certainly well taken. But I see them – following Lijphart (1977) – neither as necessary nor as sufficient but as 'favourable' conditions. In my view, they do not imply that Belgium is a lost case and that introducing direct democracy would make things even worse. Moreover, what if Ms Calmy-Rey's implicit[12] causal mechanism is wrong? What if direct democracy has been, in the Swiss context, if not the cause then at least a 'favourable condition' that has critically *supported* both (1), (2), and (3)?

Regarding (1), one could argue that direct democracy prevented the creation of linguistic blocs, given that it has prevented the merger of cantons. In fact, in recent decades, economic, political, and bureaucratic elites have been pushing for a Switzerland of seven or nine (instead of 26) cantons.[13] But whenever a merger of

12 'Implicit' because her point was to explain why Swiss democracy generally speaking, and not necessarily Swiss *direct* democracy, works better than democracy in Belgium. But given that direct democracy is at the very core of Swiss democracy, I think that we can take her remarks as referring to the functioning of direct democracy, too.

13 See e.g. 'Vers une fusion des cantons?', RTS radio, 30 September 2011 [online]. Available at: https://www.rts.ch/play/radio/le-journal-du-matin/audio/vers-une-fusion-de-cantons?id=3411920; 'Has Switzerland's 26-cantons model had it day?', Swissinfo, 28 January 2015 [online]. Available at: https://www.swissinfo.ch/eng/directdemocracy/federalismo-cantoni-svizzera-quanti-ce-ne-vogliono/41237576; 'Un chercheur a imaginé une Suisse à neuf ou treize cantons au lieu des 2[6] actuels', *Le Nouvelliste*, 7 August 2015 [online].

cantons was put to a popular vote, the results were "devastating" (Vatter, 2018, §4.1). In 2014, 68% of voters in the canton Basel-Country rejected the proposal to merge with the canton Basel-City. Twelve years earlier, in 2002, only 20% of Geneva's voters were in favour of the popular initiative '*Oui à la region (Genève-Vaud)*', which proposed to merge the canton of Geneva with the neighbouring canton of Vaud. Notice that the hypothetical canton Geneva-Vaud would have been the home of 6 out of 10 French speakers in Switzerland. In other words, it would have come close to being an institutionalised linguistic bloc, not quite as linguistically homogeneous as Wallonia (where 8 out of 10 French speakers in Belgium live) but not too far from it either.[14] To sum up, "these referendums on cantonal mergers clearly express that Swiss citizens still strongly identify with their canton" (Vatter, 2018, §4.1).

As for the importance of countrywide parties (2), my thesis is that direct democracy has been a crucial factor in explaining why Swiss parties become and remain national and multilingual, contrary to what has happened with national political parties in Belgium (see Stojanović and Bonotti, 2020). The main reason for this is that popular votes are held within a single, countrywide voting district (Stojanović, 2009: pp. 17–18; see also Lacey, 2014). This creates a powerful incentive not only for political parties but also for associations, to cross language borders and be present in all parts of the country. This incentive is in line with the centripetal approach to institutional design for divided societies (Reilly, 2012) and is comparable to the kind of incentive, and the effects it is intended to trigger, that the Pavia Group, a Belgian group of academics, has been advocating for – that is, the creation of a single, federal electoral district in which 10% of seats would be allocated (Horowitz, 2009).

The last favourable condition mentioned by Ms Calmy-Rey (3), namely, the perception that the Swiss form a single *demos*, is also strongly influenced by direct democracy (Stojanović, 2009, pp. 15–17). The thesis is that it is "the frequent

Available at: https://www.lenouvelliste.ch/articles/suisse/un-chercheur-a-imagine-une-suisse-a-neuf-ou-treize-cantons-au-lieu-des-22-actuels-343298.

14 Population censuses in Belgium do not include the language question, whereas in Switzerland the last complete (individual-based) census was held in 2000. Hence the numbers that I gave are rough approximations based on the principle of territoriality. To calculate the number of French speakers in Switzerland, I considered French speaking the population of all officially monolingual (French) cantons (Geneva, Vaud, Neuchâtel, Jura) plus the officially monolingual (French) districts of the cantons of Fribourg, Valais, and Berne. Hence, as of 2018, the share of the population of Geneva and Vaud within the *Suisse romande* (French-speaking Switzerland) was 61.0% (1,298,625 out of 2,129,848). Source: Swiss Federal Statistical Office (https://www.bfs.admin.ch/bfs/fr/home/statistiques/population/effectif-evolution/repartition-territoriale.assetdetail.9635942.html). To calculate the number of French speakers in Belgium, I considered the population of Wallonia minus the German-speaking community, plus 80% of the population of the region of Brussels. Hence, as of 2020, the share of Wallonia's French speakers within the French-speaking community of Belgium is 78.5% (3,567,294 out of 4,541,898). Source: StatBel (https://statbel.fgov.be/en/themes/population/structure-population).

exercise of direct democracy at the national level which makes the emergence of such a *demos* possible" (Stojanović, 2009, p. 16). It makes it possible because it makes it constantly 'visible'. When, in the aftermath of a popular vote, politicians and the media say that "the people has decided", the 'people' they have in mind are the Swiss as a political nation and not an ethno-linguistic community. There are also, of course, other factors that explain why Switzerland has become a multilingual nation-state and not a multinational state composed of different linguistically defined nations (Dardanelli and Stojanović, 2011), but direct democracy is an important part of the puzzle.

To sum up, my point is that each of the three arguments that have been used to explain why direct democracy works in Switzerland can be turned upside down in order to argue that each of them has also been strongly influenced by direct democracy itself.

Nevertheless, Van Parijs (2018, p. 86) remains sceptical regarding the potential use of direct democracy in Belgium and mentions "perversities" that "do not spare Switzerland". He thinks that it could only be put in place in conjunction with institutions of deliberative democracy (such as a randomly chosen second chamber) and that direct democracy should not be allowed to "prevail over representative democracy" unless it becomes an extension of the deliberative process itself (ibid.).

I agree that caution is warranted if direct democracy is to be introduced into a political system that has hardly ever used it, especially in countries such as Belgium with structural (e.g. ethnic or linguistic) minorities. For this reason, in the next section, I will turn to a number of practical recommendations that take that caution into account.

But first, I would like to spell out more clearly why I think that direct democracy could be an inspiration for Belgium. The reasons are closely linked to points (2) and (3) discussed above. First, the institutional stability of democracy in Belgium would benefit from closer ties between Dutch- and French-speaking political parties (see Pilet et al., 2009). A government coalition, for one, would be easier to form. We could also expect to see a less segmented public space. Hence, ideally, a system of national parties would gradually re-emerge.

Second, national cohesion would benefit from direct democracy, provided that popular votes were held frequently. (Remember also the importance of multiple majorities and minorities discussed above.) In fact, direct democracy has the potential to enhance the formation of a single *demos* and contribute to "the formation of a common identity" (Papadopoulos and Magnette, 2010, p. 725). Of course, a common Belgian identity has existed for a long time. But it has been eroding. Moreover, supporting the emergence of a *demos* does not mean that the linguistically defined *demoi* would or should disappear. Rather, the idea is that direct democracy could further foster the "demoi-within-demos constellation", where "a thin demos coexists with multiple demoi" (Stojanović, 2020, p. 30). It is important to stress, also in relation to the first part of the chapter, that the kind of *demos* that direct democracy brings about is not 'the people' that populists have in mind, but rather a plural political community that, as I have argued elsewhere, divided societies need in order to have a functioning democracy (Stojanović, 2011; see also Van Crombrugge, 2020).

Of course, direct democracy can be defended on many other grounds not linked to the specific kind of problems that Belgium's democracy has been facing. For example, it can be seen as an additional check on the power of political elites, or as a way to address the rising legitimacy problems besetting the institutions of representative democracy (see e.g. Budge, 1996).

Practical recommendations

I would like to conclude this chapter by advancing a couple of recommendations which, I believe, could be useful if Belgium's institutional designers should want to introduce direct democratic tools (Stojanović, 2011, pp. 109–110).

Think of direct democracy as a slow, gradual, long-term process. A possible introduction of direct democracy in Belgium should not be rapid and abrupt. In Switzerland, direct democracy has been introduced gradually, step by step, and it has taken decades for its centripetal effects to become visible. In other words, do not expect to see its effects immediately and do not be discouraged by one or another negative experience. Also, do not end the experiment too early, as the authorities of the Netherlands did in 2018 after two national referendums that had not produced the results for which they had hoped.

Start at the local level. Even though the thesis of this chapter speaks of the benefits of direct democracy at the national level, it is necessary that citizens get accustomed to it first and foremost at the local level. If citizens see that they can decide on the construction of a new bridge in their local community, or vote on the local budget, or start an initiative for eliminating a disliked parking place, they might be more open to extending direct democratic tools to higher levels of government. The federal set-up of Belgium, which grants important autonomy to the regions and to the linguistic communities, is particularly inviting in this context.[15]

Exclude 'communitarian' issues from the reach of direct democracy. In order to prevent direct democracy from becoming a (further) source of ethnic or linguistic division, instead of centripetal integration, some highly divisive issues should

15 As mentioned earlier (fn. 2), it is now possible to launch referendums at the local, provincial, and regional level in Belgium. In light of the present chapter, that is a positive development. But there are many aspects of this that are not in line with the kind of direct democracy discussed in this chapter: Financial and budgetary issues are excluded (even if they create no 'communitarian' problems), parliament has the veto power, some decisions require a majority of two-thirds (which is far above the kind of qualified majority that I favour). Also, referendums are purely consultative. Of course, it is better to have non-binding referendums than no referendums at all. But the problem with non-binding referendums, as well as with other hurdles mentioned above, is that they can be very frustrating for people who spend their time and other resources collecting signatures. So the risk is that such referendums are rarely used. Now, most beneficial effects discussed in this chapter necessitate a *frequent* use of popular votes.

be put out of reach of popular votes, at least in the initial phase. In the context of Belgium, such issues are typically related to language or territory. Of course, there will likely be many borderline cases so it might be difficult to clearly distinguish communitarian from non-communitarian issues. One could even argue that any issue can be regarded as 'communitarian' in the Belgian context. There are indeed many examples showing that "media (and politics) are [...] inclined to interpret issues through the lens of the community divide [...] even when [...] confronted with figures that do not support or even contradict this interpretation" (Sinardet, 2009, p. 53). But I do not think that we should stop thinking about democratic innovations just because we anticipate misleading framing by media and politics. Instead, we should think of mechanisms that allow us to distinguish truly communitarian issues from other issues. Devices such as the 'alarm bell' procedure that already exist in the Belgian federal parliament could be very helpful in this regard.[16]

Provide a qualified majority for votes on constitutional amendments. The constitution (or an equivalent set of norms and documents) is of central importance in every democracy. Hence, in many democratic systems, a constitutional amendment is subject to a qualified majority. In some cases, depending on the exact nature of the qualified majority and the size of minority groups, this can reassure minorities that important reforms will not be adopted without their consent. In direct democratic procedures, this implies that pure majoritarian rule (50% plus one always wins) should be abandoned in favour of a more complex majority rule. In Switzerland, as already noted, any change in the Constitution is subject to a 'double majority' of the people and the cantons. Of course, the Swiss solution is hardly transferable to Belgium, given that its federal structure is based on only three regions and three communities. But it could become a source of inspiration and could lead to the adoption of a specific (Belgian) rule of qualified majority. For example, constitutional amendments could require the approval of the majority of voters and of at least 35% of citizens in each of the three regions.

Conclusion

In the last two sections, I have put forward arguments in favour of direct democracy in the context of Belgium. What are the obstacles to this (for now rather imaginary) path that Belgium's institutional designers might wish to take? In the current context, in Belgium (see De Cleen and Van Aelst, 2016) as elsewhere, I believe that the danger of populism will be the main argument against direct democracy. For this reason, the first sections of the chapter challenged this thesis.

16 The alarm bell procedure gives to each of the two main linguistic groups in parliament (Flemish or French) the right to suspend the parliamentary procedure if at least three quarters of its members sign the motion. In practice, it has been applied only twice, and both times by French speakers (Veny and Warnez, 2016, p. 230).

I argued that direct democracy is not per se a door opener for populists. On the contrary, it can constantly undermine the populist logic – and its political success – by breaking the myth of a homogeneous people. In certain culturally (linguistically, ethnically, religiously, etc.) heterogeneous societies, however, direct democracy presents both risks and opportunities. Hence, in countries such as Belgium, it would make sense to introduce it at the local level first so that citizens can gradually become accustomed to this instrument. To avoid the risk of minority oppression, it is possible to introduce qualified majorities and to exclude communitarian issues from popular votes.

But I also see opportunities in such societies: direct democracy could make a significant contribution to developing a functioning *demos* – a viable political community of equals. Without a common *demos*, democracy can hardly survive (Stojanović, 2020). In my view, this is where the greatest potential of direct democracy can be found.

Think of democracy in the European Union, where it is commonplace to speak about the 'democratic deficit'. The European Citizens' Initiative (ECI), introduced in the Lisbon treaty, is a first step towards more direct democracy in the EU. But it is still far too modest to have any effect on the emergence of a common *demos*, especially since a successful ECI is never put to a popular vote; it is merely a non-binding recommendation to the EU parliament and the EU Commission (Stojanović and Bonotti, 2020).

In other words, not all forms of direct democracy can have the effects that I have illustrated in this chapter. In particular, the experience of Switzerland shows that one should focus on the bottom-up rather than the top-down instruments of direct democracy. Decisions should not be made only by the political elite: 'ordinary citizens' should also be able to launch popular initiatives and referendums as a corrective to the elites' power. This is where I see a crucial political advantage of direct democracy over the form of democracy dominant today, i.e. purely representative democracy.

Let me conclude this chapter with a note on *availability heuristics* – a cognitive shortcut that can generate biased judgements due to the fact that people tend to evaluate events or proposals by considering the availability of instances of that event that can readily be brought to mind (Tversky and Kahneman, 1974). So, if today somebody tries to advocate direct democracy, the typical critic will say, "Bad idea! Look at what happened with Brexit!".[17] In the context of Belgium, the critic will probably refer to the only national referendum held in the history of the country: on 12 March 1950, in a referendum on the return of King Leopold III (Sinardet, 2009; Van Parijs, 2018, p. 85),[18] the Flemish part of Belgium voted

17 See e.g. Van Parijs (2018, p. 85): "Certes, la démocratie directe n'est pas le *nec plus ultra* de la démocratie. Le vote sur le Brexit en aura sans doute convaincu un bon nombre de ceux qui ne l'étaient pas encore".

18 As Philippe Van Parijs puts it (2018, p. 85), Belgium came out of this experience "traumatized". Sinardet (2009, p. 54) notes that this referendum "is often considered as the first plain and explicit externalisation of the regional-linguistic cleavage in Belgium".

in favour of the king's return by 72% while the Francophone part voted against it by 58%.

It seems evident to me that it is not rational to reject an institution on the basis of only one or two 'bad' examples. Especially when even those examples are ill-chosen. In fact, Sinardet himself notes that the linguistic divide is too superficial an interpretation of what happened in 1950, given that various municipalities or districts in Flanders voted against the king while many Francophone areas were in favour.[19]

Also, one could say that the Brexit referendum has nothing to do with the kind of direct democracy discussed in this chapter. Apart from many problems that accompanied it (especially the fact that it was not clear that a 'no' vote would be irreversible and that the new deal with the EU would not be put to a popular vote; see Offe, 2017), I should emphasise that Brexit was a typical example of a top-down referendum, where a prime minister (or a president) has the power to decide whether or not to hold a referendum. The alternative is a bottom-up version, coming from the citizens themselves (see fn. 4). And even if popular initiatives and referendums are launched by elites (parties, trade unions, associations, etc.), they can hardly bypass the hard grassroots democratic work of collecting signatures and convincing citizens to support their cause.[20] Hence, probably the most difficult task for advocates of direct democracy is to convince their critics to abandon availability heuristics and to evaluate both the merits and the shortcomings of direct democracy in a less passionate and a more objective way.

Bibliography

Budge, I. (1996) *The New Challenge of Direct Democracy.* Cambridge: Polity Press.

Bühlmann, M. (2015) 'Reformbedarf in der direkten Demokratie? Elitistische Einsprüche, partizipatorische Ansprüche und prozedurale Gelassenheit', *Leges*, 3, pp. 571–583.

Caroni, F. and Vatter, A. (2016) 'Vom Ventil zum Wahlkampfinstrument? Eine empirische Analyse zum Funktionswandel der Volksinitiative', *Leges*, 2, pp. 189–210.

Chollet, A. (2011) *Défendre la démocratie directe.* Lausanne: Presses polytechniques et universitaires romandes.

Dardanelli, P. and Stojanović, N. (2011) 'The acid test? Competing theses on the nationality–democracy nexus and the case of Switzerland', *Nations and Nationalism*, 17(2), pp. 357–376. DOI: 10.1111/j.1469-8129.2010.00453.x.

19 "Indeed, the more rural Walloon provinces had also voted in favour of bringing back Leopold III: Namur by 58 % and Luxemburg by 65%. It is true that in the 1950s the urban-rural divide largely coincided with the division in language regions, but on this vote the community divide was secondary to the urban-rural one" (Sinardet, 2009, p. 54).

20 In Switzerland, the only possible bypass is when parliament adopts amendments to the Constitution. In that case, the mandatory referendum is automatically triggered, requiring the double majority of the people and the cantons (see fn. 4). Much less frequent are referendums launched by the executives of at least eight cantons against laws adopted by parliament.

De Cleen, B. and Van Aelst, P. (2016) 'Belgium: The Rise and Fall of Populism Research', in Aalberg, T. et al. (eds.) *Populist Political Communication in Europe.* New York: Routledge, pp. 99–110. DOI: 10.4324/9781315623016-16.

Donovan, T. and Karp, J.A. (2006) 'Popular Support for Direct Democracy', *Party Politics*, 12(5), pp. 671–688. DOI: 10.1177/1354068806066793.

Garessus, E. (2016) 'Les Suisses ont une confiance record à l'égard de la politique', *Le Temps*, 30 November [online]. Available at: https://www.letemps.ch/economie/2016/11/30/suisses-ont-une-confiance-record-legard-politique (Accessed: 2 January 2020).

Ginori, A. (2015) 'Ich höre nur auf das Volk, das keine weiteren Einwanderer mehr will', *Die Welt*, 22 May [online]. Available at: https://www.welt.de/print/die_welt/politik/article141323017/Ich-hoere-nur-auf-das-Volk-das-keine-weiteren-Einwanderer-mehr-will.html (Accessed: 2 January 2020).

Hooghe, M. and Sinardet, D. (eds.) (2009) *Public Opinion in a Multilingual Society. Institutional Design and Federal Loyalty.* Brussels: Rethinking Belgium.

Horowitz, D.L. (2009) 'A Federal Constituency for Belgium: Right Idea, Inadequate Method', in Deschouwer, K. and Van Parijs, P. (eds.) *Electoral Engineering for a Stalled Federation. A Country-wide Electoral District for Belgium's Federal Parliament.* Brussels: Rethinking Belgium, pp. 25–28.

Kley, A. (2015) 'Die Umsetzung von Volksinitiativen aus politisch-historischer Sicht', *Leges*, 3, pp. 497–520.

Korsch, F. (2016) '"Natürliche Verbündete"? Die Pegida-Debatte in der AfD zwischen Ablehnung, Anziehung und Ablehnung', in Häuser, A. (ed.) *Die Alternative für Deutschland. Programmatik, Entwicklung und politische Verortung.* Wiesbaden: Springer, pp. 111–134.

Kriesi, H. (1993) *Citoyenneté et démocratie directe. Compétence, participation et décision des citoyennes et citoyens suisses.* Zurich: Seismo.

Laborderie, V. (2012) 'Changer de système–changer de pays. Réformer le mode de scrutin de Belgique: La nécessité première', in Baele, S. (ed.) *Belgique: Sortir de crise(s).* Louvain-la-Neuve: Presses Universitaires de Louvain, pp. 13–41.

Lacey, J. (2014) 'Must Europe be Swiss? On the Idea of a Voting Space and the Possibility of a Multilingual Demos', *British Journal of Political Science*, 44(1), pp. 61–82. DOI: 10.1017/s0007123412000798.

Lijphart, A. (1977) *Democracy in Plural Societies.* New Haven: Yale University Press.

Linder, W. (2012) *Schweizerische Demokratie. Institutionen – Prozesse – Perspektiven.* 3rd rev. ed. Bern: Haupt.

Mansbridge, J. (2015) 'Should Workers Represent Workers?', *Swiss Political Science Review*, 21(2), pp. 261–270. DOI: 10.1111/spsr.12160.

Müller, J.W. (2016a) *Was ist Populismus?* Berlin: Suhrkamp.

Müller, J.W. (2016b) 'Wie die Populisten ticken', *NZZ Folio*, November issue [online]. Available at: http://folio.nzz.ch/2016/november/wie-die-populisten-ticken (Accessed: 2 January 2020).

Offe, C. (2017) 'Referendum vs. Institutionalized Deliberation: What Democratic Theorists Can Learn from the 2016 Brexit Decision', *Dædalus*, 146 (3), pp. 14–27. DOI: doi.org/10.1162/daed_a_00443.

Papadopoulos, Y. and Magnette, P. (2010) 'On the Politicisation of the European Union: Lessons from Consociational National Polities', *West European Politics*, 33(4), pp. 711–729. DOI: 10.1080/01402381003794571.

Pilet, J.B., Jaumain, S. and De Waele, J.M. (eds.) (2009) *L'absence de partis nationaux: Menace ou opportunité?* Brussels: Editions de l'Université de Bruxelles.

Reilly, B. (2012) 'Institutional Designs for Diverse Democracies: Consociationalism, Centripetalism and Communalism Compared', *European Political Science*, 11(2), pp. 259–270. DOI: 10.1057/eps.2011.36.

Reuchamps, M. (2011) 'Referendum as a Tool for Building European Identity. The case of Belgium, Luxembourg, and the Netherlands', *Cahiers de Science Politique*, 6 [online]. Available at: https://popups.uliege.be:443/1784-6390/index.php?id =91 (Accessed: 6 January 2020).

Rothchild, D. and Roeder, P.G. (2005) 'Dilemmas of State-Building in Divided Societies', in Roeder, P.G. and Rothchild, D. (eds.) *Sustainable Peace*. Ithaca and London: Cornell University Press, pp. 1–25.

Sartori, G. (1987) *The Theory of Democracy Revisited*. Chatham NJ: Chatham House.

Schmidt, M. G. (2010) *Wörterbuch zur Politik*. 3rd edn. Stuttgart: Alfred Kröner Verlag.

Sinardet, D. (2009) 'Direct Democracy as a Tool to Shape a United Public Opinion in a Multilingual Society? Some Reflections Based on the Belgian Case', in Hooghe, M. and Sinardet, D. (eds.) *Public Opinion in a Multilingual Society. Institutional Design and Federal Loyalty*. Brussels: Rethinking Belgium, pp. 47–60.

Stojanović, N. (2009) 'Is Democracy Possible in a Multilingual Country? The Swiss Experience and the Paradox of Direct Democracy' in Hooghe, M. and Sinardet, D. (eds.) *Public Opinion in a Multilingual Society. Institutional Design and Federal Loyalty*. Brussels: Rethinking Belgium, pp. 9–22.

Stojanović, N. (2011) 'Limits of Consociationalism and Possible Alternatives: Centripetal Effects of Direct Democracy in a Multiethnic Society', *Transitions*, 51(1–2), pp. 99–114.

Stojanović, N. (2014) 'When Non-Nationalist Voters Support Ethno-Nationalist Parties: The 1990 Elections in Bosnia and Herzegovina as a Prisoner's Dilemma Game', *Southeast European and Black Sea Studies*, 14(4), pp. 607–625. DOI: 10.1080/14683857.2014.974379.

Stojanović, N. (2020) 'Democracy, Ethnoicracy and Consociational Demoicracy', *International Political Science Review*, 41(1), pp. 30–43. DOI: 10.1177/0192512119881730.

Stojanović, N. and Bonotti, M. (2020) 'Political Parties in Deeply Multilingual Polities: Institutional Conditions and Lessons for the EU', *Journal of Common Market Studies*, 58(3), pp. 599–615. DOI: 10.1111/jcms.12944.

Theile, C. (2017) 'AfD-Vorbild wider Willen'. 21 June [online]. Available at: http://www.tagesanzeiger.ch/ausland/standard/vorbild-wider-willen/story/10139152 (Accessed: 2 January 2020).

Tversky, A. and Kahneman, D. (1974) 'Judgment under Uncertainty: Heuristics and Biases', *Science*, 185(4157), pp. 1124–1131.

Van Crombrugge, R. (2020) 'Are Referendums Necessarily Populist? Countering the Populist Interpretation of Referendums through Institutional Design', *Representation*. Early view. DOI: 10.1080/00344893.2020.1720789.

Van Grieken, T. (2019) [Video interview], 4 January 2019. Available at: https://www.hln.be/nieuws/binnenland/vlaams-belang-wil-totale-immigratiestop-van-minstens-tien-jaar~a7dccf7b/?referer=https%3A%2F%2Fwww.google.com%2F.

Van Parijs, P. (2018) *Belgium. Une utopie pour notre temps.* Brussels: Académie royale de Belgique.
Vatter, A. (2018) *Swiss Federalism: The Transformation of a Federal Model.* Abingdon: Routledge.
Veny, L. and Warnez, B. (2016) 'Techniques for Protecting Minority Languages under Belgian Federalism', *International Journal on Minority and Group Rights*, 23(2), pp. 211–236. DOI: 10.1163/15718115-02302002.

14 Democratic constitution-making under the Belgian Constitution

Utilising its untapped potential

Ronald Van Crombrugge

Introduction

What role – if any – should citizens play in the making or amending of constitutions? This question is the subject of ongoing debate. Although no true consensus has as yet emerged, there seems to be a genuine trend towards more democratic forms of constitution-making. Increasingly it is argued that "a democratic constitution is no longer simply one that establishes democratic governance. It is also a constitution that is made in a democratic process" (Hart, 2003, pp. 3–4). An increased level of public participation is seen by several authors as one of the important common features of modern constitution-making (Ginsburg et al., 2008; Klein and Sajó, 2012; Saunders, 2012).

The reasons why democratic constitution-making is now so actively endorsed are numerous. First of all, democratic constitution-making is seen as instrumental in achieving other goals. It is argued that popular participation in the constitution-making process is essential to ensure that a constitution is effective and that the population endorses the principles it enshrines – in other words, to ensure that it is seen as legitimate by the citizens who are subject to it (Ginsburg et al., 2009a, p. 78; Landemore, 2014; Saunders, 2012). For this reason, democratic constitution-making is also said to assist in a smooth transition from conflict or autocracy to democracy (Ghai et al., 2006; Samuels, 2005). Lastly, it is argued that the process of constitution-making has an effect on the actual content of the constitution itself. A more democratic process of constitution-making would result in a constitution that is itself more democratic, recognising more fundamental rights for its citizens as well as providing more avenues for citizens to influence public policy (Ginsburg et al., 2008, p. 381).

Even though the empirical evidence for these claims is still limited – but nonetheless cautiously positive (Ginsburg et al., 2009a, p. 219) – it can still be argued that the active participation of citizens in the making of a constitution is of intrinsic value to a democratic society. Of course, such a normative argument in favour of democratic constitution-making already presupposes a certain understanding of democracy itself. While more 'participatory' theories of democracy[1] may be

1 While the term 'participatory democracy' is often used to refer to a specific model of democracy, for pragmatic reasons I employ the term here in a broader sense to refer to a larger set of

committed to democratic constitution-making, other theories do not necessarily share this commitment. This being so, it is important to note that this chapter looks at the constitution-making process from the perspective of participatory democracy – understood in its broadest sense – and that this choice is, of course, not normatively neutral.

In sharp contrast with the norms of participatory democracy stands the Belgian approach to constitution-making. Both the practice and the theory of constitution-making in Belgium could be considered citizen-averse. On the practical side of things, we have the process of state reform which has held Belgium in its grip for over 50 years. Through this process, the unitary Belgian state has, over time, been gradually transformed into a federation through a number of 'state reforms'. Yet, all of these reforms – which fundamentally altered the nature of the Belgian Constitution – were the result of political bargains struck between party leaders behind closed doors. From the perspective of theory, several of the chapters in this book have vividly illustrated how Belgian constitutional doctrine has had the effect of minimising the role of citizens in the democratic system. Moreover, practice and theory mutually reinforce one another in this respect. Existing practices of elite-led constitutional change are legitimised by a theory of national sovereignty which presents citizen participation as incompatible with the logic of the Constitution and the beliefs of the framers. At the same time, the impetus to develop this theory was provided precisely by the divided nature of Belgian society and the debacle of the 1950 referendum on the Royal Question more specifically, a prominent example of citizen participation gone wrong. It is, therefore, no surprise that in its jurisprudence on the constitutionality of referendums, the Council of State voiced both of these concerns. Aside from its arguments about the nature of sovereignty and the exercise of state power, the Council also referred to the principle of 'federal loyalty' or 'Bundestreue' which was implicit in the Belgian Constitution (now recognised in article 143) and which would be undermined when a referendum pits the different communities against one another.

Belgium could thus rightly be considered a hard case for participatory constitution-making. Not only is it a deeply divided society, for which some sort of power-sharing or grand compromise between elites is often considered the only realistic option for peaceful coexistence,[2] but any argument in favour of a more democratic process of constitution-making also has to face up against a longstanding constitutional tradition which is hostile to citizen participation. In this chapter, I address these challenges. In the first part of the chapter, I engage the

democratic theories that emphasise the importance of citizen participation in public decision-making, not just through regular voting at elections, but also through discussion and debate. Important examples are participatory democracy (in the strict sense), civic republicanism, deliberative democracy, or discursive democracy. See Banks (2008) for a similar approach of grouping these different theories together for the purpose of discussing democratic constitution-making.

2 For a more complete discussion of consociationalism and its impact on Belgian democracy, see Chapter 13.

theoretical arguments. My argument proceeds in three steps. In the first step, I present article 195 of the Constitution – which contains the amendment procedure – and look at it from the perspective of the original intentions of the framers and their positions on constituent power. I show why the current practice of constitution-making fails to realise the framers' objectives. In the second step, I argue that – somewhat paradoxically perhaps in light of the framers' concerns – a more participatory form of constitution-making could be seen as a modern-day translation of these original objectives, which is moreover better adapted to deal with the sort of lasting conflicts characteristic of deeply divided societies. In the third step, I argue that despite the national sovereignty doctrine and the Council of State's jurisprudence, the existing amendment procedure offers plenty of room for a more active involvement of citizens. After presenting the theoretical argument for a more democratic process of constitution-making, I look at the practical side of things in the second part of this chapter. More specifically, I present two recent cases of participatory constitution-making, namely Iceland and Ireland. These examples not only showcase some of the forms a participatory process can take but also how such practices can be integrated within existing constitutional structures; thus corroborating the theoretical arguments developed in the first part. By way of conclusion, I present a short outline of how the lessons learnt from these examples could be put into practice in the Belgian context.

Democratic constitution-making, a form of realistic idealism

Article 195 of the Belgian Constitution and its objectives

As mentioned before, article 195 of the Belgian Constitution sets out the procedure for amending the constitution. This procedure consists of three distinct phases, namely the adoption of a 'declaration of revision' by the existing legislature, the dissolution of parliament followed by elections, and the actual revision of the Constitution by the newly formed parliament. In the first phase, each branch of the legislature has to adopt (by simple majority) a declaration of revision, containing all the articles deemed opportune for revision. Only those articles that appear identically in each of the three declarations will eventually be able to be revised. The adoption of the three declarations automatically triggers the second phase of the procedure, namely the dissolution of parliament and – consequently – the holding of elections. Once the newly elected parliament is convened, the third and final phase of the procedure can take place: the actual revision of the Constitution. In order to amend the Constitution, a double two-thirds majority is required in each of the parliamentary chambers: two-thirds of the members have to be present, and two-thirds of the votes have to be in favour of the revision (Alen and Muylle, 2011; Blero, 2011; Van Nieuwenhove, 1997).

This procedure was intended to fulfil two different functions. Firstly, to ensure the stability of the Constitution (stabilising function) and secondly, to legitimise constitutional revisions (democratic function). Stability was to be ensured in several ways. First of all, the heightened majority requirement ensures that the Constitution can only be amended if a broad consensus exists. The dissolution of parliament supplements this and adds a temporal element to the required consensus, by requiring that a consensus lasts through two legislatures (Blero, 2011; Popelier, 2012; Van Nieuwenhove and Voermans, 2016). Additionally, the spreading of the procedure over two different legislatures ensures that no random majority – however large it may be – can adapt the Constitution with the sole purpose of maintaining power or entrenching its policies (Rimanque, 2004). The democratic function was to be fulfilled by the holding of elections (Alen and Muylle, 2011, p. 231). This would allow the electorate to make its voice heard on the issue of constitutional reform. The newly elected parliament would then take the opinion of the voters into account.

How do these two functions map onto the framers' positions with regard to constituent power? As shown by Maes and Leijssenaar, the position of the majority of the framers could be summarised as one of locking away the constituent power of the people (see Chapter 7). They sought not only to establish their own legitimacy as a 'National Congress' but also to prevent any future exercise of constituent power outside the structures created by the newly established Constitution. This view fits perfectly with the concern for stability. While the amendment procedure introduced an element of flexibility into the Constitution, enabling it to adapt to societal changes, this was intended to be an exceptional occurrence. As Jean-Baptiste Nothomb put it, "a constitution whose fundamentals are exposed to daily amendments cannot be considered a constitution" (Huyttens, 1844, p. 424). At first sight, the democratic function is more difficult to square with the framers' views on constituent power, since the amendment procedure was conceptualised as a purely constituted power. The idea that the constituent power of the people could be channelled through the procedures of the Constitution (in the form of constituted constituent power) was foreign to the majority position in the National Congress. How then can article 195 still be said to perform a democratic function?

The important point to note here is that not every form of influence from the public on the decision-making process amounts to an exercise of (constituted) constituent power. This can be gleaned from the fact that the National Congress itself never sought to shield its debates from public opinion, even while reserving for itself the exclusive right to exercise the constituent power. The discussions within the National Congress were published in the most important newspapers and provoked a lively public debate; while members of the Congress themselves participated in this public debate by publishing proposals in newspapers before discussing them within the Congress. In other words, the idea that constitutional amendments should be informed by public opinion is not at odds with the view that the people's constituent power was exhausted by the formation of the National Congress. Nor does the Congress' position on constituent power preclude the assignment of a specific power to the people, such as the election of a new constitutional assembly as foreseen in article 195. It merely entails that when the people perform such a role, it acts as a constituted power in the sense of article 33, second paragraph. As a constituted power, the people can only exercise the powers granted to it by the Constitution, and in doing so does not take priority over other state powers – which is illustrated, among other things, by the complete absence of any sort of imperative mandate from the electorate towards the newly elected assembly. With these two caveats in mind – influence is not power, and power is constituted power – we can understand how the stabilising and democratic functions of article 195 fit within the framers' overarching vision on constituent power.

Over the last few decades, however, constitutional practice has increasingly diverged from the concerns and intentions of the framers. Since around 1965, Belgium has been engaged in a continuous process of constitutional reform where each reform carries within it the seeds for the next (Delgrange and Dumont, 1999). As a result, a consistent practice has developed of adopting a declaration of revision at the end of each legislature. What was originally supposed to be an exceptional event, has now become the normal means of dissolving parliament. Because of this, it has become difficult for the procedure of article 195 to fulfil its stabilising and democratic functions. While the need for consensus among two successive legislatures still provides protection against abuse of the Constitution, and thus furthers the goal of stability, it could be argued that it is not the right instrument to achieve this result because it makes it impossible for elections to effectively fulfil their democratic function. While the newly elected parliament is supposed to take the election results into account, the possibilities to actually do so are limited, because it can only adapt those provisions that are included in the declaration of revision, even when there is a very broad societal consensus that it is opportune to adapt other articles as well. At the same time, it has also become clear that the holding of elections is simply not an effective means to organise the participation of citizens. While elections should in principle offer a powerful democratic mandate to the drafters of the Constitution, this is often not the case in Belgium. Because the declaration of revision is generally adopted at the end of every single legislature, elections are most often dominated by questions of normal policy while the issue of constitutional reform gets pushed to the background (Blero, 2011). Moreover, because negotiations for constitutional reform are typically led by a select group of high-ranking party officials and take place behind closed doors, public scrutiny of the constitution-making process through the informal public sphere is made impossible, while the involvement of parliament is reduced to rubber-stamping the resulting compromise *ex-post facto*.

Democratic constitutional change in divided societies

It has already been noted that Belgium is engaged in a continuous process of constitutional reform. How should one look at the objective of ensuring the stability of the constitution in such a context, when practice has shown that the dissolution requirement – which was precisely intended to safeguard stability – can frustrate changes that enjoy a broad consensus and even cause a constitutional crisis? An answer can possibly be found in what authors have termed 'democratic constitutionalism' (Hutchinson and Colón-Ríos, 2011; Colon-Rios, 2012; Zurn, 2016). While this theory still rests on a clear distinction between the constitution and ordinary legislation through some form of (moderate) entrenchment of the former, the focus is placed less on the longevity of the constitution and more on the possibilities that exist for citizens to participate in the process of constitution-making, so that they can see themselves not only as subject to, but also as 'co-author' of the constitutional text. Hutchinson and Colón-Rios, for example, have argued that:

> [F]rom a democratist standpoint, the merit of a constitution is to be found not so much in its longevity and its force towards stability, but in its capacity for both democratic participation and constitutional transformation. [...] [T]here must be adequate mechanisms and processes in place to maximize these opportunities.
>
> (Hutchinson and Colón-Ríos, 2011, p. 57)

Unlike traditional constitutionalism, the stability of the constitutional order is no longer defined by the endurance of the constitution.[3] According to democratic constitutionalists, a stable constitution is not so much a constitution that is able to prevent change, but a constitution that has the necessary mechanisms in place that enable it to retain its legitimacy and the commitment for its respect throughout these changes. This is especially important in divided societies or multinational states such as Belgium. Because these states cannot be based on a 'thick' notion of national identity, it is necessary "that citizens share a common civic allegiance to the rules and procedures by which democratic decisions are arrived at, rather than to some thicker, substantive account of civic identity" (O'Flynn, 2006, p. 75).[4] Allowing for these rules and procedures to be established through an inclusive and open constitution-making process – which involves the broader public in some way – could be seen as an important instrument to ensure that the constitution enjoys the necessary degree of legitimacy to make such constitutional patriotism possible (Chambers, 2004). Another proponent of democratic constitution-making in divided societies is James Tully. According to him, opportunities for civic participation and deliberation during moments of constitutional revision (or formation) are an important ground for stability in multinational societies. According to Tully, constitutional stability in a multinational society should not be sought in some grand pact between political leaders that is meant

3 See Ginsburg et al. (2009b), who, despite their general argument in favour of endurance, also stress the need for flexibility to amend or replace the constitution when it no longer fits the society for which it was drafted.

4 Habermas calls this 'constitutional patriotism' (Habermas et al., 1994). Also see Müller (2007).

to last throughout the centuries, but rather in the mutual freedom of citizens to talk to each other about the basic norms of their coexistence.[5]

The untapped democratic potential of the existing amendment procedure

We do not have to try and pretend that the framers would consider a continuous and open process of constitution-making a valid institutionalisation of the value of stability. As argued before, the National Congress intended the amendment of the Constitution to be a rare occurrence. While it could be argued that the principles of democratic constitutionalism are better adjusted to deal with the challenges of a deeply divided society and can better accommodate the process of continuous constitutional reform that Belgium is currently engaged in, it should be pretty obvious that they stand in tension with the views of the National Congress. This raises the difficult question of whether there is any room for a democratic constitutionalist approach under the current amendment procedure, especially given the Council of State's strict interpretation of article 195. The Council of State has ruled that article 195 of the Constitution regulates the procedure for amending the Constitution in an exhaustive manner and, moreover, that this procedure has a strictly representative character. At first sight, both these arguments seem to preclude greater participation of the citizen, but this is not necessarily the case. Even within the framework outlined by the Council of State, there remains a large and hitherto untapped democratic potential.

According to the Council, article 195 determines in an exhaustive way how the Constitution should be amended. Consequently, the role of citizens within this procedure is also strictly limited: "Citizens participate in the procedure of constitutional revision only in their capacity as voters". However, the scope of this exhaustiveness should not be overestimated. In support of its interpretation of article 195, the Council of State refers to article 33, second paragraph, of the Constitution, according to which all powers "shall be exercised in the manner laid down in the Constitution". In my view, this means that the exhaustive nature of article 195 only applies to the actual exercise of powers, but not to the process which precedes it. Indeed, as argued previously, influencing the exercise of powers cannot be equated with the use of state power itself.[6] At this preparatory stage, where constitutional amendments are debated and discussed, there is room to involve political actors who are not explicitly mentioned in article 195, such as (in current practice) political parties, and – if one so wishes – the broader public. In that case, the formal role of citizens is still limited to electing the parliamentary

5 Tully bases these claims on the experience in Canada. According to him, it is precisely when the process of constitutional dialogue is closed off, that the feeling of citizens in Québec of belonging to Canada decreases and their exclusive identification with Québec increases (Tully, 2001).

6 In a similar vein, see Velaers (2019, p. 18).

assembly, but this does not prevent citizens from taking on an informal role and helping to shape the proposal to amend the Constitution, a proposal on which parliament must then – autonomously – express an opinion.

That leaves us with the strictly representative nature of the procedure enshrined in article 195, and of the Belgian democratic system in general. Does this representative nature oppose – almost by definition – any sort of citizen participation? Not necessarily. While this is true for a purely trustee-based understanding of representation, it is not the case for a communicative or relationship-based understanding of representation as defended, for example, by Iris Marion Young (Young, 2000, p. 132). Since, under this view, the legitimacy of representation is built over time through dialogue between representatives and the broader public, the basis on which representatives can claim to act on behalf and in the name of the people needs to be continuously reconstructed as well (Saward, 2010). This requires that representatives engage in a publicly visible process of 'listening'. As John Parkinson and André Bächtiger put it, representatives should ask citizens: "Here is what we think you are saying – did we get it right?" (Bachtiger and Parkinson, 2019, p. 101). From this perspective, the demand for more citizen participation when amending the Constitution is not about diminishing the legitimate role of elected representatives, but rather about providing a strong institutional basis for the process of listening that good representation requires. Nor does it imply that representatives should automatically defer to 'the Will of the People', since there is no single will which can be represented in its entirety. While representatives should listen to what citizens have to say, and in this sense show respect to them, good representation might just as well require that the representatives in the end defend their own judgment – and the collective judgment of the parliamentary body they are a part of – and try to persuade the public of the rightness of this judgment (Gutmann and Thompson, 1997; Urbinati, 2000; Young, 2000).

Neither the exhaustive nor the representative nature of article 195 provides a convincing reason to exclude all forms of citizen participation. It does, however, put a certain limit on the forms such citizen participation can take. It is clear that the majority in the National Congress attributed the power to amend the Constitution to parliament, and that they resisted any sort of binding or imperative mandate originating in the electorate. This means that citizen participation cannot go so far as to completely erode the decision-making power of the elected representatives – which, according to the Council of State, would be the case when a legally non-binding referendum is nonetheless treated as *de facto* binding in practice. Even so, this upper limit should be interpreted strictly and narrowly, and cannot extend so far down as to prevent citizens from having a genuine impact on the constitution-making process. After all, it was precisely the intention of article 195 to give citizens a say on constitutional amendments by means of elections. If the facts show that elections no longer fulfil this function, there must be room to restore the citizen's say over the Constitution through other forms of participation and consultation.

Again, it is important to stress that the framers of the Belgian Constitution would probably not have agreed with these recommendations. As the debate between the republican and the more conservative liberal and Catholic factions illustrates, the majority was certainly not concerned with maximising the potential for constitutional transformation and democratic participation, rather on the contrary. Yet, at the same time, the approach to citizen participation defended in this section – one that is grounded first and foremost in a communicative understanding of representation – is compatible with the framework established by the National Congress on a more fundamental level. Most importantly, the approach defended here does not fall prey to the anti-representative rationale which sometimes characterises arguments for democratic constitution-making. It does not present the people as a collective entity which – as the ultimate holder of constituent power – is superior to its elected representatives. Rather, it emphasises *people* – in the plural – who, in all their diversity, enter into a dialogue with each other and their representatives. As such, it is less radical than arguments for democratic constitutionalism which are precisely intended to keep the constituent power of the people alive (Hutchinson and Colón-Ríos, 2011). This is not a concession to the elitism of the framers, however, but rather a recognition of their valid concern that grand claims about being able to represent the 'Will of the People' – even when backed by a majority of the population in a referendum – can become just as much a source of despotism as a claim to the divine right to rule.[7] By placing the open-ended and contestable nature of the representative process front and centre, the approach defended here seeks to avoid this risk.

Learning from practice

Experimentation with democratic constitutional change

That these are more than just theoretical arguments is shown by international practice, where experimentation with democratic forms of constitution-making is becoming more and more prevalent. Two examples in particular stand out: the constitutional process in Iceland set up after the 2008 financial crisis and the process which took place in Ireland in 2012 (and resulted in the legalisation – by referendum – of same-sex marriage in 2015). Both were notable for combining a variety of forms of citizen participation – deliberative assemblies, opinion polls, public hearings, workshops, petitions, consultative referendums – and for doing so within the framework set out by the amendment procedure provided for in the Icelandic and Irish constitutions, respectively.

The Icelandic constitutional process of 2012 was a direct result of the 2008 global financial crisis and subsequent protests, also known as the 'Pots and Pans Revolution', which created strong public demand for a new constitution

7 On the dangers of understanding referendums in terms of the 'Will of the People', see Van Crombrugge (2020).

(Blokker, 2012). The widespread mistrust of the political class (which was held responsible for the country's financial crisis) brought with it the additional demand that the new constitution should be drafted through a participatory process (Landemore, 2014, p. 7; Valtysson, 2014, p. 53). The drafting of the new constitution started with the organisation of a National Assembly consisting of 950 citizens selected by lot who gathered for one day to discuss in small groups which values should be reflected in the new constitution. The recommendations of the National Assembly, together with the advice of various experts, were incorporated into a report that was to serve as a basis for the negotiations on the new constitution.

These negotiations were conducted within the 'Constitutional Assembly', later renamed the 'Constitutional Council', which consisted of 25 directly elected citizens who – as one of the eligibility requirements – could not hold a political office. Because professional politicians were excluded from the Council, the elections could not be based on existing political parties. Instead, the electorate could vote for 522 individuals who had put themselves forward as candidates, 25 of whom were eventually elected through a proportional electoral system. However, the turnout for these elections was very low (30%), precisely because the political parties showed very little interest and because they were insufficiently covered by the media (Landemore, 2014, p. 21). The low turnout undermined the legitimacy of the Council from the start and provided an argument for politicians – who were often very sceptical about the whole citizen-led process – to reject the eventual draft constitution.[8]

This tumultuous start forced the Constitutional Council to strengthen its legitimacy by acting in an open and transparent manner. Among other things, it invited the public to get involved and make suggestions via the Council's website and through social media. These suggestions could then be commented on by other citizens. However, the possibilities for genuine public deliberation through social media platforms remained limited at best, and numerous suggestions were dismissed out of hand without any real justification. This indicates a weakness in the design of the whole process, namely that the feedback given was irregular, informal, and limited (Suteu, 2015, p. 262; Valtysson, 2014, p. 53). More successful was the fact that the Constitutional Council also regularly published the current version of its draft text. Since citizens could respond to a concrete proposal – rather than merely submit a general idea – this second round of public consultation elicited a greater response from the public, and enabled more in-depth discussions between the public and members of the Council (Valtysson, 2014, p. 65). According to Hélène Landemore, this incremental way of working created a kind of 'feedback loop' (Landemore, 2014, p. 9).

8 The legitimacy of the assembly was further undermined when the Icelandic Supreme Court annulled the election results due to irregularities during the election campaign. After much discussion, the Icelandic parliament finally decided to appoint the 25 elected citizens as members of the Constitutional Council to replace the Constitutional Assembly.

Despite the overall transparency and openness that marked the whole process, it is important to note that the actual drafting of the constitution still took place within the Council. Moreover, the Council's deliberations were not always open to the public in real time. However, this was not necessarily a weakness of the process, since a degree of privacy can be beneficial to the internal workings of a deliberating assembly.[9] Moreover, since the discussions within the Council were eventually published and could therefore become the subject of public discussion, this limited and temporary secrecy – or, as Landemore calls it, 'lag-time transparency' – had a positive effect on the quality of internal deliberations within the Council without unduly undermining the participatory qualities of the whole process (Landemore, 2014, p. 20).

In the end, the Constitutional Council reached agreement on a final text, which was adopted by consensus. Although consensus was not a formal requirement, the members of the Council opted to present a 'united vision of the Icelandic people' to parliament. After all, it was parliament which ultimately had to formally adopt the constitution. The Council's proposal was submitted to parliament, together with the recommendation to submit the proposal to the people by way of referendum. That referendum took place on 20 October 2012. The draft constitution was approved by a large majority of two-thirds of the votes, despite the fact that political parties (again) failed to inform their voters about the proposal. After the referendum, the draft text returned to parliament for a first vote, since the amendment procedure in article 79 of the Icelandic Constitution – somewhat similar to the Belgian amendment procedure – provides for the dissolution of parliament, followed by elections and a second vote. However, parliament was divided, and after the elections the whole project fell into the background. The reasons given for the final failure of the draft differ, but a generally accepted reason is that the whole citizen-led process had alienated the realm of professional politics (Suteu, 2015, p. 273; Thor Bergsson and Blokker, 2013, p. 11; Tushnet, 2015, p. 13).

Compared to the constitutional process in Iceland, the objectives in Ireland were more modest. Instead of drafting an entirely new constitution, the Irish process focused on a limited number of specific amendments to the existing Constitution. The extent to which the public was involved in this process was also less far-reaching than was the case in Iceland. The process was launched by the Irish parliament in July 2012 with the creation of a Constitutional Convention which was to make recommendations on these matters.[10] The agenda of the convention was set in the first place by parliament, although the convention was free to add additional issues if it deemed this opportune. The Constitutional Convention consisted of 100 members. In addition to the chairman, 33 seats were taken by

9 On the role of privacy in deliberation, see Elster (1995, p. 364) and Gutmann and Thompson (1997).

10 Resolution of the Houses of the Oíreachtas of July 2012, https://www.constitution.ie/Documents/Terms_of_Reference.pdf.

elected representatives. The democratic innovation, however, came from the fact that two-thirds of the seats were reserved for ordinary citizens selected by lot.

This mixed composition had a number of important advantages compared to a citizens' assembly which relies entirely on sortition. First of all, the presence of a number of elected members of parliament ensured that the main ideological currents were represented in the debate. Secondly, in this way, the Constitutional Convention was embedded within the broader system of representative democracy, which increased the legitimacy of the decision-making process as a whole. Indeed, the support of elected members of parliament and political parties proved indispensable when the recommendations made by the Constitutional Convention had to be transposed into law. Like the Constitutional Council in Iceland, the Constitutional Convention did not have any genuine decision-making powers. It could merely adopt recommendations which were then handed over to parliament. Parliament, for its part, was obliged to respond to these recommendations and, if it considered that an amendment of the Constitution was required (be it in the form of the original proposal made by the convention, or a proposal as amended by parliament), to submit the question to the Irish people in a referendum, as required by article 46 of the Irish Constitution.

The support of elected representatives was, therefore, crucial throughout the process. In the first instance, this support was direct, since parliament still had to confirm the convention's recommendations. Later, the support was indirect, since elected representatives and political parties naturally were important political actors during the referendum campaign. At the same time, however, care was taken to make sure that professional politicians would not dominate the entire process (Farrell, 2014; Suiter et al., 2016). Most obviously, since elected politicians made up only one-third of the members of the convention, the randomly selected citizens held a *de facto* veto. In addition, the learning process which preceded the actual deliberations, the egalitarian way of working within the convention, and the moderating effect of the chairperson also ensured that the selected citizens could participate in the discussions on an equal footing with politicians.

The way in which citizens participated in amending the Irish Constitution was thus twofold. On the one hand, a select group of citizens – as a statistically representative sample of the wider population – took on a representative role themselves as members of the Constitutional Convention, thereby making a substantial contribution – on an equal footing with the elected representatives – to the formulation of the various proposed amendments (Urbinati and Warren, 2008). On the other hand, all citizens entitled to vote were subsequently given the choice of whether or not to ratify these proposals by referendum. In addition, as in Iceland, citizens could also submit their own proposals to the Constitutional Convention.[11] Moreover, a series of regional public hearings were organised in which the public was invited to express its views on the Constitution. Organised civil society was also given the opportunity to present its views directly to the

11 https://www.constitution.ie/Submissions.aspx.

convention in a series of hearings (together with other experts) (Suteu, 2015, p. 267).

However, the Constitutional Convention did not achieve the same level of transparency as the Constitutional Council in Iceland. The Constitutional Council succeeded in triggering a real feedback loop by regularly publishing draft texts and incorporating comments in subsequent versions, so that consultation and deliberation followed each other repeatedly. In Ireland, however, there was only one consultation round to speak of. As a result, members of the public were unable to comment on how the Constitutional Convention had dealt with certain comments or proposals, apart from making a final judgment at the time of the referendum. This was – at least in part – the result of the limited agenda of the Constitutional Convention. Since the convention could only pronounce itself on a limited number of constitutional amendments, its proceedings were also structured around these themes, with each theme being discussed over one or more weekends. This made it impossible to reconsider earlier recommendations in response to reactions from the public.

In the end, the experiment with the Constitutional Convention turned out to be a mixed success. The Constitutional Convention succeeded in making specific proposals for constitutional amendments on all seven subjects. Commentators were also generally impressed by the quality of the debates within the convention.[12] The Irish experience has thus shown that it is feasible for ordinary citizens who have been selected by lot – and therefore, unlike in Iceland, have not put themselves forward as candidates – to discuss the most fundamental constitutional questions and formulate recommendations on these matters. Less positive is the fact that both parliament and government largely failed to formulate a proper response to these recommendations. Despite the government's earlier promise that it would respond to the convention's proposals within four months of receiving the reports, this was the case for only four of the nine reports. The last four reports were not debated in parliament until 14 January 2016, almost two years after having been submitted to it by the convention. Moreover, only 2 of the 18 proposals requiring a constitutional amendment to become law were effectively submitted to the people by way of referendum. Of these two, only the referendum on same-sex marriage was successful, with a majority of 62% in favour of legalisation (Elkink et al., 2017). This example once again shows that citizen participation fails to attain its goals if it is not or insufficiently linked to the broader representative democratic system. Despite the institutional linkage between the Constitutional Convention and parliament – especially in the form of the 33 elected members of parliament who sat in the convention – the

12 See for example: Wall, M. (2013) 'Column: Change We Can Believe In? Ireland's Constitutional Convention Has Delivered', *Journal*, 23 July. Available at: https://www.thejournal.ie/readme/column-change-we-can-believe-in-ireland%E2%80%99s-constitutional-convention-has-delivered-1003278-Jul2013/.

government and parliament ultimately remained largely indifferent to the proposals made by the convention (Carolan, 2015).

Since then, the Constitutional Convention has had a successor in the form of the citizens' Assembly, which – among other things – deliberated on the ban on abortion. Unlike the Constitutional Convention, the citizens' assembly was made up of 100 randomly selected citizens, without the direct participation of politicians. As with the convention, the assembly's recommendations were submitted to the Irish parliament where they were further discussed. The work of the assembly took place between October 2016 and April 2018. The most notable outcome of this process was the successful referendum of 25 May 2018, where 66.4% of the population voted in favour of revoking the so-called Eighth Amendment, the provision in the Irish Constitution which recognised the equal right to life of the pregnant woman and the unborn child.

Some critical remarks

There are many lessons to be learnt from these experiments with democratic constitutionalism. Perhaps the most important concerns the role of formal representatives in the whole process. Although the radical participatory nature of the constitutional process was widely applauded in Iceland, it can at the same time be seen as one of the reasons for its eventual failure. Indeed, the draft constitution failed to gather the necessary support in parliament to be effectively ratified. Disagreement between the various parties only surfaced after the Constitutional Council had already submitted its draft to parliament. At that time, however, it was too late to renegotiate the text. Citizen participation must, therefore, be combined with negotiations between elites. This is not merely a practical response to political reality; it is also desirable from a normative point of view. As mentioned previously, political representation is best approached as a communicative relationship between representatives and citizens. However, this communication should be a two-way street. The role of representatives should, therefore, not be reduced to passively ratifying whatever is suggested to them through a consultative process.

This vision of representation was expressed more clearly in the design of the Irish Constitutional Convention. As a mixed body, the convention allowed both professional politicians and ordinary citizens to engage in debate on an equal footing. There was also room for discussion after the convention had finalised its recommendation, particularly within the Irish parliament itself. After all, the convention's proposals were not automatically submitted to the referendum. Doing so remained the prerogative of the elected representatives. Although defensible from a normative perspective, in practice this turned out to be problematic. As in Iceland, the political interest in the participatory process quickly declined after the Constitutional Convention had begun its work. While commentators were impressed by the professionalism with which the citizens in the convention had carried out their task and the expertise they had displayed in the process, the same degree of seriousness was absent in the elected parliament. The government's response to the recommendations was often no more than a brief statement, and there was rarely any real debate in parliament either. There is therefore no chance of a participatory process succeeding if there is no political will to actually address the recommendations afterwards. If such political will is lacking, participation becomes nothing more than 'window dressing', and the cynicism of the population towards the political system will only increase (Carolan, 2015).

Respect for existing constitutional structures

At the same time, these critical observations show that these experiments with democratic constitutionalism did not irreparably damage the decision-making power of formal representatives (as suggested by the Council of State). In Ireland, it was up to parliament to autonomously decide which proposals would ultimately be submitted to the people via referendum. Although the final decision in this case was made by the people themselves, this was in accordance with article 46 of the Irish Constitution. The example of Iceland is even more revealing. From the outset, it was clear that the final decision would be taken in accordance with the amendment procedure laid down in the current Icelandic Constitution, which – like the Belgian Constitution – does not attribute any role to the citizen aside from electing a new parliamentary assembly (unlike the Belgian amendment procedure, the role of this second assembly is limited to deciding whether or not to ratify – by a simple majority – the text adopted by the previous assembly). This did not prevent the preparatory work for this amendment from being outsourced by parliament to a newly created institution, namely the Constitutional Council. It was also the Icelandic parliament which decided to submit the draft constitution to the citizens in an advisory referendum – albeit at the request of the Constitutional Council. Ultimately, it was also this parliament which decided to ignore the outcome of this referendum and not to ratify the new constitution.

The problem with this decision was not that it went against 'the Will of the People'. As the elected representatives of the people, the Icelandic parliament could legitimately conclude that the draft constitution as elaborated by the Constitutional Council did not constitute a good basis for the new Icelandic Constitution. Indeed, according to a communicative understanding of representation, representatives have the right – and even the duty – to go against the will of those who elected them when they consider this necessary, provided of course that in doing so they continue to treat citizens as their equal, and thus ensure that their decision is adequately motivated and justified to the citizens who are subject to it. It is particularly in this respect that the Icelandic parliament (and to a lesser extent the Irish parliament) was at fault.

Applying these lessons to Belgium

How can all this be translated to the Belgian context? As discussed previously, the exhaustive and representative nature of the procedure laid down in article 195 does not prevent citizens from being extensively involved in the revision of the Constitution. The most logical way to do this would be to set up a consultative process before the adoption of the 'declaration of revision'. At this first stage, the consultative process could serve an agenda-setting role, highlighting the various constitutional issues which are of greatest concern to the public, while at the same time exploring a number of possible forms amendments could take. The outcome of this process can then be relied on to identify the articles which have to be included in the declaration in order to successfully carry out the constitutional revision. After the election of the new assembly, it is possible to – partly – abandon the current practice of secret negotiations. It would be advisable to adopt a more transparent working method by regularly publishing draft texts and inviting the public to comment on them. The Icelandic example, in particular, with its successful 'feedback loop', is a useful inspiration in this regard. While a certain degree of secrecy or privacy will likely remain important to provide the necessary space for difficult negotiations, it is possible to open the process up at regular intervals to ensure that negotiators remain in touch with the outside public. A more ambitious proposal would involve citizens directly in the drafting of the amendments. On this point, however, the Icelandic example constitutes a powerful warning. It shows the dangers of an exclusive reliance on citizen participation to the detriment of elected representatives: professional politics should not be alienated from the constitutional process. The use of a mixed body, such as the Constitutional Convention in Ireland, which allows ordinary citizens and elected representatives to engage in dialogue is therefore recommendable. Yet, even in this case, the final decision will continue to lie with the elected representatives. This short outline shows how – without the need for any prior amendment of the amendment procedure itself – the process of constitutional change can be democratised and the say of the citizen over the Constitution restored.

Bibliography

Alen, A., Muylle, K. (2011) *Handboek van het Belgisch staatsrecht*. Mechelen: Kluwer.

Bachtiger, A., Parkinson, J. (2019) *Mapping and Measuring Deliberation: Towards a new Deliberative Quality*, New product ed. New York: Oxford University Press.

Banks, A.M. (2008) 'Expanding Participation in Constitution Making: Challenges and Opportunities', *William & Mary Law Review*, 49(4), pp. 1043–1069.

Blero, B. (2011) 'L'article 195 de la constitution, une pierre angulaire à retailler?', in De Becker, A. and Vandenbossche, E. (eds.) *Scharnier- of Sleutelelementen in Het Grondwettelijk Recht*. Bruges: die Keure, pp. 1–58.

Blokker, P. (2012) *Grassroots Constitutional Politics in Iceland*. SSRN Working Paper. Available at: http://ssrn.com/abstract=1990463.

Carolan, E. (2015) 'Ireland's Constitutional Convention: Behind the Hype of Citizen-Led Constitutional Change', *International Journal of Constitutional Law*, 13(3), pp. 733–748. DOI: 10.1093/icon/mov044.

Chambers, S. (2004) 'Democracy, Popular Sovereignty, and Constitutional Legitimacy', *Constellations*, 11(2), pp. 153–173. DOI: 10.1111/j.1351-0487.2004.0370.x.

Colon-Rios, J.I. (2012) *Weak Constitutionalism: Democratic Legitimacy and the Question of Constituent Power*. New York: Routledge. DOI: 10.4324/9780203120132.

Delgrange, X., Dumont, H. (1999) 'Le rythme des révisions constitutionnelles et l'hypothèse de l'accélération du temps juridique', *Administration Publique*, 3, pp. 210–235.

Elkink, J.A., Farrell, D.M., Reidy, T., Suiter, J. (2017) 'Understanding the 2015 Marriage Referendum in Ireland: Context, Campaign, and Conservative Ireland', *Irish Political Studies*, 32(3), pp. 361–381. DOI: 10.1080/07907184.2016.1197209.

Elster, J. (1995) 'Forces and Mechanisms in the Constitution-Making Process', *Duke Law Journal*, 45(2), pp. 364–396.

Farrell, D.M. (2014) 'The 2013 Irish Constitutional Convention: A Bold Step or a Damp Squib?', in Ferrari, G.F., O'Dowd, J. (eds.), *75 Years of the Constitution of Ireland: An Irish Italian Dialogue*. Dublin: Clarus Press.

Ghai, Y., Galli, G., International Institute for Democracy and Electoral Assistance (2006) *Constitution Building Processes and Democratization*. Stockholm: International Institute for Democracy and Electoral Assistance.

Ginsburg, T., Blount, J., Elkins, Z. (2008) 'The Citizen as Founder: Public Participation in Constitutional Approval', *Temple Law Review*, 81(2), pp. 361–382.

Ginsburg, T., Elkins, Z., Blount, J. (2009a) 'Does the Process of Constitution-Making Matter?', *Annual Review of Law and Social Science*, 5(1), pp. 201–223. DOI: 10.1146/annurev.lawsocsci.4.110707.172247.

Ginsburg, T, Elkins, Z., Melton, J. (2009b) *The Endurance of National Constitutions*. Cambridge: Cambridge University Press. DOI: 10.1017/CBO9780511817595.

Gutmann, A., Thompson, D. (1997) *Democracy and Disagreement*. Cambridge, MA: Harvard University Press.

Habermas, J., Nicholsen, S.W., Wolin, R. (1994) *The New Conservatism: Cultural Criticism and the Historians' Debate*. 4. print. ed. Studies in Contemporary German Social Thought. Cambridge, MA: MIT Press.

Hart, V. (2003) *Democratic Constitution Making*. USIP Special Report 107.

Hutchinson, A.C., Colón-Ríos, J. (2011) 'Democracy and Constitutional Change', *Theoria: A Journal of Social and Political Theory*, 58(127), pp. 43–62.

Huyttens, E. (1844) *Discussions du Congrès National de Belgique 1830–1831. Tome premier*. Brussels: Société Typographique Belge.

Klein, C., Sajó, A. (2012) 'Constitution-Making: Process and Substance', in Rosenfeld, M., Sajó, A. (eds.) *The Oxford Handbook of Comparative Constitutional Law*. Oxford: Oxford University Press. DOI: 10.1093/oxfordhb/9780199578610.001.0001.

Landemore, H. (2014) 'Inclusive Constitution-Making: the Icelandic Experiment', *Journal of Political Philosophy*, 23(2), pp. 1–26. DOI: 10.1111/jopp.12032.

Müller, J.-W. (2007) *Constitutional patriotism*. Princeton: Princeton University Press.

O'Flynn, I. (2006) *Deliberative Democracy and Divided Societies*. Edinburgh: Edinburgh University Press.

Popelier, P. (2012) 'De truc met artikel 195: een lapje voor het bloeden met de zegen van Venetië', *Chroniques de Droit Public – Publiekrechtelijke Kronieken.*, 2012(3), pp. 421–443.

Rimanque, K. (2004) *De Grondwet toegelicht, gewikt en gewogen*. Antwerp: Intersentia.

Samuels, K. (2005) 'Post-Conflict Peace-Building and Constitution-Making', *Chicago Journal of International Law*, 6(2), pp. 663–682.

Saunders, C. (2012) 'Constitution Making in the 21st century', *International Review of Law*, 4, pp. 1–10. DOI: 10.5339/irl.2012.4.
Saward, M. (2010) *The Representative Claim*. Oxford: Oxford University Press. DOI: 10.1093/acprof:oso/9780199579389.001.0001.
Suiter, J., Farrell, D.M., Harris, C. (2016) 'The Irish Constitutional Convention: A Case of "high legitimacy"?', in *Constitutional Deliberative Democracy in Europe*. Colchester: ECPCR Press.
Suteu, S. (2015) 'Constitutional Conventions in the Digital Era: Lessons from Iceland and Ireland', *Boston College International and Comparative Law Review*, 38(2), p. 251.
Thor Bergsson, B., Blokker, P. (2013) *The Constitutional Experiment in Iceland*. SSRN Working Paper, https://papers.ssrn.com/sol3/papers.cfm?abstract_id=2320748.
Tully, J. (2001) 'Introduction', in Gagnon, A., Tully, J. (eds.) *Multinational Democracies*. Cambridge: Cambridge University Press. DOI: 10.1017/CBO9780511521577.
Tushnet, M. (2015) *New Institutional Mechanisms for Making Constitutional Law*. SSRN Working Paper, https://papers.ssrn.com/sol3/papers.cfm?abstract_id=2589178 .
Urbinati, N. (2000) 'Representation as Advocacy: A Study of Democratic Deliberation', *Political Theory*, 28(6), pp. 758–786.
Urbinati, N., Warren, M.E. (2008) 'The Concept of Representation in Contemporary Democratic Theory', *Annual Review Political Science*, 11(1), pp. 387–412. DOI: 10.1146/annurev.polisci.11.053006.190533.
Valtysson, B. (2014) 'Democracy in Disguise: The Use of Social Media in Reviewing the Icelandic Constitution', *Media, Culture, and Society*, 36(1), pp. 52–68. DOI: 10.1177/0163443713507814.
Van Crombrugge, R. (2020) 'Are Referendums Necessarily Populist? Countering the Populist Interpretation of Referendums Through Institutional Design', *Representation*, pp. 1–22. DOI: 10.1080/00344893.2020.1720789.
Van Nieuwenhove, J. (1997) 'De herziening en de coördinatie van de Grondwet', in Veny, L., Van Der Hulst, M. (eds.) *Parlementair Recht. Commentaar En Teksten*. Ghent: Mys & Breesch, p. 120.
Van Nieuwenhove, J., Voermans, W. (2016) 'De grondwetsherzieningsprocedure in 1815 en de latere ontwikkelingen in België en in Nederland: Op het spanningsveld tussen rigiditeit en soepelheid', in Alen, A., Heringa, A.W., Heirbout, D., Rotteveel Mansveld, C.J. (eds.) *De Grondwet van het verenigd koninkrijk Dèr Nederlanden van 1815: Staatkundige en historische beschouwingen uit België en Nederland*. The Hague: Boom Juridische uitgevers, pp. 57–103.
Velaers, J. (2019) *De Grondwet: een artikelsgewijze commentaar. Deel II. De machten (de federale staat, de gemeenschappen en de gewesten)*. Bruges: Die Keure.
Young, I.M. (2000) *Inclusion and Democracy*. Oxford: Oxford University Press. DOI: 10.1093/0198297556.001.0001.
Zurn, C. (2016) 'Democratic Constitutional Change: Assessing Institutional Possibilities', in Bustamante, T., Fernandes, T.B. (eds.) *Democratizing Constitutional Law: Perspectives on Legal Theory and the Legitimacy of Constitutionalism*. Cham: Springer International Publishing, pp. 185–212.

15 Sovereignty without sovereignty

The Belgian solution

Raf Geenens

"Let us delete the word sovereignty from our vocabulary"
Benjamin Constant (1830)

At least since 1950, Belgian constitutional law is in the grip of a myth: the myth of national sovereignty.[1] Framed as an originalist claim about the meaning of article 25 at the time of its ratification, scholars and judges alike hold that sovereignty in the Belgian context means 'national sovereignty'.[2] National sovereignty is here understood as the opposite of popular sovereignty, in line with the conceptual dichotomy expounded by, among others, French legal theorist Raymond Carré de Malberg. In recent years, several authors have demonstrated that this interpretation of the Constitution is highly anachronistic (De Smaele, 2000; Deseure, 2016; Geenens and Sottiaux, 2015). The Belgian drafters, when working on the Constitution in 1830–1831, did not understand sovereignty in the terms that are now routinely ascribed to them. The national sovereignty myth, it seems, is a product of muddled thinking. In order to stave off the push for more – and more direct – democracy, subsequent generations of legal scholars applied ever thicker conceptual layers to the Constitution, up to the point where it has come to say nearly the opposite of what it said in 1831.

Although the myth is increasingly criticised for its lack of historical accuracy, some scholars cling to it (e.g. Clement and Van de Putte, 2018; De Schepper, 2018; Keunen and Bijnens, 2017). Others have abandoned the originalist claim and instead now suggest that the national sovereignty interpretation derives its authority from *opinio juris*: through a long line of precedents, the vague notion

1 As author of this text, I am solely responsible for all potential errors. However, to the extent that it contains something valuable, this is certainly owing to the colleagues and PhD students with whom I have been collaborating on this topic in the past years. I want to thank them explicitly for this: Olga Bashkina, Brecht Deseure, Bas Leijssenaar, Christophe Maes, Stefan Sottiaux, Nora Timmermans, and Ronald Van Crombrugge.

2 Article 25 is today article 33. When referring to articles of the Belgian Constitution, I will always use the numbering of 1831. The full text of the 1831 version of the Constitution can be consulted in Stevens et al. (2008, pp. 71–97). I will sometimes use '1831' as shorthand for the 1831 Belgian Constitution. Likewise, '1791' is shorthand for the 1791 French Constitution.

of sovereignty in article 25 has "crystallized" into the doctrine of national sovereignty, and this is enough to give the myth legal weight (Alen, 2015; Velaers, 2019, p. 8). This willingness to maintain the concept of national sovereignty suggests that the wide gulf that separates it from the mental world of 1831 is still not fully appreciated.

This, then, is the central aim of this chapter. I intend to present a coherent picture of what the authors of the Belgian Constitution thought about sovereignty so as to lay bare the multiple differences between the drafters' ideas on sovereignty and the national sovereignty myth. These differences are important not only for historical reasons, but also for practical ones. If the conflict between the drafters' understanding of sovereignty and the national sovereignty myth is as big as I claim it to be, resorting to *opinio juris* is a wrong-headed approach. It requires one either to discard the 1831 meaning of the text as irrelevant, or to accept as legally valid two incompatible interpretations of the Constitution. Both options are an affront to legal integrity. Understanding these differences also matters for philosophical reasons. The Belgian drafters' thinking on sovereignty had a richness to it which the national sovereignty myth has completely obscured. Both 1831 and the myth can be understood as conceptual strategies to keep the full effects of popular sovereignty at bay, yet strategies that are far from identical. Of the two, 1831 is certainly the more elegant one.

In the following sections, I begin by interpreting article 25 in light of the intellectual and political circumstances in which the drafters found themselves in 1830–1831. I then seek support for this interpretation by looking at the debates in contemporary newspapers and by situating it in the drafters' broader constitutional vision. In the second half of this chapter, I discuss the national sovereignty myth. After briefly presenting its core tenets, I explain why it is untenable and why it remains, even with slight alterations, indefensible. By way of conclusion, I turn to the constitutionality of referendums, as this is the question that has become the litmus test for interpretations of article 25.

Article 25 in 1830–1831

From 1815 to 1830, lawyers, journalists, clerics, and other members of the educated classes in the southern part of the Netherlands went through a roller coaster of political experiences and new ideas. The Belgian Constitution is, before anything else, a reflection of their collective trajectory. Two elements are particularly important in that trajectory. First, they were privileged witnesses to the decline of monarchical rule. As Markus Prutsch explains elsewhere in this book, constitutional monarchism might have looked attractive in 1814, but was doomed to be a transitional phenomenon.[3] With tradition no longer available as a source of legitimacy, and the public – helped by the press – constantly watching over political decisions, kings lost their independence. Their legitimacy now depended on

3 See Chapter 2 and Prutsch (2013).

gaining the support of popular opinion and they were forced to find an entente with the press. William I, coming at the head of the newly united Netherlands in 1815, proved spectacularly inept at this, at least in the southern half of his realm. His attempts to concentrate all power in his own hands, his stubbornness in the debate on ministerial responsibility, and his heavy-handed tactics against the opposition press, taught his southern subjects that centralised power was to be distrusted, that parliamentarisation was the only way forward, and that a free press and public opinion were crucial guarantees for liberty. These 15 years were also formative for a second reason. In the course of the nineteenth century, citizens across Europe came to discover that constitutions are uniquely powerful tools: they can be used not only to justify political and legal institutions, but also to denounce incautious rulers (cf. Grotke and Prutsch, 2014). Southern activists learnt this lesson early. Their conflicts with King William I almost invariably concerned constitutional values: no matter whether they clashed about ministerial responsibility, freedom of the press, or clerical appointments, the interpretation of the Constitution was always involved. Publicists disseminated these conflicts through the numerous newspapers, thereby creating, in what would soon become Belgium, a politically aware public and a strong constitutional culture.[4]

If, shortly after the Belgian Revolution, the drafters managed to produce an exemplary and coherent constitution within a short span of time, it is because they had been writing and talking about constitutional matters for 15 years.[5] The constitution that came out of this long gestation period expressed their central concerns: it was to guarantee liberty and stability by setting up counterbalancing institutions, by shuffling power away from the king, and by cementing the force of public opinion into the constitutional edifice. The keystone of this programme was article 25: “All powers emanate from the Nation. They are to be exercised as prescribed by the Constitution”.

In order to get a clear view of what this article is aiming at, we should start by carefully looking at its formulation. The second half of the article is, of course, rather straightforward: it reflects the drafters’ awareness of the importance of constitutions in maintaining liberty. But the meaning of the first half is more disputable. This first sentence is usually presented as a statement about sovereignty, but most commentators have failed to notice the obvious, namely that the word sovereignty is absent. This absence is significant because many other constitutions of the era (see, most famously, the French Constitution of 1791) contain lengthy, explicit statements about sovereignty, for instance claiming

4 The most striking illustration is the extensive courses in constitutional theory which Pierre-François Van Meenen published in serialised form in *L’Observateur belge* from 1815 to 1820.

5 The Belgian Constitution is often described as an “eclectic” or “mosaic” creation because fragments of the text can be traced to divergent sources (cf. Descamps-David, 1891; Gilissen, 1968; De Smaele, 2005). Even Joseph Lebeau, one of its authors, already described it as “eclectic” in December 1830 (Huyttens, 1844a, p. 416, 13 December 1830). Retrospectively, however, it is clear that the Constitution, at the level of content, is rather loyal to a coherent set of ideas, namely those of the so-called Coppet-liberals.

that it is indivisible or unalienable. Nothing similar can be found in the Belgian Constitution. Only the word "powers", in the plural, is used. Equally remarkable is the choice of "emanate from" (in French: "émanent de"). Again, the comparison with other constitutions is instructive. The Revolutionary Constitution of 1791 states that sovereignty "belongs to" ("appartient à") the nation. The constitutions of 1793 and 1795 use the even stronger formula "resides in" ("réside dans").[6] And then there is the choice of the term "nation" ("nation") over alternatives such as "people" ("peuple"), which was used in 1793, or "the totality of citizens" ("l'universalité des citoyens") as in 1795. The importance of this choice should not be overplayed. The members of the constituent assembly, as well as the contemporary newspapers, consistently used the terms 'people' and 'nation' interchangeably. And in the Constitution's Dutch translation, produced by the provisional government in 1831, article 25 contains the word "people" (in Dutch: "volk") rather than nation.[7]

What to make then of the entire statement? What does it say about sovereignty? My hypothesis is that this sentence is not about sovereignty strictly speaking. It does not indicate who is holding the highest office or who is wielding supreme command, nor does it name the author of all legislation.[8] It is rather a statement about the origin of all constituted powers, that is, it is a statement about what can more accurately be called original constituent power. This is not surprising. The congressmen clearly thought that it was important to be aware of the source of their power. Again and again, they describe the constituent assembly as "emerging from the people" or "originating [...] from the nation".[9] Moreover, they made key declarations – such as the two eternity decrees – "in the name of the Belgian people". Their constant references to the people (or the nation), both in speech and in article 25, unambiguously recognise the people as the origin of all powers and thereby confirm the modern idea that there can be no other source of legitimacy.

At the same time, the congressmen clearly believed that the people's constituent power had been transferred to the National Congress and would, once its work was done, be relegated "to a nearly inaccessible sphere", as Jean-Baptiste Nothomb, one of the leading drafters, put it (Huyttens, 1844a, p. 424, 14 December 1830). In other words, the founders did not believe that

6 Even though republican congressmen, like Pierre Seron, tried to claim that article 25 should be read to mean that sovereignty "resides in" the nation and that "sovereignty is inalienable" (Huyttens, 1844b, p. 15, 3 January 1831).

7 It does not follow that the choice of the word 'nation' was arbitrary. In French, as in other European languages, the word 'people' can refer not only to the citizenry as a whole but also to the lower classes. 'Nation', in contrast, always had more dignified connotations.

8 Of course, a lot depends on the definition of terms. According to Richard Tuck, sovereignty (in opposition to "government") was the term that Hobbes and Rousseau used to indicate what is now usually called constituent power, i.e. the power to create or alter society's basic laws and institutions (Tuck, 2016).

9 See the discussion in Chapter 7 of this book.

the people's constituent power would continue to play a substantial role. It had emerged out of the people into the constituent assembly and was meant to stream, beyond the assembly, into a constitutional system of powers. However, if the people's constituent power has no real role in this system, it is not obvious why it has to be mentioned in the Constitution. After all, a constitution is supposed to become useful once the constituent work is done. It seems that the drafters wanted to constantly remind all power-holders of the ultimate source of their powers. This means that the role of the people, *qua* constituent power, becomes primarily a symbolic one. The people are the discursive anchoring point that permanently provides the constitutional project with its legitimacy.

If article 25 is not truly a statement about sovereignty, how can we know what the drafters thought about sovereignty? First of all, we should give full weight to the observation that they chose not to say anything explicit about sovereignty in the Constitution. The fact that the Constitution's vocabulary does not include the word sovereignty suggests that its authors disliked this word or, at the very least, that they did not find it helpful in expressing their constitutional vision. This already tells us something about their constitutional vision. Secondly, we can look at what they said about sovereignty in the constituent assembly. As Brecht Deseure (2016) has demonstrated, the debates in this assembly show that an overwhelming majority of members accepted popular sovereignty as an indisputable principle for which there is, in modern times, no alternative. They clearly believed that the political regime they were creating encompassed the principle of popular sovereignty and that its norms and rules and all elements of its functioning would be compatible with this principle.[10] With one lonely exception to confirm the rule, no member of the constituent assembly ever put into question the people's sovereignty.

This creates something of a riddle. If the drafters accepted the principle of popular sovereignty, why did they not explicitly include it in the constitutional text? What to make of this refusal to express the role of the people in terms of sovereignty? The context is crucial here. The Belgian constitutional project was driven by a double fear. On the one hand, the congressmen feared the concentration of excessive state power in the hands of a monarch, as they had so recently seen exemplified by the autocratic rule of William I. On the other hand, in line with post-revolutionary sentiment across Europe, they continued to be haunted by the Reign of Terror. The term 'sovereignty' was associated with both these dangers. Whether sovereignty belonged to a king or was exercised in the name of the people, either way it could collapse into despotism. Sovereignty, it seemed, was intrinsically connected with a monolithic 'will', with the concentration of all authority in one point, and with unlimited and arbitrary power. As the debates in

10 Speakers in the National Congress stated, for instance, that a parliamentary monarchy is always based on the "sovereignty of the people", or even that all modern societies are based on the "sovereignty of the people", without meeting any resistance or correction (cf. Huyttens, 1844a, pp. 216, 603).

the National Congress demonstrate, the abhorrence for uncontrolled, centralised power was shared across the political spectrum, with the possible exception of the republican minority and some ardent monarchists.

The dominant liberals and liberal-Catholics also had their own, additional reasons for disliking sovereignty. Liberals were primarily concerned with individual liberty. And as they associated sovereignty with a strong state, they naturally viewed it as inimical to the liberty of individuals. Moreover, they feared the volatility and capriciousness of a strong collective will. If liberals were in favour of monarchy, it is because they believed the stability provided by a neutral king would help to curb the unpredictable effects of popular sovereignty: "Heredity and inviolability are two political fictions, two public necessities [...]. Opposite these fictions appears, ever menacing, the sovereignty of the people" (Huyttens, 1844a, p. 193, 19 November 1830). This statement by Nothomb is exemplary of the views of the liberal congressmen, who were worried about the potential hazards that come with an unrestrained collective will.

The Catholic position was less uniform, running from liberal-Catholics who supported modern political ideas to deeply anti-modern, 'intransigent' ultramontanes. Almost all of them quickly perceived the practical benefits of a liberal constitution: a weaker state would give them more leeway in, say, the running of schools or the appointment of priests. Liberal-Catholics also embraced individual liberty in a principled way, as a formal recognition of human dignity. But they also had principled reasons to rail against sovereignty. Leo de Foere, a leading Catholic, had argued in 1821 that popular sovereignty should not be understood in too strong – i.e. too collectivist – a way, because social order necessarily originates from individual wills: "One would judge me wrong [...] by attributing to me the doctrine of the exclusive and absolute sovereignty of the people. I believe sovereign power resides in the individual, or in individuals according to the modalities established by contracts" (De Foere quoted in Marteel, 2009, p. 313). This dislike of popular sovereignty remained widespread among liberal-Catholics. It seems that they associated sovereignty with the stifling, top-down imposition of homogeneity and uniformity. True vitality and unity, in contrast, "results from the autonomous life of every part of the social body", as Lamennais put it in *L'Avenir* in December 1830, emphasizing the rich variety of "habits" and "moeurs" of different localities.[11] Liberal-Catholics did not join ultramontanes in fantasising about a corporatist, neo-medieval utopia,[12] but they did hope for a decentralised society, based on "the 'sovereign' rights of organic social units like family, commune and province", who should be allowed "to administer their

11 Félicité de Lamennais quoted in Viaene (2001, p. 69).

12 Among intransigent ultramontane Catholics, the rejection of sovereignty was even stronger. In *De l'esprit de vie et de l'esprit de mort* (1831), Henri de Merode and Ernest de Beauffort explicitly deplore the replacement of God's sovereignty by popular sovereignty, which they call "the sovereignty of individual reason" and which they see as an expression of the "spirit of death" (quoted in Viaene, 2001, p. 47).

own affairs as much as possible" (Viaene, 2001, p. 69). Thus, even if they mostly paid lip service to the principle of popular sovereignty, the idea of a unitary collective will ran counter to their preferred vision of a liberated, "bottom-up" community of Christians (cf. Marteel, 2018, p. 237).

Article 25 should be read as the joint outcome of these liberal and liberal-Catholic attitudes towards sovereignty. By wording article 25 as they did, they could recognise the people's power as the legitimate basis of government, and thereby nod to the principle of popular sovereignty (a principle which they took for granted), without having to rely on the notion of sovereignty. They had no problem accepting the citizens as the source of legitimacy, but they feared the idea of a monolithic, supra-individual collective agent. Given this negative attitude towards sovereignty, it is not surprising that the Belgian Constitution is not about constructing a strong state that can channel the people's united will, but rather about restraining sovereignty and cutting it up into a plurality of powers.

The newspaper debate

This picture is confirmed by the opinion pages of contemporary newspapers, where there was a vivid debate about sovereignty. Some newspapers assumed that the constitutional text simply enunciated the sovereignty of the people. But sharp-sighted observers noted that something more was going on.[13] A good example is the exchange between the establishment newspaper *Courrier des Pays-Bas* (*CDPB*),[14] with which many of the drafters were affiliated, and the conservative, ultramontane *Courrier de la Meuse* (*CDM*). This latter newspaper maintained that all power comes from God[15] and argued that a regime of popular sovereignty would have disastrous consequences. In their editorials, journalists at *Courrier de la Meuse* repeatedly attacked what they perceived to be the majority position, namely the idea that the negative effects of popular sovereignty could be prevented by creating a system of opposing powers. According to them, this Montesquieu-inspired strategy was a mere illusion as sovereign power, in actual practice, is always located in one specific place: "Sovereignty is here, or it is there; but it is never in two places at the same time. It cannot be shared, it cannot be divided" (*CDM*, 9 December 1830, no. 296). *Courrier de la Meuse* insisted on the impossibility of dividing sovereignty from October 1830 all the way to March 1831, making this a leitmotiv of its opposition to the draft constitution. In an editorial at the beginning of March 1831, *Le Courrier des Pays-Bas* criticised them head-on for this. Sovereignty might be unitary in its source, but its

13 I owe the newspaper citations in this section to research by Christophe Maes (see Maes 2020).

14 Note that "des Pays-Bas" was dropped from its official name on 1 January 1831. I will refer to this newspaper by its original name.

15 Within the constituent assembly, this position had no traction. It was voiced only once, by Pierre Vander Linden. Arguing against popular sovereignty, he solitarily claimed that all power has its origin in God (Huyttens, 1844b, p. 14, 3 January 1831).

institutionalisation should be guided by the insight that power can only be limited by means of other powers. In absence of such a distribution of powers, we end up in despotism:

> In a system of dependent powers [...] only the superior power is truly a power because only its will has to be executed: the inferiors can also will, but they can only will what the superior wills. This is exactly what we call unlimited or absolute or despotic power.
>
> (*CDPB*, 5 March 1831, no. 64)

Thus, a system of independent powers is needed, rather than a system in which all powers can be traced to one, central seat of sovereignty. In the same piece, *Courrier des Pays-Bas* noted that all powers were currently vested in the National Congress, which flew in the face of the principle of power distribution which this assembly was preaching. As was to be expected, the journalists at *Courrier de la Meuse* saw this as a good opportunity to mock their opponents. In the process, they gave the best possible summary of the majority position on sovereignty:

> The *Courrier des Pays-Bas* notices that our Congress possesses sovereignty ("est en possession de la souveraineté") and is displeased by this. This is natural, for it wants sovereignty to be only in the nation, or rather, *it wants sovereignty to be nowhere*; because it actually wants there to be only powers that counterbalance each other, so as to assure order and liberty.
>
> (*CDM*, 10 March 1831, no. 59, italics modified)

In the remainder of this opinion piece, they deride once again the idea of a division of powers by emphasising, in a political-realist way, that final authority is always located *somewhere*.

In contrast to this ultramontane view, republican newspapers insisted on the unity of sovereignty out of principle. Although some republicans were heartened by the fact that the Constitution sanctioned the principle of popular sovereignty, many of them realised that things were not that simple. Already in mid-November 1830, the republican journalists at *L'Emancipation* (*EMP*) warned their readers that they should not be so naïve as to think that "All powers emanate from the nation" means the same thing as "sovereignty resides in the nation". The difference, they write, is "enormous" (*EMP*, 15 November 1830, no. 26).[16] For *L'Emancipation*, sovereignty equals legislative power equals the general will equals the nation: "(T)he sovereign has no other force than the legislative power, it is simply the general will, and it is obvious that the general will or sovereignty can only exist in a general form, that is, in the universality of the nation" (*EMP*, 15 November 1830, no. 26).

16 This shows that even committed republicans did not think that the choice of the term 'nation' was meaningful. Much more important for them was the omission of the term 'sovereignty' and the choice of the verb 'emanate'.

Over time, republicans will increasingly oppose the constitutional project as it moves further away from this simple scheme in which sovereignty, a unitary legislative will, and the nation are identified with each other. In the run-up to the vote over bicameralism, a desperate *L'Emancipation* argues once again that the general will is necessarily "one" and "indivisible" (*EMP*, 10 December 1830, no. 51). This plea is of no avail: the constituent assembly overwhelmingly votes in favour of creating a senate.

Although I am only providing snippets here, I believe these newspaper exchanges do help us to pin down how well-informed observers perceived the Constitution at the time of its writing. In the next section, I want to demonstrate how the meaning of article 25, as construed above, fits into the broader web of constitutional ideas advocated by the dominant drafters.

Public opinion and individual interests

Throughout the months of the constituent assembly, the drafters' core ideas always displayed the same duality: they recognised the citizens as the permanent anchoring point of legitimacy, but they refused to define the citizens' role in a holistic manner. Their recognition of the citizens as the source and the ultimate touchstone for every exercise of power, is most visible in the importance they attached to public opinion. The new Constitution was to create a variety of channels through which public opinion would play a political role. For starters, the Constitution gives the press a maximum amount of freedom. This is because newspapers, pamphlets, and books serve both to build and to express public opinion. Liberty, in the words of Catholic leader Etienne de Gerlache, would find a "guarantee in the omnipotence of public opinion through the press" (Huyttens, 1844a, p. 471, 15 December 1830).[17] The freedom of the press, in turn, would find a guarantee in the jury. Whereas William I had muffled journalists with the help of the courts, in Belgium they would be protected by the better judgment of their co-citizens. Jury trials, it was hoped, would become a reliable check on judicial and executive power (Delbecke, 2012). Public opinion would also have other conduits. Petitions, for instance, were seen by the founders as an important tool for correcting and steering public powers. And then there was, of course, the second chamber, often dubbed "the chamber of opinion". Liberal heavyweight Charles de Brouckère, when describing its role in the constitutional edifice, writes that the second chamber will be "the expression of public opinion" because it "represents the nation from which all powers emanate" (Huyttens, 1844a, p. 427, 14 December 1830). For good measure, he repeats: "public opinion, that is,

17 The term 'guarantee' is very recurrent in the drafters' speeches and betrays their common way of thinking: their global concern is to establish guarantees that would maintain liberty and stability. In Van Meenen's lectures on constitutional theory (published in *L'Observateur belge*), the theme of 'guarantees' was already omnipresent. On the role of "garantisme" in Coppet-liberalism, see Lacchè (2000, p. 141 f.).

the nation" (ibid.). The second chamber was not just involved in lawmaking but also, importantly, in holding the government to account through the mechanism of ministerial responsibility. This latter mechanism was crucial, as it meant that all holders of executive power were, ultimately, accountable to the opinion of the electorate.

The overall result, as Charles Blargnies put it in the constituent assembly, would be that "the law is the result of enlightened public opinion, as expressed by those who the people elect, by the press, and by petitions" (Huyttens, 1844a, p. 238, 22 November 1830). In the same speech, he described public opinion as the "true will of the people" (Huyttens, 1844a, p. 236, 22 November 1830). The theme of public opinion is also prominent in the publications of the key drafters. Charles-Hippolyte Vilain XIIII, in his *Appel au Congrès* published in the fall of 1830, writes that, through the jury and the press, "public opinion becomes the state's greatest asset" (Vilain XIIII, 1830, p. 30). Joseph Lebeau, in his book on royal power, describes how, apart from counterbalancing powers, there is a further guarantee for liberty, namely "opinion", which is connected to the press and works on parliament from the outside (Lebeau, 1830, p. 85). He even goes so far as to say that "representative government is the government of opinion" (Lebeau, 1830, p. 65).

Lebeau's formulations betray how close the drafters' ideas on public opinion sit to those of Benjamin Constant, who is probably the main intellectual inspiration for the Belgian Constitution.[18] Although adopting Montesquieu's division of powers, Constant discovered an additional, even more potent force that protects freedom, namely public opinion (Constant, 1815, p. 31).[19] Arthur Ghins has recently brought to light just how important the notion of public opinion was for Constant. According to Ghins, public opinion came to function in Constant's mind as an alternative to popular sovereignty (Ghins, 2021). Of course, Constant recognised the sovereignty of the people. His *Principes de Politique* starts, not incidentally, by explicitly stating that the principle of popular sovereignty cannot be contested (Constant, 1815, p. 13). But Constant was always worried about the voluntarist implications of sovereignty. In an article published in *Le Temps* in 1830, shortly before his death, he even goes so far as to "deny" popular sovereignty and he proposes to "delete the word sovereignty from our vocabulary" (Constant, 1989, pp. 176–177).

Constant's preferred conceptual substitute for popular sovereignty was public opinion, and it seems that the Belgian drafters followed him on this point. And just as was the case for Constant, their attachment to public opinion had everything to do with their unwavering belief in the power of individual judgment. For

18 It has already been demonstrated that the Belgians were heavily influenced by Constant when it came to ministerial responsibility (Van Velzen, 2005) and freedom of the press (Delbecke, 2012).

19 On Constant and public opinion, see Fontana (1991, pp. 81–97), Fink (1998), Tenenbaum (1998), and Rosenblatt (2011).

Constant, as for other members of the Coppet Group, freedom found its ultimate guarantee in the individual's "right to judge and control laws and power" (Jaume, 2012, p. 42). Indeed, this is what distinguishes Coppet-liberalism from other currents of French liberalism, in particular from the Doctrinaires, who favoured and trusted the state as the final underwriter of freedom (cf. Jaume, 1997; Garsten, 2015). Similarly, in the debates in the National Congress, the idea of 'judgment' by the citizens is a recurrent trope. See, for instance, its appearance in Lebeau's intervention on bicameralism. In this imposing speech, arguably one of the high notes of the entire constituent period, Lebeau claims that a bicameral system turns the nation into a judge, which is a decisive advantage over a unicameral system. When the chambers disagree, each chamber will defend its opinion with reasons, majority against majority, giving the court of public opinion the opportunity to judge the strength of these opposing reasons (Huyttens, 1884a, pp. 413–414, 13 December 1830).

While the drafters emphatically wanted to empower the judgment of individual citizens, they never characterised the working of these judgments in a collectivist manner. In line with this, they always avoided talking in terms of a 'general interest' which the nation could come to recognise.[20] Instead, they repeatedly stated that the plurality of societal interests cannot be superseded. This theme was already prepared by Pierre-François Van Meenen's constitutional lectures, published in *L'Observateur belge* from 1815 to 1820. According to Van Meenen, terms such as "the state", "raison d'état", "general will", and "the common good" (and even "liberty" and "independence") can become dangerous abstractions, in the name of which too much blood has already been shed. The only entities that really exist, he emphasises, are individuals, as well as individual rights, individual interests, and individual happiness (Van Meenen, 1815, pp. 29–30). Some Catholics might have found this all a bit too individualistic, but this metaphysics clearly underpinned the dominant liberal view in Congress. This is, for instance, the basis of Nothomb's case for bicameralism and, more generally, of his preference for "mixed government" (Huyttens, 1844a, p. 192, 19 November 1830). According to Nothomb, "there is in society a plurality of interests" (Huyttens, 1844a, p. 425, 14 December 1830). Multiplying the sites of representation is therefore highly desirable. Rather than believing that any one representative institution can overcome this plurality, the different societal

20 And when they do use a term such as "general interest", they avoid using it in the singular. De Gerlache, for instance, talks of "the general interests of the nation" (Huyttens, 1844a, p. 472, 15 December 1830). Similarly, Van Meenen says "public interests" rather than "the public interest" (Huyttens, 1844a, p. 429, 14 December 1830). But not all speakers are so careful. Occasionally, one does find 'monolithic' expressions. Charles Destouvelles, for instance, describes the law as the outcome of "the general will" (Huyttens, 1844b, p. 253, 24 January 1831). Compare this with the more scrupulous formulation of De Brouckère, who speaks of "the wills of the nation" (Huyttens, 1844a, p. 427, 14 December 1830).

interests should find separate institutional expression. As Nothomb puts it: "I give to each the right of being represented" (ibid.).[21]

Again, this brings the drafters close to Constant. As Lucien Jaume has abundantly demonstrated, Constant's individualism was directed against the French Revolutionary conception of representation as embodied in the Constitution of 1791. In the 1791 conception, there is an obsession with unity, "a Unity that can be read from the representative operation". It is the state, and only the state, that "can define the general interest". Thus, "representation can never be the expression of separate interests" (Jaume, 1998, pp. 159–160). Constant's crucial move was claiming that particular interests do have a right of expression. Rather than organising politics in such a way that the true or correct interpretation of the general interest can be found and imposed in a uniform manner, priority should be given to individuals with their own local interests and ideas (cf. Garsten, 2016, p. 254 f.; Ghins, 2018).[22] In line with Constant, the Belgian drafters were convinced that no unity or generality exists detached from the individuals involved (cf. Van Meenen, 1815, p. 30). When looking inside the black box of the so-called 'general interest', one finds nothing but a plurality of particular interests. Hence, unity can only be the result of a constant dialogue between different and opposing forces.

The republican minority clearly felt that this was the dominant mood in the constituent assembly and occasionally tried to push back. Eugène Defacqz, for instance, dedicated an entire speech to the theme of unity. He was careful enough to show his agreement on other key themes, explaining how the Constitution, the press, and public opinion would function as interlocking guarantees for freedom. But he was tired of the constant emphasis on plurality, on divisions, and on counterbalancing powers. Instead, he claimed that "unity" was "natural", that the "truth" was "one", and that "discord has to be weeded out" from all institutions if the citizens wanted to act in "unison" (Huyttens 1844a, pp. 421–424, 14 December 1830). Obviously, this solitary republican cry from the heart achieved nothing. It only emphasized how far all other drafters had moved away from the 'unitarian' spirit of the French Revolution.

In summary, the intent behind the whole constitutional framework was to activate individual judgments and give them political weight, without succumbing to any form of holistic thinking. Rather than excluding citizens from the legislative process and leaving it for representatives to proclaim the 'general will', the 'public interest', or other such dangerous abstractions, the aim was to mobilise public opinion as a permanent and reliable force in the political game. Article 25 naturally fits into this constitutional programme. It recognises the citizens

21 Compare this with the formulation of Sieyès in *Qu'est-ce que le tiers-état*: "citizens only have the right to being represented in virtue of the qualities they have in common, not in virtue of the qualities that distinguish them" (Sieyès, 1988, p. 173).

22 See also Chapter 3 of this book.

as the ultimate anchoring point of public powers, while avoiding the collectivist metaphysics of the sovereignty formulations from the French Revolution.

The national sovereignty myth

Surprisingly, most Belgian public law textbooks present an interpretation of article 25 that claims loyalty to the founders' intentions while clearly going against the grain of this constitutional programme. This 'mythical' interpretation gradually emerged in the nineteenth century and gained near-universal acceptance after the referendum on the royal question in 1950. From then on, virtually all textbooks – as well as the courts – have come to read article 25 in light of the doctrine of national sovereignty. The key tenets of this doctrine are as follows. The Belgian drafters consciously adopted the view on sovereignty embedded in France's 1791 Constitution (see e.g. Wigny, 1952, p. 223). In this view, purportedly developed by Sieyès (see e.g. Alen, 1995, p. 20), sovereignty is "unitary, indivisible, and unalienable" (Mast, 1966, p. 25) and belongs to "the nation" (see e.g. Van Goethem, 2002, p. 236; Velaers, 2006, p. 190), understood as an "indivisible collectivity comprising the citizens of the past, the present and the future" (Tilleman and Alen, 1992, p. 11). Because the nation, defined in this way, is an "abstract entity" – or even simply a "fiction" – that is "distinct from the individuals that compose it", it can only express itself through representative institutions (Uyttendaele, 2005, pp. 34–35). This latter point is what distinguishes, in practice, national sovereignty from popular sovereignty, which supposedly entails direct democracy (see e.g. Vande Lanotte et al., 2015, pp. 208–209).

The textbooks regularly quote Carré de Malberg to give more substance to this doctrine.[23] In its full Malbergian version, the doctrine of national sovereignty is bound up with a positivist legal philosophy that sees the state as the supreme source of law. This state finds its legitimacy in the fact that it embodies the nation, a nation that is, however, nothing more than an intra-legal effect. It is postulated by law and expresses itself through legally constituted representatives or rather, in Carré de Malberg's preferred terminology, *organs*. It is only through its organs, such as parliament, that the nation comes to have a will. This will, Carré de Malberg stresses, is "general": it "cannot be understood as the sum of particular wills", but "is itself part of the unity and indivisibility of the nation" (Carré de Malberg, 1922, p. 255). Thus, elected politicians do not represent "the totality of citizens individually considered, but their indivisible and extra-individual collectivity as a whole" (Carré de Malberg, 1922, p. 223).[24] And it is in this whole, "in this total and indivisible body, that exclusively resides sovereignty" (Carré de Malberg, 1922, p. 255). Note that this positivist logic deliberately presents law

23 It is generally assumed that Carré de Malberg has provided the authoritative formulation of the national sovereignty doctrine, but the doctrine is of course not exclusively his (see the work of Adhémar Esmein, Julien Lafferière, Paul Bastid, and others).

24 Translation taken from Brunet (2016, p. 434).

as a closed system without an outside. Although the will of the nation should be considered the joint will of all its members, Carré de Malberg's theory cannot provide resources to connect the content of the law to any reference point that exists outside or before it (cf. Mineur, 2012). The will of the representatives can be attributed to the nation only on the basis of constitutional rules, "not in virtue of the conformity which that particular will may have with the actual will of the people who elected the representatives" (Brunet, 2016, p. 434).

In a bold anachronistic move, Carré de Malberg traces this positivist theory of the state to 1791 and to Sieyès. In passing, he also names Belgium's 1831 Constitution as an example of his doctrine (Carré de Malberg, 1922, p. 169). Jurists in post-war Belgium got Carré de Malberg's hint and gratefully pushed the doctrine to its full practical conclusions. For instance, the Council of State would come to claim that the Belgian drafters consciously bestowed "sovereignty" on "the nation", a nation that "encompasses past and future generations of citizens".[25] And it used this as an argument against the introduction of referendums, stating that it is "impossible to give a certain number of today's citizens the power to replace the national representation, which is constitutionally established to express the will of that abstract being which our foundational act calls 'the nation'".[26] Similarly, André Alen, the former president of Belgium's Constitutional Court, writes that from "a constitutional perspective, there is an irrefutable presumption that the will of the representatives is the will of the people" (Alen, 1995, p. 21). In this way, the national sovereignty doctrine became an important brick in the constitutional line of defence against demands for direct participation in Belgium.

It is not a coincidence that many of the textbook authors quoted above held influential positions in Belgium's legal and political institutions. In the decades after the Second World War, in an increasingly divided Belgium, elite compromise-formation was seen as a crucial mechanism to pacify social relations and to maintain stability, a stability that was never more threatened than by the 1950 'royal' referendum. For those wishing to operate in the name of raison d'état, shielded from democratic pressure, Carré de Malberg's state-centric doctrine provided a convenient theoretical framework.[27] Thus, the misreading of article 25 in the national sovereignty myth was, just like the original formulation, moti-

25 Opinion of 15 May 1985, Part. Doc. Chamber 1983-84, no. 783/2, 8.

26 Ibid.

27 Note that, in post-war Italy and France, the anti-democratic implications of Carré de Malberg's conception of national sovereignty were clearly perceived and actively challenged by, among others, Costantino Mortati and Georges Vedel (see Rubinelli, 2020, pp. 147–150). Nothing similar has happened in Belgium. Note also that, later in life, Carré de Malberg became a critic of his own doctrine. Frustrated with its anti-democratic effects and with the increased power of parties in France, he started to advocate the introduction of popular referendums (Carré de Malberg, 1931). As Olga Bashkina explains in Chapter 10, Carré de Malberg came to the conclusion that one either had to provide a stronger connection between the parliament and the actual citizens, or else stop pretending that the parliament is democratically legitimate.

vated by a desire to keep the potentially threatening effects of popular sovereignty at bay. Having said that, the national sovereignty interpretation differs too greatly from the drafters' views on sovereignty to be tenable. But before going into these differences, let me point out some of the minor problems that beset the national sovereignty interpretation.

For starters, there is no textual or circumstantial evidence to support it, other than the choice of the word "nation" in the Constitution. However, no one in 1830–1831, not even staunch republicans, seemed to find this choice particularly significant. It is also difficult to claim, on the basis of the text, a direct connection between the Belgian understanding of sovereignty and the French Revolutionary Constitution of 1791. In fact, the Belgian Constitution differs from this latter Constitution in at least three important respects. (i) In the 1791 Constitution, article 1 of the third section extensively defines sovereignty (as, *inter alia*, "indivisible" and "unalienable"). The Belgian Constitution contains no trace of this article. If the Belgian drafters took their conception of sovereignty from the 1791 Constitution, it is at least remarkable that they did not copy any material from its article on sovereignty. (ii) Likewise, the Belgian drafters failed to copy any of the formulas that emphasise the representative nature of the regime. The Constitution of 1791 explicitly states that all powers can only be exercised "by means of delegation" and that the "French Constitution is representative". This is the core message of article 2 of the third section. Nothing similar can be found in the Belgian Constitution.[28] (iii) In order to defend the proximity of 1831 to 1791, scholars also point to article 32 of the Belgian Constitution. This article states that "(t)he members of the two Chambers represent the Nation, and not only the province or the subdivision of the province that has appointed them".[29] The corresponding article in the 1791 Constitution reads as follows: "The representatives [...] are not the representatives of a particular department, but of the entire Nation". What I find most striking is not the similarity but rather the difference between the two articles. In France, representatives are supposed to represent only the nation, whereas the Belgian Constitution declares that they simultaneously represent a specific locality. In other words, Belgian representatives are *not* supposed to purify themselves of partial interests. This should not surprise us. Many Belgian founding fathers believed that local powers (provinces

28 There is, of course, a textual semblance between the Belgian formulation "All powers emanate from the Nation" and the French sentence "The nation, from which all powers emanate, can only exercise them by means of delegation". The 1791 formulation might be the inspiration for the Belgian formulation, but the emphasis is certainly different. The French sentence is formulated to stress the element of representation, whereas the Belgian drafters left out the part about representation. Gilissen (1968, pp. 126–127) lists various potential sources of inspiration for the Belgian formulation and concludes that it is impossible to know which example the Belgian drafters followed.

29 This is the original formulation of article 32. The current formulation (of what is now article 42) reads as follows: "The members of the two chambers represent the Nation, and not only those who elected them".

and communes) were a useful counterweight against centralising tendencies. In this regard as well, the Belgians were in tune with Benjamin Constant.[30]

The national sovereignty doctrine also has an important conceptual weakness. Its advocates assume that popular sovereignty is necessarily associated with direct democracy, while national sovereignty would have a necessary connection with representative procedures. But this assumption is unwarranted: citizens expressing themselves in a referendum could just as well be construed as an organ of the nation.[31] A further problem for the national sovereignty doctrine is posed by Carré de Malberg's various historical inaccuracies. As is now generally acknowledged, he misread the views of the French revolutionary constituent assembly (which were more democratic and more influenced by natural law than he could allow for) and he distorted Sieyès' views (who cannot be presented as an advocate of the national sovereignty doctrine) (cf. Bastid, 1939; Bacot, 1985; Maulin, 2003; Rubinelli, 2020).

The major problem with the national sovereignty interpretation, however, is its utter incompatibility with the ideas of the Belgian founding fathers. The doctrine of national sovereignty, as worded by Carré de Malberg, involves a commitment to the logical priority of the state and a specific, positivist view on legal validity: the law derives its legitimacy from a fictive subject that only appears once its organs have been created and authorised by the law to speak on its behalf. Such views are alien to the Belgian drafters, who were decidedly not legal positivists. Their ideas had the shape of a political theory: individual liberty has to be safeguarded through interlocking institutional guarantees and through modern forms of democratic participation. Moreover, the ultimate basis of legitimacy was not an intra-legal construction (a postulated nation), but was to be found in pre-legal, empirical reality: the opinions of actual citizens. The dominant groups in Congress, including liberal-Catholics, clearly operated on a liberal scheme: everything that is relevant – individuals, individual interests, associations between individuals – already exists outside and before its appearance in the political or legal sphere. Moreover, they assumed that the most basic norms (in particular: the fundamental rights of individuals and the sovereignty of the people) do not derive their legitimacy from positive law, but are valid independently of it.

Even when cutting away Carré de Malberg's legal-positivist conceptualisation, the doctrine of national sovereignty continues to clash with the drafters' deep-rooted convictions. What the three references traditionally used to explain the Belgian conception of sovereignty – the Constitution of 1791, Sieyès's theory of the nation, and Carré de Malberg's model of representation – ultimately have in

30 On an anecdotal note it can be mentioned that Charles Rogier, an important liberal congressman, begins his 1826 dissertation in law with a long quote by Benjamin Constant. In this passage, Constant claims that politicians need to have very strong local attachments (Discailles, 1893, p. 112, n. I; cf. Garsten, 2016, pp. 255 f.). I owe this reference to Christophe Maes.

31 Inversely, it is perfectly conceivable for Carré de Malberg that the people are sovereign but transfer the exercise of their power to representatives.

common, is a typically French belief in the unity of the will: a will that is indivisible and that transcends, in some way or other, the wills and interests of individual citizens (cf. Mineur, 2010, pp. 89–144). In 1791, this unitary tradition expressed itself by writing a monolithic conception of sovereignty into the Constitution. In the case of Sieyès, this belief in unity can be perceived throughout his early writings and speeches. In a crucial passage in *Qu'est-ce que le tiers-état*, he writes that we need "*one* nation, *one* representation, and *one* common will" (Sieyès, 1988, p. 157). In a 1791 speech defending unicameralism, he stresses that "the general will has to be one"; bicameralism inevitably leads to "counteractions" and therefore threatens the necessary unity of the law (Sieyès quoted in Rubinelli, 2020, pp. 63–65).[32] In the work of Carré de Malberg, this unitarianism shows itself in the need for an indivisible, supra-individual subject as the holder of sovereignty. It also reveals itself in his emphasis on the unity of the general will, a point on which he openly agrees with Rousseau (cf. Carré de Malberg, 1922, p. 255).

Belgium's drafters, with their post-revolutionary sensibilities, wrote a constitution that is the exact antithesis of this French unitarianism. In doing so, they were inspired by Montesquieu and his disciples in the Coppet Group, who are the only ones to have systematically challenged this deep unitarian instinct in France. The Belgian Constitution can without exaggeration be described as a living monument to the Montesquieu-Coppet philosophy. In light of this, it is truly astonishing that so many textbooks use a combination of terms such as 'sovereignty', 'unitary', 'will', and 'indivisible' to explain the views of the Belgian founders. Paradoxically, such an explanation sits in many respects closer to the minoritarian republican position of 1830-1831 than to the majoritarian liberal and liberal-Catholic position.

In defence of the myth

The national sovereignty myth is premised on an originalist approach to the Belgian Constitution. When interpreting article 25 in light of the national sovereignty doctrine, authors and judges claim to explain the meaning of the text in the way its original authors, and well-informed readers at the time of writing, understood it. It is clear by now that this originalist strategy is untenable. The national sovereignty doctrine is simply too different from how the drafters thought about sovereignty. Does it follow that the national sovereignty interpretation cannot be defended at all? Actually, I believe there are three minimally plausible strategies one could follow if one really wished to hold on to it.

32 But note that Sieyès was also concerned with limiting the excesses of sovereign power (*inter alia* by means of the division between constituted and constituent power) and did come to see that the "very idea of general will was inherently wrong" (Rubinelli, 2020, p. 70). As such, he became an important source of inspiration for Constant and other Coppet-thinkers, cf. Pasquino (1988, 31 f.) and Laquièze (2005).

1. A first possibility would be to tone down the national sovereignty doctrine to a mere belief in representation.[33] The claim would then be as follows: 'The Belgian drafters did not find direct decision-making by the citizens desirable. Instead, they believed that formal political power should be exercised by elected representatives'. This claim is probably correct, but it is also very trivial. Virtually all nineteenth-century constitutions would then be examples of 'national sovereignty', so why use this particular term, with all its intellectual baggage? Moreover, by stating the claim in this way, detached from a more comprehensive view on sovereignty and political participation, it becomes difficult to assess how important representation was for the drafters in comparison with some of their other views.

2. Another slightly plausible strategy would consist in pointing out that elements of the national sovereignty doctrine were already available in 1830–1831. Even before the French Revolution, Jacques Necker toyed with the idea of the "wish" ("vœu") of the nation, which he opposed to the short-term interests of the currently living citizens (Grange, 1974, pp. 269–270). Sieyès's claim that indivisible representation is a precondition for national unity, which he formulated during the French Revolution, inspired the later doctrine of national sovereignty and could also have inspired the Belgian drafters. Moreover, in the French Revolutionary assembly there was a heated debate between supporters and critics of the imperative mandate,[34] a debate that contains *in nuce* the opposition between popular and national sovereignty.[35] Maybe the drafters never explicitly endorsed these ideas, but they might have silently absorbed them.

One could also mention the French Doctrinaire liberals, whose work gained steam and prominence during the 15 years leading up to the Belgian Revolution. According to the Doctrinaires, democracy and popular sovereignty contained "the seeds of tyranny" and might lead to the destruction of "the balance of opinions, interests, and classes" (Craiutu, 2004, p. 105). As an alternative, they proposed the sovereignty of reason and justice: rationality should become the norm for lawmaking and political power should be reserved, in perpetuity, for the

33 This seems to be the core of the strategy pursued by Clement and Van de Putte (2018) who, in a recent article, defend the national sovereignty doctrine against various criticisms. They emphasise the fact that the Belgian founders were deeply elitist. This is, of course, true. Despite accepting the principle of popular sovereignty, the founders defined the suffrage in a very narrow way. But it is not obvious that their elitism was a matter of constitutional principle. Many of them were convinced that, over time, further enlightenment would allow for a broad extension of the vote.

34 Note that, as opposed to what is often assumed, Sieyès did not fully side with the group that opposed the imperative mandate. Instead – because of his dislike for sovereignty – he sidestepped the debate by focusing on the distinction between constituent and constituted power (Rubinelli, 2020).

35 It appears that the first recognisable formulations of this opposition are to be found in an 1836 book by Simonde de Sismondi (cf. Paulet-Grandguillot, 2010, pp. 142 f.) and in an 1838 book by the Brussels-based philosopher Heinrich Ahrens (cf. Maes, 2020).

rational few.[36] These ideas, which would later be assimilated into the theory of national sovereignty, might have sounded tempting to Belgium's drafters. Thus, it is factually possible that they developed a view on sovereignty that was at least isomorphic to what would eventually become the national sovereignty doctrine.

However, one would have to show that some or all of these elements were indeed picked up by the Belgian drafters. This remains a tall order. The closest one probably gets is by explaining that the drafters rejected the imperative mandate and entrusted representation to assemblies whose members were elected by limited suffrage. These members were representatives, not just because they had been elected, but also because they carefully deliberated about the interests of the population. These points do betray the influence of the French Revolution and its intellectual aftermath. Proving more, however, seems difficult, as there is a wide gulf separating the Belgian drafters from the French cult of 'unity', 'nation', 'indivisibility', and 'sovereignty' that would eventually culminate in the national sovereignty doctrine. There is also a fundamental dissensus between the authoritarian Doctrinaires and the mood of 1830–1831: the newly minted Belgians distrusted the state, believed that the judgment of actively involved citizens is the ultimate and irreplaceable touchstone for political decisions, and would never sacrifice individual interests and opinions to an official policy of truth, reason, or justice.[37]

3. A third strategy would be to abandon all originalist ambitions and instead claim that the national sovereignty interpretation receives its legal weight only from the accumulated opinions of later interpreters. This seems to be the option picked by André Alen (2015) and Jan Velaers (2019). Of the three strategies, this is certainly the most feasible one. After 1831, certain Belgian liberals (including some of the founding fathers themselves) tilted towards a raison d'état perspective and became concerned that article 25 would be interpreted in an overly populist way, which led to the emergence of a Doctrinaire interpretation of the Constitution.[38] This Doctrinaire view gained influence in the second half of the nineteenth century and, together with other elitist and socially conservative tendencies, contributed to the adoption of the national sovereignty doctrine as the main conceptual scheme for understanding article 25. Thus, the national

36 A good introduction to the notion of "sovereignty of reason" is provided by Aurelian Craiutu (2004, pp. 123–153), although he might be overstating the proximity to Constant (cf. Jaume, 2012; Ghins, 2018).

37 Surprisingly, Els Witte claims that the Doctrinaire liberals were the dominant group among Belgian liberals during the run-up to the Belgian Revolution, that article 25 expresses the "sovereignty of reason", and that liberals in the National Congress championed the idea of "sovereign reason" (Witte, 2018, pp. 94, 105–106, 108). Unfortunately, she does not provide any evidence for these claims. Patricia Popelier also tends to read 1831 in Doctrinaire terms (Popelier, 2007).

38 The Doctrinaire reading seems to have emerged after the 1848 Revolution. The leading Catholic De Gerlache also moved away from the principle of popular sovereignty around 1850.

sovereignty account can indeed be presented as the product of a long, collective process of reinterpretation.

Despite its plausibility, this strategy has serious downsides. If one admits that the meaning of the constitutional text can be altered in unrecognisable ways through later interpretations, then one also has to accept that the national sovereignty view might wither away in light of changing needs and circumstances. One could even argue that the constitutional changes allowing non-binding referendums at the local level (article 41, since 1999) and at the regional level (article 39bis, since 2013) already signal the demise of the national sovereignty doctrine. My main objection to this strategy, however, is that it obscures the specificity and the ingenuity of the drafters' take on sovereignty in 1831. This is especially unfortunate because the ideas of 1831 might well be more appropriate and inspiring for today's needs than the stale doctrine of national sovereignty. Of course, two conflicting interpretations can flourish side by side, but only one can be granted legal validity.

Conclusion

Bruce Ackerman has famously stated that the American founding fathers "failed" in one important respect (Ackerman, 2007; 2010). Convinced that Congress would be "the most dangerous branch", they went to great constitutional lengths to contain its power. Yet the presidency has become much more dangerous as the rise of the party system turned it into a quasi-plebiscitary office. The founding fathers could not foresee this because "they were legislating for a world without national political parties" (Ackerman, 2007, p. 30).

Their distant Belgian heirs, it seems, made a similar error. They believed that setting up counterbalancing institutions would contain the threat of power concentrations, but they failed to foresee that well-organised parties could thwart their design. With their members sitting in all political bodies, the power of parties cuts across traditional divisions of power. In Belgium, this has created a situation where party leaders, who lack electoral accountability towards citizens and whose office is not described in the Constitution, have amassed astonishingly large amounts of power. Even the power-dividing mechanisms added after 1831, such as the Constitutional Court or federalism, have largely fallen victim to these same dynamics, leading some to claim that parliamentary democracy in Belgium is now a mere facade (Dewachter, 2001; 2014).

I believe these unforeseen circumstances should play a role in the interpretation of the Constitution, especially when it comes to the constitutionality of referendums – a question that is inextricably linked with article 25. Since 1950, all discussions about referendums have been conducted in light of the national sovereignty doctrine, which supposedly excluded referendums. But with the doctrine dislodged, we can again ask whether referendums are compatible with the principles of the Belgian Constitution.[39] Referendums are not mentioned in the text of the Constitution, but neither is the role of political parties. And the discussion was never merely about the letter of the text: referendums were deemed irreconcilable with the general conception of participation and representation expressed in the national sovereignty doctrine.

Ultimately, when deciding upon the constitutionality of referendums, one has to weigh several elements against each other. The fact that the drafters only provided representative mechanisms for formal lawmaking, is one such element. Another element is the observation that the Belgian Constitution – in contrast to some of the constitutions that inspired it – does not explicitly state that lawmaking, as a matter of principle, should happen in an exclusively representative manner. If the drafters thought representation was crucial, it would have been logical for them to import the formulas on representation from 1791 into the Belgian Constitution, but they did not. A further relevant element is the prominent role the drafters wished to give to public opinion. They consciously created several channels through which the opinions of citizens would be expressed, would contest and would influence policy. And then there is, of course, the division of powers: deeply concerned about power concentrations, the drafters set up various power-dividing mechanisms.

There are more elements that can be taken into consideration, and it is certainly not obvious how much weight should be given to each. The only way to make such a judgment, as Ronald Dworkin has never stopped repeating, is by rising above the concrete elements at play and by stepping up on "the ladder of theoretical ascent" (Dworkin, 1997, p. 359). In difficult cases, triggered by new and unforeseen circumstances, one can only judge correctly by making use of abstract moral or political principles (Dworkin, 1996). Some claim that such a normative judgment is not necessary and that looking at the text is enough to declare referendums unconstitutional. But this smacks of hypocrisy. It means that one places all the weight on the first element to the exclusion of all other elements. Hence, one is making a normative judgment, albeit without admitting it and without disclosing the principles that motivate this judgment. Fortunately, most opponents of referendums have never claimed to be only looking at the words of the text. They usually acknowledge that it is necessary to climb up to the level of more abstract principles. This is precisely why they invoke the doctrine of national sovereignty. According to them, this doctrine, as a systematic articulation of the drafters' views on sovereignty, provides a comprehensive scheme for thinking about representation and participation in the Belgian context.

My claim is that the doctrine is not at all suited to this purpose. The core of the drafters' constitutional programme was to avoid power concentrations by

39 Of course, one can introduce referendums regardless of the ideas of the founders, especially because changing the Belgian Constitution is relatively easy. However, even in this scenario coherence with its general principles should be a matter of concern. Moreover, the argument against referendums was never simply "that they are not yet in the text".

means of interlocking institutional guarantees and by empowering the judgment of individual citizens. It is only in light of this broad idea that we can cogently understand their concrete decisions, starting with the omission of the word sovereignty from the Constitution. I do not wish to take a position here on whether contemporary Belgians remain bound to the decisions of their long-deceased founders. But if the goal is to continue the 1831 constitutional project in a coherent way, then it is from this broad idea that one should start. When applying this idea to the question of referendums, the problem of particracy looms large. The rise of parties has created the very power concentrations and lack of accountability which the drafters ardently wished to prevent.[40] Referendums naturally offer themselves as part of the solution. They are a strong means of activating and empowering public opinion, and they serve as a pillar in the decision-making process that cannot be colonised by professional politicians.[41] Thus, rather than a break with the constitutional project, referendums might well be an effective continuation of it in today's circumstances.[42]

Bibliography

Ackerman, B. (2007) *The Failure of the Founding Fathers: Jefferson, Marshall, and the Rise of Presidential Democracy.* Cambridge, MA: Harvard University Press.

Ackerman, B. (2010) *The Decline and Fall of the American Republic.* Cambridge, MA: Harvard University Press.

Alen, A. (1995) *Handboek van het Belgisch Staatsrecht.* Deurne: Kluwer.

Alen, A. (2015) *Hoe "Belgisch" is het "Belgisch Staatsrecht" nog?* Antwerp: Intersentia.

Bacot, G. (1985) *Carré de Malberg et l'origine de la distinction entre souveraineté du peuple et souveraineté nationale.* Paris: CNRS.

Bastid, P. (1939) *Sieyès et sa pensée.* Paris: Hachette.

Brunet, P. (2016) 'Raymond Carré de Malberg (1861–1935)', in Pattaro, E. and Roversi, C. (eds.) *Legal Philosophy in the Twentieth Century: The Civil Law World. Tome 1: Language Areas.* Dordrecht: Springer, pp. 428–436.

40 When political parties emerged in Belgium in the course of the nineteenth century, many argued that this new, alternative way of organising political power was unconstitutional because it was incompatible with the distribution and the exercise of power prescribed by the Constitution (Van Goethem, 2002, p. 242).

41 Referendums are often associated with the monolithic or even populist expression of a collective, not fully rational will. This association is clearly outdated. Referendums, when well regulated and properly organised, can be useful building blocks in an encompassing "deliberative system" (Parkinson, 2020) and are compatible with a pluralistic understanding of the people (Van Crombrugge, 2020). One can also claim, as Hans Lindahl and Bert Van Roermund (2000) have done in the context of the Netherlands, that referendums are a form of representative democracy: just like other procedures and institutions, a referendum creates *a* representation of the people. Thus, the fact that parliament represents the Dutch people does not exclude setting up other channels of representation next to it.

42 This conclusion requires more arguments than I can provide here. But see the many relevant considerations in Chapters 12–14.

Carré de Malberg, R. (1922) *Contribution à la théorie générale de l'Etat. Tome deuxième*. Paris: Sirey.

Carré de Malberg, R. (1931) 'Considérations sur la question de la combinaison du referendum avec le parlementarisme', *Revue du droit public et de la science politique*, 48, pp. 225–244.

Clement, J. and Van de Putte M. (2018) 'The Constitution of the Belgian People. The Nation as Legitimisation', *Journal of Constitutional History*, 35(1), pp. 113–128.

Constant, B. (1815) *Principes de Politique*. Paris: Eymery.

Constant, B. (1989) 'De la souveraineté (*Le Temps* – 12 février 1830)' (edited by Harpaz, E.), in Cockerham, H. and Ehrman, E. (eds.) *Ideology and Religion in French Literature. Essays in Honour of Brian Juden*. Camberley: Porphyrogenitus, pp. 173–179.

Craiutu, A. (2004) *Liberalism under Siege: The Political Thought of the French Doctrinaires*. Lanham, MD and Oxford: Lexington.

De Schepper, V. (2018) 'Art. 33', in Dalle, B., Keyaerts, D., Pas, W., Theunis, J., Verrijdt, W. (eds.) *Duiding federale staatsstructuur 2018*. Brussels: Larcier, pp. 14–18.

De Smaele, H. (2000) *'Omdat we uwe vrienden zijn': religie en partij-identificatie*, 1884–1914. Faculty of Arts, Unpublished PhD-thesis. Leuven: KU Leuven.

De Smaele, H. (2005) 'Eclectisch en toch nieuw. De uitvinding van het Belgisch parlement in 1830–1831', *Bijdragen en Mededelingen betreffende de Geschiedenis der Nederlanden*, 120(3), pp. 408–416. DOI: 10.18352/bmgn-lchr.6253.

Delbecke, B. (2012) *De lange schaduw van de grondwetgever. Perswetgeving en persmisdrijven in België, 1831–1914*. Ghent: Academia Press.

Descamps-David, E. (1891) *La mosaïque constitutionnelle. Essai sur les sources du texte de la Constitution Belge*. Leuven: Peeters.

Deseure, B. (2016) 'National Sovereignty in the Belgian Constitution of 1831. On the Meaning(s) of Article 25', in Müßig, U. (ed.) *Reconsidering Constitutional Formation*. Berlin: Springer, pp. 93–156. DOI: 10.1007/978-3-319-42405-7_2.

Dewachter, W. (2001) *De mythe van de parlementaire democratie. Een Belgische analyse*. Leuven: Acco.

Dewachter, W. (2014) *De trukendoos van de Belgische particratie. Een Europese schande*. Kapellen: Pelckmans.

Discailles, E. (1893) *Charles Rogier (1800–1885) d'après des documents inédits. Tome premier*. Brussels: Lebègue.

Dworkin, R. (1996) *Freedom's Law. The Moral Reading of the American Constitution*. Cambridge, MA: Harvard University Press.

Dworkin, R. (1997) 'In Praise of Theory', *Arizona State Law Journal*, 29, pp. 353–376.

Fink, B. (1998) 'Benjamin Constant: mobilisation et mediation du mot', in Tilkin, F. (ed.) *Le Groupe de Coppet et le monde moderne*. Geneva: Droz, pp. 333–346.

Fontana, B. (1991) *Benjamin Constant and the Post-Revolutionary Mind*. New Haven and London: Yale University Press.

Garsten, B. (2015) 'The "Spirit of Independence" in Benjamin Constant's Thoughts on a Free Press', in Kemp, G. (ed.) *Censorship Moments. Reading Texts in the History of Censorship and Freedom of Expression*. London: Bloomsbury, pp. 117–124.

Garsten, B. (2016) 'From Popular Sovereignty to Civil Society in Post-Revolutionary France', in Bourke, R. and Skinner, Q. (eds.) *Popular Sovereignty in Historical*

Perspective. Cambridge: Cambridge University Press, pp. 236–269. DOI: 10.1017/CBO9781316418024.011.
Geenens, R. and Sottiaux, S. (2015) 'Sovereignty and Direct Democracy: Lessons from Constant and the Belgian Constitution', *European Constitutional Law Review*, 11(2), pp. 293–320. DOI: 10.1017/s1574019615000188.
Ghins, A. (2018) 'Benjamin Constant and the Politics of Reason', *History of European Ideas*, 44(2), pp. 224–243. DOI: 10.1080/01916599.2017.1416309.
Ghins, A. (2021) '"Popular Sovereignty that I Deny": Benjamin Constant on Public Opinion, Political Legitimacy and Constitution Making', *Modern Intellectual History.* (forthcoming).
Gilissen, J. (1968) 'La Constitution belge de 1831: ses sources, son influence', *Res Publica*, 10, pp. 107–141.
Grange, H. (1974) *Les idées de Necker.* Paris: Klincksieck.
Grotke, K.L. and Prutsch, M. (eds.) (2014) *Constitutionalism, Legitimacy, and Power: Nineteenth-Century Experiences.* Oxford: Oxford University Press.
Huyttens, E. (1844a) *Discussions du Congrès National de Belgique 1830–1831. Tome premier.* Brussels: Société Typographique Belge.
Huyttens, E. (1844b) *Discussions du Congrès National de Belgique 1830–1831. Tome deuxième.* Brussels: Société Typographique Belge.
Jaume, L. (1997) *L'individu effacé, ou, Le paradoxe du libéralisme français.* Paris: Fayard.
Jaume, L. (1998) 'Le problème de l'intérêt général dans la pensée de Benjamin Constant', in Tilkin, F. (ed.) *Le Groupe de Coppet et le monde moderne. Conceptions–Images–Débats.* Geneva: Droz.
Jaume, L. (2012) 'The Unity, Diversity and Paradoxes of French Liberalism', in Geenens, R. and Rosenblatt, H. (eds.) *French Liberalism. From Montesquieu to the Present Day.* Cambridge: Cambridge University Press, pp. 36–54. DOI: 10.1017/CBO9781139084178.004.
Keunen, S. and Bijnens, D. (2017) '"Ceci est une fiction". Grondwetgevende referenda in de Belgische rechtsorde', *Tijdschrift voor Bestuurswetenschappen en Publiekrecht*, 5, pp. 248–260.
Lacchè, L. (2000) 'Coppet et la percée de l'état libéral constitutionnel', in Jaume, L. (ed.) *Coppet, Creuset de l'esprit libéral.* Aix-en-Provence: Presses Universitaires d'Aix-Marseille, pp. 135–155.
Laquièze, A. (2005) 'La réception de Sieyès par la doctrine publiciste française du XIXème et du XXème siècles', *Historia Constitucional*, 6, http://hc.rediris.es/06/index.html (Last viewed on 11 August 2020.).
Lebeau, J. (1830) *Observations sur le Pouvoir Royal ou Examen de quelques questions relatives aux droits de la couronne dans les Pays-Bas.* Liège: Lebeau-Ouwerx.
Lindahl, H. and Van Roermund, B. (2000) 'Is er een plaats voor het referendum in de representatieve democratie?', *Openbaar bestuur. Tijdschrift voor beleid, organisatie en politiek*, 10(1), pp. 26–29.
Maes, C. (2020) *Het soevereiniteitsbegrip in de Belgische Grondwet van 1831.* Faculty of Law, Unpublished PhD thesis. Leuven: KU Leuven.
Marteel, S. (2009) *"Inventing the Belgian Revolution". Politics and Political Thought in the United Kingdom of the Netherlands (1814–1830).* Unpublished PhD thesis. Florence: European University Institute.
Marteel, S. (2018) *The Intellectual Origins of the Belgian Revolution.* Basingstoke: Palgrave.

Mast, A. (1966) *Overzicht van het grondwettelijk recht*. Ghent: Story-Scientia.

Maulin, E. (2003) *La Théorie de l'état de Carré de Malberg*. Paris: Presses Universitaires de France.

Mineur, D. (2010) *Archéologie de la représentation politique*. Paris: Presses de Sciences Po.

Mineur, D. (2012) 'De la souveraineté nationale à la volonté générale. L'évolution de Carré de Malberg, du projet positiviste au parti-pris démocratique', *Jus politicum* (8), http://juspoliticum.com/article/De-la-souverainete-nationale-a-la-volonte-generale-536.html (Last viewed on 11 August 2020).

Parkinson, J. (2020) 'The Roles of Referendums in Deliberative Systems', *Representation*, 56(4), pp. 485–500. DOI: 10.1080/00344893.2020.1718195.

Pasquino, P. (1988) *Sieyes et l'invention de la constitution en France*. Paris: Odile Jacob.

Paulet-Grandguillot, E. (2010) *Libéralisme et démocratie. De Sismondi à Constant, à partir du Contrat Social (1801–1806)*. Geneva: Slatkine.

Popelier, P. (2007) 'De (ir)rationele wetgever vroeger, vandaag en in de toekomst', in Peeters, B. and Velaers, J. (eds.) *De grondwet in groothoekperspectief: liber amicorum discipulorumque Karel Rimanque*. Antwerp and Oxford: Intersentia, pp. 57–98.

Prutsch, M. (2013) *Making Sense of Constitutional Monarchism in Post-Napoleonic France and Germany*. Basingstoke: Palgrave Macmillan.

Rosenblatt, H. (2011) 'Rousseau, Constant, and the Emergence of the Modern Notion of Freedom of Speech', in Powers, E. (ed.) *Freedom of Speech: The History of an Idea*. Plymouth: Rowman and Littlefield, pp. 133–164.

Rubinelli, L. (2020) *Constituent Power. A History*. Cambridge: Cambridge University Press. DOI: 10.1017/9781108757119.

S.A. *Le Courrier de la Meuse* (CDM).

S.A. *Le Courrier des Pays-Bas* (CDPB).

S.A. *L'Emancipation* (EMP).

Sieyès, E. (1988) *Qu'est-ce que le tiers-état?* Paris: Flammarion.

Stevens, F. et al. (2008) *Constitutional Documents of Belgium, Luxembourg and the Netherlands 1789–1848*. München: K.G. Saur.

Tenenbaum, S. (1998) 'The Coppet Circle: Public Opinion and the Modern State', in Tilkin, F. (ed.) *Le Groupe de Coppet et le monde moderne*. Geneva: Droz, pp. 223–234.

Tilleman, B. and Alen, A. (1992) 'General Introduction', in Alen, A. (ed.) *Treatise on Belgian Constitutional Law*. Deventer and Boston: Kluwer, pp. 1–22.

Tuck, R. (2016) *The Sleeping Sovereign. The Invention of Modern Democracy*. Cambridge: Cambridge University Press. DOI: 10.1017/CBO9781316417782.

Uyttendaele, M. (2005) *Précis de droit constitutionnel belge. Regards sur un système institutionnel paradoxal*. Brussels: Bruylant.

Van Crombrugge, R. (2020) 'Are Referendums Necessarily Populist? Countering the Populist Interpretation of Referendums Through Institutional Design', in *Representation*, online first. DOI: 10.1080/00344893.2020.1720789.

Van Goethem, H. (2002) 'De gehele natie of de partij? Het parlementaire mandaat in België', in De Smaele, H. and Tollebeek, J. (eds.) *Politieke representatie*. Leuven: Leuven University Press, pp. 233–247.

Van Meenen, P.-F. (1815) 'Droit Public – Art. 6 – Constitution (suite 3)', in d'Elhoungne, A.-F., Doncker, P. and Van Meenen, P.-F. (eds.) *L'Observateur*

politique, administratif, historique et littéraire de la Belgique par une société de jurisconsultes et d'hommes de lettres (Vol. II). Brussels: De Mat, pp. 29–40.
Van Velzen, P. (2005) *De Ongekende ministeriële verantwoordelijkheid. Theorie en praktijk 1813–1840.* Nijmegen: Wolff.
Vande Lanotte, J. et al. (2015) *Belgisch publiekrecht. Deel I.* Bruges: Die Keure.
Velaers, J. (2006) *Staatsrecht.* Antwerp: Universitas.
Velaers, J. (2019) *De Grondwet. Een artikelgewijze commentaar. Deel II.* Bruges: Die Keure.
Viaene, V. (2001) *Belgium and the Holy See from Gregory XVI to Pius IX (1831–1859): Catholic Revival, Society and Politics in 19th-Century Europe.* Leuven: Leuven University Press.
Vilain XIIII, C.-H. (1830) *Appel au Congrès par un ami de la patrie.* Ghent: Van Ryckegem-Hovaere.
Wigny, P. (1952) *Droit constitutionnel.* Brussels: Bruylant.
Witte, E. (2018) 'Republic and Popular Sovereignty. The Belgian Case: 1830–1831', *Journal of Constitutional History*, 35(1), pp. 89–112.

Publications without a specific, personal author (such as newspapers and official documents) are listed under S.A.

Index

For Product Safety Concerns and Information please contact our EU representative GPSR@taylorandfrancis.com
Taylor & Francis Verlag GmbH, Kaufingerstraße 24, 80331 München, Germany

www.ingramcontent.com/pod-product-compliance
Ingram Content Group UK Ltd.
Pitfield, Milton Keynes, MK11 3LW, UK
UKHW020152200926
475702UK00016B/2678

* 9 7 8 0 3 6 7 7 1 2 2 8 0 *